Design Roots

CW01496784

Design Roots

Culturally Significant Designs, Products, and Practices

Edited by
*Stuart Walker, Martyn Evans,
Tom Cassidy, Jeyon Jung, and
Amy Twigger Holroyd*

BLOOMSBURY VISUAL ARTS
LONDON · NEW YORK · OXFORD · NEW DELHI · SYDNEY

BLOOMSBURY VISUAL ARTS
Bloomsbury Publishing Plc
50 Bedford Square, London, WC1B 3DP, UK
1385 Broadway, New York, NY 10018, USA

BLOOMSBURY, BLOOMSBURY VISUAL ARTS and the Diana logo are trademarks
of Bloomsbury Publishing Plc

First published in Great Britain by Bloomsbury Academic 2018
This edition published by Bloomsbury Visual Arts 2018

© Editorial content and introductions: Edited by Stuart Walker, Martyn Evans, Tom Cassidy,
Jeyon Jung, and Amy Twigger Holroyd

© Individual chapters: their authors

Stuart Walker, Martyn Evans, Tom Cassidy, Jeyon Jung, and Amy Twigger Holroyd have asserted
their right under the Copyright, Designs and Patents Act, 1988, to be identified as Authors of
this work.

Cover design: Louise Dugdale
Cover image © Martyn Evans

All rights reserved. No part of this publication may be reproduced or transmitted in any form or by
any means, electronic or mechanical, including photocopying, recording, or any information storage
or retrieval system, without prior permission in writing from the publishers.

Bloomsbury Publishing Plc does not have any control over, or responsibility for, any third-party
websites referred to or in this book. All internet addresses given in this book were correct at the
time of going to press. The author and publisher regret any inconvenience caused if addresses have
changed or sites have ceased to exist, but can accept no responsibility for any such changes.

A catalogue record for this book is available from the British Library.

A catalog record for this book is available from the Library of Congress.

ISBN: PB: 978-1-3501-0341-2
         ePDF: 978-1-4742-4181-6
         eBook: 978-1-4742-4183-0

Typeset by Integra Software Services Pvt. Ltd.
Printed and bound in Great Britain

To find out more about our authors and books visit www.bloomsbury.com
and sign up for our newsletters

CONTENTS

ILLUSTRATIONS

FIGURES

TABLES

NOTES ON CONTRIBUTORS

Jeyon Jung currently works as a design consultant in design management, service design and design for sustainability. Prior to this, she was a senior research associate in ImaginationLancaster at Lancaster University, working on several AHRC-funded research projects. Broadly, her research explores the strategic use of design in different contexts. She is also keenly interested in the relationship between place, culture, and designed products, and how design can be applied to enhance and sustain this relationship. She completed her Ph.D. in design, exploring the disciplinary core of design as a field of research and practice, in 2015.

Amy Twigger Holroyd is a designer, maker, and researcher. Through her "craft fashion" knitwear label, Keep & Share, she has explored the emerging field of fashion and sustainability since 2004. Her work has been featured in many books, publications, and exhibitions, from *Vogue* to *Fashion Theory*. Following her Ph.D., Amy joined the University of Leeds as a research fellow on the Design Routes project. She is now a senior lecturer in design, culture, and context at Nottingham Trent University. Her monograph, *Folk Fashion: Understanding Homemade Clothes*, was published by I.B.Tauris in 2017.

Stuart Walker is chair of design for sustainability at Lancaster University, UK where he co-founded a design department and the dedicated design research centre ImaginationLancaster, of which he is a director. He is also visiting professor of design for sustainability at Kingston University, London and emeritus professor at University of Calgary. His distinctive practice-based research explores the environmental, social and spiritual aspects of sustainability. His conceptual designs have been exhibited in Canada, Australia, Italy, at the Design Museum, London, and most recently at Brantwood, John Ruskin's house in the English Lake District. His books include: *Sustainable by Design*, *The Spirit of Design*, *The Handbook of Design for Sustainability* (ed. with Jacques Giard), and *Designing Sustainability*. His most recent book is *Design for Life*, published by Routledge in 2017. He is the Principal Investigator for the AHRC (UK) funded projects 'Living Design' and 'Design Ecologies' that have informed the making of this book.

Patrick Dillon is a visiting professor in the Faculty of Philosophy at the University of Eastern Finland and emeritus professor at the University of Exeter. He has a first degree in biology and doctorates in economic history and education. He has been a university academic since 1981. His research is in cultural ecology, which is concerned with the interactions between people and their environments that give rise to generative, transactional, relational and co-constitutional ways of knowing and being. Patrick's work in cultural ecology is closely allied to research in crafts, design, the arts, and heritage.

Siún Carden is a research fellow in the Centre for Rural Creativity, University of the Highlands and Islands. An anthropologist, her current research interests are Shetland textiles, maker cultures, and the application of the 'creative industries' concept to rural contexts. Past publications include "Making space for tourists with minority languages: The case of Belfast's Gaeltacht Quarter" (2012) *Journal of Tourism and Cultural Change* 10(1), "Cable Crossings: The Aran jumper as myth and merchandise" (2014) *Costume* 48(2), and "The Gaeltacht Quarter of Mural City: Irish in Falls Road Murals" (2017) in *Visiting Murals: Politics, Heritage and Identity*, eds. Jonathan Skinner and Lee Jolliffe, Ashgate. She teaches on UHI's MA in art and social practice.

Disaya Chudasri is a lecturer in the Animation and Game Program at the College of Arts, Media and Technology in Chiang Mai University, Thailand. Disaya received a BArch (Industrial Design) from the King Mongkut's Institute of Technology Ladkrabang (KMITL), Thailand, a MDesign from the University of Technology Sydney (UTS), Australia, and a Ph.D. in design from Lancaster University, UK. Disaya's research interests include involved design for education, craft and sustainability, well-being and healthcare, and knowledge management. Previously, Disaya worked in design companies for 10 years and dealt with commercial projects such as packaging design, corporate identity, and branding.

Hazal Gümüş Çiftçi holds a Ph.D. in design from Lancaster University (2017). She received her bachelor's degree in industrial design from Istanbul Technical University and her master's degree in product/service/system design from Politecnico di Milano. She has also taught at Izmir University of Economics' Industrial Design Department (2012—15). Her research interests are practice-based design research, design for sustainability, grassroots production, participatory design, and social innovation.

Poone Yazdanpanah is a senior research associate in ImaginationLancaster in Lancaster University, UK. Previously she taught in the Department of Architecture at Isfahan Art University in Iran where she also served as Head of Department. Her research interests span crafts and architecture, human meanings and holistic thinking, tradition and transition. She holds a Ph.D. in design for sustainability from Lancaster University which investigated the relationship between human meanings and sustainability in architecture, and which included an in-depth case study of the traditional Iranian domestic courtyard known as the Miān-Sarā.

Sara Kristoffersson is professor of design history at Konstfack University College of Arts, Design and Crafts in Stockholm, and holds a Ph.D. in art history and visual studies from the University of Gothenburg. Her recent book *Design by IKEA. A Cultural History* (Bloomsbury 2014) investigates the brand IKEA and how the corporation has come to define a nation. In an ongoing project, Kristoffersson analyzes the relation between ideology and design, with the Swedish Cooperative Movement as an example.

Anne Marchand is an associate professor in industrial design and vice-dean of research at the Université de Montréal's Faculty of Environmental Design. An industrial designer by training (Université de Montréal), she holds a doctoral degree in environmental design (University of Calgary). She teaches research in design methodologies, including user-centred approaches. Her work in action research and research-creation addresses contemporary creation inspired by local and traditional know-how. She is cofounder of the Tapiskwan Collective, a non-profit Aboriginal organization whose mission is to implement a sustainable development strategy based on the cultural heritage and creativity of members of the Atikamekw Nation.

Karine Awashish is co-founder of the Nitaskinan Coop, an organization set up and driven by the desire of three Atikamekw and Québécoises female entrepreneurs to support Atikamekw socio-cultural and economic development. She is from the Opitciwan community. Holding a Master's degree in leisure, culture and tourism (Université du Québec à Trois-Rivières) and a Bachelor's degree in business administration (Université du Québec à Montréal), she has professional experience in the area of Aboriginal social economy enterprises.

Christian Coocoo is the coordinator of cultural services for the Atikamekw Nation Council. He works actively to promote and sustain his nation's culture. As cultural coordinator for the Atikamekw Nation Council, he initiates and coordinates documentation, transfer and dissemination activities for traditional knowledge and know-how.

Solen Roth is a postdoctoral fellow in the School of Design at the Faculty of Environmental Design, Université de Montréal. An anthropologist specializing in material culture and intercultural relations, she received a Master's degree from the Louis Lumière University in Lyon and a Ph.D. from the University of British Columbia in Vancouver. Her doctoral thesis focused on the Aboriginal art market in Canada, with particular emphasis on the commercialization of Northwest Coast art. She has been a postdoctoral researcher at the Université de Montréal since January 2015.

Renata Marques Leitão is a postdoctoral researcher at HEC Montréal. A graphic designer by training, she is interested in social innovation processes through design. She is originally from Brazil and holds a Ph.D. in environmental design (Université de Montréal), a Master's degree in design (Université de Montréal) and a Bachelor's degree in graphic design (Universidade Mackenzie, São Paulo).

Cédric Sportes holds a Bachelor's degree in product design (Kingston University). He is the founder of *Sportes Outdoor Tools*, a business and design laboratory for outdoor products inspired by ancient concepts. He teaches product design at the Université de Montréal and the Université du Québec à Montréal.

Caoimhe Isha Beaulé has a Bachelor's degree in design (Concordia University) and is currently pursuing her Master's degree at the Université de Montréal. Strongly influenced by her childhood in Canada's Far North and her studies at the University of Lapland in Finland, her interests revolve around design from the North.

Adhi Nugraha is a product designer and teacher. He trained as a product designer in Bandung and received his Doctor of Arts from Aalto University Finland in 2012. In

Indonesia, he established a design studio and workshop in Bandung. He also teaches in the Department of Industrial Design at Bandung Institute of Technology (ITB). He is also actively involved in various projects focused on the development of the creative economy in Indonesia.

Meong Jin Shin is a researcher in design management related to culture, textile and fashion product design, digital design, and consumer behavior research. She has authored journal articles on cultural reinvention, digitizing traditional cultural designs, consumer color preferences, and electronic resources for fashion education in the expanding remit of design management for textile and fashion designs.

Sebastian Cox is a furniture designer and maker, based in south London. Sebastian founded his workshop and design studio in 2010 on the principle that the past can be used to design and make the future. He is deeply motivated by the way generations of craftspeople have used a limited palette of biodegradable and renewable materials in a creative way, turning them into objects that are functional, simple, understandable and as a result, beautiful. He produces his own collections of furniture, lighting and home accessories, available for purchase through his own website and showroom; other collections are stocked by Heal's, The New Craftsmen and Benchmark; he has produced bespoke pieces of design for clients including Sir Terence Conran; he recently designed an award-winning kitchen for deVOL.

Patty Johnson is a designer and educator who is interested in the interchange between research, design, commerce, and culture. Based in the US and Canada, she has developed design projects in Africa, the Caribbean, and Central and South America. Johnson designs product lines for manufacturers like Keilhauer, Nienkamper, David design, and Mabeo. In 2016, she joined the faculty at the Rhode Island School of Design and is the graduate program director in the Department of Furniture Design. Johnson was educated at the University of Toronto, and received her Master's from Central Saint Martins College of Art and Design, London.

Jacques R. Giard is professor of industrial design in The Design School at Arizona State University. Professor Giard received his undergraduate education in furniture design in Montreal (1969), completed a Postgraduate Diploma in industrial design (engineering) in Birmingham, UK (1971), and earned a Ph.D. from Concordia University in Montreal (1987). He is the author of four books on design as well as over forty articles and papers published in various journals and magazines in North America and Europe. Previously, Professor Giard was director of the School of Industrial Design at Carleton University in Ottawa, Canada and president of the Association of Canadian Industrial Designers.

Steve Marotta is a Ph.D. candidate at Portland State University in Portland, OR. His current research examines the cultural and economic complexities of "Made in" branding as a facet of craft manufacturing and maker culture in Detroit (MI) and Portland (OR).

Austin Cummings is a doctoral student and research assistant at the Toulan School of Urban Studies and Planning at Portland State University in Portland, Oregon. He has a Bachelor of Science in philosophy and psychology and Master of public administration from the University of Oregon. His research interests focus on the intersection between the creative economy, urban revitalization, community development, and the policing of cultural expression.

Charles Heying is emeritus professor in the Nohad A. Toulan School of Urban Studies and Planning at Portland State University, Portland, Oregon. He has co-authored a book and numerous articles on the politics and development of Olympic cities. Professor Heying's current research combines his interest in the arts with his passion for community-based economic development. His book, *Brew to Bikes: Portland's Artisan Economy*, describes how the transformation from an industrial to a post-industrial economy is being articulated in the trend-setting edges of Portland's artisan production.

Sirpa Kokko works as a senior lecturer at the University of Helsinki in the Faculty of Educational Sciences/Craft Teacher Education. She has vast experience of craft education from primary to higher education in Finland, Europe, South America, and Africa. She has conducted research on various topics of arts and crafts and their education: gender and crafts, cultural heritage of crafts, and current developments of craft education in comprehensive schools and higher education.

Tom Cassidy holds the chair in design at the University of Leeds, School of Design. He has been carrying out research in design and design related areas for over thirty years and is a fellow of the Design Research Society. He has had twenty-five Ph.D. student completions and has published many papers in academic journals, chapters in books, and has co-authored a book. Professor Cassidy is a member of a number of editorial boards and has reviewed many journal papers, conference papers, and research grant applications and has been a principal investigator or co-investigator on six research council awarded grants.

Tracy Diane Cassidy is a trained knitwear designer experienced in knitwear and bespoke bridal-wear design, manufacture, and retail. She obtained her Ph.D. through the investigation of color forecasting and is the first author of the book *Colour Forecasting* (Blackwell). Tracy is a reader in fashion and textiles, departmental lead for research and innovation, and centre director of the Textiles Thinking Research Centre at the University of Huddersfield, and continues to conduct research in fashion and textile design, trends, and marketing. While trends and color have remained particular areas of research interest in both design and marketing applications, more recently research interests include home furnishings and interiors encompassing fashion and textiles in a much broader context. Tracy is an established author with international presence, a reviewer for many reputable journals, and editorial board member.

Marsha C. Bol is the director emerita of the Museum of International Folk Art, Santa Fe, New Mexico. Over the past thirty-four years, she has worked as a director or curator in four US museums (the New Mexico Museum of Art, the Carnegie Museum of Natural History, and the Maxwell Museum of Anthropology) and as an associate professor at the University of Texas at San Antonio. She has a Ph.D. in art history from the University of New Mexico and is a specialist in Native American art/architecture and Spanish Colonial art/architecture.

Daniela Selloni is a service designer, research fellow and adjunct professor at the School of Design of Politecnico di Milano, where she teaches the Master's degree in product service systems design. She is member of POLIMI DESIS Lab within the Department of Design of Politecnico di Milano, where she works in international and Italian research programs. Her research interests cover service design and social innovation, focusing on citizen activism, methods and tools for co-design, public services, design for democracy, and shared economy. She also acts in an advisory capacity for start-up incubation programs and organizations from the private and third sectors.

Anna Meroni is an architect with a Ph.D. in design. She is also associate professor of design in the Department of Design at the Politecnico di Milano. Her research focus is on service and strategic design for sustainability to foster social innovation, participation, and local development. She is the head of the international Master of Science program in product service system design and coordinator of the POLIMI-DESIS Lab, the Milan-based research laboratory of the DESIS-Design for Social Innovation and Sustainability Network. Anna is on the board of the Ph.D. program in design, principal investigator of research projects, chair of conferences, and author of several publications.

Çağla Doğan is a design educator and researcher, with knowledge and experience at undergraduate and graduate levels. She has several years of teaching experience, including industrial design studios and related theory courses, as well as graduate thesis supervision. She has a well-established research focus on design research and education for sustainability. She holds a Ph.D. in product design for sustainability from the Faculty of Environmental Design, University of Calgary, and MSc and BID degrees in industrial design from the Department of Industrial Design, METU in Ankara, where she has been founder and projects coordinator of the Sustain Design Research Lab.

Emma Murphy is a senior lecturer and program leader in design innovation at the Glasgow School of Art. Her research interests are based around the convergence of design, management, and policy, including design research methods and methodology, business models, design procurement and commissioning, and managing creativity and innovation. Emma was previously a lecturer and researcher at ImaginationLancaster, a creative design research lab within Lancaster University, and head of marketing and business development at international design consultancy Graven. Over the last fourteen years, Emma has led and managed projects for both industry and academia, and has worked for clients including Volkswagen AG, RBS, and BBC Scotland. Emma supervises Ph.D. students in the areas of design management and design education.

Martyn Evans is professor of design and head of Manchester School of Art Research Centre at Manchester Metropolitan University, Manchester. As a trained product designer, his research interests explore the strategic approaches designers use to consider the future, in particular the ability of designers to envision potential social, cultural, technological and economic futures. He has led a number of funded research projects, both in the UK and Europe, and was principal investigator for the AHRC-funded Design Routes project. In 2017, he was elected as a council member of the Design Research Society.

Editorial Introduction

Stuart Walker

Some decades ago, before the full effects of Reagan–Thatcher market deregulation and the growth of neoliberal economics, I had the opportunity to circle the world, stopping in the Middle East, the Indian subcontinent, Southeast Asia, China, North America, and Europe. What struck me at that time was the cultural distinctiveness of the places I visited. The character of each place was quite unique, and all were new and unfamiliar to me. This could be unsettling and somewhat stressful, but it was also invigorating and deeply illuminating. It opened my eyes and made me realize that the way I had been looking at the world and the things I had been taking for granted were not universal. People elsewhere often saw things very differently and had other priorities, dreams, and expectations. And this realization enabled me to see my own world from a new perspective. Unquestioned understandings suddenly came into view for the first time. It was a revelation. I began to see things in a new way. It was a true education.

Since those days, there has been the fall of the Iron Curtain; the rise of globalization and free markets and the expansion of international trade; a transformation in the economies of Asia; and the advent of digital culture. All these developments can have both economic and intercultural benefits but, as with most things, there is a price to pay. In recent decades, as people around the world have enthusiastically embraced the Western-style, growth-based economic system that is so dependent on consumption, there has been a very significant flattening and homogenizing of cultures. Differences in dress, products, ways of living, and daily work routines have diminished, and standards and expectations have become unified within and among professions. As a consequence, much of the color and character of different cultures, perspectives and ways of seeing the world have been lost. Language may also be a contributing factor to this decline. English has become the standard for international communication and is the language of higher education in schools, colleges and universities that aspire to internationalization. With this mode of expression comes a way of framing perceptions, and ways of thinking that are implicitly, perhaps unconsciously, inculcated into our ways of doing (Weiler 2015). The use of language—or indeed its absence—can be a critical factor in appreciating traditional knowledge and practices. Barry Lopez, who has traveled for many years with indigenous peoples, has noted that there are often long periods without conversation. Reflecting on this, he says that if an observer does not attempt to immediately convert sensory information into language, "into the vocabulary and syntactical framework we all employ when trying to define our experiences, there's a much greater opportunity for minor details, which might at first seem unimportant, to remain alive in the foreground of an impression, where, later, they might deepen the meaning of an experience" (Lopez 2015: 13).

In addition, consumption-based economies are generally more urban in nature, with employment opportunities, shopping malls and bright lights, so there is a migration from the villages and countryside to the cities. And with this migration, aspects of identity, tradition, tacit knowledge and intergenerational wisdom become lost—perhaps for ever.

Yet, human beings are, if anything, unpredictable and hopeful, and consequently they continually confound linear, simplistic trajectories and predictions of gloom. Amid and concurrent with powerful forces taking us towards homogeneity, today we also see strong inclinations towards, and myriad examples of, the local, the situated, and the traditional (Hawken 2007). Around the world, we are seeing re-learnings, re-appreciations and revivals of practices that are culture-specific, place-based, often ancient, and deeply meaningful. These exist alongside and, perhaps paradoxically, because of and in concert with globalization, international trade, and homogenization. Indeed, digital communications are enabling new ways of sharing, learning and reviving cultural practices.

Our research in Santa Fe and northern New Mexico demonstrates a particularly successful example of art, design and traditional practices (Design Routes 2016). Here, culturally significant North American Indian, Hispanic and Anglo arts are flourishing, but their recognition and appreciation in this particular region are not entirely by chance. Their prominence is partly due to historical and geographical circumstance, but is also the result of conscious effort. Gradually over the last century, a variety of initiatives helped create what is today an internationally renowned center for traditional arts, crafts, products, and practices. These have included attention to architectural aesthetics, the instigation of juried arts markets, the appearance of a plethora of private galleries, the creation of world-class museums, and the promotion of the region as a destination, with hotels, restaurants, local foods, and a wide variety of other arts and cultural events.

In the UK, there has been a revival in traditional British foods. Restaurants and pubs commonly include locally sourced ingredients, and regional recipes that were once ignored are now prominently and proudly featured on menus. Long-forgotten British cheeses have also seen something of a rebirth. Internationally trained specialists are using their skills to great effect, presenting and promoting varieties of cheese that often appear new but are, in fact, traditional, which in turn supports and encourages independent farmhouse cheesemakers (e.g. Swinscoe and Swinscoe 2016).

In Albania, chefs who learned their trade in top restaurants in Western Europe are moving back to their home country, seeing its gastronomic potential from a new perspective, and using locally grown ingredients to create distinctive menus for their restaurants (Petrini 2015).

Shanghai, one of the most dynamic, economically driven cities in Asia, is re-appreciating many of the traditional crafts and practices that were either discouraged during the Cultural Revolution of 1966–76 or left behind in the more recent rush to economic development. It has started to recognize and recover these practices. In 2003, UNESCO issued the *Convention for the Safeguarding of Intangible Cultural Heritage,* which it defines as "the practices, representations, expressions, as well as the knowledge and skills (including instruments, objects, artifacts, cultural spaces), that communities, groups and, in some cases, individuals recognise as part of their cultural heritage." Intangible cultural heritage includes traditional craftsmanship as well as performing arts, oral traditions, social practices, rituals, festivals, and worldviews (UNESCO 2015). In the Shanghai area, there are fifty-five recognized examples.

In this volume, we have captured examples and case studies from all over the world that help illuminate the importance and value of culturally significant designs, products and practices, and their relevance to contemporary society. We have brought together a wide range of contributions from an international field of authors and researchers, which detail diverse approaches for positive development and sustainable change in material culture. This collection offers an extensive review of practices that are rooted in community and place, and shaped by their use of local materials, techniques, and custom. It introduces the reader to important context-related issues that affect and, potentially, can help foster future opportunities for developing culturally meaningful designs, products, and practices.

We are especially concerned here with creative roots, place-based creative ecologies, and deep understandings of cultural significance, not only in terms of history and tradition but also in terms of locale, social interactions, innovation, and change—change that is respectful and supportive of culturally significant practices and material productions, their longevity, their embodied knowledge and local wisdoms, and their contributions in creating a better future. Importantly, these practices are not locked in time by sentimentality and nostalgia but are innovative, adaptive to new technologies and changing circumstances, and in a continual state of becoming. It is our view that these case studies and traditions—all connected to community, local know-how, and culture—have much to offer for the future in terms of sustainability, cultural identity, personal well-being and new opportunities in design.

In the following pages we will read about the foundations of such designs, products, and practices; their emerging directions; amateur and professional endeavours; enterprise models; business opportunities; and the changing role and contribution of design in helping to create material cultures of significance, meaning and value.

A truly global vista is provided through case studies and research from North and South America, Africa, Europe, Asia, and Australasia. Hence, this collection of invited writings offers a timely international survey of culturally significant designs, products and practices, and their potentially positive role in shaping the future of material cultures. The essays are arranged into five sections, although, inevitably with this kind of subject matter, the topics under discussion do not necessarily fit neatly into just one section but will often spill over into the others. The sections are:

1   Culturally Significant Designs, Products, and Practices
2   Authenticity and Tradition in Material Culture
3   Revitalization by Design
4   Enterprise, Policy and Education for Positive Development
5   Design Futures

Part 1: Culturally Significant Designs, Products, and Practices begins with a contribution by Jeyon Jung and Stuart Walker. The authors consider these kinds of designs, products and practices in relation to the local, place-based creative ecology; that is, the associated structures, organizations, activities and interactions that help support and enable the work of individual makers. Their chapter looks at the origins and history of practices, their characteristics, and the internal, mutually reinforcing relationships that facilitate productive activity. This is followed by Amy Twigger Holroyd's personal reflection on the factors at play when we attempt to revitalize culturally significant practices, the kinds of interventions that might be considered, and notions of authenticity and origin. In my own chapter, I look at the relationship of culturally significant artifacts to modernity, tradition, and contemporary understandings of sustainability. In particular, I consider the potential future of such artifacts and, with them, practices, beliefs, and values. Patrick Dillon discusses such artifacts in terms of "transactions" between people and the resources of their environments. He sees such making practices as part of an historical continuum in which traditions become established, and he explores the constant interplay between established ways of doing things and new possibilities and innovations.

Part 2: Authenticity and Tradition in Material Culture begins with Siún Carden's case study of the Aran jumper. Many will be surprised to learn that this quintessentially "traditional" symbol of Irishness was actually developed as a clever marketing ploy in the 1930s. From Ireland we journey to Thailand for Disaya Chudasri's chapter on northern Thai weaving and textile enterprises. Disaya reports results from an in-depth study of handicrafts in this region. She also includes a consideration of the potential areas in which creative design can contribute in ensuring the continuity of weaving communities and production of textile products in ways that are compatible with the principles of sustainability. Our next stop is Turkey and Hazal Gümüş Çiftçi's study of the traditional carving of the black Oltu-stone *tasbih* or prayer beads. Hazal conducted a series of interviews with the makers to identify the challenges they are facing, and the opportunities and potential for constructive design interventions. We then travel to Iran and Poone Yazdanpanah's discussion of the Miān-Sarā—the inner courtyard of a traditional Iranian extended family home. This is a housing form that goes back several millennia but it has been in severe decline since the late nineteenth century. In particular, Poone considers the relationship of the Miān-Sarā to practical, social and spiritual aspects of contemporary sustainability. Part 2 comes to a close with Sara Kristoffersson's chapter on the mass production of national design identity. More specifically, she looks at "Scandinavian Design" and how it is packaged and sold to consumers around the world by the Swedish company IKEA.

Part 3: Revitalization by Design examines if and how traditional practices might be revived and sustained, and whether design can make a constructive and meaningful contribution. We begin in northern Quebec with Anne Marchand's work with indigenous communities and, in particular, with members of the Atikamekw Nation. She presents *Tapiskwan*, an intergenerational participatory action research project, and discusses the issues, challenges and opportunities raised by this collaboration. Indonesia is our next port of call with Adhi Nugraha's "ATUMICS"—a tool he has developed for artists, craftspeople, designers and students to help them transform various aspects of tradition into new artifacts. Meong Jin Shin takes us to South Korea with her chapter on design reinvention as applied to traditional fabric patterns of *bojagi* or Korean wrapping cloths. She has developed a web-based application that enables a library of traditional patterns to be viewed and applied to contemporary clothing. Sebastian Cox is a designer-maker in the south of England. He considers how old and new are combined in his own practice in order to take us, product by product, towards a more sustainable material culture. Patty Johnson then whisks us to the Caribbean for the final chapter in this section. She presents a case study that looks at the revitalization of place-related products and the way design has played a role in the development of culturally significant artifacts in this region.

Part 4: Enterprise, Policy and Education for Positive Development begins in Arizona with a chapter from Jacques Giard on the Hohokam people of the American Southwest. Using his own beautifully rendered illustrations, Jacques describes the evolution of Hohokam pottery production and reflects on what it can teach contemporary designers about sustaining cultural significance in the design and making of everyday things. We stay in the United States for the next chapter, in which Steven Marotta, Austin Cummings and Charles Heying tell us about three artisan sectors in Portland, Oregon: craft brewing, the handmade bicycle industry and food carts. While their deeply contextual interpretation of the development of Portland's artisan economy at first appears to yield no lessons for transferability to other places, in fact they conclude that the opposite is true. Sirpa Kokko then takes us to Estonia to consider the role of higher education in sustaining culturally significant crafts. Crafts form an important part of Estonian heritage and national identity, and the Department of Estonian Native Crafts at the Viljandi Culture Academy is devoted to researching and raising the profile of this country's craft traditions. Tom Cassidy and Tracy Diane Cassidy provide a reflection on the role of intellectual property rights (IPR) as they apply to culturally significant products and practices. They recognize that outcomes of IPR cases in this field are rarely fully resolved, they point out the pitfalls and complexities of such cases, and suggest that a robust research methodology may improve outcomes. For the last chapter in this section, we return to the United States for Marsha Bol's discussion of the relationship between the museum, the artist, and the marketplace. She considers how the Museum of New Mexico and other local cultural institutions have played a significant role in sustaining the health and economic viability of traditional arts practices in the region.

Part 5: Design Futures is the final section of this collection, where we look forward. Tom Cassidy begins by considering research approaches for culturally significant design. He discusses eight approaches and includes case studies to illustrate how they are being used. Amy Twigger Holroyd looks at digital transformations and revitalization. Amy's focus is textile crafts, including knitting, sewing, and mending, and she suggests that digitally enabled amateur making communities can lead to new opportunities for revitalization. This is followed by a comparative study of three design projects rooted in the local context. In their chapter, Anna Meroni and Daniela Selloni explore the contribution of design in the current transition from creative communities to social innovation ecosystems, and from communities of experience to evolved communities of expertise. Çağla Doğan takes us to Turkey to discuss her graduate design work that focuses on lighting and the integration of scales of production for sustainability. Çağla provides a comprehensive review of the design explorations that emerged out of a research through design method. Emma Murphy then offers a perspective on how designerly approaches can be employed to develop an authentic brand identity. She considers how the principles and context of authentic branding can be taught in the curriculum in order to promote authentic branding practice in business and design contexts. Finally, Martyn Evans and the rest of the editorial team wrap up the collection with a series of strategies for revitalizing culturally significant designs, products, and practices, and emerging themes are identified that will be important in addressing future challenges.

It has been a great pleasure to bring this collection together, to work with the different authors, and to learn about their work and areas of interest. We are exceedingly grateful to all the contributors, who have been so generous with their time, their commitment, and the sharing of their knowledge and ideas. We have thoroughly enjoyed reading their chapters and we trust that you, the reader, will be fascinated, surprised and encouraged by these inspiring examples from around the globe.

References

Design Routes (2016), *Design Routes: Culturally Significant Designs, Products and Practices.* Available online: http://designroutes.org/ (accessed July 22, 2016).

Hawken, P. (2007), *Blessed Unrest*, New York: Penguin Group.

Lopez, B. (2015 Autumn), "The Invitation," in *What Have We Done*, Vol. 133, 13–17, London: Granta Press.

Petrini, C. (2015), "Heroes of the Future: Bledar and the Albanian Gastronomic Renaissance," article first published in *La Repubblica Milano*, July 8, 2015. Available online: http://www.slowfood.com/expo2015/en/heroes-of-the-future-bledar-and-the-albanian-gastronomic-renaissance (accessed September 9, 2016).

Swinscoe, A. and K. Swinscoe (2016), *The Courtyard Dairy*, Settle, Yorkshire. Available online: http://www.thecourtyarddairy.co.uk/ (accessed July 22, 2016).

UNESCO (2015), *UNESCO at 60: Definition of Intangible Heritage*. Available online: http://www.unesco.org/services/documentation/archives/multimedia/?id_page=13 (accessed September 9, 2016).

Weiler, N. (2015), "Speaking A Second Language May Change How You See The World," *Science*, American Association for the Advancement of Science, March 17, 2015. Available online: http://www.sciencemag.org/news/2015/03/speaking-second-language-may-change-how-you-see-world (accessed September 10, 2016).

Culturally Significant Designs, Products, and Practices

Editorial Introduction

Martyn Evans

The chapters in *Part I* explore key concepts that underpin culturally significant designs, products, and practices, and provide a foundation for considering how cultural significance and design interfaces with broader factors are created, including: place-based creative ecologies; the evolving characteristics of authenticity and origin; the disconnect between tradition; sustainability and modernity; and the relationship between making and the contexts in which culturally significant artifacts exist. The authors consider how the past has shaped the current understandings of cultural significance and, in turn, the prospective contribution that design may bring to revitalizing future traditions, values, and beliefs.

Jeyon Jung and Stuart Walker examine how designs and products that emerge from place-based practices may be culturally significant if they contribute to a sense of local identity. In *Creative Ecologies: Contextualizing Culturally Significant Designs, Products, and Practices,* they consider how locally produced design and products need not necessarily be distinct in terms of materials, processes, aesthetics and skills, as very similar examples can be often found in other places. However, if through materials, patterns or design, or indeed through their use, there arises a sense of cultural particularity associated with custom and tradition, this can contribute to a local sense of identity and strengthen the cultural contribution of such artifacts. Moreover, if they serve to continue a tradition that is rooted in the history of people and place, this will further add to their importance. This chapter looks at examples of such designs and products, their origins and history, and the characteristics and mutually reinforcing relationships of the creative ecology in which they exist.

In *Forging New Futures: Cultural Significance, Revitalization, and Authenticity,* Amy Twigger Holroyd explores how culturally significant designs, products and practices are important to particular communities because of their social, historical, and/or aesthetic values. Revitalization initiatives bring new life to these cultural forms while aiming to retain, or even enhance, the values associated with them. Designers often play a key role in such initiatives and thus their work can have far-reaching implications in terms of cultural significance. As a reflective exploration of various factors at play within these revitalization interventions, there is a particular focus on the notion of authenticity. Although "authentic" traditions are often thought to be static, culturally significant designs, products, and practices must change if they are to remain relevant. Likewise, consideration of "origin" suggests that designs, products, and practices are uniquely and authentically linked to a single place when in fact their histories—and futures—are much more complex.

In *Culturally Significant Artifacts and Their Relationship to Tradition and Sustainability,* Stuart Walker looks at how the modern worldview is inextricably linked to the demise of traditional knowledge and current concerns about sustainability, and can be seen as an obstacle to more meaningful and more lasting interpretations of material goods. Following this critique, the meaning of the term "culturally significant artifacts" is considered and it becomes apparent that it not only involves tradition but also accords with comprehensive understandings of design for sustainability. Such artifacts recombine facts and values, which became disconnected in the modern era. Contrary to common perceptions of "tradition," its integration in the creation of our material culture is fundamentally future facing. The chapter demonstrates that the recovery and incorporation of tradition in how we create functional artifacts is not only concerned with the present, and creating more fulfilling ways of life today, it is also integrally related to the future and the continuation of our beliefs and values by future generations.

Concluding this section, *Making and Its Cultural Ecological Foundations* looks at culturally significant making in the wider frame of cultural ecology. Patrick Dillon contests that a cultural ecology is concerned with transactional relationships between people and the resources of their environments. Transactions in making practices are viewed as part of an historical continuum in which long-term traditions may be set. However, there is a constant interplay between established ways of doing things, i.e. working in a "tradition," and new possibilities arising from improvisations and innovations. Market mechanisms have typically been used to explain these tensions between tradition and change. A cultural ecological framing takes account of a wider complex of human values, tastes, attitudes, social and cultural norms and patterns of consumption to theorize dynamic relationships between people, place, resources, techniques, and processes of making.

1

Creative Ecologies

Contextualizing Culturally Significant Designs, Products, and Practices

Jeyon Jung and Stuart Walker

Introduction

Designs and products that emerge from place-based practices may be "culturally significant" if they contribute to a sense of local identity. They may have rich historical links with communities and cultures and, as a consequence, have much to offer for the future in terms of sustainability, cultural resilience, and well-being (Gould 2001). However, these kinds of traditional designs, products, and practices are often regarded as being out of step with contemporary society and, in many places, traditional practices are not being taken up and continued by younger people. Over the years, there has been a variety of efforts to revitalize these kinds of designs, products, and practices, with varying degrees of success.

The Design Routes project, and the more recent Living Design and Design Ecologies projects, all supported by the Arts and Humanities Research Council, UK have been investigating the potential role of design in contributing to and helping to develop and revitalize culturally significant designs, products, and practices, which, within the scope of this study, are defined as:

- *designs* refer to distinctive features of products such as surface patterns, three-dimensional forms, materials specifications, and aesthetic detailing;
- *products* are confined to those that are durable (i.e. not food and drink), portable (i.e. not buildings), tangible (i.e. not music, dance, language or religion), and visually creative (i.e. not books, scripts or texts);

- *practices* refer to activities that relate to these designs and products, including their creation, use, and preservation.

The term cultural significance here refers to attached values (Kroeber and Kluckhohn 1952) that are, first, essential to the culture in which the designs, products, and practices exist and, second, transmitted from one generation to the next, up to the present. Such transmission is vital to the preservation of situated, culturally relevant knowledge, skills, and beliefs, as well as cultural, and often religious, identity. During this transmission process, meanings and interpretations formed by individuals, communities and society as a whole will change and evolve over time, albeit slowly (Spencer-Oatey 2012). As they do so, local traditions and knowledge rooted in the history of people and place are perpetuated. During the course of this process, there may well arise some distinctive qualities in material combinations, making processes, use patterns and so on, which will contribute to a local sense of cultural identity. Cultural significance and meaning can be understood as a multifarious set of interrelated factors related to tradition, place, community, sense of identity, spiritual well-being, aesthetics, local conditions, materials, technologies, skills, and exchange of goods and services. While many studies have been conducted that examine the continuation of cultural value attached to designs and products, these often focus on individual designs and products (Kokko and Kaipainen 2015; Lin 2007; Shin, Cassidy, and Moore 2011). Here, we suggest that there is also an opportunity for design to contribute at a much broader level—a level that looks at and attempts to visualize the wider context in which the artisans and artifacts reside.

This chapter proposes and discusses a place-based creative ecology as an effective approach to revitalize culturally significant designs, products, and practices. We begin by describing several initial examples that led to the development of the place-based creative ecology approach. Here, design is employed not to create new artifacts but to visualize and synthesize a wide range of context-specific information that can, potentially, be used as a diagnostic tool for identifying where new initiatives are needed. In addition, we present an in-depth case study, conducted in Santa Fe, New Mexico, that was used to inform the process and serve as an exemplar. From this work, a series of factors are identified that can contribute to a successful place-based creative ecology.

Initial study examples

This section describes five initial study examples of the successful revitalization of culturally significant designs, products, and practices, and how they offered a starting point for considering place-based creative ecologies. Insights from these, based mainly on secondary sources, provided a basis for developing our understandings. They also provided a basis for further data collection in order to develop the concept in greater depth. Table 1.1 summarizes some of the key findings of each study example selected.

TABLE 1.1 *Summary of initial study examples*

Example	Description
Graham and Brown Ltd, Blackburn, UK (est. 1946)	• One of the largest independent wallpaper manufacturers in Britain operating internationally, with their success rooted in a place that was once an important center for textile manufacturing and textile printing; the cotton industry flourished in this region in the late eighteenth century. • Despite the decline of the textile industry, the skills and equipment remained well preserved in the region, providing a basis for the development of wallpaper production. • The successful revitalization of the necessary techniques and skills is strongly rooted in the historical development of the place.
Morgan Motor Company Ltd, Malvern, UK (est. 1910)	• The only family-owned British motor manufacturer, which has been producing in the same factory for more than 100 years and exporting their products worldwide. • Renowned for sustaining production of traditional, hand-built motorcars, despite the car industry shifting towards hi-tech mass production (Ranchhod and Gurău 2007). • The company serves as a foundation for building a traditional culture of craftsmanship in the area and, in doing so, is a provider of good-quality work, which enhances employment in the local economy. For example, an apprenticeship program is operated with close links to the local community, which in turn contributes to developing a local tradition of craftsmanship.
Cyber Valley, Malvern, UK (est. 2011)	• In the Second World War, due to concerns over bombing raids, the leading research laboratory for radar development was moved from London to the rural location of Malvern (Day 2014). • Expertise here has grown and adapted to deal with new security threats, especially cybercrime. • Due to government policy, many government-run operations have become privatized. Many small firms have resulted, creating a center of expertise, which in turn attracts other expertise. • A high concentration of small- and medium-sized enterprises (SMEs) in the area enables collaborative activities in designing and making security-related products and services, leading to the development of a collective of specialized practices by contemporary, non-craft, cyber-security enterprises concentrated in a specific location.

TABLE 1.1 (*Continued*)

Example	Description
Joseph, Oregon, USA	• After the collapse of the timber industry, relatively inexpensive property in this small rural town started to attract artists who, commonly, have relatively limited financial means. Of particular note, a fine-art bronze foundry was established. • The foundry was used to produce the owner's own artwork and also the work of others, and the town gradually gained a national reputation for bronze casting with high-quality patinas. Today, the town attracts not only other bronze artists but also painters, ceramicists, and sculptors. • The town has become a thriving arts community with a high concentration of artists, galleries, and festivals, e.g. the *Bronze, Blues & Brews* festival held in August each year, which enriches the arts and culture of the place and attracts visitors from far and wide.
Crawford Bay, British Columbia, Canada	• This small community is known for its vibrant culture of arts and crafts by local artisans, especially its handmade broom maker—the Northern Woven Broom Company. There is also a blacksmith, potter, weaver, glass blower, copper enamel artist, saddler, and several jewelry makers. • Even though the population is only about four hundred, its arts and crafts-based community is thriving, with close connections between artisans, shops, galleries, cafes, restaurants, and hotels.

Emergence of place-based creative ecology

These examples feature designs, products and related practices that are sustained through a strong rootedness to a particular place. From these initial investigations, some contributing factors for the successful revitalization of cultural products and practices were identified.

First, the importance of historical events and tradition is specifically illustrated in the case of Graham and Brown Ltd. This example illustrates not only the utilization of existing capacity that is present in a place, but also its adaptation to changing needs and markets. In this case, skills and knowledge in textile pattern printing were adapted to wallpaper production, as Blackburn transformed from a cotton town to a modern industrial town. It demonstrates how enterprise can change over time while still being rooted in the history and development of industry in the area. Thus, in this example we see both continuity and change, which is the very essence of tradition; traditions have to adapt in order to stay relevant. Historical development, however, is often quite serendipitous; it is not planned as such. In this particular example, there are a host of different historical factors related to enterprise, invention, empire, and even climate (see "Climate and Cotton"). This chance element can greatly influence the nature of local practices as well as their continuity and subsequent developments. Similarly, in the example of the Cyber Valley, the basis of this expertise in security in Malvern stems from a mixture of historical events. However, there is a second, politically related contributing factor in this latter example. Changing government policy towards privatization led to the establishment of a host of independent and interrelated enterprises, which work both independently and collaboratively. The creative enterprises are more service-based, and dependent on accumulated knowledge and expertise, with less emphasis on tangible products. Due to the proximity between companies, their knowledge and expertise are easily shared, enabling a collective growth through collaboration, rather than simply competing with each other. Here, we find competition and independent enterprise along with cooperation and collaboration. This effect of geographical concentration of similar skills and expertise is also evident in the last two examples. In the art town of Joseph and the crafts community of Crawford Bay, the collective efforts of creative people result in the growth of a local culture of arts and crafts, which attracts visitors and customers as well as other related businesses such as galleries, shops, museums, festivals, and other events.

A further contributing factor identified from the initial examples is related to adaptation and value-driven innovation. In the Morgan Motor Company, the cultural traditions of skilled practices, high-quality products and apprenticeships are highly valued by the organization. This craftsmanship-based value also forms a basis for their decision-making, which includes a strong commitment to ethical, social and environmental considerations to sustain their business, not just profit-driven considerations or a wish to continually grow and expand. Furthermore, the family business model allows more independent decision-making based on longer term thinking, not just the short-term maximization of shareholder profits.

The success of culturally related products and practices is dependent not just on the individual products but also:

- the history of the place;
- the interrelationships and interdependencies that occur through a geographical concentration of similar specialties;
- innovation driven by values rather than just profits.

CLIMATE AND COTTON

The high rainfall and consequent high humidity of Lancashire were found to be suitable for cotton spinning. In a drier climate, the threads would tend to break because, due to the hygroscopic nature of cotton thread, they would have a lower tensile strength.

From these initial findings, a need for an in-depth study arose to fully understand how the identified factors contribute to the success of traditional craft enterprises. We identified a particularly successful example, namely Santa Fe, New Mexico, which has a vibrant arts and crafts-based culture. A study of this location would potentially allow us to identify additional factors, which in future could inform revitalization efforts in places where arts and crafts are in decline. A study of this region, however, required a broader approach beyond individual designs and products. We therefore expanded the scope of our study to include place and its environs within which traditional designs and products are created and practiced. In other words, we were examining a wide range of interrelated factors that collectively enable individual craft makers to flourish. We set out to build an overall picture of these factors, which we have called "a creative ecology." The next section will discuss what we mean by this term and how this approach helped guide our research in more detail.

Place-based creative ecology

Defining a creative ecology

An ecology refers to the interrelationships between (living) entities in their environment; it is a term used in biology. In anthropology, the concept of cultural ecology has been used to address the interrelationships between human, culture, and environment (Gunn 1980; Steward 1972). The purpose of cultural ecology is "to explain the origin of particular cultural features and patterns which characterise different areas rather than to derive general principles applicable to any cultural-environmental situation" (Steward 1972: 36). Thus, emphasis is placed on the particulars of local environments, in which their cultural phenomena should be analyzed by applying appropriate concepts and methods rather than borrowing those from biology. For example, the concept of "community"—one of the key concepts in a biological understanding of ecology—needs to be understood as a culturally determined factor rather than a mere biotic assemblage or physical environment (Tansley 1935). This is illustrated in Titon's study on ecology of music, which adapted the concept of community to refer to "various worlds of music, including both physical and cultural factors of the musical environments, e.g. ideas about music, sound instruments, recording studios, musical education and so on" (2009: 122–3), meaning the highest level of ecosystem of musical heritage.

Based on these understandings, here, we use the term "creative ecology" to refer to the interrelationships between people, enterprises, practices, environment and so on that, together, serve to facilitate and support individual creative practitioners in their activities. Also, adapting Titon's (2009) work, we consider three levels of interaction in a creative ecology:

1. **Individuals**—who interact with other people concerning creative practices (i.e. woodcarvers interact with one another at markets, learning skills from each other).

2. **Groups**—that are interdependent with other groups of practitioners or enterprises in sustaining their creative practices (i.e. woodcarver groups, galleries and markets are all dependent on each other).

3. **Environs**—includes both physical and cultural factors of practice-related environments.

Place-based creative ecology

As discussed, we use the term creative ecology to describe our approach to studying the multiplicity of interrelated elements that enable the development and survival of a flourishing arts and crafts sector. In doing so, "place" becomes an important factor that specifically locates any particular "creative ecology" by embracing the local culture that is unique to that place, i.e. local distinctiveness that is integrated in people's ways of living (Clifford and King 1993). It was clear from our initial studies that designs, products, and practices that are still thriving nowadays have usually emerged and evolved by being rooted to a particular place. In addition, the mutual relationship between culturally related products and place is acknowledged as an input–output model: "on the one hand, cultural products industries constantly create and recreate images of a place; and on the other hand, these industries consume the same place-specific cultural phenomena as input" (Scott 1996: 306).

We also consider the role of a place as both a geographical location and a "repository of particular kinds of production capabilities, skills, and know-how" (Scott 1996: 306). It has long been studied and discussed that the performance of "cultural products enterprises" benefits from locational concentration, described in various terms: transactions-intensive agglomerations (Scott 1996), regional advantage (Saxenian 1994), and creative clusters (Chapain et al. 2010). Examples include book and magazine publishing in London and the high-fashion businesses of Paris. In relation to this, identifying the attributes and features of successful cases of cultural clusters and their creation and sustainment have emerged as interesting areas of study (Porter 1990; Scott 1996). Some of the findings from these studies indicate that geographical concentration of cultural industries is an important facet of competitive advantage of regions and nations.

Having described our place-based creative ecology approach, the next section discusses our field research in Santa Fe, New Mexico in which we identified a complex set of supportive elements that, together, allow the arts and craft sector in this particular location to thrive.

In-depth case study: Santa Fe, New Mexico, USA

The site selected for this study was Santa Fe and its environs in New Mexico, USA. Arts and cultural industries in New Mexico have long enjoyed a national and global reputation, one that is linked to the unique culture and heritage of the place. Nearly one in ten jobs (9.8 percent) in the state are employed by arts and cultural industries (Mitchell et al. 2014), including professionals working as artists and artisans, in galleries and museums, and in other activities that are closely associated with the creative aspects of arts and culture. Despite greater competition imposed by globalization and emerging technologies, New Mexico is succeeding in the sustainment and development of its creative economy, supported by its unique history and a strong cultural reputation.

Among regions in New Mexico, Santa Fe is extraordinary in terms of the level of concentration of its creative economy. Nearly six percent of the workforce is employed in arts and cultural occupations and it has the greatest concentration of professional artists (2.6 percent) in the entire country, which is higher than in New York, Los Angeles or Miami. There are also 128 art dealers in the city, making it the seventh highest in the nation (Mitchell et al. 2014). Particularly with its heritage of Indian and Spanish Colonial Arts, Santa Fe is recognized as a place with a highly developed, flourishing arts scene, where government policy, history, migration, heritage, culture, music, design, art, a festival, and design identity all come together to form a unique place-based creative ecology.

We conducted sixteen semi-structured key informant interviews with twenty-two participants in order to profile policy makers, arts leaders, and craft makers from various fields of practice, including weaving, woodcarving, tinware, metalwork, ceramics, museums, and galleries. The interviews with craft makers were mostly conducted in their homes or workplaces, which are located in Santa Fe or its environs, including the nearby towns of Chimayo and Taos. This provided us with an opportunity to observe closely how the artisans work; we saw many demonstrations of them using various materials and tools. In conjunction with interviews, we also visited galleries, museums, and some historical sites (e.g. the UNESCO World Heritage site of Taos Pueblo), and learned about the history of the region. From this, we were able to draw out information relating to culturally significant product collections and making practices, and to build a picture of the interrelationships and interdependencies that contribute to this vibrant creative ecology.

Artisan

Our focus is on individual artisans and the various factors and elements that enable them to flourish in what they do. Therefore, the artisan is at the center of our creative ecology model. In the Santa Fe region, we encountered many individual artisans with highly specialized expertise in their particular art form. With large Native American populations in New Mexico, there are numerous artisans producing goods such as jewelry and pottery. In this study, we focused on Spanish Colonial artists in particular and interviewed a selection of those who regularly participate in the annual Spanish Market, which is a high-quality, juried event. These artisans hold a great depth of knowledge in materials, tools, and practices. Many of their resources are sourced locally, some are gathered from the natural environment, others are made by the artisans themselves or bought from local suppliers, and only rarely are they imported from outside the locale. For most of them, their knowledge of local designs, materials, tools and techniques was passed down from their parent(s) and/or grandparent(s). For some, it was acquired by self-learning through observing other artisans' practices and/or studying artifacts in museum archives, and books. Their knowledge often extended to the history, geography, and economy of the local area. With this specialized knowledge and expertise, they are often invited to give lectures and talks to the public and people interested in becoming a professional artist.

Other supporting elements of Santa Fe's creative ecology

With artisans at the centre, we identified ten important categories of elements that informed the development of Santa Fe's creative ecology: geography, history, economy, education and training, competencies, communications, cultural events, hospitality, policy and development, and resources and supplies. This section discusses these categories and provides a brief description of each. The locale-particular elements that populate these categories are crucial in supporting and sustaining the craft-based economy of Santa Fe; they complement each other to provide beneficial conditions for the community to flourish.

Geography

Supporting aspects of geography include unique local flora and fauna that influence the development of a specific style or making process. The natural beauty of the region, its culture, heritage, landscape, and way of life provide both a source of inspiration and an essential component of the artists' and makers' identity. The dry and sunny climate also proves an attractive environment for large numbers of tourists who participate in cultural events (Mitchell et al. 2014).

History

Santa Fe has a distinct history that has resulted in three cultures living side-by-side and influencing the identity of the city. The early seventeenth century saw Spanish soldiers and Catholic missionaries seeking to convert the Pueblo Indians of the region, who lived in the still-visible adobe buildings. However, a revolt by the Pueblo Indians saw the colonizers driven out. This history is part of New Mexico's rich Indian, Spanish, and Anglo tri-culture that influences much of the art and craft of the region (Jenkins and Schroeder 1973).

Economy

Art and culture are significant contributors to the local economy. The traditional Spanish Market was referred to as a primary source of income; up to fifty percent of local artisans' annual income can be made on this one weekend in the summer. It is a juried event and being selected for inclusion is an important affirmation of the artisan's skill and the quality of work. The Spanish Market attracts approximately 75,000 visitors over the course of the weekend (Horton 2005: 102). This, and other arts markets in Santa Fe and the larger region, serve as focal points for selling and buying, and for artisans to meet, socialize, and share knowledge. Other markets in Santa Fe include the International Folk Art Market, the Winter Spanish Market, the Santa Fe Indian Market, and in nearby Albuquerque there is the Rio Grande Arts and Crafts Festival.

Galleries are also important to the local economy, although less preferred by craftspeople due to high commission fees. Despite these fees, exhibiting their work in a high-quality gallery is an important affirmation of the quality of their work, through which they may gain regional, national, and even international prestige. Artists and craftspeople also valued exchanging their work and bartering with other artisans. We found that the work of other artisans is frequently displayed in their homes and workplaces. Significantly, we found only a few artisans whose practice was their primary source of income. These produced high-quality work, often to special commission, and some were producing innovative forms that spoke to contemporary issues. For most, however, selling their work provided only a secondary source income and for some, income from their work was not a primary consideration; they pursued it for the love of the craft and for the continuity of their cultural traditions. Consequently, they were not under pressure to produce or to alter their work to suit market demands.

Education and training

Santa Fe is also home to a strong informal and formal education tradition. Artists were often invited to give lectures and talks to share their knowledge. Informal education and training would occur through observing an experienced practitioner at work, being taught by them, and working alongside them. This would be the case within families, where knowledge was passed down through generations. Much of this informal learning was often augmented by college courses where students could learn in formal settings.

Similarly, numerous museums are dedicated to presenting the history and development of the area, a major part of which is the arts and crafts culture. Examples include The Palace of the Governors in the main central plaza, the Museum of Contemporary Native Art near the cathedral, and the Museum of Spanish Colonial Art on Museum Hill. There are numerous other related museums such as the International Folk Arts Museum, the Georgia O'Keeffe Museum, and the Museum of Indian Arts and Culture.

The presence of so many high-quality museums in the city and surrounding areas has many benefits, including:

- the conservation and presentation of original artifacts from the area is itself an affirmation of the importance and value of these artifacts in the history and contemporary culture of the region;
- the extensive archives in these museums, along with highly informed curatorial staff facilitates study and provides artisans with a resource for studying and understanding traditional techniques;
- research by academics and the production of books, journals, and papers leading to an additional archive of related written materials.

Competencies

The extensive competencies of local craft makers were a crucial part of this ecology. Their knowledge and skills range from the use of materials and tools in their practices to understanding the history, geography, and economy of the region.

This knowledge, much of it gained from their own experiences, often serves as a source of inspiration for their practice. We also identified that their passion and desire to continue the art and craft traditions of Santa Fe were strong drivers of their practices. Some participants mentioned religious faith as a motivation for their work; the subject matter of Hispanic arts and crafts in the region is predominantly based on religious themes—ornamental crosses, panel paintings (*retablos*), and carvings (*bultos*) of saints etc. Some participants are passionate educators of young people in the community, ensuring their specialist practice is passed down through the generations.

Communications

Santa Fe was a historically isolated community, bypassed by the railway line and with limited road access. Allied to this was a scarcity of resources within the surrounding region. This isolation encouraged the community to become self reliant and find a way to build the local economy and work together to meet local needs, with limited outside help. One historian we interviewed spoke of how this geographical isolation generated a strong sense of cultural identity and was a key contributing factor in Santa Fe becoming a well-preserved arts and culture community.

Cultural events

More broadly, Santa Fe can be considered an Arts City, home to a number of other arts and cultural events. These include music (traditional Spanish music), dance (Flamenco), theatre (Santa Fe Lensic, Santa Fe Playhouse), and opera (Santa Fe Opera). Distinctive regional food and wine also form an important part of the cultural milieu, with frequent food-focused events and festivals in the city alongside other arts markets (Native American, contemporary paintings, sculptures etc.), and classic car shows. These combine with the arts community to create an Arts City.

Hospitality

Santa Fe is home to a thriving hospitality industry that caters to large numbers of visitors. There are hundreds of hotels, as well as campsites and RV parks close to the city center. It also has dozens of restaurants and food outlets close to the central plaza, including popular street food stands on the plaza itself. There are also food-centered events, and food culture is often an important aspect of other events such as the folk arts markets and festivals. We identified productive partnering among local restaurants, galleries, and attractions. For instance, during the season, the Santa Fe Opera will host receptions that provide business for local food and wine enterprises. In addition, we found that the Santa Fe Opera was an important draw to the city that helped ensure the commercial success of some of the higher end galleries; visitors who come to Santa Fe for the opera will often also buy art. Tourists are also provided with well-developed services, such as tours to Chimayo, Taos, Taos Pueblo—a UNESCO World Heritage Centre—and Bandelier National Monument, amongst other nearby venues.

Policy and development

A series of municipal policies has contributed to a flourishing arts and crafts culture in Santa Fe and in New Mexico more widely. Funding programs to run different arts and cultural events are available at both the city level and the state level for public and cultural institutions. One of our interviewees, from the New Mexico Department of Cultural Affairs, mentioned that a large number of legislators are from the Hispanic or Native American communities. They represent cultural communities that value traditional arts and culture, and this emphasis is reflected in the legislation, which aims to support and promote cultural activities related to tradition and history. Architectural policy has also contributed significantly to creating a unique atmosphere in the city, especially through the maintenance of adobe-style construction. This has been encouraged since early in the twentieth century and was later ensured, through regulation introduced in 1957.

Resources and suppliers

Equally important to all of these is the existence of a number of related businesses, which fulfil a significant need for the artists and craftspeople. These focus mostly on supplies such as art materials and tools, as well as on the people who help facilitate events, markets, and receptions through the provision of marquees, cranes, portable toilets, safety, event management, food, drink, tables, chairs, and so on.

Mapping creative ecologies of Santa Fe

The various categories discussed above emerged by analyzing different aspects of the city's culture. This analysis included museums, galleries, markets, festivals, historical events, and natural settings, all of which help support and contribute to artistic and artisanal practices in the region. While these supporting elements are specific to Santa Fe, the broader categories are more generally applicable themes that can be useful to other communities. For example, the adobe-style of building in Santa Fe may be considered to provide the "Aesthetics and Atmosphere of Place" important in the development of a creative ecology. Likewise, certain aesthetic characteristics of a place may also be considered to contribute to a creative ecology in that place. In Figure 1.1, we present our Creative Ecology concept diagram.

In addition to these outer or externally verifiable factors, we also include in our study inner factors, interpreted from our reading of relevant literature and from our field observations and interviews. These include the sense of community, perceptions, beliefs, values, motivations, and outlooks of those who are involved in the sustainment of these culturally significant traditions. These may be considered more intrinsic factors that underlie artisans' practices, which also support a creative ecology of the place to emerge and to be sustained. For example, Spanish Colonial artists and craft makers in Santa Fe share beliefs and values that are based on a common religion, history, and culture, which contribute to their cultural identity and sense of belonging to place. This, in turn, reinforces a sense of being part of the community through learning from each other by sharing ideas and skills, bartering, and swapping work, and bonding through the various events and markets in which

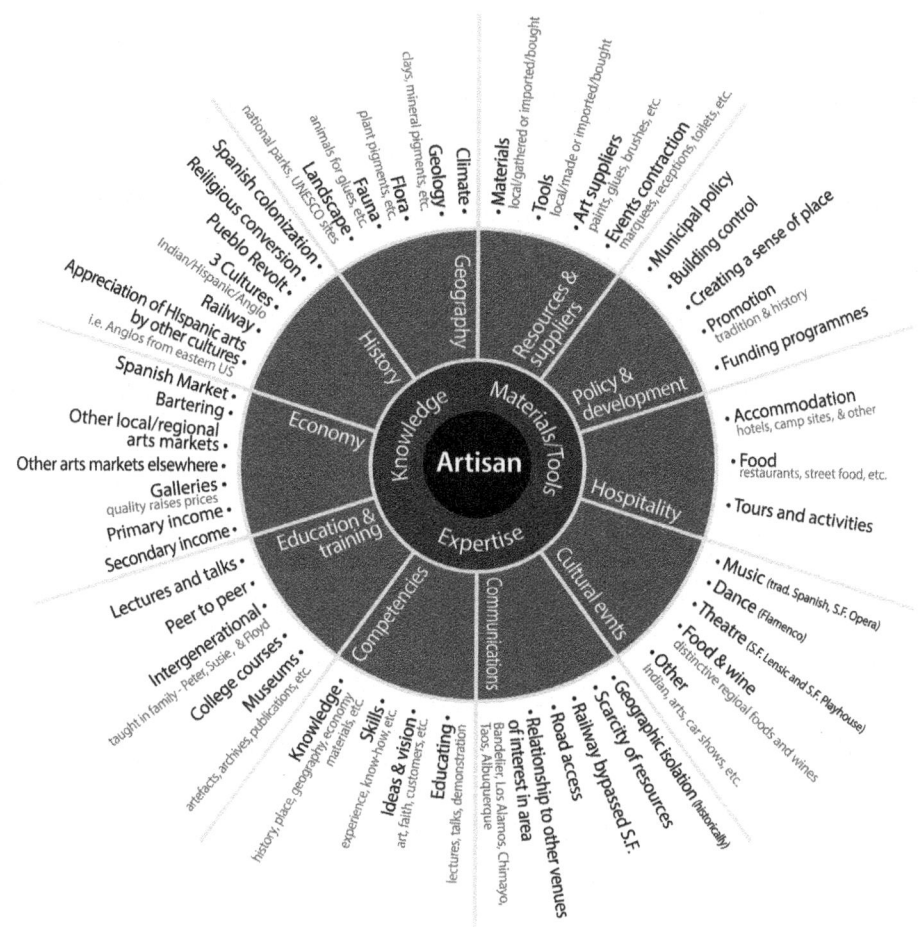

FIGURE 1.1 Creative Ecology of Santa Fe—conceptual mapping. © Jeyon Jung and Stuart Walker.

they participate. Therefore, a place-based creative ecology needs to take into account both extrinsic and intrinsic factors that are preserved and accumulated in a place over time.

This chapter has discussed our approach to studying culturally significant designs, products, and practices, and how initial study examples have shifted our focus from individual designs and products to the place in which those products are produced and practiced. A conceptual mapping of the Creative Ecology of Santa Fe presents artisans' knowledge and expertise at its core, together with ten other supporting elements identified as pertinent to the development of this flourishing art community. While this mapping has been developed from identifying case-specific examples, more generalized themes emerged as extrinsic supporting factors of a creative ecology. This creative ecology map has the potential to be used as a diagnostic tool to evaluate the conditions of other creative ecologies of practice in different places rather than to be applied as a universal framework.

References

Chapain, C., P. Cooke, L. De Propris, S. MacNeill, and J. Mateos-Garcia (2010), *Creative Clusters and Innovation. Putting Creativity on the Map*, London: NESTA.

Clifford, S. and A. King (1993), "Losing Your Place," in S. Clifford and A. King (eds.), *Local Distinctiveness: Place, Particularity and Identity*, London: Common Ground.

Day, P. (2014), [radio] "Cyber Town Malvern," World of Business, Radio 4, BBC London, broadcast Thursday, 16 January at 20:30 GMT.

Gould, H. (2001), "Culture & Social Capital," in F. Matarasso (ed.), *Recognising Culture: A Series of Briefing Papers on Culture and Development*, London: Comedia.

Gunn, M. C. (1980), "Cultural Ecology: A Brief Overview," *Nebraska Anthropologist*. Paper 149.

Horton, S. (2005), "Where is the 'Mexican' in 'New Mexican'?: Enacting History, Enacting Dominance in the Santa Fe Fiesta," in A. Gulliford (ed.), *Preserving Western History*, 98–106, Santa Fe, NM: University of New Mexico Press.

Jenkins, M. E. and A. H. Schroeder (1973), *A Brief History of New Mexico*, Albuquerque, NM: UNM Press.

Kokko, S. and M. Kaipainen (2015), "The Changing Role of Cultural Heritage in Traditional Textile Crafts from Cyprus," *Craft Research*, 6 (1): 9–30.

Kroeber, A. L. and C. Kluckhohn (1952), "Culture: A Critical Review of Concepts and Definitions," Papers, Peabody Museum of Archaeology & Ethnology, Harvard University.

Lin, R. T. (2007), "Transforming Taiwan Aboriginal Cultural Features into Modern Product Design: A Case Study of a Cross-Cultural Product Design Model," *International Journal of Design*, 1 (1): 45–53.

Mitchell, J., G. Joyce, S. Hill, and A. M. Hooper (2014), *Building on the Past, Facing the Future: Renewing the Creative Economy of New Mexico*. Albuquerque, NM: University of New Mexico, Bureau of Business & Economic Research.

Porter, M. E. (1990), "The Competitive Advantage of Notions," *Harvard Business Review*, 68 (2): 73–93.

Ranchhod, A. and C. Gurău (2007), *Marketing strategies: A Contemporary Approach*, New York, NY: Pearson Education.

Saxenian, A. (1994), *Regional Advantage: Culture and Competition in Silicon Valley and Route 128*, Cambridge, MA: Harvard University Press.

Scott, A. J. (1996), "The Craft, Fashion, and Cultural-Products Industries of Los Angeles: Competitive Dynamics and Policy Dilemmas in a Multisectoral Image-Producing Complex," *Annals of the Association of American Geographers*, 86 (2): 306–23.

Shin, M. J., T. Cassidy, and E. M. Moore (2011), "Cultural Reinvention for Traditional Korean Bojagi," *International Journal of Fashion Design, Technology and Education*, 4 (3): 213–23.

Spencer-Oatey, H. (2012), *What is Culture? A Compilation of Quotations*. GlobalPAD Core Concepts. Available online: http://go.warwick.ac.uk/globalpadintercultural (accessed November 12, 2016).

Steward, J. (1972), "The Concept and Method of Cultural Ecology," in *Theory of Culture Change: The Methodology of Multilinear Evolution*, 30–42, Champaign, IL: University of Illinois Press.

Tansley, A. G. (1935), "The Use and Abuse of Vegetational Concepts and Terms," *Ecology*, 16 (3): 284–307.

Titon, J. T. (2009), "Music and Sustainability: An Ecological Viewpoint," *The World of Music*, 119–37.

2

Forging New Futures

Cultural Significance, Revitalization, and Authenticity

Amy Twigger Holroyd

Introduction

This chapter discusses the revitalization of designs, products, and practices that are "culturally significant": deemed to be important to particular communities because of their social, historical, and/or aesthetic values. These values are frequently associated with traditional artifacts and craft processes, and with items that have a strong association with a particular place. Today, for a variety of reasons, many of these designs, products, and practices are in decline. Yet, across the globe, countless initiatives are seeking to revitalize them. Designers are frequently involved in these initiatives, often playing a key role in shaping the interaction between tradition and innovation.

This chapter is a personal reflective exploration of various factors at play within these revitalization interventions. It emerges from the research undertaken in collaboration with other authors featured in this volume, and is based on a wide-ranging review of literature, both within and outside the sphere of design. I will begin by exploring the meaning of cultural significance in more detail, along with the impacts of globalization on local and traditional designs, products, and practices. I will then discuss revitalization initiatives, focusing on the motivations behind such projects and the complex considerations that designers must deal with when working in this field. Finally, I will use the notion of authenticity to challenge widespread assumptions about tradition and origin—and, particularly, the implications of these assumptions for revitalization. While my focus here is material culture, it is important to recognize that debates are taking place in other cultural spheres—such as food, architecture, and music—that yield many productive parallels concerning decline, revitalization, tradition, and modernity.

Defining cultural significance

I will start by identifying the type of products being discussed in this chapter. These products have three key characteristics:

- *tangible* (rather than intangible "products" such as dance and music);
- *durable* (rather than products that are completely consumed in one use such as food and drink);
- *portable* (rather than permanent structures such as buildings).

I am, therefore, talking about physical artifacts such as tableware, furniture, and jewelry. It is important to stress that the concern here is not with singular artifacts, but rather *types* of artifacts, of which there will be countless individual examples. By "designs," I mean the surface patterns and three-dimensional forms associated with such products; by "practices," I mean the processes involved in their construction, use, and repair.

I am especially interested in designs, products, and practices that are significant to particular place-based cultures: local, regional, and national communities. But what does "significant" mean? The notion of cultural significance is widely discussed in relation to the conservation of heritage sites, and this work provides a useful starting point. De la Torre and Mason (2002: 3) propose that "Cultural significance … mean[s] the importance of a site as determined by the aggregate of values attributed to it." Borrowing this logic, a culturally significant design, product or practice is one considered to be important due to the various values attributed to it. This raises the next question: what are these values? Mason (2002: 7) explains that in this context, values mean "the qualities and characteristics seen in things, in particular the positive characteristics (actual and potential)." He argues that values are multiple and diverse: "In a given moment, a given heritage site, building, or object has a number of different values ascribed to it" (Mason 2002: 10). Furthermore, values are not absolute; rather, they are always in flux and contingent on their cultural surroundings.

Although values cannot be objectively measured, they can be productively explored and assessed. Various typologies of values—which enable a range of perspectives to be understood—have been developed in terms of heritage sites. As Mason (2002: 10) indicates, there are many commonalities between these typologies: "In most instances, they describe the same pie, but slice it in subtly different ways." The Australian National Committee of the International Council on Monuments and Sites (Australia ICOMOS 2013), for example, organizes values into five categories: aesthetic, historic, scientific, social, and spiritual. The categorization used by English Heritage (2008) comprises aesthetic, historical, evidential and communal value. Mason emphasizes that one typology will not speak equally well to all cultural milieus, and encourages the development of new typologies, where required. With this in mind, I have adapted the typologies identified above for the domain of designs, products, and practices. The resulting categorization comprises social, historical, and aesthetic values, as briefly described below:

- *Social value* refers to the associations that a design, product or practice has for a particular cultural group and the social, cultural or spiritual meanings that it holds for them. Social value may reflect a sense of identity, distinctiveness, and social interaction.

- *Historical value* derives from the ways in which aspects of life from the past can be connected to the present through designs, products, and practices. It may be based on the length of time a tradition has developed, its association with specific people or events, or its rarity or uniqueness.

- *Aesthetic value* refers to the visual, sensory, and perceptual experience of a design, product or practice. It includes artifacts and patterns with uncommonly attractive or distinctive qualities that evoke strong feelings or special meanings.

To be deemed culturally significant, a design, product or practice would need to have a strong sense of value across these three categories. Because I am primarily interested in significance felt within and amongst a community, I place the greatest emphasis on social value; historical and aesthetic values should be seen—for this purpose—as supporting elements. By using this typology, cultural significance is guided by the values felt by the communities in question and thus can be adapted to diverse contexts. Despite this flexibility, I have noted two characteristics that are frequently associated with cultural significance: designs, products, and practices that are traditional—especially traditional crafts—and those that originate in a specific place. These characteristics provide useful indicators of social, historical, and aesthetic values, and thus help to establish my field of interest. Yet—as I will explain—both tradition and origin are rather slippery concepts that must be approached with a degree of critical curiosity.

Impacts of globalization

Many, but by no means all, culturally significant designs, products, and practices can be traced back to pre-modern times, before the far-reaching transformations in society associated with the processes of modernization. Transitions to modern life occur differently across countries and regions due to the influence of countless geographical, social, economic, and political factors. Yet, taking a broad view, modernization involves a shift towards consumer capitalism and industrialization. While in rare cases craft traditions may be sustained outside a market economy, in the vast majority of contexts, culturally significant products and practices must adapt to an emergent consumer society. Three key factors in this change can be identified.

First, traditional craft products have to compete with cheaper mass-produced goods, whether produced in the region or imported. There is competition, too, in terms of work, with paid employment in other sectors often offering a reliable income and a better material standard of living than a precarious living based on craft production. Second, modernization carries with it an innate sense of progress. This can cause communities to make a conscious break with traditions, including local crafts and vernacular designs, which come to be seen as old-fashioned and backwards-looking (Borges 2011; Taylor 1997). Third, the changes associated with modernization often bring about significant changes in lifestyle. As traditional practices, which had been embedded in everyday life, become obsolete, the products associated with them fall out of use, along with the motifs and patterns that adorn them, and the underpinning meanings of these designs are gradually lost.

Globalization, described by Albrow (1990: 9) as "all those processes by which the peoples of the world are incorporated into a single world society," has brought about further fundamental changes in everyday life.

> In each case, something distinctive has been replaced by something bland; something organic by something manufactured; something definably local with something emptily placeless; something human scale with something impersonal. The result is stark, simple and brutal: everywhere is becoming the same as everywhere else (Kingsnorth 2008: 7).

Scrase (2003: 449) takes the producer's perspective, detailing the multiple ways in which "the globalization of production exacerbates, rather than diminishes, the marginal status of artisan communities" in less economically developed countries. Thus, the impact of globalization on culturally significant designs, products, and practices is arguably the central impetus and challenge for contemporary revitalization initiatives.

Yet alternative perspectives suggest that the impacts of globalization are more complex than they may first appear. Robins (1991) points out that it is not just the standardized products of multinational companies that spread across the world, but also the vernacular creations of particular cultures—such as (to pick two undeniably global examples) pizza and jazz. As Levitt (1983: 31) argues: "globalization does not mean the end of segments. It means, instead, their expansion to worldwide proportions."

Perhaps most importantly in the context of revitalization, many argue that the processes of modernization and globalization actually stimulate desire for tradition, diversity, and local distinctiveness.

> For a period, many believed that industrialization would kill craft. Similarly, globalization would kill local cultural expressions ... However, this prognosis of extinction was not confirmed. There are many clues to the contrary; that the place of craft in our modern society is expanding (Borges 2011: 203).

There are various reasons for this recent growth of interest, which warrant in-depth examination and explanation. While such examination falls beyond the scope of this present discussion, there are several important aspects of modernization and globalization that positively support revitalization.

First, in many cultures—particularly those that have enjoyed the trappings of modern life for several decades—the "gloss" is starting to wear off mass-produced, globalized products.

> In a world filled with generic, throwaway goods, where our relationship to the things that populate our everyday environment (not to mention their origins) has become more and more abstract, there is a rising demand for design that communicates and upholds a deeper connection to our personal identities – objects that bring value to both the creators and the users over and above a price tag (Carpenter 2014).

Hence, the contemporary movement to revitalize culturally significant designs, products, and practices is not (or not *just)* the latest instalment in an age-old anxiety about progress and change, which laments the loss of particular ways of life as they approach extinction (Williams 1973). Rather, there is evidence that this movement is an inherent part of a shift to a post-industrial era, in which "the success and contradictions of the Fordist system are resolved in a new set of economic and institutional relationships" (Heying and Ryder 2010: 25).

Second, it is important to note that modern, globalized life—and particularly the emergence and development of the internet—presents "new opportunities to articulate national and local identities" (Kaiser 2012: 173). Hence, while multinational corporations may find it easier than ever to market their products to a worldwide audience, the "long tail" effect of the internet (Anderson 2006) is turning conventional marketing on its head and allowing individual makers and micro-enterprises to connect directly with distant customers and collaborators (Luckman 2012). The internet is also enabling amateur enthusiasts to connect around niche interests, bringing new life to traditional crafts and place-related designs. For example, members of the Heirloom Knitting group on the knitting-related social network Ravelry reverse-engineered a highly complex Shetland lace shawl pattern from an archival image in a matter of weeks by working remotely yet collaboratively (Fleegle 2009), thus contributing to the revival of a culturally significant tradition.

The third point concerns the relationship between modernity and tradition, which can be explored using insights from the field of sociology. As discussed above, the transition to modern life involves transformations in society and the "leaving behind" of traditional ways of living. Giddens (1991) is particularly interested in this transition. He argues that in traditional societies, our choices are largely restricted by existing structures of class, religion, occupation, and so on; in modern societies, by contrast, tradition becomes less important and we have much more freedom in how to live. While this characterization may appear somewhat over-simplistic today, Giddens's central thinking about the impact of this freedom holds true: that it leads to uncertainty. Indeed, uncertainty and fragmentation have been widely identified as the characterizing features of modern (described by some as postmodern or late-modern) life. However, tradition—which modernity supersedes—can offer a sense of stability to individuals and societies. As West (2012: 13) argues, "tradition ... can be of great use in a liquid modern world, a questioning, solidifying force, and a reminder that society cannot spend its entire time in the fast lane." Similarly, globalization—which breaks down borders and appears to combine us into one homogenous culture—simultaneously increases the significance of place (Harvey 1990). Hence, it can be argued that modernization and globalization unexpectedly, and paradoxically, *fuel* our appetite for the tradition and sense of place associated with culturally significant designs, products, and practices (Scrase 2003).

In summary: modernization and globalization have multiple, and sometimes conflicting, impacts on place-related cultures. As Ascherson (1993: 49) argues, the world is "becoming more uniform and less uniform, at once coagulating into larger entities and breaking down into smaller ones." Hence, the impact of these processes on culturally significant designs, products, and practices is complex, acting both to suppress and to support them.

Revitalization

I use the term "revitalization" to describe any initiative that brings new life to a culturally significant design, product or practice, while aiming to retain (or even enhance) the values associated with it. Building on the flexible and contingent understanding of cultural significance discussed above, a revitalization initiative could be assessed by studying the social, historical, and/or aesthetic values associated with the emergent cultural form. If the values were sustained, it could be considered to be a success. This is an intentionally broad view of revitalization, which allows for changing dimensions of cultural significance. It encompasses approaches that translate a culturally significant design to an entirely new context alongside those which invigorate a craft in its traditional guise. Revitalization strategies might include the redesign of products, the application of patterns and forms in new contexts, or new uses for traditional craft practices. They could address the production process, the selection of materials, promotion and branding, routes to market, enterprise and business models, and the transfer and development of relevant skills. By allowing for radical reinventions, my definition of revitalization is notably different to the conservation approach generally applied to heritage sites. As explained in the Australia ICOMOS Burra Charter for culturally significant sites, conservation "requires a cautious approach of changing as much as necessary but as little as possible" (Australia ICOMOS 2013: 3).

A range of stakeholders can be identified in revitalization initiatives. While some projects are initiated by individuals, communities or commercial businesses, in many cases governmental or non-governmental organizations have played an instrumental role. In the global South, the revitalization of local crafts has been widely seen as a way of sustaining elements of traditional culture, while providing a useful and accessible means of economic and social development (Friel and Santagata 2008). These projects often aim to open up new markets, beyond the local community (Cohen 1989) or improve the goods on offer in terms of aesthetic appeal, quality or utility. Some revitalized products are kept under the control of one particular business or organization, but in many cases the instigators aim for updated designs and practices to be appropriated by the wider community. Although there are instances of revitalization being led by members of the community to which a tradition is connected, projects frequently involve outsiders coming in to provide professional expertise, investment, and crucial links to distant consumers.

Designers are often involved in revitalization initiatives, bringing their skills to bear on specific tasks such as developing new product designs or branding, as well as applying their design thinking to generate holistic strategies to address the challenges faced by culturally significant designs, products, and practices. In many cases, designers will find themselves collaborating with traditional craft makers; these collaborations have recently been described by one company that is active in this area as a "growing, widespread practice" (Carpenter 2014). Some design-led projects are successful and positive; others are less so. Borges (2011), for example, describes a wide range of revitalization projects in Brazil and highlights many issues that arise in these encounters, particularly relating to the differences in formal education and status between designers and artisans. Borges highlights the problem of short-term projects that produce eye-catching results, but do not provide any lasting benefit to the communities in question. Similarly, Ladd (2012) questions whether well-intentioned Western designers working with craftspeople in African countries might inadvertently collude in promulgating an idea of Africa as dependent. This view chimes with that of Nussbaum (2010), who asks: "is humanitarian design the new imperialism?" Of course, not all cases of revitalization through design involve professional designers being "parachuted in" to less economically developed countries. Yet these considerations relating to status and impact highlight the need for those seeking to engage with culturally significant designs, products, and practices to consider the wider ramifications of their work.

Authenticity

A dominant concept in popular discourses surrounding culturally significant designs, products, and practices is authenticity. This is frequently a key element in the marketing of culturally significant designs, products, and practices, and an interest in authenticity often extends to those initiating revitalization projects. Yet the traditions and origins on which this authenticity is based are often far from straightforward. For example: many practices that are generally considered to have enduring and well-established traditions are revealed, upon closer inspection, to be relatively recent developments. Hobsbawm (1983) argues that these "invented traditions" consciously seek to join the present with the past through links with history that are artificially staged. Tartan is a classic example of an invented tradition; the association of tartan with particular Scottish clans—popularly assumed to date back to antiquity—only came about as part of a pageant devised by Sir Walter Scott in 1822 (Trevor-Roper 1983: 19). Similarly, the matreshka doll (Figure 2.1), often believed to be a traditional Russian folk symbol, was invented by an individual designer in 1891 as part of the kustar initiative to revitalize local "peasant" crafts (Salmond 1996).

Furthermore, while we tend to think of traditions as static, Shils (1981) explains that they evolve in the process of transmission. Indeed, it is this ability to adapt that allows traditions to remain relevant in the long term. Detailed accounts of specific

FIGURE 2.1 Matreshka dolls, purchased in Moscow, 2012. Courtesy Twigger Holroyd.
© Amy Twigger Holroyd.

craft traditions describe cultures of creativity and innovation. According to basket
maker Joe Hogan, who has studied the diversity of vernacular baskets in Ireland,
"from the outside, traditional work can look very static, but the closer you get, the
more you realise that it's experimental" (quoted by Lloyd-Jones 2014: 35).

Likewise, delving into the histories of "local" products generally reveals instances
of intracultural diffusion—whether through colonization, migration or trade—
through which patterns and processes have moved around the world (Hann 2013).
Take, for example, the Paisley pattern. While the pattern is now most frequently
used in printed textiles (Figure 2.2), it gained its name because of its association
with weavers producing shawls in the Scottish town of Paisley in the nineteenth
century. However, the pattern did not originate in Scotland; in fact, the distinctive
designs used by the Paisley weavers—along with weavers in Norwich, Edinburgh,
and Paris—were copied from shawls imported from Kashmir. Tracing the story
further, evidence suggests that the pattern actually originated in ancient Babylon
(Reilly 1987). Interestingly, the shop owner who commissioned the matreshka doll
instructed the designer to take inspiration from a Japanese nesting toy (Salmond
1996). Thus, even in cases of invented traditions, there are frequently far more
enduring stories to be uncovered.

The issue of authenticity can be useful: it reminds us that there is a limit to
how far and how fast culturally significant designs, products, and practices can be

FIGURE 2.2 Paisley pattern, detail of men's dressing gown, 1974. Courtesy The Marks & Spencer Company Archive. © Amy Twigger Holroyd.

changed without losing the identity and meaning that underpin social, historical, and aesthetic values. It reminds us, too, to question the portrayal of particular designs, products, and practices as "traditional" or "local," remembering that these claims may be deceptively overblown or even entirely invented—especially as, according to Hobsbawm (1983), invented traditions occur more frequently in post-traditional societies. The desire for authenticity acts as a counterbalance to the temptation to appropriate traditional designs and crudely translate them into new contexts, which have no link to the "original" culture. Although this practice is widespread in all fields of design, and particularly fashion and textiles, serious concerns have been raised about the political and ethical implications of the use of indigenous cultural heritage in commercial and external contexts. Shand (2002), for example, discusses the complex issues arising from the appropriation of Maori graphic patterns for products, including swimwear, perfume packaging, and rugby boots. This desire also acts to protect—to some extent—artisan communities whose livelihoods are threatened by mass-produced copies of local crafts, often imported from distant countries with lower labor costs (Rhodes 2011).

On the other hand, authenticity can be a problematic notion. It tends to present a normalizing force that closes down complexity and difference in favor of a more easily digestible and romanticized image (Goodrum 2005). For example, Luckman (2012) describes the ways in which the desire for authenticity amongst tourists in the English Lake District inadvertently sidelines the work of those craftspeople who—through factors such as ethnicity, sexuality or style—fall outside their stereotypical expectations. Reflecting on the desire for authenticity also reveals a hidden issue relating to innovation and tradition that is particularly pertinent to the topic of revitalization. Baker (1997: 132) argues that "makers in a western society employing non-European pattern motifs will be understood to be inspired by the ideas, philosophies and symbolisms of other cultures, but the non-European maker will be seen as betraying tradition." Many people have concerns about the "inauthentic" commodification of tradition when culturally significant artifacts are adapted for consumption by Western tourists (Howes 1996). However, as Baker points out, such concerns can mask an unspoken assumption that non-Western communities should remain traditional and authentic, and should not evolve and adapt to changing times. This assumption can also be made by those working within revitalization projects; Ladd (2012) discovered such attitudes while contributing as a practicing designer to a charity-led project seeking to revitalize "authentic" traditional weaving in Burkina Faso.

Of course, the "trinketization" of crafts (Urry and Larsen 2011: 61) can lead to a loss of meaning and diversity, and a consequent decline in the social, historical, and/or aesthetic values associated with designs, products, and practices. This issue arises frequently, and designers are rightly wary of contributing to this trend. However, Cohen (1989) argues that in cases where designs, products, and practices are already falling out of use—thus, in some ways, losing the values associated with them—reinvention for external markets may be a valuable means of sustaining a traditional craft. Cohen also argues that we should not jump to conclusions about tourist products, explaining that "craft styles ... at first produced for the market, become in some instances reintegrated into the ethnic culture and used by the local people" (1989: 166). He cites the example of the "bula-shirts" made for tourists from industrially printed fabric by Fijian tailors, which were subsequently adopted for everyday wear by Fijians themselves. Meanwhile, Taylor (1997) describes a situation in which Romanian makers produced "authentic" forms of traditional weaving and embroidery for the tourist market, while experimenting with alternative versions—using "modern" synthetic materials—for their own use. Examples such as this demonstrate that multiple versions of culturally significant products, created for different applications and audiences, can coexist.

Concerns about authenticity can create an unhelpful hierarchy of "genuine" tradition over invented tradition, or products with demonstrably long origins in a single place over those that have complex cross-cultural routes. Arguably, the most important indicator of cultural significance is perception: if those within a community consider a design, product or practice to carry social, historical, and/or aesthetic values, this should surely outweigh any misgivings about its authenticity. As Faiers (2008: 279) proposes in relation to the reinvention of the kilt, the myths surrounding invented traditions quickly become "embedded in popular consciousness," and it is more fruitful to work *with* these myths than pedantically seeking to dispel them. Similarly, when we assess revitalized designs, products, and practices, perhaps we should concern ourselves less with the distance that a new interpretation has traveled from its "original" form and focus more on whether it is valued by the community in question.

Conclusion

In this chapter I have proposed a typology of values to define culturally significant designs, products, and practices. Taking a global view, I have examined the challenges facing these aspects of material culture and considered the role of designers in revitalization initiatives. A critical discussion of the notion of authenticity—in terms of both tradition and origin—has revealed the complexity of this field.

Reflecting on this discussion, it becomes apparent that evolution and change are integral elements of tradition. While the initial response to an "endangered" design, product or practice may be preservation, such an approach would arguably degrade its cultural significance and harm its chances of surviving and thriving. If we fall into the trap of forcing these cultural forms to become static, we effectively turn them into invented traditions, existing only to offer a hollow sense of history. As anthropologist Antonio Arantes points out, "practice as social action cannot be preserved. It has to change in order to stay the same" (quoted by Borges 2011: 139). Hence, it can be argued that if culturally significant designs, products, and practices are to be truly relevant to their communities, they must be allowed to change.

Likewise, cross-cultural interactions are part and parcel of human life: the influences of "outsiders" have long shaped our cultures. "Origin" is a largely misleading concept, suggesting that designs, products, and practices are uniquely linked to a single place, when in fact their histories are much more complex. When thinking about this topic, it is useful to consider the words of the cultural theorist Stuart Hall, who suggested: "instead of asking what are people's roots, I ought to think about what are their routes, the different points by which they have come to be" (1999). This idea translates directly to culturally significant designs, products, and practices: rather than thinking only of their roots, we should recognize the complex routes that have carried them to the present day. Furthermore, we can think about how we, as designers, can contribute to the continuation of these routes: developing new ways forward for culturally significant designs, products, and practices, keeping the past in mind but looking towards the future.

References

Albrow, M. (1990), "Introduction," in M. Albrow and E. King (eds.), *Globalization, Knowledge and Society: Readings from International Sociology*, 3–13, London: SAGE.

Anderson, C. (2006), *The Long Tail: How Endless Choice is Creating Unlimited Demand*, London: Random House.

Ascherson, N. (1993), "The Failure of the Melting Pot," in S. Clifford and A. King (eds.), *Local Distinctiveness*, 47–54, London: Common Ground.

Australia ICOMOS (2013), *The Burra Charter: The Australia ICOMOS Charter for Places of Cultural Significance*, Burwood.

Baker, P. L. (1997), "20th Century Myth-making: Persian Tribal Rugs," in T. Harrod (ed.), *Obscure Objects of Desire: Reviewing the Crafts in the Twentieth Century*, 126–35, London: Crafts Council.

Borges, A. (2011), *Design + Craft: the Brazilian Path*, São Paulo: Editora Terceiro Nome.

Carpenter, W. (2014), "The Past is the Future," *Pamono*. Available online: http://www. pamono.com/stories/the-past-is-the-future (accessed May 10, 2016).

Cohen, E. (1989), "The Commercialization of Ethnic Crafts," *Journal of Design History*, 2 (2/3): 161–8.

de la Torre, M. and R. Mason (2002), "Introduction," in M. de la Torre (ed.), *Assessing the Values of Cultural Heritage*, 3–4, Los Angeles, CA: The Getty Conservation Institute.

English Heritage (2008), *Conservation Principles: Policies and Guidance for the Sustainable Management of the Historic Environment*, London: English Heritage.

Faiers, J. (2008), *Tartan*, Oxford: Berg.

Fleegle (2009), [blog] "The Queen Susan Shawl," *Fleegle's blog*, November 28. Available online: http://fleeglesblog.blogspot.co.uk/2009/11/queen-susan-shawl.html (accessed May 10, 2016).

Friel, M. and W. Santagata (2008), "Making Material Cultural Heritage Work: From Traditional Handicrafts to Soft Industrial Design," in H. Anheier and Y. Isar (eds.), *The Cultural Economy*, 274–283, London: SAGE.

Giddens, A. (1991), *Modernity and Self-Identity: Self and Society in the Late Modern Age*, Stanford, CA: Stanford University Press.

Goodrum, A. (2005), *The National Fabric: Fashion, Britishness, Globalization*, Oxford: Berg.

Hall, S. (1999), "A Conversation with Stuart Hall," *The Journal of the International Institute* 7 (1), available online: http://hdl.handle.net/2027/spo.4750978.0007.107 (accessed August 10, 2017).

Hann, M. (2013), *Symbol, Pattern & Symmetry: the Cultural Significance of Structure*, London: Bloomsbury Academic.

Harvey, D. (1990), *The Condition of Postmodernity*, Oxford: Blackwell.

Heying, C. and M. Ryder (2010), "Genesis of the Concept," in C. Heying (ed.), *Brew to Bikes: Portland's Artisan Economy*, 23–9, Portland, OR: Ooligan Press.

Hobsbawm, E. (1983), "Introduction: Inventing Traditions," in E. Hobsbawm and T. Ranger (eds.), *The Invention of Tradition*, Cambridge: Cambridge University Press.

Howes, D. (1996), "Introduction: Commodities and Cultural Borders," in D. Howes (ed.), *Cross-Cultural Consumption: Global Markets, Local Realities*, 1–16, London: Routledge.

Kaiser, S. B. (2012), *Fashion and Cultural Studies*, London: Bloomsbury Academic.

Kingsnorth, P. (2008), *Real England: the Battle Against the Bland*, London: Portobello Books.

Ladd, K. (2012), "A Handmade Future: the Impact of Design on the Production and Consumption of Contemporary West African Craft as a Tool for Sustainable Development," Ph.D. thesis, University of Brighton, Brighton.

Levitt, T. (1983), *The Marketing Imagination*, New York, NY: The Free Press.

Lloyd-Jones, T. (2014), "Joe Hogan: A Way with Willow," *Crafts*, 248: 30–5.

Luckman, S. (2012), *Locating Cultural Work: the Politics and Poetics of Rural, Regional and Remote Creativity*, Basingstoke: Palgrave Macmillan.

Mason, R. (2002), "Assessing Values in Conservation Planning," in M. de la Torre (ed.), *Assessing the Values of Cultural Heritage*, 5–30, Los Angeles, CA: The Getty Conservation Institute.

Nussbaum, B. (2010), "Is Humanitarian Design the New Imperialism?" *Fast Company*. Available online: http://www.fastcodesign.com/1661859/is-humanitarian-design-the-new-imperialism (accessed May 10, 2016).

Reilly, V. (1987), *The Paisley Pattern*, Glasgow: Richard Drew.

Rhodes, S. (2011), "Beyond 'Nourishing the Soul of a Nation': Craft in the Context of South Africa," *Making Futures*, 2.

Robins, K. (1991), "Tradition and Translation: National Culture in its Global Context," in J. Corner and S. Harvey (eds.), *Enterprise and Heritage: Crosscurrents of National Culture*, 21–44, London: Routledge.

Salmond, W. R. (1996), *Arts and Crafts in Late Imperial Russia: Reviving the Kustar Art Industries, 1870–1917*, Cambridge: Cambridge University Press.

Scrase, T. J. (2003), "Precarious Production: Globalization and Artisan Labour in the Third World," *Third World Quarterly*, 24 (3): 449–61.

Shand, P. (2002), "Scenes from the Colonial Catwalk: Cultural Appropriation, Intellectual Property Rights, and Fashion," *Cultural Analysis*, 3: 47–88.

Shils, E. (1981), *Tradition*, London: Faber.

Taylor, L. (1997), "State Involvement With Peasant Crafts in East/Central Europe 1947–97: the Cases of Poland and Romania," in T. Harrod (ed.), *Obscure Objects of Desire: Reviewing the Crafts in the Twentieth Century*, 53–65, London: Crafts Council.

Trevor-Roper, H. (1983), "The Invention of Tradition: the Highland Tradition of Scotland," in E. Hobsbawm and T. Ranger (eds.), *The Invention of Tradition*, 15–42, Cambridge: Cambridge University Press.

Urry, J. and J. Larsen (2011), *The Tourist Gaze 3.0*, 3rd edn, London: SAGE.

West, G. (2012), *Voicing Scotland: Folk, Culture, Nation*, Glasgow: Luath Press.

Williams, R. (1973), *The Country and the City*, London: Chatto and Windus.

3

Culturally Significant Artifacts and their Relationship to Tradition and Sustainability

Stuart Walker

Were not the gods responsible for that,
weaving catastrophe into the pattern of events
to make a song for future generations.
HOMER, *THE ODYSSEY*[1]

Introduction

In this chapter we will be considering artifacts, which embody knowledge, practices, and modes of living that, for one reason or another, are regarded as meaningful and culturally significant. These artifacts will be discussed in relation to tradition and contextualized within contemporary understandings of sustainability. It will be demonstrated that, in addition to any functional benefit they may offer, objects we tend to consider as culturally significant are manifestations of human values and deeper notions of human meaning. As such, their modes of making, their use, and their presence in our lives can teach us much about more sustainable approaches to material culture. Here, we will be focusing mainly on smaller functional objects of everyday use but many of the points raised will also apply to non-utilitarian artifacts that are appreciated for their symbolic meanings.

The discussion begins with a brief overview of the problem, which is addressed in two parts. The first part considers the inadequacies of the "modern" outlook and sets the scene for the second part, which considers the loss of a meaningful material culture, the loss of associated knowledge and practices, and, with them, the loss of social and environmental sustainability. It continues with an elaboration of the term *culturally significant artifacts* to reach an understanding of the various elements that this term encompasses. It will become apparent that a key ingredient of such artifacts is *tradition*. This word is often mistakenly construed as being only about the past, with negative connotations of nostalgia and mawkish sentimentality. We will show that tradition is actually deeply concerned with the present, with values that matter to us, and with those who come after us. Hence, *culturally significant artifacts* are relevant to our lives today and to future generations and so are critically connected to contemporary challenges of *sustainability*. In addition, because such artifacts can be understood as bearers and expressions of human values and meanings, they are vital to the creation of a more meaningful material culture.

The modern outlook and its shortcomings

There can be little doubt that we are living through a period of highly disruptive transformation. The priorities of scientific rationalism, materialism, and the narrowed worldview propagated by modernity are becoming less and less tenable (Ward 2014: 126). The consumption-driven, overly wasteful ways of living generated by modernity's emphasis on individualism cannot be sustained. The human and environmental costs of rising social disparities (Piketty 2014: 294), and loss of biodiversity and ecosystems are all too evident and increasingly worrying—as a recent World Bank report makes clear, "Forecasts of future changes in biodiversity are generally alarming" (2014: 70). Additionally, secularization, the hegemonic influences of globalization, and so-called "free trade", which characterize the market-based systems of corporate capitalism, are being challenged in many parts of the world—by those who react through retrenchment into fundamentalism; by those who choose to respond with violence; and by those looking for deeper, more peaceful paths forward that afford a greater sense of fulfilment than those proffered by consumerism (e.g. Pullella and Marsh 2015).

With its prioritization of science, technology, and instrumental rationality, a central principle of the modern era, which remains prevalent in today's period of late-modernity, is its deference to seemingly objective, evidence-based research, which compartmentalizes and categorizes data and is often seen as the sole basis of legitimate knowledge. This "detached observer" view of reality not only fails to take into consideration the fact that we are part of, not separate from, the world but also that our claimed objectivity is always affected by the theories we bring, the interpretations we make, and the values we hold (Cottingham 2014: 19–20). The dominance of these priorities in many aspects of contemporary life has created a constricted, abstracted view of reality and an inadequate understanding of the human condition, one that offers a rather colorless and disenchanted worldview (Taylor 2007: 25). Undeterred by these disturbing attributes, the transition to the modern tends to be framed in positive terms, at least in the Western account. It is also frequently seen as a culture-neutral development that those in any traditional culture would surely choose to undergo once they have understood the veracity of the empirical-scientific approach, the effectiveness of instrumental rationality, and the absurdity of many traditional ways of thinking such as religious beliefs that heed intuitive insights or involve leaps of faith. In this interpretation, the change to the modern is not about the rise of a new distinctive culture among others. It is a type of change "not defined in terms of the specific cultures it carries us from and to, but is rather seen as of a type any traditional culture could undergo" (Taylor 1995: 24).

Therefore, while fully recognizing the extraordinary scientific advances that have occurred in the modern period, it is important to acknowledge that the modern outlook has some serious deficiencies. These have been detailed by various authors, including philosopher Charles Taylor (1995: 26–32) and involve:

- a predisposition to separate facts from values;

- an emphasis on individualism, in which we see ourselves as "beings whose behavior is ultimately to be explained as individuals" rather than being shaped and defined through our relationships with others, including family, community, and the time and place in which we live;

- a lack of recognition that science has developed within a culture that involves not only the individual but also society, nature, and notions of morality and goodness, which are related to personal and cultural values—a point that echoes the concerns about objectivity mentioned above;

- a devaluing of embodied understandings, ritual, symbolism, and non-explicit evocative forms of expression;

- insensitivity to the disastrous effects of modernity on other cultures through a one-size-fits-all transition towards societal secularization and atomization in which our own ethnocentric forms are projected onto others, and traditional beliefs are marginalized or lost.

Indeed, the severe impact of colonialism, imperialism and the imposition of Western values on traditional cultures in the modern era has become an area of academic study in its own right under the rubric of *Postcolonialism* or *Postcolonial Studies* (SOAS 2015; Young 2003). These considerable, often debilitating, consequences of modernity tend to be overlooked in the "culture-neutral" account.

In acknowledging the inadequacies of the modern outlook, and despite a pervasive impression to the contrary, it is important to recognize that human beings are not simply or wholly rationally acting, self-interested individuals. We are also social beings who are intuitive, emotional, creative, and imaginative. We experience the world in the first person, i.e. subjectively, and in a holistic rather than a compartmentalized manner. Individual facts and details are seen and understood not as separate, discrete elements but within and as part of a larger context of significance and value. These broader, integrated ways of knowing are associated with "right-hemisphere" understandings of reality, in contrast to the detailed but piecemeal ways of knowing characteristic of the modern era, which are associated with left-hemisphere brain activity (McGilchrist 2009: 41–2). By valuing and emphasizing the contributions of both, we gain a more comprehensive picture—one in which knowledge derived from meticulous analysis is contextualized within an overall, synthetical understanding.

Today, the overly narrow modern perspective is slowly giving ground to these broader understandings. While this is certainly a necessary development if we are to more effectively address pressing issues of sustainability, it is also disconcerting and disruptive. Established certainties are dissolving and new understandings and priorities are coming to the fore. Inevitably, there will be those that resist this shift and try to hold on to outmoded approaches, but as in any period of transition, when a belief system or worldview reaches a point where it no longer makes sense, things change (Ward 2014: 125).

The loss of a meaningful material culture

In the latter half of the twentieth century and the early years of the twenty-first, the period generally referred to as late-modernity, the Western economies underwent a transition from a creative, production-based economy to an illimitable, consumption-based economy. This emphasis on consumption—of products, services, entertainments, and experiences—has led to inordinately wasteful lifestyles that are having extremely damaging effects on natural places and ecosystems. The same period also witnessed divisive, often unscrupulous, social-economic developments, resulting in rising inequalities in most countries with developed economies, as well as in many countries with developing economies. According to former chief economist and senior vice president of the World Bank, François Bourguignon, these retrograde directions can be attributed to a number of interrelated events and occurrences that include globalization, technological progress, expansion of the financial sector and the shift to free-market economic doctrines (2015: 47, 117–18). Yet, faced with very considerable social and environmental ills, two important associated factors tend to hamper our effective responses.

First, modernity is synonymous with a rejection of tradition and the long-established, often deep-rooted, modes of living and acting that tradition represents. In the early years of the twentieth century, the past—our history, traditions and long-held values—were effectively consigned to the rubbish heap. Marinetti's influential *Futurist Manifesto*, which appeared in *Le Figaro* on February 20, 1909, was an outspoken condemnation of the accumulated knowledge, learning and wisdom that had been handed down from past generations (Italian Futurism 2014). It expressed something of the mood of the times and helped spur a view that the well of knowledge, stories, values, and traditions of a particular community or society were essentially irrelevant. As we have seen, the progress of modernity is characterized by a strengthening of individualism, increased secularization, and a decline in common patterns of thought, mutual understandings, and shared values, all of which have fuelled societal fragmentation. But to address today's social and environmental concerns more effectively, there will need to be collective action and common purpose. Tradition is associated with just such common understandings, shared values, community, and the common good, as we will discuss. All these factors contribute to one's sense of identity and belonging within a particular social group, and they can give a sense of depth, meaning, and worth to our activities.

Second, the incessant distractions offered by consumer society, especially in a digitally connected world, tend to hinder more contemplative and reflective modes of being. But contemplation and reflection, including self-reflection, are important for ensuring a worthwhile life. That is, a life worth living that accords with individual flourishing, social well-being, and humanity's enduring search for meaning, encompassed by what Huxley referred to as the highest common factor and the perennial philosophy (1945: 9). The rise of digital devices, social media, and web-based services that enable communication, convenience, and personalization has done little to stave off the atomization of social life. Sherry Turkle, a psychologist who studies the effects of digital culture, has pointed out that with the escalation of demands created by these technologies we have more online contacts but less time to ourselves and fewer friends (2011: 180). She asks, "is it really sensible to suggest that the way to revitalize community is to sit alone in our rooms typing at our networked computers and filling our lives with virtual friends?" (1996: 387). Distraction, atomization, and lack of real community ties are all antithetical to building common understandings and a sense of common purpose by which we can more effectively address environmental and social concerns.

These factors—from the rejection of tradition to the myriad distractions and trivia of consumer society—not only affect our personal outlook and sense of identity and purpose, they also affect the nature of our activities, including the design, production, tenor and meaning of our material goods. The relationship of these concerns to the loss of a meaningful material culture is summarized in Figure 3.1.

Given these shortcomings, it is perhaps unsurprising that in recent years there has been renewed interest in ways of doing, ways of making, and in the creation and use of artifacts that are representative of what we might refer to as "non-modern" or "after-modern" outlooks.[2] They emerge from a different way of thinking, which represents or perhaps strives to achieve a more balanced outlook: an outlook that sees value in the subjective as well as the objective; the

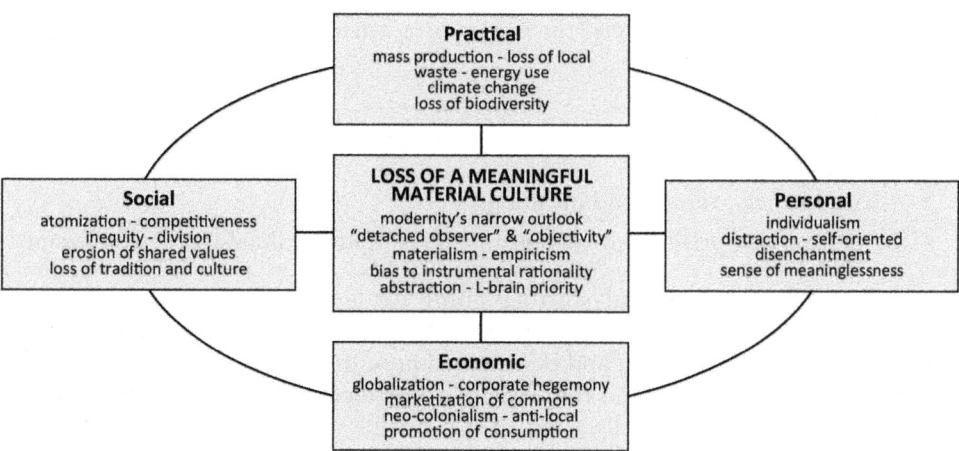

FIGURE 3.1 The loss of a meaningful material culture. © Stuart Walker.

intuitive as well as the rational; continuity as well as innovation; spontaneous insight as well as methodical development; and synthesis as well as analysis. As will become evident, this is not a nostalgic looking back but is critically linked to the present and the future, to the preservation and passing on of values that we believe to be important, and to infusing our lives and activities with meaning and purpose.

In this context, the recovery, preservation, and continuance of traditional practices can be seen as a positive, forward-looking approach that is capable of restoring balance and equilibrium to a system that is out of kilter not only with the natural environment but also with feelings and intuitively apprehended ideas about meaningful ways of living—today and into the future—for individuals, communities, and society as a whole.

Culturally significant artifacts

In line with normative understandings of the term "culture," we can say that culturally significant artifacts are those that embody, express, and help sustain the beliefs, knowledge, and activities of a particular social group. Interestingly, Ward describes cultural power as "access to knowledge and tradition and the possession of abilities that are not widely available to all but are socially esteemed" (2014: 19). With regard to the making and use of such artifacts, therefore, this power or the driving forces that help sustain a culture will include the knowledge and ability to design, create and/or use artifacts that help maintain tradition and the activities, customs or rituals that are valued and regarded as worthwhile by the community. These artifacts may be functional, symbolic or a mix of both. Indeed, traditional, craft-based making techniques bring together and assimilate functionality with the expression of enduring human values (Risatti 2007). In other words, they combine practical utility with attitudes and dispositions that are linked to beliefs and motivations and have context-dependent emotional and deliberative dimensions (see Scheffler 2013: 16–17). Therefore, we can say that "culturally significant artifacts" incorporate a variety of overlapping elements that include:

- tradition;
- context-related factors;
- shared beliefs, values, and meanings;
- expertise, comprising knowledge and skills, that is valued by the community.

This would seem a useful starting point for understanding the basis of a more meaningful material culture, particularly in response to relatively recent developments in globalization and the expansion of marketization and competition into virtually all walks of life. The design and production of culturally significant artifacts in or close to their location of use can be seen as a positive, restitutive route for creating good work, alleviating social disparity, and reducing waste and environmental degradation.

Tradition—and its relationship to modernity and the future

It is apparent from the foregoing that tradition is an important facet of culturally significant artifacts. Even so, tradition is often seen as rather "old hat"—something that has become irrelevant in our modern, fast-paced, future-oriented world of technological progress and possibility. This ill-founded assumption is at the heart of the modern outlook and can be understood as a gross error of judgement that is inextricably linked to today's disturbingly ambivalent responses to sustainability. Moreover, while it is certainly the case that aspects of modern design can now be understood as historical and culturally significant, and could also be construed as representative of their own "traditions," the very placelessness and detachment from the nuances of any particular culture make modern design a somewhat problematic fit with conventional understandings of traditional practices related to material culture. In fact, despite growing contestation in some quarters since the 1960s, the modern outlook remains the principal characteristic of our market-driven, consumption-based society. Its penetration and dominating influence in all quarters of the world through globalization is sometimes seen as a new form of colonialism (Pullella and Marsh 2015; Young 2003: 3, 130–7) that rides roughshod over local customs, eliminates cultural distinctiveness, and poses a serious threat to long-standing making practices and forms of expression and livelihoods that are embedded in social, historical, and geographical contexts, and deeply related to local culture.

It is critical to this discussion to understand that tradition is not simply about the past. It is very much concerned with the future—with continuity and with extending *contextualized, embodied knowledge, practices and values* to coming generations. As American philosopher Samuel Scheffler has explained, "Traditions are ... human practices whose organizing purpose is to preserve what is valued beyond the life span of any single individual or generation. They are collaborative, multigenerational enterprises devised by human beings precisely to satisfy the deep human impulse to preserve what is valued" (2013: 33). Hence, traditions are embodiments of values to which people feel a strong commitment, and human enterprises that express and substantiate traditional knowledge and practices are concerned with the defence and preservation of those values. Furthermore, those values will have a better chance of being preserved if efforts to do so are pursued not just by individuals but by collective enterprises, which are self-evidently more capable of enabling a tradition to flourish over the long term.

Individuals who contribute to such a tradition are, then, upholders of values that are seen to be important and worth preserving. These values are manifested through the artifacts of traditional practices—songs, dances, paintings, crafts, rituals—and are taken forward in the knowledge or the hope that those who come after us will share our values. As Scheffler says,

> In this sense, participation in a tradition is not only an expression of our natural conservatism about values but also a way of achieving a *value-based* relation to

those who come after us. We can think of our successors as people who will share our values, and ourselves as having custodial responsibility for the values that will someday be theirs.

Significantly, the idea that the collective values of the community in which the traditional practices take place will persist after we as individuals have passed away provides us with a personal stake in the future (2013: 33–34) and this, too, is important to us—to our own lives and activities today, as we shall see in the following section.

Sustainability—and its relationship to culturally significant artifacts and tradition

The implications of Scheffler's contentions are critically connected to our contemporary concerns about sustainability. In fact, they suggest that the reason for addressing sustainability in a timely and substantial manner is effectively turned on its head. While most of us might assume, without giving it too much deliberate thought, that the human race will continue to exist in the future, after our own lifetimes, Scheffler's studies suggest that this idea is actually very important to us and to the way we live our lives. The belief that humanity will continue well into the future matters to us. It affects our sense of well-being and gives value and purpose to our own lives and the kinds of activities we find worthwhile (*Samuel Scheffler on the Afterlife* 2015). If this is the case, then it is vital to ensure that the nature of our activities, our policy decisions and our individual and collective actions are not destroying but rather helping to protect and preserve the means by which the human race will continue into the future. Hence, the reasons for addressing sustainability today should not be seen simply in terms of our own self-sacrifice for the sake of future generations, which seems to be an implication of the oft-quoted definition of sustainable development in the Brundtland Commission's 1987 report *Our Common Future*: "Sustainable development is development that meets the needs of the present without compromising the ability of future generations to meet their own needs" (WCED 1987: 43). Instead, we should act because doing so not only helps ensure a future for humankind but also *because knowing that we are helping to ensure that future adds meaning, value, and a sense of purpose to our own lives in the here and now*. Put the other way round, the idea that humankind's future is under threat because of the way we live today can create a sense of existential angst in us—gnawing away at our sense of happiness and well-being, and diminishing the values and activities we hold dear.

The term "sustainability" is much used but its implications are often not fully appreciated. Contemporary, informed interpretations of sustainability refer to an interwoven set of issues that, for our activities to be meaningful, involve: (1) **practical considerations**: serving our physiological needs of food, water, warmth, and shelter, as well as reasonable or moderate wants, in ways that take into account and strive to ameliorate the negative environmental consequences of their provision; (2) **social considerations**: acting in morally responsible ways that recognize the social nature of being human. This means, for example, upholding the dignity of the person, striving towards social justice and equity, acting with conscience, and curbing our tendencies towards selfishness and self-interest in order to uphold the common good; (3) **personal considerations**: recognizing that we are also individuals who have a capacity for reflection and intuitive apprehension of "beyond self" and "beyond now"—which raises existential questions about purpose, matters of ultimate concern, and the living of a meaningful life. Down the ages, these have been expressed through individual practices, as in the contemplative traditions, and through collective practices that involve symbolism and ritual, as in religious worship. However, the following of such practices is not independent of social responsibilities because the inner quest and personal fulfilment are incompatible with selfishness and the exploitation or harming of others (Eagleton 2007: 97); and (4) **economic considerations**: recognizing that money is a useful and important means of exchanging things of value between people—but only that, a means rather than an end in itself, which facilitates the provision of our practical, social, and personal requirements and obligations. These four components comprising the three primary considerations of practical, social, and personal matters, and the necessary but secondary consideration of economic matters, constitute the *Quadruple Bottom Line of Sustainability*, which I have introduced and expanded upon elsewhere (Walker 2011: 190, 2014: 41–53).

We can see that, taken together, these considerations support both the individual and the social nature of the human condition. To a great extent, they rest on collective understandings and practices; shared values and preserving the common good; and the acquired knowledge and practices that have come down to us from previous generations. This latter point is certainly true of religious practices but it is also true of many traditional practices employed in the production of our material culture. We often find that such practices have been refined over generations until a "fit" has been achieved, such that on the one hand practical needs and reasonable wants are satisfied and on the other the effects on the local environment are harmless or even have long-term positive impacts. For example, many traditional housebuilding techniques around the world can be traced back hundreds or even thousands of years. They tend to be context sensitive and utilize local materials and skills. In their design, they frequently employ entirely passive means for maintaining comfortable living conditions. As a case in point, in the deserts of Iran a traditional form of adobe housing features wind-catcher towers that cool the rooms by directing the hot desert winds over water. They also incorporate an inner courtyard or *Miān-Sarā*. This is planted to create shade and almost always features a pool of water. These techniques help create a micro-climate that supports comfortable living within a harsh landscape that would otherwise remain barren (Yazdanpanah 2014). The relationships between culturally significant artifacts, tradition and the various dimensions of sustainability are summarized in Figure 3.2.

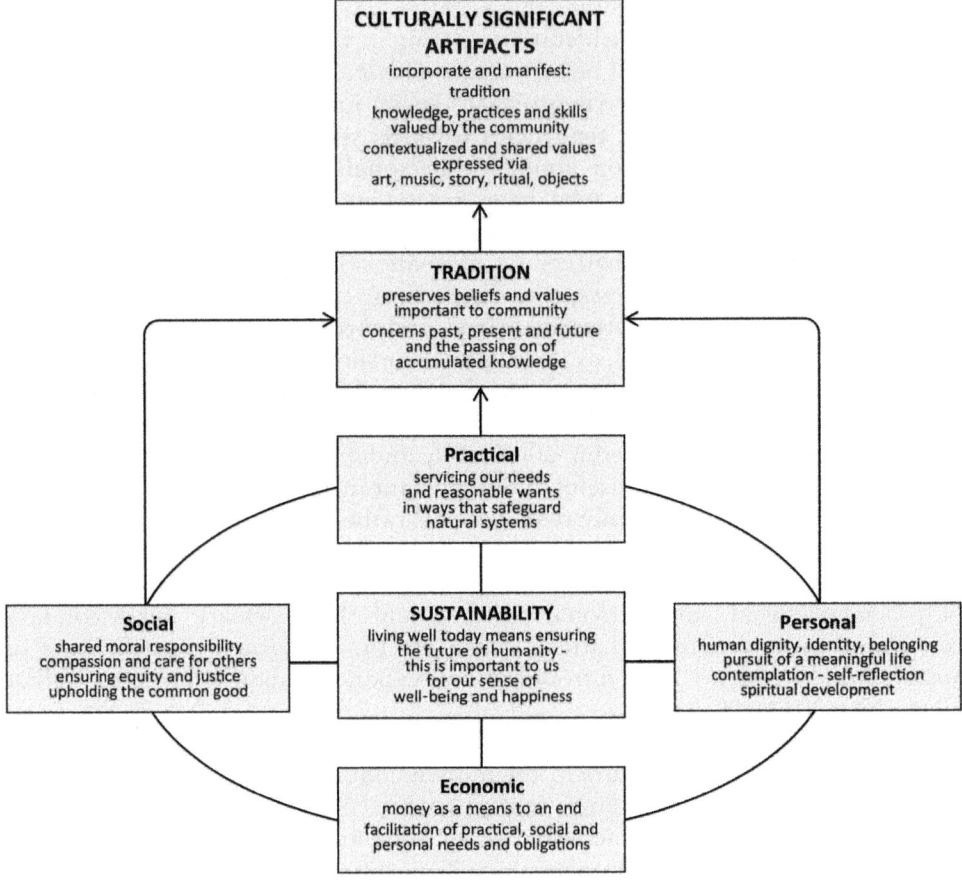

FIGURE 3.2 Culturally significant artifacts and their relationship to tradition and sustainability. © Stuart Walker.

Conclusions

The modern worldview emerged from changes in understandings that occurred as a result of new scientific developments and discoveries—perhaps especially the heliocentric model of Copernicus. Rapid progress in the sciences was accompanied by advancements in technological capabilities and in modes of manufacturing. Modernity saw a shift away from traditional handicrafts and a rise in factory-based mass production techniques along with huge changes in social patterns and economic systems (World Bank 2015: 72). These technological developments, which altered the nature of work, encouraged urbanization and eventually led to consumer society, were not the result of detached, objective observer findings and decisions. Rather, they were fundamentally based in human values and judgements about notions of the good life and what we regard as worthwhile and, of course, these decisions were often inseparable from the desire for wealth and power.

There are indications that, in the present time, we are undergoing another transition— spurred again, to a great extent, by scientific developments and discoveries that are affecting our understandings. We are becoming increasingly aware and, perhaps too slowly, coming to terms with the fact that our modes of production and ways of living are creating enormous damage to ecosystems and leading to unpredictable changes in climate patterns. At the same time, they are causing impoverishment for millions and unconscionable social inequities and injustices within and between nations. These developments, which have become increasingly clear in recent decades, represent a considerable threat to the future of human societies and this knowledge, as we have seen, can affect our own individual sense of well-being and happiness, as well as our motivation and the kinds of activities we regard as worthwhile.

We must not forget that these developments are the result of human actions and human decision-making. And the increasingly worrying consequences of these actions and decisions suggest that the philosophical outlook and the values that have characterized modernity and late-modernity, right up to the present, are seriously flawed and deeply harmful. They have created a culture of exorbitant waste in which shopping has become the pre-eminent social and economic activity, where short-lived products are unrepairable and destined for the dump, the quality of human work has drastically diminished, and socio-economic divisions have risen steeply (Wilkinson and Pickett 2009: 221–2).

For change that is in accord with the principles of sustainability, it will be crucial in the areas of design and making to recognize that many of the priorities of current product development, innovation, manufacturing, and marketing are inherently destructive and representative of outdated thinking. And it will be important to demonstrate, through high-quality, imaginative design, that affordable, beautiful, and meaningful alternatives are possible. Hence, it will be important for designers to employ their creative skills to help develop a material culture that is inspiring, long-lasting, repairable, and worth repairing, and that is grounded in local capacity. It is the local context where culturally appropriate solutions can be developed, where interpersonal relationships and communities flourish, and where environmental impacts can be recognized and alleviated. Working at the local level also means that packaging and shipping can be significantly curtailed or even eliminated. While it is essential, of course, to see such approaches in terms of functional benefits and economic livelihoods, it is equally essential to see them as expressions of culture- and context-related beliefs and values that are considered important and worth sustaining. Through such means we can develop not only culturally significant artifacts but also culturally significant and deeply meaningful *goods*.

Notes

1   Homer's *The Odyssey*, Book VIII, p. 138, translated by E. V. Rieu [1946], Penguin Group, London.

2   Examples include context and community-centered architecture, exemplified in the work of Welsh architect Christopher Day (www.christopherday.eu/, accessed July 17, 2015), and the sensitive rural architecture of Irish architect Dominic Stevens (2007). There have also been numerous recent Ph.D. studies on traditional ways of making and their relationship to social and environmental care. For example, in relation to architecture, such as Yazdanpanah (2014), and in relation to the revitalization of traditional crafts, such as Nugraha (2012) and Chudasri (2015).

References

Bourguignon, F. (2015), *The Globalization of Inequality*, Princeton, NJ: Princeton University Press.

Chudasri, D. (2015), *Design and Sustainable Development in the Craft Industry: A Case Study in Upper Northern Thailand*, Lancaster: Lancaster University.

Cottingham, J. (2014), *Philosophy of Religion*, New York: Cambridge University Press.

Eagleton, T. (2007), *The Meaning of Life*, Oxford: Oxford University Press.

Huxley, A. ([1985] 1945), *The Perennial Philosophy*, London: Triad, Grafton.

Italian Futurism (2014), *The Founding and Manifesto of Futurism by F. T. Marinetti*. Available online: http://www.italianfuturism.org/manifestos/foundingmanifesto/ (accessed July 1, 2015).

McGilchrist, I. (2009), *The Master and His Emissary*, New Have, CT: Yale University Press.

Nugraha, A. (2012), *Transforming Tradition: Methods for Maintaining Tradition in a Craft and Design Context*, Helsinki: Aalto University.

Piketty, T. (2014), *CAPITAL in the Twenty-First Century*, Cambridge, MA: The Belknap Press of Harvard University Press.

Pullella, P. and S. Marsh (2015), "Pope Calls for New Economic Order, Criticises Capitalism," *Reuters*, July 10. Available online: http://uk.reuters.com/article/2015/07/10/us-pope-latam-bolivia-idUKKCN0PJ29B20150710 (accessed July 10, 2015).

Risatti, H. (2007), *A Theory of Craft*, Chapel Hill, NC, quoted on p. 627 of: K. Niedderer and K. Townsend (2014), "Designing Craft Research: Joining Emotion and Knowledge," *Design Journal*, 17 (4): 624–48.

Samuel Scheffler on the Afterlife (2015), [radio] BBC Radio 4, June, 28, 21:30.

Scheffler, S. (2013), *Death and the Afterlife*, Oxford: Oxford University Press.

SOAS, (2015), *MA in Postcolonial Studies*, Centre for Cultural, Literary and Postcolonial Studies (CCLPS), The School of Oriental and African Studies (SOAS), University of London, UK.

Stevens, D. (2007), *Rural*, Cloone, Ireland: Mermaid Turbulence.

Taylor, C. (1995), "Two Theories of Modernity," *The Hastings Center Report*, 25 (2): 24–33.

Taylor, C. (2007), *A Secular Age*, Cambridge, MA: The Belknap Press of Harvard University Press.

Turkle, S. (1996), "Virtuality and its Discontents," in J. Turow and A. L. Kavanaugh (eds.), 2003, *The Wired Homestead: An MIT Press Sourcebook on the Internet and the Family*, 385–97, Cambridge, MA: MIT Press.

Turkle, S. (2011), *Alone Together*, New York, NY: Basic Books.

Walker, S. (2011), *The Spirit of Design*, Abingdon, Oxford: Routledge.

Walker, S. (2014), *Designing Sustainability*, Abingdon, Oxford: Routledge.

Ward, G. (2014), *Unbelievable: Why We Believe and Why We Don't*, London: I. B. Tauris.

WCED, (1987), *Our Common Future*, World Commission on Environment and Development, Oxford: Oxford University Press.

Wilkinson, R. and K. Pickett (2009), *The Spirit Level*, London: Allen Lane, Penguin Group.

World Bank (2014), *4° Turn Down the Heat*, Washington, DC: World Bank, License: Creative Commons Attribution CC BY-NC-ND 3.0 IGO.

World Bank (2015), *World Development Report 2015: Mind, Society, and Behavior*, doi: 10.1596/978-1-4648-0342-0, License: Creative Commons Attribution CC BY 3.0 IGO.

Yazdanpanah, P. (2014), *Architecture, Sustainability and Substantive Values: A Case Study – The Traditional Iranian Domestic Courtyard* (Miān-Sarā), Lancaster: Lancaster University.

Young, R. J. C. (2003), *Postcolonialism*, Oxford: Oxford University Press.

4

Making and its Cultural Ecological Foundations

Patrick Dillon

Introduction

Diverse forms of social organization and "making things" are said to be two defining characteristics of the human condition. Much of what a society deems to be its cultural heritage derives from traditions of making and the lifestyles associated with them. In the long prehistory of making, the appropriation of materials and the fashioning of tools to procure food and build shelters are prominent themes. These activities, in turn, lead to processes of acquisition and accumulation. Even the nomad has to travel with a basic toolkit for survival. But settlement encourages accumulation and accumulation produces surplus. Surplus generates trade—trade not just in resources, consumables and artifacts, but also in techniques and ideas. Once an artifact has been made for a particular purpose there is always the challenge of designing and making something that does a better job. And then there is embellishment. Ornamentation makes an artifact more desirable, or at least gives it novelty value. As Phillips (2015) observes: "Ornament is born of a primary and elemental urge. It tries to make sense of the world and make the world make sense." Artifacts are thus as much repositories of imagination and meaning as they are material "things"; they can be "read" and their stories revealed (Dillon and Howe 2003).

Trade requires theatres for its transactions, i.e. markets. Markets are not just places where goods and services are sold and exchanged, but any state of competition between beliefs and ideas and forms of behavior, or the arenas in which interaction takes place between the people who hold or practice them (Jones 2006: 49). Markets are voracious; they demand ever more variety—new ideas, new ways of working, differentiation in form and function, specialization. Markets and their associated institutions become ever more complex and are now the primary socio-economic entities that determine not just patterns of production and consumption but the human values and norms that underpin systems of social organization.

This is a cultural ecologist's take on the history of making. Cultural ecology is closely allied to anthropology and sociology but differs subtly from them in having a focus on the *transactions* between people and the material, social and psychological resources of the environments they inhabit. "Environment" means more than just physical surroundings and economic activities. It includes social relations and the collective capabilities of all the people who inhabit it—their lifestyles, beliefs, ideas, and aspirations (Dillon 2015). In his provocative history of humankind, Harari (2014: 42) sees it like this:

> Biology sets the basic parameters for the behaviour and capacities of *Homo sapiens*. The whole of history takes place within the bounds of this biological arena. However, this arena is extraordinarily large, allowing Sapiens to play an astounding variety of games. Thanks to their ability to invent fiction, Sapiens creates more and more complex games, which each generation develops and elaborates even further.

Harari's "complex games" are transactions based on social norms, economic conditions, material resources, means of exchange, institutional structures, human resources, beliefs, values, attitudes, tastes, needs, wants, patterns of production and consumption, and so on. Transactional games are what delineate design from making and the crafted artifact from the artifact as art. A cultural ecological exploration of these relationships, with its broad definitions of both environment and market, as given above, helps place the activity of making in the wider frame of cultural enterprise. However, in common with the views of Sennett (2008) and others, cultural ecology does not make judgemental distinctions between manual and mechanized forms of making, both of which may be deemed "culturally significant." Rather it sees them as lying at opposite ends of a continuum of possible engagements between people and their environments. Space does not permit a detailed examination of the relationship between the two, and the focus in this chapter is primarily on making as a manual craft activity, although even here there are definitional pitfalls. I look at mechanisms behind making as a transactional process, specifically its phenomenological basis at the level of the individual, and, at the collective level, the way markets act as agents of selection on ideas and practices.

The phenomenology of transactions

Transactions are generally thought of as happening between people—a conversation, an exchange of goods, payment for a service. The cultural ecological definition is wider, taking in the possibility of individuals transacting with any component of their environment—animate and inanimate, tangible and intangible. Take the case of a person working with simple tools and materials, weaving a rug. Here the transactions are between the capabilities of the individual (determined not only by knowledge and skill, but also by disposition etc.) and the affordances of the materials and tools (the properties of the materials and the functionalities of the tools). The transactions, i.e. the person working with the materials and the tools and weaving the rug, can be explored through two interrelated modes of engagement, "conceptual" and "perceptual." Much of what is going on is conceptual, the person is drawing on experience, the work is largely routine and it is *relational*, that is, it relates to normative ways of working and established bodies of knowledge. Simultaneously, there is a perceptual mode, the person is "living the moment." This is *co-constitutional* engagement. The term "co-constitutional" means that the environment and the "in the moment" behaviors of the person concerned mutually shape or co-construct each other. It follows that the conceptual/relational and the perceptual/co-constitutional ways of engaging with the work, or ways of "being in the world," do not happen in isolation of each other. The two modes are constantly re-forming each other in ways that are themselves relational and co-constitutional. Put another way, systematic understanding of the world is derived through cumulative organization and rearrangement of experientially acquired understandings of the world (Marton 1993). This cultural ecological account of the act of making does not distinguish between thinking and doing, or between the application of knowledge and the expression of skill. Rather it sees them all as integral, often subliminal, parts of an *embodied* process. "Movement is knowing," as Ingold (2013) would say, and making is intentional movement.

A simple analogy: an individual can walk through a landscape on a marked footpath, a planned journey. However, what the individual encounters on the walk cannot be predicted in detail—it is a combination of what the environment presents at that time (affordances) and how the person engages with it (sensory, dispositional etc.). Although the detail of the walk cannot be predicted, the individual nevertheless brings with him or her past experiences that in turn condition expectations about what might be encountered. In other words, experiences of the present are part of a temporal continuum building on the past and anticipating a future. This example introduces some of the fundamental ideas in phenomenology that are broadly confirmed by research in neuroscience. The relationship between what there is and how an individual experiences it is known as *intentionality*, and intentionality is *superpositioned* with multiple meanings derived from prior experiences.

To return to the rug: it may be made to a "plan," but through the process of making the individual adds something unique to it. Figure 4.1 is a diagrammatic representation of why this is so: the two interrelated modes of engagement, the conceptual (relational) and the perceptual (co-constitutional), which define the way an individual transacts with his or her environment, are shown in Figure 4.1. In the bottom diagram, the star shape represents the transaction and the circle containing it the context in which the transaction takes place. This is the conceptual mode where the transaction is based on accumulated knowledge and established patterns of behavior. This mode of transaction is defined relative to the context in which it takes place, i.e. it is context dependent. As any given context is different from any other context, conceptual modes of transaction may be defined relatively to each other, i.e. they are relational. So, for example, crafting the rug in a workshop

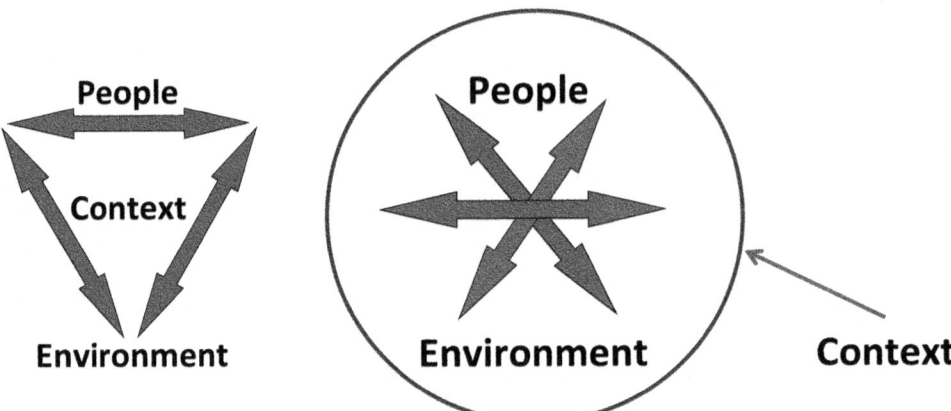

FIGURE 4.1 Co-constitutional (left) and relational (right) modes of engagement with the environment (adapted from Dillon 2012). © Patrick Dillon.

is a different context from selling the rug in a market. The behaviors in each context, and the ways in which knowledge and skill are applied, are specific to those contexts. Each context can be "conceptualized," i.e. it can be described in words, as narratives, instructions, prescriptions etc. When we look back at situations and reflect on them, we typically describe them relationally, i.e. according to the contexts in which they took place. But these relational descriptions are abstractions of reality; they cannot capture experience as it is lived in the moment. The "in the moment" mode of transaction is depicted in the top diagram. Here, the context emerges out of the transaction itself, literally constructed out of the individual's engagement with the affordances of the environment in distinct "moments of being." These unique, personal contexts exist simultaneously alongside relational contexts, fleeting thoughts and actions, which typically are of no consequence, but occasionally can be profound. In the moment transactions are "co-constitutional," they are manifestations of the moments in which they happen.

As soon as co-constitutional transactions occur, they immediately interact with relational constructs. In other words, through rationalization and conceptualization we "make sense" of what we do. Although the co-constitutional is fleeting its influence is far reaching. Not only is it constantly "updating" our relational constructs, but creativity, improvisation, ingenuity, insight etc. typically occur "in the moment" or in the "flow." The interrelationship between co-constitutional and relational ways of being in the world is represented by enclosing the symbols for each mode of engagement in circles and then overlapping the circles (Figure 4.2). The composite symbol is a variation on mandorla/mandala iconography, which has been used in many cultures to signify unity or wholeness. But the relationship between relational and co-constitutional is more than one of overlap. They are continually re-structuring each other. In the composite diagram (Figure 4.2), this reciprocal relationship is represented by two mutually referring arrows placed in the intersection of the two circles.

The reciprocal relationship between spontaneity and rationality is part of the magic of how people interact with their environments. However, no individual

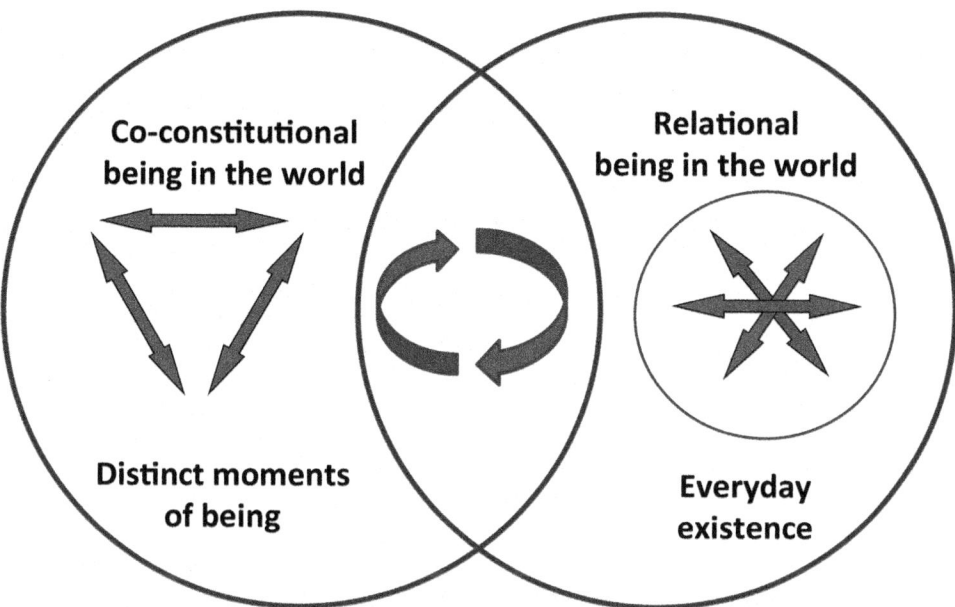

FIGURE 4.2 Cultural ecology as the reciprocal relationship between co-constitutional and relational modes of engagement with the environment (adapted from Dillon 2012). © Patrick Dillon.

exists in isolation therefore, in order to model processes of continuity and change in practices of making, it is necessary to look at how collective mechanisms operating through markets act as agents of selection on what we make and how we make.

Market selection

The extended definition of market given above, which includes beliefs and ideas and forms of behavior etc., is a cultural ecological definition rather than a purely economic one. This definition offers a number of interrelated ways of looking at the processes of selection operating on how people make things. Two are important here: the market of possibilities and the market of metrics.

The market of possibilities deals in ideas. Complex processes of selection favor certain distinct moments of being which in turn influence the relational contexts of everyday working. Of the multitude of subtle variations in moment to moment thoughts, dispositions and actions (collectively "superpositions"), most do not directly impact on the process of making. These are shown in the left-hand diagram of Figure 4.3. The triangles represent "in the moment," co-constitutional transactions. In routine making, as soon as they occur they are accommodated within the trajectory of the relational context, the task in hand (the stars in circles, linked by a directional arrow). Thus, in the relational mode, a handwoven rug is made to a set of rules, a prescription based on knowledge of "how it is done here," i.e. within the affordance of the environment in question (bearing in mind the extended definition of environment). However, if the maker allows a carry-over of some of the variations in his or her thoughts and actions there is the possibility of taking the relational context in new directions, of developing a new trajectory (right-hand diagram, Figure 4.3).

This is the "restless dynamic" that characterizes the making, or "crafting," of an artifact; a dynamic between the relational factors that contribute to maintaining stability and continuity (e.g. enduring beliefs, limitations of knowledge, availability of resources) and the "moments of being" that contribute to processes of change (e.g. new ideas, improvisations) and the generation of new relational models. Craft practice is thus positioned in the cultural ecology such that it is both a manifestation of cultural tradition and a force for forging new directions.

The market of metrics deals in mechanisms through which "value" is assigned and quantified and in the application of systems of "measurement" to processes of production and consumption. The market of metrics includes conventional monetary measures, processes of specification, and ways in which people and institutions work together to advance their economic or social interests.

A transaction involving goods and services, otherwise known as trade, requires cooperation between individuals and groups. In its simplest form cooperation is through direct exchange or barter. Most transactions are mediated and regulated through money. The economic value of a commodity, determined by supply, demand, competition etc. is referenced against a monetary equivalent. Systems of organized labor and mass production, which allow manufacturing to a specification in a factory system, offer economies of scale and the possibility of reducing the unit cost of commodities. In cultural ecological terms, factory production displaces the co-constitutional mode in the process of making. Ideas and innovations are the province of those who design the system and the products. The process of making is reduced to overseeing mechanized production, the application of a pre-defined metric.

Just as co-constitutional and relational forms of human engagement with the environment constantly interact and restructure each other, so too do markets of ideas and markets of metrics. To see how this works we can return to the example

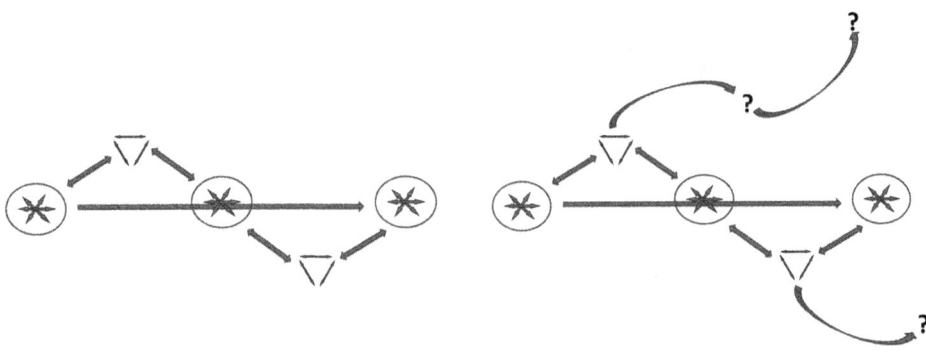

FIGURE 4.3 Working within a relational trajectory (left) and opening up the trajectory through improvisations (right) (adapted from Dillon 2012). © Patrick Dillon.

of the woven rug, this time looking at a specific case, the Finnish *ryijy*. A detailed history of the *ryijy* is given by Sopanen and Willberg (2008), from which this account is adapted. The *ryijy* is a textile woven on a loom where the long wool pile consists of rows of knotted threads on a linen, hemp or cotton warp. *Ryijy* making is part of a long-term craft tradition, which has accommodated incremental changes in technique and adapted to cumulative adjustments to context. Functionally, the *ryijy* has changed from being a sleeping blanket, to a covering for travel in boats and sleighs, to a floor covering, a chair cover, and more recently a decorative wall hanging. The economic value of the *ryijy* in late medieval Finland depended on the amount of wool it contained, and the scale and quality of its ornamentation. There was a distinction between the elaborate designs of *ryijys* belonging to the wealthy and those belonging to people of lesser financial means. Since the earliest records, the *ryijy* has been symbolic, e.g. at weddings where the couple stood on their wedding *ryijy*, into which was woven signs of luck and protection. More recently it has become a symbol of Finnishness and a representation of family lineage: as wall hangings, *ryijys* pass from generation to generation. Changes in craft practice and *ryijy* making have included loom types (upright/horizontal), knot types, warp/weft pile variations, dye types, dyeing techniques, and designs. Sopanen and Willberg (2008) describe these changes as gradual and incremental, depending on both innovations introduced from elsewhere (e.g. new dye colors) and variations developed and adopted locally. It shows the Finnish *ryijy*-rug as an enduring craft tradition that has accommodated incremental change through market selection of ideas and functionalities (see also Dillon 2012 for a diagrammatic representation of how agents of selection have operated on *ryijy* making).

A cultural ecology of making

The term cultural ecology is attributed to American anthropologist Julian Steward (1972), who applied it to the study of the biological and cultural processes that enable a human population to survive and reproduce within a given environment. The focus of early work in cultural ecology, mainly through anthropological studies of subsistence communities, was on adaptation. More recent work has taken a broader perspective on human-environment relationships, especially in terms of the global environment, where the human population is seen as a significant agent of change (e.g. Simmons 1989).

The development of a cultural ecological framework for making is a work in progress (Dillon 2012; Dillon and Howe 2003, 2007; Howe and Dillon 2001). It adopts the ecologist's notion of "niche," which in its simplest formulation describes the complete range of physical and biological conditions in which a species lives, but extends it to include social, political, moral, ethical, theological, and other "human" dimensions, i.e. the sum of all the transactions represented in the overlapping circles in Figure 4.2. These extra dimensions align the human niche closely with Bourdieu's (1977) notions of "field," "habitus", and "capital," i.e. the settings in which people acting as social agents are located and through which they engage in social, economic, and cultural transactions. The work of Steward and others in anthropology, and Bourdieu in sociology, might be termed "big picture" cultural ecology. In a cultural ecology of making, I am more concerned with individual agency, hence the phenomenology of transactions, and how this ties into the bigger picture via market mechanisms.

The phenomenological-market approach is compatible with recent work on niche theory. In their evolutionary perspective, Odling-Smee, Laland, and Feldman (2003) explore niche in a general ecological sense but include a chapter on human niche construction. Here they see niche as the interplay between the subsystems of the environment itself (which they call factors) and the traits and characteristics of the [human] population (which they call features). Particular configurations of the "feature-factor relationship" define the cultural patterns that characterize the subsystems we call making.

Because the human niche can be thought of in both ecological and evolutionary terms, the most fundamental way of exploring it is through the conditions (i.e. feature-factor relationships) that maintain human society. Boyden (1987) has proposed such a set of conditions. It includes primary needs such as clean water, clean air, and suitable climatic and dietary conditions. More significantly, in terms of how making is placed within the cultural ecology, are the social dimensions. Boyden gives these as: meeting aspirations, nurturing interests, giving and receiving, emotional support, responsibilities and obligations on individuals toward their extended families and peer and friendship groups, and an environment and a lifestyle that are conducive to a sense of personal involvement, purpose, belonging, responsibility, excitement, challenge, satisfaction, comradeship, love, enjoyment, confidence, and security, and so on.

Whereas at the most fundamental level, making is a process through which basic needs are satisfied, it is through the wider social dimensions that human creativity is expressed and processes of making may be differentiated broadly into craft, design and art. Phillips (2015) puts craft at the center from which design and art are derived. The earliest derivations he attributes to ornamentation of functional objects: "[the] syntactical elements (stripe, hatching, dot) that are all paraphrases of nature," which once divorced from nature become abstractions. As Phillips observes, the moment such markings made by one craftsman were compared and preferred to those of another, "the whole great engine of art started up." Phillips contends therefore, that aesthetics should be considered one of the most fundamental disciplines: "critical discourse, patronage, and commerce soon get underway on a road that leads to schools of style, salons, academies and our great museums."

The conceptualizations of niche offered by Odling-Smee, Laland, and Feldman (2003) and others help define "contexts" of making. In its simplest use, context is the surroundings in which human agency takes place (bottom diagram in Figure 4.1); the points of reference which help place the component parts, the boundaries, the interrelationships between traits and characteristics. Context in these terms encompasses space, place, people, and activity, where space may be regarded as a potentially unlimited area, which may (or may not) contain a person or an object, and place as a particular portion of space occupied by a person as a locus for meaningful actions. From a cultural ecological perspective, space is given definition and becomes "place" through cultural transaction. Space is "fluid"; it has potential to be utilized. Utilization, through cultural transaction, imposes predictability and continuity on elements of the human feature-factor relationship, in other words, it "fixes" parts of the environment, it creates an "infrastructure," it establishes a context. We regularize the creation of infrastructure through design. Designed infrastructure is good for being in the world *relationally*. But as noted earlier, the relationship between features and factors that define niches are subtly and constantly adjusting relative to each other. It is through these adjustments that we are able to be in the world *co-constitutionally*, to "live the moment." In this sense, there will always be a tension between fluidity (the unconstrained space of possibility) and fixity (the made infrastructure).

On the one hand, design and making are part of the tension between fluidity and fixity; on the other hand, they provide ways of overcoming it. People engage with their material surroundings both mechanistically and through individual and collective experiences, ideas, values etc. Much of human behavior is routine and predictable and artifacts are made to accommodate this behavior. Artifacts can also be designed and made to condition behavior thought to be necessary or desirable, or to align behavior with social norms or economic expediencies (as in for example fashion). Human creativity makes it possible to design and make with expressive and intellectual flexibility within a necessary infrastructure. Thus, we can think of spaces that are conducive to imagination and improvisation co-existing with places that are utilitarian and functional. Improvisation is one means through which people both adapt their behavior to, and find possibilities in, new situations and environments.

Since the co-constitutional and the relational cannot exist in isolation of each other, it follows that all human action is located in the intersection of the two circles in the mandorla (Figure 4.2). What differentiates craft, design, and art is how the "tension" between the co-constitutional and the relational is "resolved." This tension in the process of making is what educationalists used to describe as between "the hands and the head." Now, because making is seen as an embodied process, we would say, colloquially, that it is "between hands, head and heart," in other words, between cognitive, physical, and affective engagements.

Just as the relational and the co-constitutional are in a continual state of flux, so too are the cognitive, the physical, and the affective. People have a bodily dexterity that corresponds with the type of making they are engaged in. Making something manually has a different physicality to making something virtually, e.g. a computer graphic. Ideas and improvisations (allowing free rein to the co-constitutional) may be followed through "on the job," irrespective of whether the making activities are labelled craft, design or art. In some situations, specific ideas may be assigned to others for development. Making can thus be an expression of individual improvisation and it can involve systematic incremental improvement founded on scientific testing and development (based on and leading to relational models). Craft and art are ambiguous in these terms. Although craftspeople and artists seldom engage in formal, systematic testing and prototyping, they are nevertheless constantly playing with ideas, exploring the potential of materials and tools, refining techniques. Mechanization and factory line production of identical multiples represents the most extreme compromise to the co-constitutional in the making process. Here it is suppressed at the expense of pre-defined relational models.

Thus, the phenomenology of transactions shows that context is both a "given" component of making (meeting an objective, i.e. it is relational) and an emergent property of the activity and the embodiment associated with it (co-constitutional). The superpositioned meanings of a person's actions, objects, tools, and symbols are co-constituted by the role these elements play, as well as the values they accrue, in the intentionality of the activity. A context thus defined is never universally given or absolutely determined; it depends in part on how a situation is interpreted in terms of the activities to be carried out. A context is constructed by an agent every time the agent gets actively involved in a setting by determining a goal, drawing on prior experiences, looking at the means available, investigating actions etc. This is the process that van Oers (1998) calls context making or contextualizing.

The wider social dimensions of making align niche and context with the sociocultural theories that are used to explain individual and collective identities and the meanings people and groups create within the environments they inhabit. Different formulations of sociocultural theory draw on Dewey's ideas about personally significant experience, the sense that someone has about a situation, and Leontev's ideas about the collective understanding captured in language, social artifacts, and made objects (Stevenson 2004). In both formulations the emphasis is on what the individual is doing through his or her transactions within the social system or with and through artifacts. This is how the identities and meanings associated with processes of making contribute to the material aspects of "culture." Particular traditions of making may be recognized as "cultural patterns." Viewed in this way, artifacts are repositories of cultural information; they are laden with history as well as meaning. It follows that artifacts, the traditions in which they are made, and the strong associations they evoke between people, places, and activities, are windows into cultural heritage (see Kokko and Dillon 2011, 2016).

In conclusion, cultural ecology is a transactional, phenomenological way of looking at the world and, through the focus of this chapter, it has been used as a lens on culturally significant making. Making is seen as being in symbiosis with its surrounding environment. It is an embodied process and both the act of making and the environment of making continuously change relative to each other. Markets broadly defined, through which possibilities are explored and value is assigned, are important agents of change in a cultural ecology. Culturally significant making comes from tradition and generates tradition. It carries echoes from the past and offers trajectories into the future.

References

Bourdieu, P. (1977), *Outline of a Theory of Practice*, Cambridge: Cambridge University Press.

Boyden, S. (1987), *Western Civilization in Biological Perspective: Patterns in Biohistory*, Oxford: Clarendon Press.

Dillon, P. (2012), "Framing Craft Practice Cultural Ecologically: Tradition, Change and Emerging Agendas," in M. Ferris (ed.), *Making Futures: The Crafts as Change-maker in Sustainably Aware Cultures*, 72–8, Plymouth, MA: Plymouth College of Arts.

Dillon, P. (2015), "Education for Sustainable Development in a Cultural Ecological Frame," in R. Jucker and R. Mathar (eds.), *Schooling for Sustainable Development. A focus on Europe*, 630–43, Dordrecht: Springer.

Dillon, P. and T. Howe (2003), "Design as Narrative: Objects, Stories and Negotiated Meaning," *International Journal of Art and Design Education*, 22 (3): 291–8.

Dillon, P. and T. Howe (2007), "An Epistemology of Presence and Reconceptualisation in Design Education," *Interchange*, 38 (1): 69–88.

Harari, Y. L. (2014), *Sapiens. A Brief History of Humankind*, London: Vintage Books.

Howe, T. and P. Dillon (2001), "Cultural Niche and the Contexts of Craft, Design and Fine Art," *The Design Journal*, 4 (3): 50–7.

Ingold, T. (2013), *Making*, London: Routledge.

Jones, E. L. (2006), *Cultures Merging. A Historical and Economic Critique of Culture*, Princeton, NJ: Princeton University Press.

Kokko, S. and P. Dillon (2011), "Crafts and Craft Education as Expressions of Cultural Heritage. Individual Experiences and Collective Values amongst an International Group of Women University Students," *International Journal of Technology and Design Education*, 21 (4): 487–503.

Kokko, S. and P. Dillon (2016), "Engaging Trainee Teachers with Crafts and Cultural Heritage," *International Journal of Education through Art*, 12 (1): 21–37, doi: 10.1386/eta.12.1.21_1.

Marton, F. (1993), "Our Experience of the Physical World," *Cognition and Instruction*, 10 (1): 227–37.

Odling-Smee, F. J., K. Laland, and M. W. Feldman (2003), *Niche Construction: The Neglected Process in Evolution*, Princeton, NJ: Princeton University Press.

Phillips, T. (2015), "The Nature of Ornament. A Summary Treatise," *The New Bookbinder*, 35: 7–14.

Sennett, R. (2008), *The Craftsman*, New Haven, CT: Yale University Press.

Simmons, I. G. (1989), *Changing the Face of the Earth*, Oxford: Blackwell.

Sopanen, T. and L. Willberg (2008), *The Ryijy-Rug Lives On. Finnish ryijy-rugs 1778–2008*, Kuopio, Finland: Kuopio Museum of Cultural History.

Stevenson, J. (2004), "Developing Technological Knowledge," *International Journal of Technology and Design Education*, 14: 5–19.

Steward, J. H. (1972), *Theory of Culture Change: The Methodology of Multilinear Evolution*, Chicago, IL: University of Illinois Press.

Van Oers, B. (1998), "From Context to Contextualizing," *Learning and Instruction*, 8 (6): 473–88.

PART TWO

Authenticity and Tradition in Material Culture

Editorial Introduction

Amy Twigger Holroyd

Part I examined cultural significance in terms of designs, products, and practices, and explored connections with key underpinning concepts such as sustainability and cultural ecologies. Authenticity and tradition were highlighted as crucial factors that shape the ways in which culturally significant artifacts have developed in the past, are received in the present, and can potentially prosper in the future. *Part II: Authenticity and Tradition in Material Culture* provides the reader with the opportunity to explore these concepts through five case studies from Europe, the Middle East, and Asia. The examples describe traditions dating back thousands of years alongside more recently emergent phenomena, and include instances of conscious invention as well as enduring cultural forms handed down between generations. Together, these chapters provide a detailed insight into the issues of authenticity and tradition in terms of material culture in diverse cultural contexts.

In *The Aran Jumper*, Siún Carden explores an internationaly recognized symbol of Irishness, which carries emotionally charged ideas about kinship and nativeness. While many believe this culturally significant design to have medieval or even pre-Christian origins, it was actually developed in a canny act of marketing during the 1930s. Despite this surprising history, the jumper carries an important sense of cultural identity for Irish communities, both within Ireland and across the global diaspora. Siún explores the myths and meanings that surround the Aran jumper, and the fascinating political and social interconnections that have influenced its development.

Moving from Western Europe to Southeast Asia, Chok *Weaving And Textile Enterprises From Northern Thailand* presents an analysis of field research into the weaving communities of *Long* district (Phrae province) and *Mae Chaem* district (Chiang Mai province). Disaya Chudasri explains the rationale for selecting *chok* weaving as an in-depth case study and describes a number of textile enterprises, including their stakeholders, production networks, and primary markets. She discusses key issues related to the traditional production of *chok* textiles and analyzes the weaving enterprises in relation to the principles of sustainability, using the "Quadruple Bottom Line" proposed by Walker (2011) comprising personal meaning, social responsibility, environmental care, and economic viability. Finally, Disaya identifies potential areas in which design can help to ensure the continuity of the weaving communities and support the production of textile products in ways that are compatible with sustainability.

In the following chapter, *Oltu-Stone Prayer Beads: A Journey into The Art of Carving Tasbih*, Hazal Gümüş Çiftçi discusses a type of black amber found in Eastern Turkey. Prayer beads are traditionally made from this stone, and the craft has been passed down from one generation to the next. Today it provides an important source of income in the *Erzurum* district of Eastern Turkey, but the sector is unstable and faces a range of challenges. An absence of governmental regulations, declining interest among young people, the difficulty of the work, and a lack of fair wages contribute to an ongoing struggle for craftspeople. Hazal draws on semi-structured interviews with Oltu-stone prayer bead makers in order to define challenges, opportunities, and potential design interventions. She concludes by proposing a viable pathway for a sustainable future of this age-old, delicate handicraft.

A fourth case study, written by Poone Yazdanpanah and Stuart Walker, broadens the field of interest to examine an example of culturally significant architecture. *The Miān-Sarā: Tradition and Sustainability in Iranian Homes* considers the inner courtyard of a traditional Iranian extended family home. This architectural feature can be traced back thousands of years but has been in severe decline since the nineteenth century due to the influence of Westernization and modernity. Drawing once again on Walker's "Quadruple Bottom Line," the investigation demonstrates how this type of architecture—refined over the centuries—is at once locally appropriate, economically viable, environmentally benign, socially reifying, and spiritually enriching. It is a sophisticated and exceptionally appropriate way of providing comfortable living within a harsh desert landscape. Rooted in cultural mores and spiritual symbolism, it provides a beautiful example of sustainable architecture and a poignant reminder of how much has been swept aside in the rush to modernity.

The final chapter in *Part II*, written by Sara Kristoffersson, addresses a much more recently developed example of culturally significant material culture. In *IKEA: Mass-produced National Design Identity* Sara discusses the way in which "Scandinavian Design" is packaged and sold to consumers around the world by one of Sweden's top brands. IKEA products are perceived by many to represent Scandinavian design ideals and aesthetics. This notion of "Scandinavian Design" was developed in the latter part of the twentieth century and used strategically to develop a distinct design identity. Today, the products designed and sold by IKEA help to reinforce this identity. However, the stereotypical Scandinavian design identity is regarded by some as not only inauthentic but also a hindrance to its development and evolution. This chapter looks at IKEA's design-related promotional materials, including its use of objects to tell stories, in relation to broader understandings of authenticity and tradition in material culture.

5

The Aran Jumper

Siún Carden

Introduction

The Aran jumper is a pullover knitted in cream wool and elaborately textured
with cable stitch patterns. It has become almost as powerful a symbol of "Brand
Ireland" (Patterson 2011: 26) as the shamrock or a pint of Guinness (Figure 5.1). It
is also a recurrent and adaptable fashion trend whose motifs and conventions are
frequently reinvented through couture, commerce, and craft. The garment itself is
accompanied by apocryphal stories about its origins and the meanings attributed to
its stitch patterns. Ever since the popularization of this style of knitwear in the mid-
twentieth century, these patterns have been interpreted as traces of a much older
way of life, carrying meanings that "cold words" cannot manage (Kiewe 1982:
6). Turney (2009: 55) argues that when stitch patterns are "read" as if they were
text, they locate an object within a hypothesized pre-literate world, underlining
the association of knitting with Romantic concepts of nature and primitivism.
These concepts are key to nineteenth-century ideas about the "celtic" world (Kelsall
2003: 1–19) and have been influential forces in the evolution of Irish national
identity and design history (Mattar 2004; King and Sisson 2011). The meanings
that have been read into the Aran jumper also include ideas about kinship and
national identity, which resonate with the construction of contemporary Ireland as
a "diaspora nation" (Lentin 2007: 433). While it has come to symbolize a static and
homogenous Irishness, the Aran jumper is a transatlantic phenomenon, shaped by
processes of migration and tourism. This chapter explores the myths that surround
the Aran jumper, and the political and social interconnections that have influenced
its development.

FIGURE 5.1 Display of "Irish Knitwear" in Belfast souvenir shop combining classic Aran designs (bottom left) with variations including shamrock motifs, 2016. Courtesy Carden. © Siún Carden.

Myths and meanings

The garment takes its name from the Aran Islands, which lie off Ireland's western coast and have iconic status within Ireland's cultural geography. The idea of the rural west as archetypally Irish, a remote, enduring tendril of the Celtic fringe, runs through Irish politics and literature and has been compared to the role of "the west" in the national identity of the USA (Kneafsey 2002: 127; Nash 1993: 87; Wall 2011: xv). The islands' spectacular landscape, now attractive to tourists, formed an almost absurdly challenging environment for the subsistence farming and fishing by which Aran islanders long supported themselves. Kelsall (2003: 183) describes the Aran Islands as representing, in the context of English Romanticism, "the racial heartland which nourished (or starved), in uncontaminated poverty, the racially pure *Volk*, whose very poverty, sufferings and heroic powers of resistance symbolized the inextinguishable flame of nationhood." These imagined Aran Islanders are the *dramatis personae* of the Aran jumper myth, within which, as Kiewe (1982: 6) writes, the jumper "was their passport and their identity document, expressing their background through its coils and curves more vividly than cold words could manage."

The central myth about Aran knitting is the story of a fisherman lost in the Atlantic, whose drowned body is unrecognizable by the time it washes ashore, but can be identified by a pattern knitted into his pullover (or "gansaí" in Irish). The "intricate, salt-stiff/ family motif/ of a month-drowned Aranman's gansaí" (Muldoon 2011: 83) is a powerful example of what Turney calls "knitting as a sign of the familial" (2009: 55). Similar apocryphal stories are told about knitwear in fishing communities in Scotland and England, where the knit-and-purl designs of traditional ganseys have also been credited with powers of identification (Gordon 2010: 99; Stall-Meadows 2014: 261). However, the story of the drowned fisherman is today most commonly associated with the Aran Islands. Its repetition in tourist information, marketing material, knitting instructions, museum exhibitions and literature has fuelled the Aran jumper's emergence as a symbol of Irishness and a classic style of knitwear (see Carden 2014: 260). As well as the idea that the Aran-knit garment functions as a document, placing the body of the individual within the context of a family lineage, the individual stitch patterns that are combined within Aran knitting have been read as indexical signs. Stitch glossaries illustrating this "traditional" knowledge are familiar to many hand knitters and tourists visiting Ireland (Compton 1983: 63–7; Darlington 1991: 88–90). Certain themes recur: nature, the life cycle, family, and spirituality. Physical resemblances such as honeycomb and blackberry appear alongside more abstract or tenuous ideas such as the Holy Trinity, the "ups and downs of married life," and even "the unbroken chain between the Irish who emigrate and those who remain at home" (Darlington 1991: 89). The most startling claims about the symbolism of the Aran jumper were made by a German textile enthusiast, Heinz Kiewe, who saw an early Aran jumper in a Dublin shop window in 1936 and was struck by the similarities between the jumper's design, the "celtic" knotwork of illuminated manuscripts, and the swirls carved into megaliths. He concluded that Aran knitting designs were part of an unbroken chain of religious iconography stretching back for millennia, originating in the Near East and surviving in the folk memory of the west of Ireland, which he saw as a particularly primitive outpost of northern Europe (Kiewe 1971: 65–75). Kiewe began promoting this theory in 1938 and elaborated it in his later (1967/71) book, *The Sacred History of Knitting,* and became surprisingly influential given the spurious nature of many of his suggestions (see Rutt 1987: 195–6). With his vision of Aran knitting flowing from "the Celtic blood of the artistic Irish," Kiewe (1971: 71) elevated the design of the Aran jumper to cosmological status: "An interlace of netting, plaiting, cording, braiding, an illusion of a garland to heaven, became their image of life on earth bound and beautiful in their bond with God in heaven" (1971: 74).

It is unlikely that fanciful ideas about Aran knitting would have proved so resilient in the face of historical evidence if they had not resonated with particular desires within Ireland and desires for commodified versions of Irishness around the world. The Aran jumper came into being as a distinct product during the 1930s (McQuillan 1993: 24–7). At this time, most of Ireland was newly independent from the United Kingdom (six counties remaining within the UK as Northern Ireland) and "deeply wounded both physically and psychologically" (Zuelow 2009: 1) from the period of civil war that surrounded partition in 1921. The government of the Free State (as the thirty-two counties that became independent from the United Kingdom were called between 1921 and 1937) and the Republic of Ireland (as it was later known) took paternalistic attitudes towards the rural west, and pursued protectionism in trade (Giblin, Kennedy, and McHugh 2013: 40). In 1933, the *Taoiseach* (prime minister) Eamonn De Valera called for Irish women to abandon foreign fashions and wear Irish wools and tweeds "until Irish silks and cottons became available" (Daly 1992: 90; see O'Kelly 2014: 12). Textile crafts such as weaving and knitting were seen as elements of a traditional way of life, which was threatened by high emigration. Simultaneously, weaving and knitting were advocated by some as a potential way to reduce the economic need for that migration (Mitchell 1997: 77; O'Kelly 2014:12). The Aran jumper found its transatlantic market in the late 1950s to 60s, when lower cost air travel was beginning to facilitate mass tourism. At this time, Irish America was growing as a political power within America and as a self-ascribed ethnic identity (Moynihan 2013; Lee and Casey 2006). In this context, the story of a lost Atlantic traveler being named and claimed by his family, and reconnected with an ancient landscape and belief system in the process, has an emotional power. Hence, as twentieth-century Ireland was being shaped by different forms of travel, the idea of the Aran jumper as an identity document fell on very fertile ground.

Migration, tourism and Irish hospitality

Migration and tourism are very much connected in Ireland's history, and the Aran jumper emerged from their interconnections. Emigration "peaked around the time of the Great Famine" of the 1840s (Duncan 2012; Gray 2013: 102) and the famine remains the central traumatic event in migration narratives within Ireland and the USA. Irish America is seen by both as the outcome of Irish Catholic economic hardship and dispossession (Frawley 2012: 58). However, the emigration peak at the time of the famine is part of a much longer and more varied emigration trend (Akenson 1996). After partition, the continuing high levels of emigration "became a barometer of state failure" (Gray 2013: 101) for the new independent Free State/ ROI. In his 1962 book *Aran: Islands of Legend*, nationalist Padraig O'Síocháin wrote that the purpose of his Galway Bay Company, which sold Aran jumpers, was to create jobs in the west of Ireland for young people who "drift without return" (1962: 126). The additions made in the 1967 edition include a photograph captioned "*Máirín Uí Dhomhnall of Inis Mean holds a magnificent example of the Aran Folk Art Knitting*" which is credited to Bórd Fáilte, the Irish tourist board. Clearly, selling the Aran jumper as a product was already part of promoting Ireland as a destination.

In 1962, on the other side of the Atlantic, an Irish folk group called the Clancy Brothers and Tommy Makem appeared on the USA's *Ed Sullivan Show*. All four wore Aran jumpers. Their performance launched not only their music but also the Aran jumper onto a mass American market. In 2009, Liam Clancy told *Irish America* magazine that before the show, "Irish-Americans weren't really interested in us … Pete Seeger played with us. A lot of people said: 'They've got a Communist up there.' So most of our audience were folkies and liberal Jews'" (Deignan 2009). The Ed Sullivan appearance changed that. The Clancy Brothers and Tommy Makem found an Irish American fan base and the Aran jumper became their visual brand. They subsequently wore Aran jumpers on almost all of their album covers; by 1972, on the cover of *Show Me The Way*, an empty Aran jumper stands in for the band. The association of the Aran jumper with Irish national identity in the American context was secured through the Clancy Brothers' success.

The Irish tourist industry was well established as a "national interest" (Zuelow 2009: 35) by this stage. The very emptiness of the depopulated rural west could be marketed as freedom, peace and beauty, while tourism offered a means to ameliorate its economic ills (O'Connor 1993:74). "Irish hospitality" was, after all, proverbial. Interest in Irishness as a transatlantic diasporic identity underpins "roots," "ancestral," "genealogical" or "heritage" tourism (Nash 2002: 27; O'Connor 1993: 63), whereby international visitors travel to Ireland in search of a sense of homecoming. However, the mainstreaming of Irish America has been such that the American market for goods and experiences associated with Irishness is greater than even the 34.6 million US citizens who identify themselves as Irish American would suggest (United States Census Bureau 2017).

The late twentieth century saw a surge of what Patterson (2011: 27) calls a "cult of Celtic chic which sells everywhere." The global phenomenon of the Irish pub, ever more elaborate St Patrick's Day celebrations in the USA, and the growth of an "seemingly limitless Irish-themed goods market" (Casey 2006: 104) made Irishness appear less an ethnicity than a mobile, recreational commodity (Negra 2006: 4). The distinctive textures of Aran knitting provide a useful material shorthand for this consumer experience of Irishness (Figure 5.2).

FIGURE 5.2 Souvenir trinkets including a miniature knitted hat that reads "Aran Tradition," 2016. Courtesy Carden. © Siún Carden.

For example, in 2014, a Boston-based footwear company called Concepts designed a limited edition Converse trainer for St Patrick's Day, with "an Aran-sweater upper." This was explained in the specialist sneaker press with the words "Boston is a huge Irish city" (Welty 2014).

As Nash (2008: 10) argues, Irish American fascination with transatlantic family ties is fuelled from within Ireland as well as from America. In the 1990s, Ireland reframed itself as what Lentin (2007: 433) calls a "diaspora nation." This process included symbolic elements, like Irish President Mary Robinson lighting a candle in the window of her official residence for Irish people overseas; practical elements like the provision of localized facilities for family history research to encourage genealogical tourism; and, most problematically, changes to the constitution (Moynihan 2013: 11; Nash 2014: 2). In 1998, the constitution of the Republic of Ireland was amended to include the words "the Irish nation cherishes its special affinity with people of Irish ancestry living abroad who share its cultural identity and heritage" (Nash 2002: 34). This heightened focus on Ireland's diaspora in the Celtic Tiger years coincided with the emergence of Ireland as a destination for migration. In 2004, another amendment was made to the constitution, by referendum, which removed the right to Irish citizenship from people born in Ireland whose parents were born elsewhere. The result is that someone from the USA with one grandparent who emigrated there from Ireland may claim Irish citizenship more easily than a person born in Ireland to parents who were born elsewhere. The identification of national identity with genealogical descent, which extends Irish nationhood to a vast global diaspora, is less than welcoming to Ireland's newest residents (Moynihan 2013). The collapse of the Celtic Tiger economy amid the global economic crisis of the 2000s sharpened this tension, as net out-migration resumed, with huge numbers of young people (or "Generation Emigration," as the *Irish Times* (Ferriter 2015) calls its series devoted to them) leaving in search of work overseas (Gray 2013: 104). Hazy nostalgia for the hardships and triumphs of Irish mass emigration was thrown into sharp relief by anxiety about today's globalized labor market.

In 2013, the ROI government made a direct appeal for economic help from Irish emigrants and their descendants around the world, inviting the diaspora to return as tourists during a year-long event called "The Gathering." Postcards were distributed to 1.8 million households, with the intention that they would be sent as invitations to family members living overseas, and Irish people were encouraged to organize and host "reunions" (An Post 2012). Publicity material for "The Gathering" included an image, captioned "Welcome home ...," of a group of people embracing in a friendly fashion. The clothing of those in the front row forms an Irish tricolor flag as they are dressed in green, white and orange Aran jumpers (O'Kelly 2014: 9). The Gathering was criticized by some, including Ireland's Cultural Ambassador Gabriel Byrne, as "a scam" (Gray 2013: 116–17).

Scams and stories

Questions of deception and misrepresentation arise from any account of Aran knitting, which shares the "dense aura of inauthenticity" surrounding "tourist art"

(Phillips and Steiner 1999: 4). Can we interpret the popular stories about these stitches as a creative form of communal fiction, or do their inaccuracy and commercial motivation mean they lack any cultural relevance for Irish people? In her rich history of a Dublin shop called Cleo, whose high-end, hand-knitted Aran jumpers were worn by clients ranging from playwright Sean O'Casey to Marilyn Monroe, O'Kelly (2014: 35) reports that in the 1950s, the shop owners became curious about where the Aran stitches had come from. Their agent on Aran Mór responded to their enquiries with a letter recounting how her mother, Maggie Dirrane, had emigrated to America in the 1900s and learnt complex knitting stitches there, under the influence of women from different parts of Europe. On her return, her daughter said, she adapted and combined these stitches into what we see as Aran patterns (see also Rutt 1987; Darlington 1991; McQuillan 1993 on the role of Maggie Dirrane and Maggie O'Toole). O'Kelly (2014: 35) writes that: "The letter … was treasured in Cleo, and framed for safekeeping. But it was kept facing the wall in the shop, aware as the Cleo women were that a great deal of the Irish economy 'was hanging on that story.'" It is impossible to say how much of what we know as Aran knitting can be attributed to any individual, and there are various competing stories about the origins of these stitches (Mitchell 1997: 87). Questions of originality and authorship are notoriously difficult in this kind of work, where the line between invention and reverse engineering is far from obvious. What we do know is that the erasure of individual creativity from the imagined lineage of Aran knitters is not unusual, as vernacular craft skills are often associated with an ancient, communal, instinctual inheritance rather than individual innovation or intellect, particularly in the case of domestic crafts, which are identified with femininity (Chiarappa 1997: 399; Makovicky 2011: 155).

Given surging demand for Aran knitting produced in Ireland, the skilled nature of the work and low rates of pay, the Aran jumper industry quickly found itself short of Irish knitters. Muriel Gahan refused to sell Aran knitting produced outside the islands themselves through her Country Shop (Mitchell 1997: 91). Less scrupulous traders were happy to misrepresent the provenance of the finished item. Juliette Pearson (pseudonym) knitted Aran jumpers for one of these companies on a piecework basis in Sunderland, England in the late 1960s to 70s, alongside several neighbors and a cousin. She remembers her cousin writing "'Made in Sunderland' on the inside of the tags, in tiny writing, before she sewed them into place," because they "thought it was a cheek that people would pay good money for something they thought was made on a specific island" (personal communication 2015).

A darker thread in the Aran jumper's history has been glimpsed in recent years, due to inquiries into the role of the Republic of Ireland state in Magdalen laundries and other religious institutions where women and children who were believed to have transgressed (or to be at risk of transgressing) Irish Catholic social and sexual norms were confined until as recently as the 1990s (Department of Justice and Equality 2013). In press interviews, Maureen Sullivan, a former resident of two Magdalen laundries, mentions that her (unpaid) labor included knitting Aran jumpers for sale (BBC 2013). Given the absence of records, it is not currently possible to gauge how isolated or widespread such practices were, or to trace the route these garments took. However, as O'Kelly (2014: 34) observes, the role of religious institutions in Irish textile production and processing "now appears a great deal less benign than it

did even ten years ago." In Coleman (2010), Maureen Sullivan recalls a supervised
visit from her mother as a teenager:

> The nuns was (*sic*) saying, "Oh yes, she's very good and she's coming along
> great and she's getting great training and tell your mother about the lovely Aran
> sweater that you done," not *sweaters*! And I was thinking, God how many have
> I done at this stage? And my mother was saying, "Can you do an Aran sweater?"
> She was all excited because I was able to knit an Aran sweater. I think she really
> didn't know that we were knitting Aran sweaters late at night after a day's work.
> The Laundry was never mentioned.

Whatever the scale of such production, the exaltation of family ties and Irish
ancestral roots through the mythology of the Aran jumper appears cruelly ironic in
the context of a system within which women and children were separated, sometimes
across national borders, and where poor record keeping and communal silence has
resulted in gaps in many Irish family trees. The "export and sale of Irish children"
(Maguire 2002: 396) to American couples through unregulated adoptions during
the 1940s, 50s and 60s makes the idea of any inhabitant of such an institution
knitting Aran jumpers for sale disturbing. The changing public understanding of
this aspect of Ireland's history demonstrates that there is more to kinship than easy
sentimentality, and it is a mistake to assume that fantasies around the Aran jumper
have only catered to Irish-American desires.

Conclusion

Rather than being timeless or static, Aran knitting continues to be reinvented
and reinterpreted. Instead of using it to suggest a coded text, some designers have
exploited its figurative potential. Most famously, a Jean Paul Gaultier dress adds
knitted conical breast cones to the familiar repertoire of cable stitches, expanding
his "vocabulary of reassessed femininity" (Conway and Downey 2007: 42). In 2014,
Alexander McQueen produced an Aran jumper that uses cable stitches to depict
a skull, reflecting both a motif of the designer brand and the association of the
Aran jumper with death. Reinventions like these (as well as those of Irish designers
like Joanne Hynes and Lainey Keogh) play with the conventions of Aran knitting,
using its cosy kitsch to offset innovation. Reviewing Lainey Keogh's show at London
Fashion Week in 1998, the *Irish Times* remarked that until recently, "The Aran
sweater was perceived to hold a position in Irish fashion equivalent to the Catholic
Church in Irish society" (*Irish Times* 1998). It therefore lends itself to subversion,
iconoclasm and creative reflection on Irish history and society. For example, in
his 2003 installation, "United," Austin McQuinn lined a cell in Kilmainham Gaol
with a patchwork of Aran knitting, converting "the austere chamber into a warm,
barnyard-smelling 'padded' cell" as part of a group exhibition marking the 200th
anniversary of the execution of nationalist revolutionary Robert Emmet (Clancy
2003: 87). Deirdre Nelson has used an Aran jumper purchased on eBay as the
basis for part of her "*Barántúil*" ("Authentic") collection of textile "souvenirs",

shifting emphasis away from preservation and purity in "traditional" crafts towards processes of making and exchange (West 2011: 6).

While the idea of Aran stitches carrying messages to be decoded in a pre-literate society is not accurate, it is instructive to look at the ways the Aran jumper has been "read." As Jo Turney (2009: 55) argues, the idea of knitted textiles as communicative media in non-literate societies "consigns the garments to a preindustrial era of more rural and simple times," situating them in an imagined state of "stasis." Thus, the ways in which Aran stitches are "read" sometimes obscure the processes through which they are "written," whether in terms of individual authorship and creativity, or in terms of their manufacture. Regardless of the historical veracity of claims that particular Aran stitch patterns index features of the social, natural or spiritual worlds, analyzing the ways they have been "read" reveals how Aran knitting has performed broader communicative functions (see Sonja Andrew 2008). These functions continue to be subverted and elaborated by fine artists, and translated into couture and mass market fashion products. As an international symbol of Irishness that comes with its own origin myth, the Aran jumper embodies emotionally charged ideas about nativeness and diaspora. David Lloyd (1999:102), among others, writes of a "sentimental and fetishizing" interest in diasporic identities (see Moynihan 2013: 12). Catherine Nash's work on Ireland suggests that the very limitations of such an attitude, when they come up against the complexities and surprises of actual genealogical research can open up space for more nuanced understandings of relatedness to enter public consciousness. Nash writes that "In some respects at least, settler genealogies of Old World ancestry reflect a nostalgia for an imagined time when place, identity, culture and ancestry coincided" (2008: 9). This imagined time is the setting for the Aran jumper myth, which emerged from changing and unstable relationships between place, identity, culture, and ancestry.

References

Akenson, D. (1996), *The Irish Diaspora: A Primer*, London: P.D. Meany Co.

Andrew, S. (2008), "Textile Semantics: Considering a Communication-based Reading of Textiles," *TEXTILE*, 6(1), 32–65.

An Post (2012), "An Post shows support for The Gathering Ireland 2013," November 15. Available online: http://www.anpost.ie/AnPost/News/ THE+GATHERING+IRELAND+2013.htm (accessed October 31, 2015).

BBC (2013), "Magdalene Laundries: Survivor Stories," February 5. Available online: http://www.bbc.co.uk/news/world-europe-21345995 (accessed October 31, 2015).

Carden, S. (2014), "Cable Crossings: The Aran Jumper as Myth and Merchandise," *Costume*, 48 (2): 260–75.

Casey, N. (2006), "'The Best Kept Secret in Retail': Selling Irishness in Contemporary America," in D. Negra (ed.), *The Irish in us: Irishness, Performativity and Popular Culture*, 84–109, New York, NY: Duke University Press.

Chiarappa, M. (1997), "Affirmed Objects in Affirmed Places: History, Geographic Sentiment and a Region's Crafts," *Journal of Design History*, 10 (4): 399–415.

Clancy, L. (2003), "Dearcadh: Visionaries of 1791–1803 in Kilmainham Gaol," *Circa*, 106 (Winter): 86–7.

Coleman, K. (2010), *Haunting Cries: Stories of Child Abuse in Catholic Ireland*, Dublin: Gill & Macmillan.

Conway, H. and G. Downey (2007), *Weardowney Knit Couture: 20 Hand-knit Designs from Runway to Reality*, London: Anova.

Compton, R. (1983), *The Complete Book of Traditional Knitting*. London: B.T. Batsford.

Daly, M. (1992), *Industrial Development and Irish National Identity, 1922–1939*, Dublin: Gill & Macmillan.

Darlington, R. (1991), *Irish Knitting: Patterns Inspired by Ireland*, London: A & C Black Publishers Ltd.

Deignan, T. (2009), "The History of the Clancy Brothers," April/May. Available online: http://irishamerica.com/2009/04/the-history-of-the-clancy-brothers/ (accessed October 31, 2015).

Department of Justice and Equality (Republic of Ireland) (2013), "Chapter 19: Living and Working Conditions," *Report of the Inter-Departmental Committee to Establish the Facts of State Involvement with the Magdalen Laundries*. Available online: http://www.justice.ie/en/JELR/Pages/MagdalenRpt2013 (accessed April 4, 2016).

Duncan, P. (2012), "Ireland's Leaders Try to Woo Diaspora Back as Crisis Sends New Generation Packing," *Time*, March 14. Available online: http://content.time.com/time/world/article/0,8599,2108917,00.html (accessed October 31, 2015).

Ferriter, D. (2015), "Last Chance to Get Your Certificate of Irish Heritage," *Irish Times*, August 22. Available online: http://www.irishtimes.com/opinion/diarmaid-ferriter-last-chance-to-get-your-certificate-of-irish-heritage-1.2324526 (accessed October 31, 2015).

Frawley, O. (2012), *Irish Studies: Memory Ireland, Diaspora and Memory Practices*, New York, NY: Syracuse University Press.

Giblin, T., K. Kennedy, and D. McHugh (2013), *The Economic Development of Ireland in the Twentieth Century*, London: Routledge.

Gordon, J. (2010), "Maritime Influences on Traditional Knitwear Design: The Case of the Fisherman's Gansey: An Object Study," *Textile History*, 41 (1): 99–108.

Gray, B. (2013), "Towards the Neo-Institutionalization of Irish State-Diaspora Relations in the Twenty-First Century," in M. Collyer (ed.), *Emigration Nations: Policies and Ideologies of Emigrant Engagement*, 100–25, London: Palgrave Macmillan.

Irish Times (1998), "Lainey Blows Holes in Traditional Image of Irish Knitwear," *Irish Times*, February 2. Available online: http://www.irishtimes.com/news/lainey-blows-holes-in-traditional-image-of-irish-knitwear-1.137379 (accessed October 31, 2015).

Kelsall, M. (2003), "Luttrell of Arran and the Romantic Invention of Ireland," in G. Carruthers and A. Rawes (eds.), *English Romanticism and the Celtic World*, 182–95, Cambridge: Cambridge University Press.

Kiewe, H. (1971), *The Sacred History of Knitting*, Oxford: Art Needlework Industries Limited.

Kiewe, H. (1982), "Foreword," in S. Hollingworth (ed.), *Traditional Aran Knitting*, 6–8, London: Dover.

King, L. and E. Sisson (eds.) (2011), *Ireland, Design and Visual Culture: Negotiating Modernity 1922–1992*, Dublin: Cork University Press.

Kneafsey, M. (2002), "Tourism Images and the Construction of Celticity in Ireland and Britain," in D. Harvey (ed.), *Celtic Geographies: Old Culture, New Times*, 123–99, London: Routledge.

Lee, J. and M. Casey (2006), *Making the Irish American: The History and Heritage of the Irish in the United States*, New York, NY: New York University Press.

Lentin, R. (2007), "Illegal in Ireland, Irish Illegals: Diaspora Nation as Racial State," *Irish Political Studies*, 22 (4): 433–53.

Lloyd, D. (1999), *Ireland After History*, Dublin: Cork University Press.

Maguire, M. (2002), "Foreign Adoptions and the Evolution of Irish Adoption Policy, 1945–52," *Journal of Social History*, 36 (2): 387–404.

Makovicky, N. (2011), "'Erotic Needlework': Vernacular Designs on the 21st Century Market," in A. Clarke (ed.), *Design Anthropology: Object Culture in the 21st Century*, 155–68, Vienna: Springer.

Mattar, S. (2004), *Primitivism, Science, and the Irish Revival*, London: Clarendon.

McQuillan, D. (1993), *The Aran Sweater*, Belfast: Appletree Press.

Mitchell, G. (1997), *Deeds not words: the life and work of Muriel Gahan: [champion of rural women and craftworkers]*. Dublin: Town House.

Moynihan, S. (2013), *"Other People's Diasporas": Negotiating Race in Contemporary Irish and Irish American Culture*, New York, NY: Syracuse University Press.

Muldoon, P. (2011), "The Toe-Tag," in *Meeting the British*, 83, London: Faber & Faber.

Nash, C. (1993), "'Embodying the Nation': The West of Ireland Landscape and Irish Identity," in B. O'Connor and M. Cronin (eds.) *Tourism in Ireland: A Critical Analysis*, 86–111, Cork: Cork University Press.

Nash, C. (2002), "Genealogical Identities," *Environment and Planning D: Society and Space*, 20: 27–52.

Nash, C. (2008), *Of Irish Descent: Origin Stories, Genealogy, and the Politics of Belonging*, New York, NY: Syracuse University Press.

Nash, C. (2014), "Blood of the Irish: Knowing 'Ourselves' Genetically," *The Irish Review*, 48: 1–16.

Negra, D. (2006), *The Irish in Us: Irishness, Performativity, and Popular Culture*. Durham: Duke University Press.

O'Connor, B. (1993), "Myths and mirrors: Tourist images and national identity," in B. O'Connor and M. Cronin (eds.) *Tourism in Ireland: A Critical Analysis*, 68–85, Cork: Cork University Press.

O'Kelly, H. (2014), *Cleo: Irish Clothes in a Wider World*, Dublin: Associated Editions.

O'Síocháin, P. (1962/7), *Aran: Islands of Legend*, Dublin: Foilsifichain Eireann.

Patterson, A. (2011), "Brand Ireland: Tourism and National Identity," in E. Frew and L. White (eds.), *Tourism and National Identity: An International Perspective*, 26–37, Oxon: Routledge.

Phillips, R. and C. Steiner (1999), *Unpacking Culture: Art and Commodity in Colonial and Postcolonial Worlds*, London: University of California Press.

Rutt, R. (1987), *A History of Hand Knitting*, London: B. T. Batsford Limited.

Stall-Meadows, C. (2014), "Scottish Sweater," in A. Lynch and M. Strauss (eds.), *Ethnic Dress in the United States: A Cultural Encyclopedia*, 260–1, London: Rowman & Littlefield.

Turney, J. (2009), *The Culture of Knitting*, London: Bloomsbury Academic.

United States Census Bureau (2017), "Facts For Features: Irish-American Heritage Month (March) and St Patrick's Day (March 17): 2017", Release Number: CB17-FF.05. Available online: https://www.census.gov/newsroom/facts-for-features/2017/cb17-ff05. html (accessed August 14, 2017).

Wall, E. (2011), *Writing the Irish West: Ecologies and Traditions*, Notre Dame, IN: University of Notre Dame Press.

Welty, M. (2014), "The Concepts x Converse Pro Leathers Are Your Drinking Shoes for St. Paddy's Day," Complex Sneakers. Available online: http://uk.complex.com/sneakers/2014/03/concepts-converse-aran-cable-knit-st-patricks-day (accessed October 31, 2015).

West, K. (2011), "Introduction," in *Modern Languages: Reinterpreting the Irish Vernacular*, 5–6, Dublin: Crafts Council of Ireland.

Zuelow, E. (2009), *Making Ireland Irish: Tourism and National Identity Since the Irish Civil War*, New York, NY: Syracuse University Press.

6

Chok Weaving and Textile Enterprises

From Northern Thailand

Disaya Chudasri

Introduction

This chapter presents an analysis of field research into the weaving communities of *Long* district (Phrae province) and *Mae Chaem* district (Chiang Mai province) in northern Thailand. The research aimed to:

- examine weaving communities and textile enterprises in relation to the principles of sustainability, i.e. Walker's *Quadruple Bottom Line of Sustainability* (2011) comprising personal meaning, social responsibility, environmental care, and economic viability;
- develop an in-depth understanding of the relationships between textile production, design and sustainability among various interested groups in order to foster the implementation of *craft and design for sustainability*;
- identify potential areas in which design can help ensure the continuity of the weaving communities and the production of textile products in ways that are compatible with sustainability.

Research questions for the field research

- Which handwoven textiles of northern Thailand have potential for design interventions that are compatible with sustainability, and what are the selection criteria?

- What are the relationships between the textile production of northern Thailand and sustainability?

- What are potential areas in which design can contribute to the weaving communities and textile enterprises of northern Thailand?

The research methodology comprised four main phases: (i) identification of case studies, (ii) collection of information and its validation, (iii) data analysis and the formulation of findings and conclusions from the field data, and (iv) validation of the findings. A grounded theory approach (Glaser and Strauss 1967, as cited in Castree, Kitchin, and Rogers 2013; Scott 2014) was employed as a research strategy for collecting information and analyzing it. The author went into the field without any preconceived design framework or theoretical statements, but with the three research questions given above and an understanding of the *Triple Bottom Line* (Elkington 1997, 2004) and the *Quadruple Bottom Line* (Walker 2011) of sustainability. Contextual information from the field emerged from spending time with the weaving communities and textile enterprises and talking to the various people involved. This information was then related to the principles of *design for sustainability*.

Multiple research techniques and tools were employed to identify case studies and collect information about the selected case study enterprises. Research techniques included (i) enquiries and discussions (conversations, informal interviews, and collective interviews), (ii) a review of the literature identified through the field research and accessed via paper- and Web-based sources, (iii) observations, and (iv) the changing role of the researcher (from being a facilitator in group discussions, a practitioner in weaving, to a buyer of textile products). These techniques were determined in the field in relation to each situation. Of particular importance was the rapport achieved with the various informants and the types of information accessed (oral discussions, books, inspections of and discussions about textile artifacts, weaving demonstrations). Various tools were employed to acquire information in the field, including field notes, photography, video and audio recording, questionnaires, and the visualization of information (diagrams and sample pictures).

The in-depth case studies took place over a period of about eleven weeks covering (i) three sub-districts in the *Long* district of Phrae province with seventeen informants, (ii) two sub-districts in the *Mae Chaem* district of Chiang Mai province with twenty-four informants, and (iii) local markets and trade fairs in northern Thailand and Bangkok. The rationale for the selected communities is explained later in the chapter. The informants included group leaders of the weaving communities, weavers, shop owners/assistants, villagers, tourists coming to the districts for a cultural experience, buyers from outside the districts, and the staff of a government department. Information was also collected from a group of twenty weaving trainees in *Long* district. Among all these informants, five from each district were identified as key informants; these included group leaders and experienced weavers, who were able to provide in-depth and comprehensive information about and insights into weaving in Thailand.

The data analysis employed a mixed-methods approach. However, much of the analysis was qualitative. It describes and visualizes the practices of the weaving communities and the stakeholders involved in the production of *chok* textiles and clothing. Findings from the analysis were then related to theoretical ideas about *design for sustainability*. Some quantitative information was extracted from the data, which helped to inform some of the areas of interest, especially those related to financial value. Finally, the main research findings were validated with peer-reviewers who specialize in design, textiles, and sustainability.

Rationale for selecting *chok* weaving for in-depth case studies in relation to *Design for Sustainability*

Northern Thailand covers nine provinces, including Chiang Mai, Chiang Rai, Lampang, Lamphun, Mae Hong Son, Nan, Phayao, Phrae, and Uttaradit. The region is characterized by its mountain ranges and the history of the Kingdom of Lanna, which existed from the thirteenth century for more than seven hundred years (Bowie 1992; Lannaworld.com 2006).

Weaving is a tradition that has been inherited by ethnic groups in Thailand, especially women in the northern region. The Tai Yuan is a group whose relatively large population lives in the northern region (McIntosh 2012: 3–9). Over generations, *Tai Yuan* women have inherited weaving skills, especially using a technique known as "*chok*" to produce *chok* textiles with unique patterns. *Chok* textiles are commonly used to produce traditional clothes of a basic design, like a tube skirt that is called "*sin tin chok*" (Figure 6.1). The unique patterns of *sin tin chok* can distinguish the *Tai Yuan* from other ethnic groups as well as the *Tai Yuan* of other regions in Thailand (Suchitta 1989: 97). Weavers make *sin tin chok* on the understanding that it is a special, traditional cloth, which women wear only occasionally and in particular to attend religious ceremonies in Buddhist temples (McIntosh 2012: 3, 6). The *Tai Yuan* regard *chok* weaving and *sin tin chok* very highly, seeing it as part of their historical and cultural heritage and their group identity.

The weaving communities of *Long* district and *Mae Chaem* district are generally of the same ethnicity, being identified with the *Tai Yuan*. They produce *chok* textiles for personal use and, in more recent years, for trade and economic development. The *chok* weaving communities of the two districts are renowned among other textile communities in Thailand, and they are especially important for the revitalization of the weaving culture and traditional clothing as part of the identity of the *Tai Yuan* group, as well as of the whole of Thailand.

In 2010, the leader of a weaving community in *Long* district was declared a national artist in visual art (fine art and the art of handwoven textiles). Also, the leader of a weaving group in *Mae Chaem* district is recognized nationally as one of the early pioneers behind the revitalization of traditional weaving. These

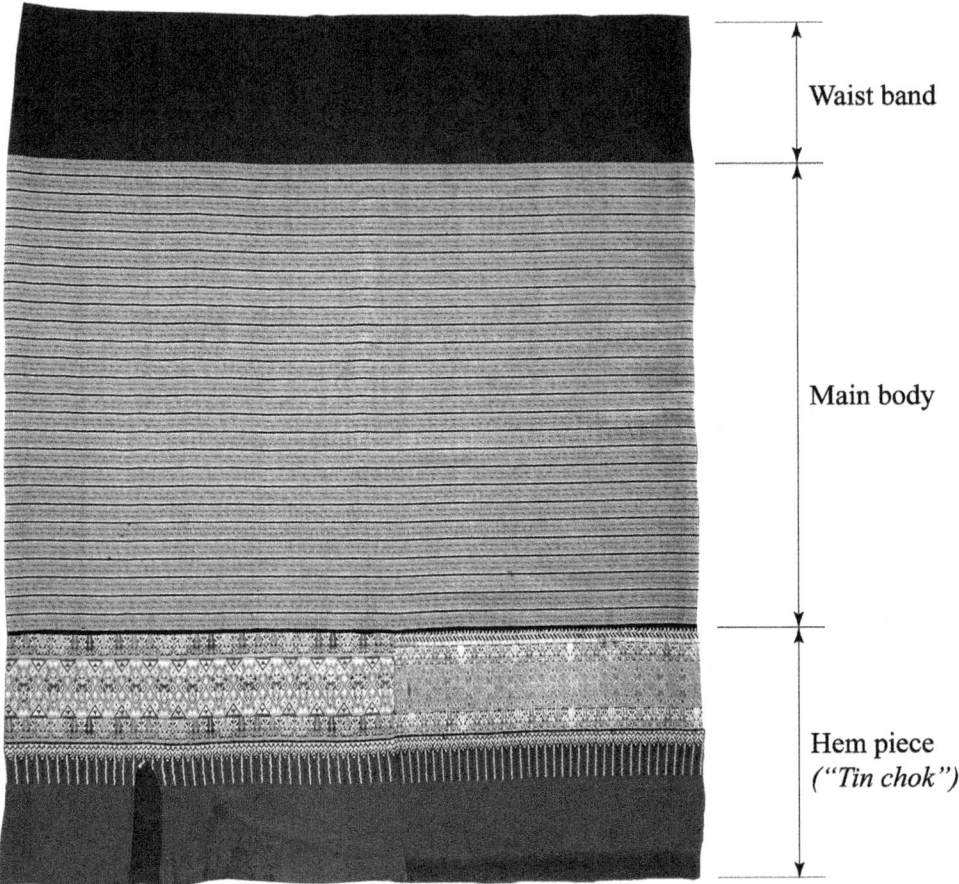

FIGURE 6.1 A vintage *sin tin chok* from c.1950s, which the weaver received from her mother. Courtesy Disaya Chudasri.

communities now produce a wide range of textile products, besides *chok* textiles and *sin tin chok,* which they supply to commercial markets. For these reasons, the weaving communities of these two districts were identified as the focus of this research.

It is clear that their textile production, especially that of *sin tin chok,* has qualities that are compatible with all the elements of Walker's *Quadruple Bottom Line of Sustainability* (comprising personal meaning, social responsibility, environmental care, and economic viability) (Walker 2011: 190). The benefits of their textile production are summarized in relation to these elements of sustainability as follows.

- **Personal meaning** can be inherent to the process of textile production in various ways, such as the (i) *spirituality* that is invoked during weaving and other craftwork, linked to beliefs in Buddhism and religious rites, (ii) *self-expression and identity* of the makers, resulting from their imagination, creativity and hand skills in weaving a fabric with unique patterns, (iii) sense of positive *fulfilment* that comes from various feelings, such as: loving what they are doing; having a sense of contentment and being at peace while engaged in the processes of making; being acknowledged within various groups; having made something, seeing one's own development, especially in terms of skill levels; seeing beauty in the art of weaving; understanding the historical and cultural heritage and having pride in it; having an appreciation of the value of traditional weaving as an identity of Thailand that goes beyond monetary value and economic indicators; having empathy with traditional weaving, wanting it to flourish and contributing to this in a globalized world.

- **Social responsibility** involves the weavers of *Tai Yuan* continuing to work in traditional weaving and passing on their knowledge and skills to the next generation—through demonstrating and teaching practices in weaving and making clothes and textile products. This occurs especially among close family members and other relatives in the villages. Making textiles and clothing by the traditional process is rather complex and difficult; it requires a number of contributors with various skills and skill levels. These include yarn-spinning, weaving, tailoring, and repairing traditional looms. Weavers and artisans can also work at home and thus are able to deal with other domestic responsibilities, such as taking care of children or aging relatives. Indeed, such textile systems serve to transfer traditional knowledge and skills, and to strengthen collaboration, solidarity and care among various communities in the locality.

- **Environmental care** is found in the principles and practices of local weavers and artisans in their self-sufficient ways of living and efficient use of natural materials, which can be sourced locally, e.g. cotton yarns for weaving, hard wood and bamboo for handlooms and weaving tools. They believe that production tools and textile products that are made from natural materials will have less harmful effects on the people and the environment, especially when textile products are disposed of and decompose in the natural environment.

- **Economic viability** and the financial income resulting from weaving are commented on by weavers, shop owners, and villagers (whether weaving is carried out as a hobby, a part-time activity or a full-time job). Their perspectives are divided into three main groups: weaving can be (i) a productive activity supporting economic development; (ii) a part-time activity providing a supplementary income and boosting savings; or (iii) not worth doing—because the income from weaving cannot cover the various expenditures incurred in day-to-day living, and so some weavers turn to other jobs that can provide a higher income. Income rates vary depending on skill levels. The weavers who do weaving as a way to earn income generally fall into two broad categories. Either they are in their twenties to forties and are capable of advanced weaving that commands higher prices, or they are older, in their sixties to seventies, and are able to do basic weaving that provides a lower rate of income.

Textile community enterprises and business activities

In the context of the study areas, a **community enterprise** is a group of neighbors in one or more villages in the same sub-district or beyond who set up a business together and manage their local capital (including natural resources, know-how, finance, and sociocultural heritage) to trade products or services so that they can earn an income and be self-reliant (Secretariat Office of Community Enterprise Promotion Board (SCEB) c.2015).

In the two districts studied, there are several community enterprises producing textile products, including traditional clothes, i.e. *sin tin chok*, clothes in folk and contemporary styles, accessories such as scarves, bags and wallets, kitchen and bedding accessories, fabric rolls such as indigo-dyed fabrics and hand-spun cotton fabrics, and handwoven textiles made specifically for textile competitions or exhibitions.

Various **stakeholders** are involved in the production and trading of textile products. They can be classified by their roles as follows (Chudasri 2015: 242):

- *makers*—artisans who supply materials such as hand-spun cotton yarns, weavers, tailors, group leaders;
- *producers/purchasers*—group leaders, local teachers, business owners, designers, government departments/officers;
- *purchasers/traders*—artisans, group leaders, local teachers, tourists, market customers, business owners, designers, government departments/officers;
- *purchasers/users*—all of the above.

One person may take several roles in the running of a textile business. For example, a group leader may be a maker who produces textile items or a producer who employs local weavers/artisans to make textile products or a purchaser/trader of textile products.

Textile production is largely based on traditional skills and skilled labor, e.g. making hand-spun cotton yarns and natural-dyed yarns, weaving, sewing and tailoring. In recent times, there have been various developments in the processes of traditional weaving, especially in *chok* weaving. Today, there are three main directions for textile production at the local level: (i) handmade production using traditional processes; (ii) handmade production that integrates weaving techniques, i.e. "*chok*" (discontinuous supplementary weft technique) and "*yok dok*" (brocade technique) to make *chok* textiles, and (iii) combinations of handmade and machine-based production.

Production networks can range from a weaving community within a village, a collection of weaving communities and textile enterprises spread over several villages within a district, to communities across districts in the same province or other provinces and regions in Thailand. Many have established long-term relationships through the employment of skilled labor, trading in raw materials and textile products, and marriage.

The primary market for handmade textile products is domestic. Textile products are distributed to individual customers within districts and beyond via shops, trade fairs and exhibitions, local festivals and cultural tours, home stays, and websites. Various groups of people can be individual customers of textile products, e.g. owners of textile shops, teachers, government officers, visitors or tourists. Events that host weaving demonstrations, such as trade fairs in Bangkok, and *Junlakathin*, a Buddhist religious ceremony held in the districts, can help to stimulate interest, facilitate knowledge exchange between weavers/artisans and individual customers, and encourage purchasing. Websites can connect local producers with various customers within the district and beyond. However, only a few local producers use the internet and websites for commerce.

Key issues related to the traditional production of *chok* textiles

These issues include:

- two different approaches to developments in the process of traditional weaving;
- developments in textile production for commerce and their impact on the weavers' knowledge, skills, and identity, and customers' understanding;
- knowledge transfer between experienced weavers and the younger generation.

Two different approaches to developments in the process of traditional weaving

The weavers of *Mae Chaem* district prefer not to alter the traditional process (Figure 6.2 (left)) in order to accelerate production and increase production capacity. Instead, they choose to continue using traditional weaving practices, which are rather complicated and time-consuming, and to make *chok* textiles in their free time ("as a hobby"), primarily for their personal use. When they are able to produce more textiles than are required for their personal use, this may be traded for income generation.

The weavers believe that traditional weaving techniques are critical to their cultural heritage, because these practices have been passed on for generations. This relates to their Buddhist beliefs and the idea of sufficiency in their way of life. They gain spiritual meaning while working on traditional weaving (as explained above). Additionally, they take historic pride in their skills, especially when the weavers supply very intricately made textiles to the royal family and aristocrats. They believe that the values (including the monetary value) of *sin tin chok* made in the traditional way will continue to increase in the future. This research finds that these beliefs relate to "a core principle of finance, namely the time value of money" (Investopedia, c.2015).

However, *sin tin chok* made by traditional techniques is noted for its increasingly high price, which may lead to it becoming too expensive for ordinary people and thus only available to a few wealthy people and the weavers themselves. They may wear *sin tin chok* only on special occasions, such as religious ceremonies. It is notable too that male buyers/collectors do not usually wear *sin tin chok*. Instead, they keep it in their textile collections at home and occasionally show *sin tin chok* to visitors. Such small, elite markets for traditional handmade textiles could mean that the popularity and relevance of such textiles will fade from the minds of ordinary people.

In contrast, the weaving communities of *Long* district have seized opportunities to benefit from developments in traditional weaving that can reduce production times and increase their production capacity for *chok* textiles for trade and income generation. This approach also complies with a vision of Queen Sirikit of Thailand to revitalize traditional weaving and textile culture in ways that can alleviate poverty in rural communities.

In the 1990s, the weavers of *Long* district adopted a brocade technique, known locally as "*yok dok.*" Using this technique in *chok* weaving (Figure 6.2 (right)) resulted in a reduction in production times of around sixty percent for weaving a piece of *chok* textile comprising seventy repeated patterns. *Chok* textiles made in this way, however, have a different quality as the patterns of fine quality appear on only one side.

In the 2010s, a weaving community in *Long* district initiated another method of textile production that uses both machinery and skilled hand labor to produce products such as pleated blouses, tube skirts, and printed bags—in parallel with their existing production method that is based on handmade techniques alone.

FIGURE 6.2 *Chok* textiles made in 2012 from: traditional process in *Mae Chaem* district (left); integrated techniques in *Long* district (right). Courtesy Disaya Chudasri.

Such developments result in greater quantities of *chok* textiles being produced at more affordable prices, at the rates of which weaving communities can still earn supplementary income, make savings and improve their economic status. Also, larger numbers of ordinary people can now afford to buy *chok* textiles and use them to make contemporary dresses. Hence these developments in traditional weaving help not only to alleviate poverty in rural areas, but also contribute to revitalizing the popularity of traditional textile culture across Thailand.

Developments in textile production for commerce and their impact on weavers' knowledge, skills, and identity, and customers' understanding

These developments mean that textiles of different quality enter the market and are sold at different prices. It is found that these developments can result in some erosion of weavers' knowledge, skills, and identity. The various ranges of textiles can confuse customers, who may not understand the differences in techniques and quality and the reasons why some *chok* textiles are very expensive and others are relatively inexpensive.

The erosion of weavers' knowledge, skills and identity is a particular issue for weavers in *Long* district. Because weaving communities are keen to employ the faster integrated techniques to produce *chok* textiles, the buyers and traders of *Tai Yuan* groups in other provinces, such as Sukhothai, place orders with producers in *Long* district to produce *chok* textiles with patterns related to Sukhothai identity. Many weavers in *Long* district have become "supply weavers," knowing that they are making *chok* textiles in *Long* district, but are unaware of and no longer identifying with the traditional characteristics of *chok* textiles of *Long* district, which can be distinguished by textile patterns and motifs. Some weavers broadly say that there are two types of patterns, "traditional" and "new," but they cannot articulate the names and meanings of many *chok* textile patterns and motifs unless they check in books.

Customers' understanding of the value of *chok* textiles in the market is challenged, especially given the ranges of *chok* textiles and their different qualities and prices resulting from different production techniques. The research finds that individual customers lack sufficient information in many ways. Customers are keen to know more about product quality and appropriate pricing. Moreover, some customers are interested in product pricing in relation to production processes, the practices of ethical production and fair trade, the personal meanings associated with weaving communities and customers, the historical and cultural heritage of weaving communities, the ethnicity and unique identity of weaving communities that are revealed through textile products. Without clear and sufficient information about textile products and their production, customers tend to put off purchasing decisions. Thus, it is necessary to convey adequate information about textile products and production in ways that are relevant and clear to the customer. This will enable them to have a better understanding of the textiles that interest them and lead to more informed purchasing decisions. Such information can also assist the weaving communities to explain and differentiate their products from those of other communities and industrial craft-producers.

Knowledge transfer between experienced weavers and the younger generation

This is found to be an important issue requiring urgent attention because of the rapidly declining numbers of experienced weavers. Many weavers are over fifty years of age and few younger people are being trained. There is a shortage of young people willing to consider weaving as a career option, especially those in their twenties. Moreover, training novices to become proficient weavers takes time. The transfer of weaving knowledge and skills can take "years or decades" until the trainees become proficient and knowledgeable. Training weavers is usually done through demonstration, oral instruction and regular practice, which occur in a home or a shared space available to weaving communities. It is the weavers themselves who possess the skills and knowledge derived from training. To prevent the loss of weaving knowledge and skills in the near future (i.e. over the next twenty to thirty years), it is critical to develop appropriate platforms and activities so that experienced weavers can pass on their knowledge and skills to the next generation. To this end it will be necessary to develop weaving courses and training, including tools that are appropriate and attractive to the younger generation. This is explained further in a later section.

Potential areas to which design can contribute

Five potential areas are identified where design can make a useful contribution and be compatible with sustainability principles. These are: product design and development; design for marketing and sales; production development; producers' understanding of new kinds of knowledge; knowledge transfer of traditional weaving.

Product design and development: In the general context of handmade textile production, product design and development is identified as an area that can help increase the value and sales potential of textile products through, for example, designing forms and functions of textile products that are better suited to the lifestyles of potential customers. Likewise, in the specific context of *chok* textiles, producers are less certain about using *chok* textiles as part of other products, other than *sin tin chok*. It is found that the production of *chok* textiles is time-consuming and strongly related to the beliefs and cultural heritage of local people. These textiles are associated with historical pride and local traditions. Hence the monetary value of these traditional handmade textiles is high. If pieces of *chok* textiles were used as raw material to make other products, such as book covers and bags, these products would generally be too expensive for the market to bear. And it is questionable whether such products are fitting with regard to the cultural significance, especially in the view of local people.

It should also be borne in mind that there are many product ranges on the market, especially mass-produced goods with fashionable designs that are available in greater quantities and at more affordable prices. Rather than trying to compete directly with such products, weavers prefer to produce *chok* textiles for making *sin tin chok*, traditional clothing with a long-established market in Thailand and neighboring countries. In the context of *chok* textiles, designers should take factual information from local producers into account and carefully consider to what extent and in what direction product design and development can make a positive contribution to help ensure the continuity of weaving communities and textile products that are compatible with sustainability.

Design for marketing and sales: This involves the design of product information for marketing and sales purposes, e.g. product lists describing the features and qualities of handmade textiles, telling stories about the values of textile products in terms of historical and cultural values and community development. This can also involve the design of communication channels such as packaging, exhibitions and especially websites to help local producers to better connect with potential customers within the district/province and beyond using a variety of languages. This can include branding and identity design that reveals the essence of local producers, informs potential customers of the reputation of local producers and distinguishes them from other textile enterprises.

Production development: This includes various areas, such as workforce, raw materials, production standards and quality control, production capacity, original equipment and technology for production. Designers can contribute to:

- the development of strategies to persuade the younger generation and experienced weavers to become involved in weaving and textile activities for knowledge and skills transfer;
- the development of textile products with an action plan that entails the management of natural resources that are available locally, the consistent use of specified materials and the delivery of textile products for trade;
- the acquisition of information and effective presentation of information about the quality and specifications of raw materials;
- the exploration of choices of materials that might be used in production for new product directions (these materials could be from natural sources or, potentially, be synthetic if they are in accord with sustainable principles, e.g. fibers derived from recycled sources).

These various areas, if addressed, might increase the quality and quantity of textile products, enhance customer satisfaction and promote the reliability and market competitiveness of local producers. However, production development hinges on the views of local producers, especially group leaders, and how much they wish production to be developed. This, of course, may be beyond the scope of designers' influence. Other aspects, which local producers take into consideration, include the potential impact of development on their way of life, the sufficient number of skilled workforce, trust and long-term relationships among various stakeholders.

Producers' understandings of new kinds of knowledge: Local producers should develop their understanding of new kinds of knowledge, which they may learn from other stakeholders involved. This includes areas of technology, product design and development for marketing, trading systems, foreign languages, and sustainability.

- *Design aided by new technologies* includes the use of computer software, the internet and digital photography to: illustrate/design textile patterns; keep track of purchase orders and financial management; visualize the concept of a textile supply chain and areas for development; develop websites for e-commerce; produce photographs of textiles to showcase; develop online databases so that people can search for information about potential markets, products, and customers.

- *Product design and development for marketing* is usually concerned with the materials, form, appearance and functions of textile products, as well as production techniques and costs, pricing, and the preferences of potential customers—to help local producers develop a more entrepreneurial approach and increase the perceived value of their textile products and boost sales potential. However, in the context of *chok* textiles, designers need to consider carefully the extent to which *chok* textiles can and should be developed further in relation to trade (see above).

- *Design in relation to trading systems* refers to design activities that support the distribution of textile products to help ensure that products reach potential customers. This might include the development of websites and e-commerce platforms, areas of which local producers have little understanding.

- *Designing information in multiple languages,* especially Chinese and English, which are applicable to various groups of potential customers. This can be done through packaging design for textile products, visual information in textile shops, and exhibitions (including digital media) about weaving communities and local textiles.

- *The significance of traditional weaving and* chok *textiles* in relation to the twenty-first-century global agenda for sustainability can be strengthened through design, in collaboration with the weaving communities themselves, in all the aforementioned areas. Specifically to Thailand, traditional weaving and textiles are found to be highly significant. They are part of a social foundation linked to traditional arts and culture, historical and cultural heritage, ethnic and national identity, manufacturing, tourism and economic development. All of these aspects contribute to national development strategies and the soft power of Thailand.

Knowledge transfer of traditional weaving: In this context, traditional knowledge includes:

A range of knowledge areas such as production (including materials, techniques and processes), products (including materials, form and function, patterns and colors), and the identity of ethnic groups in localities (characterized by, for example, the techniques they use and the features of what they make). These areas of traditional knowledge are in need of attention with respect to knowledge preservation, knowledge management and knowledge transfer, and this will require repositories of information and a system for knowledge transfer between skilled craftspeople and younger practitioners and also other stakeholders. (Chudasri 2015: 235)

Designers can contribute to developing repositories of information and a system for knowledge transfer. Mechanisms may include **books** that contain both textual and visual/photographic information about ethnic textiles and their identity/ history; **weaving courses and training** that foster interaction between experienced weavers and the younger generation to transfer knowledge about and skills in weaving; **knowledge centres** in which the environment is attractive and practical for the various stakeholders, especially the younger generation. These could be local libraries, coffee shops and galleries, textile shops, and weavers' houses that are open to particular groups of tourists/customers for short stays; **local events** that offer weaving demonstrations, e.g. at textile exhibitions, trade fairs, and religious ceremonies; **websites and social media** that contain archives of documents, photographic information and videos about weaving and ethnic textiles; and **mass media** such as magazines, newspapers, and documentary TV programs that discuss weaving and ethnic textiles.

Among these mechanisms, weaving courses and training are identified by the group leaders as particularly important because they can be effective in connecting the various interested groups and bridging knowledge gaps—traditional and new knowledge—and allowing for skill transfers between groups. However, the challenges faced in developing such courses are related to course content and the management of training courses that can generate sufficient income for local communities over the long term. This presents an opportunity for further research.

Conclusion

In conclusion, this chapter reveals that the handmade textile production of *Long* district (Phrae province) and *Mae Chaem* district (Chiang Mai province) in northern Thailand, especially of *sin tin chok,* has qualities that are compatible with all the elements of Walker's *Quadruple Bottom Line of Sustainability* (comprising personal meaning, social responsibility, environmental care, and economic viability).

The weaving communities usually produce textile products for their personal use as well as for trade, especially in domestic markets. Their textile businesses are operated on a community enterprise system. Their production network may be in the same village or connected with various groups in other villages in the same district, other districts or other provinces. The methods of textile production at the local level can be classified into three groups: (i) hand-skilled labor and traditional processes; (ii) hand-skilled and the integration of weaving techniques, such as "*chok*" and "*yok dok*"; (iii) hand-skilled labor and machine-based production.

Regarding the traditional production of *chok* textiles, three main issues are identified: (i) whether the traditional process of weaving should be preserved and continued in order to present a traditionally cultural heritage, or it should be altered in order to accelerate production and increase production capacity for commerce and income generation; (ii) developments in the traditional textile production for commerce and their impact on the erosion/confusion of weavers' knowledge, skills, and identity and of customers' understanding; (iii) knowledge transfer between experienced weavers and the younger generation.

Five potential areas to which design can make a useful contribution to the continuity and development of weaving communities in ways that are compatible with sustainability principles are identified. These are in: (i) product design and development; (ii) design for marketing and sales; (iii) production development; (iv) producers' understanding of new kinds of knowledge; (v) knowledge transfer of traditional weaving.

References

Bowie, A. K. (1992), "Unraveling the Myth of the Subsistence Economy: Textile Production in Nineteenth-Century Northern Thailand," *The Journal of Asian Studies, Association for Asian Studies*, 51 (4): 797–823.

Castree, N., R. Kitchin, and A. Rogers (2013), *A Dictionary of Human Geography*, Oxford: Oxford University Press. Available online: http://www.oxfordreference.com.ezproxy. lancs.ac.uk/view/10.1093/acref/9780199599868.001.0001/acref-9780199599868-e-775?rskey=gHhFls&result=2 (accessed June 27, 2015).

Chudasri, D. (2015), "An Investigation into the Potential of *Design for Sustainability* in the Handicrafts of Northern Thailand," Ph.D. thesis Lancaster University, Lancaster, UK.

Elkington, J. (ed.) (1999, 1st edn 1997), *Cannibals with Forks: The Triple Bottom Line of 21st Century Business*, Oxford: Capstone.

Elkington, J. (2004), "Enter The Triple Bottom Line," in A. Henriques and J. Richardson (eds.), *The Triple Bottom Line, Does It All Add Up?: Assessing the Sustainability of Business and CSR*, 1–16, London: Earthscan.

Investopedia, LLC. (c.2015), "What is the 'Time Value of Money—TVM.'" Available online: http://www.investopedia.com/terms/t/timevalueofmoney.asp (accessed March 21, 2016).

Lannaworld.com (2006), *History of Lanna, Chiang Mai*. Available online: http://www. lannaworld.com/history/lannahist.htm (accessed June 24, 2011).

McIntosh, S. D. (2012), "*Tai Yuan* textiles of Thailand." *Textiles Asia Journal*, 4 (2): 3–9.

Scott, J. (2014), *A Dictionary of Sociology*, 4th edn, Oxford: Oxford University Press. Available online: http://www.oxfordreference.com.ezproxy.lancs.ac.uk/view/10.1093/ acref/9780199683581.001.0001/acref-9780199683581-e-957?rskey=gHhFls&result=5 (accessed June 27, 2015).

Secretariat Office of Community Enterprise Promotion Board (SCEB) (c. 2015), "The meaning of community enterprise: Bangkok." Available in Thai language at: http://www. sceb.doae.go.th/Ssceb2.htm (accessed August 5, 2015).

Suchitta, P. (1989), "Mental Template: The Case of the Tai Lao Pha Sin." *Asian Folklore Studies*, 48: 95–105.

Walker, S. (2011), *The Spirit of Design: Objects, Environment and Meaning*, London: Earthscan.

7

Oltu-stone Prayer Beads

A Journey into the Art of Carving Tasbih

Hazal Gümüş Çiftçi

Introduction

In the future, the role of the craftsman will be more important than ever before. (McLuhan cited in Vencatachellum 2005)

For hundreds of years traditional handicrafts have been considered as an honorable, though intangible, heritage. Over the years, especially after the hardships of the Industrial Revolution and a period of environmental degradation, social inequity and economic instability, traditional handicrafts began to diminish and in some parts of the world almost disappeared. In particular, the tiring and demanding work was considered to be of no value. As a result, many practitioners stopped performing their craft and training future generations.

However, in many ways traditional handicrafts still continue to conform to a more sustainable lifestyle. Their use of local, often natural materials, proximity to the market and the small-scale nature of the work all tend to comply with practical, social, and personal understandings of sustainability. Prior to post-modern "consumer society" that is so reliant on the import of inexpensive goods, such practices were also economically viable. Unlike the scale of production and waste, craftspeople do not over-produce; handcrafted goods are usually generated out of necessity— generally they are not "luxury" objects but are produced to serve local needs, both practical and spiritual.

One of the main reasons for the disappearance of traditional handicrafts is migration. The major consequence of migration from underdeveloped rural areas to developed urban regions is the socio-economic disorder and the difficulty people find in adapting to a different region and lifestyle. In Turkey, more developed western regions welcome the human labor but often make poor use of these people's skills, many of which are important in terms of Turkish traditions and culture. Instead, most migrants are employed in manual labor and are given menial tasks that contribute to economic growth. The subsequent loss of local knowledge, traditions, and customs also includes a tragic loss of traditional handicrafts (Özkan Tağı and Erdoğan 2008). The making of Oltu-stone prayer beads is an example of these traditional handicrafts in Eastern Turkey.

Field trips to the region revealed not only a variety of challenges but also potential opportunities for this sector. Therefore, this research investigates if and how design can contribute to the revival and development of the making of prayer beads.

Oltu-stone

Oltu-stone is a type of amber (Kalkan, Bilici, and Kolaylı 2012) and is excavated in Erzurum, a province in Eastern Turkey. It has been processed for over two centuries in this region for the production of prayer beads, jewelry, and houseware (Alparslan 2009). Oltu-stone is "a coal-like stone … black in colour and velvety to the touch" (McKanna 2011). According to Kalkan, Bilici, and Kolaylı (2012), this stone is soft when first carved out of underground galleries. Later, it solidifies when exposed to the air during engraving (2012: 2387).

This stone is called various names including "Oltustone, Erzurum Stone, Black Amber, Gagat, Jayet and Jet" (Ethem cited in Kalkan, Bilici, and Kolaylı 2012: 2388). In Turkey it is also known as: "Oltutaşı, Erzurum Taşı, Kara Kehribar and Sengi Musa" (Ibid. 2012). It is categorized as a plant fossil and the Mineral Research and Exploration Institute (MTA) lists it as a semi-precious and opaque gemstone (MTA and Doğanay cited in Kocaman 2013: 117).

Oltu-stone quarries are around 80 cm in diameter and the tunnels go as far as 150 meters deep, which makes them difficult to work in (Menteşeli cited in Kocaman 2013: 118). Workshops for the production of Oltu-stone accessories are found in the Oltu district of Erzurum, and retail stores are found in Taşhan, in a historic building in the center of Erzurum, as well as in some other shops in Oltu (Kocaman 2013: 118). During the nineteenth century, forty craftspeople worked as Oltu-stone carvers (Parlak cited in Alparslan 2010: 182) and in 1996 there were reported to be around 150 workshops in the Oltu district alone (Kılıç 1996: 111). This craft is still being carried out in workshops and homes, and is generating employment for thousands of people (Alparslan 2009: 32).

Oltu-stone prayer beads

Prayer beads are known to have been used within various belief systems and as charm objects for over four thousand years (Tekin 2014). Although there is a diverse range of souvenir products made out of Oltu-stone, the most commonly produced artifacts are the prayer beads in Erzurum; these are known globally (Kalkan, Bilici, and Kolaylı 2012: 2387). Prayer beads are considered as an "enduring object" that has survived throughout the centuries due to its "functional, social/positional, and inspirational/spiritual" features (Walker 2006: 44–8). Walker says:

> It is an object that crosses boundaries of time, belief, gender, culture, and class .... It is variously known as the mala, the tasbih, the rosary, or simply as "prayer-beads". Throughout the centuries, it has carved out a unique place in human culture as an object that ties the physical or outer person with the inner, contemplative, and spiritual self (2006: 44).

Although prayer beads were once considered culturally significant, unique, handmade accessories, machines are increasingly being used for their mass production (Bell cited in Bağlı 2015: 307). As culturally significant objects, they portray a public image of their user and, accordingly, their spiritual functions have become diminished (Bağlı 2015). However, Penington says "prayer beads offer a kinesthetic comfort; they are a means in the material world to remember one's place in the spiritual worlds" (cited in Wiley and Shannon 2002: 24).

Islamic prayer beads consist of thirty-three or ninety-nine beads representing the ninety-nine names of Allah (Kuşoğlu cited in Alparslan 2009: 72). Tekin claims that the word "prayer beads" is associated with Islam: therefore, Turkish prayer beads are "privileged" (2014: 1010). The making of prayer beads qualifies as a fine art in Turkey as well as serving a religious purpose (2014: 1016). The value of prayer beads is determined by the materials (from ivory to fossilized wood), the beads' similarity to each other, and the alignment of all the elements (Sarici cited in Tekin 2014: 1016). Akbulut observes that imported raw materials are used to make religious products, along with imported labor (2013). Therefore, Akbulut claims that domestication of the production of culturally important objects is a sign of authenticity (2013: 237).

Tekin (2014: 1016) mistakenly claims that all these materials are imported into Turkey; forgetting that Oltu-stone is found exclusively in Turkey (Anadolu Ajansı 2013). In fact, Oltu-stone prayer beads are the most commonly produced accessories in Erzurum— 85.4 percent according to research done among craftspeople (Alparslan 2009: 103).

The making of Oltu-stone prayer beads

Oltu-stone is excavated by hand and found in the Oltu district of Erzurum (Alparslan 2009; Eymirli, Gürbüz, and Toy 2013); the galleries in which it is quarried are narrow and steep (*Yol Arkadasim Oltu Episode* 2014; Menteşeli cited in Kocaman 2013). This black, velvety amber is sold to craftspeople in tins (*Yol Arkadasim Oltu Episode* 2014) and is turned into rings, earrings, necklaces, bracelets, tie pins, smoking pipes, cigarette holders, and prayer beads (Kalkan, Bilici, and Kolaylı 2012: 2394). According to Doğanay, the production of jewelry and accessories began in the 1960s, along with prayer beads and pipes (cited in Kocaman 2013).

Oltu-stone is fairly easy to work with since it is soft prior to exposure to air (Alparslan 2009: 33). However, the whole process involved in making a bead consists

FIGURE 7.1 A master cutting Oltu-stone before lathing, c. 2011. Courtesy Gümüş Çiftçi. © Hazal Gümüş Çiftçi.

of lathing (Figure 7.1), polishing, and drilling (Kalkan, Bilici, and Kolaylı 2012: 2394), all of which vary according to the beads' ornamentation (Alparslan 2009: 55); in some workshops these phases are done side by side.

Displaying these delicate prayer beads (Figure 7.2) in an appropriate manner is as much a work of art as it is to make them. Oltu-stone gets brighter over time as it is used and the stone hardens as it is exposed to air (Alparslan 2009, 2010). Therefore, exhibiting the amber prayer beads requires careful attention so as to avoid damaging them (Durbaş cited in Tekin 2014: 1016). Traditionally, knowledgeable retailers lay a piece of soft cloth under the prayer beads (Ibid.).

> If the heart breaks, there is a remedy. A good prayer bead is a sign of the heart but it is more delicate, and valuable like the heart, if damaged no mending will be possible (Durbaş cited in Tekin 2014: 1013).

Turbulent times for prayer bead making

In Eastern Turkey, some craft work has diminished due to the arrival of mass-produced products in the local markets (Devlet Planlama Teşkilatı Müsteşarlığı 2000: 281). However, these substitutes cannot replace unique handcrafted goods, such as the handwoven carpets, kilims or blankets produced in Siirt, which will continue to be wanted (Ibid.).

Oltu-stone prayer beads are considered as one of the most unique and famous products of the region. Various sources state that from excavation to carving and trading, Oltu-stone creates jobs in the region (Alparslan 2009; Anadolu Ajansı 2013;

FIGURE 7.2 Oltu-stone prayer beads in display for customers, c. 2011. Courtesy Gümüş Çiftçi. © Hazal Gümüş Çiftçi.

Eymirli, Gürbüz, and Toy 2013). Around Oltu, where excavation sites are found, migration is reported to be lower than for other villages in the region (Kocaman 2013: 125). The stone is excavated only in the Oltu district and is processed both in Oltu and Erzurum. Craftspeople who were interviewed acknowledge that there is no support or incentives for their work to continue. Although there are some retailers who would sell these handmade, unique prayer beads online, their market is restricted to local buyers. All the craftspeople interviewed agreed that over time the value and size of the market for the prayer beads has dropped. One of the craftspeople says:

> If we produce 100 pieces in a month then 20 of them will go to Taşhan and the rest will go to all over Turkey. We rarely send these abroad and it could also be that tourists from Germany or other places come here, buy it and take it with them.

Craft is described as "a social activity" since it is learned through apprenticeship (Bonanni and Parkes 2010: 180). This explains the need for craftsmen and women to find young people who are interested in and enthusiastic about their crafts in order to be able to pass on their skills. Smith makes her point clearly for creating a future in crafts, stating that: "Making a decent living is the major factor in the survival of artisans and their work; demonstrating that a future is possible in craft encourages the next generation to continue in the field" (2009). The time required to become a master may vary; however, the master-trainee relationship remains a constant. Over time, making Oltu-stone prayer beads has lost its status, and in most cases, the masters could not find apprentices. All the craftspeople who were interviewed agreed that the young people had no interest in learning this age-old knowledge, and attempts at passing it on by training young people seem useless. A junior craftsperson says there were courses to train people but these never worked out due to a number of constraints. Some masters even gave up and opened a retail shop to trade a variety of prayer beads – not only ones made out of Oltu-stone. Unfortunately, they have a pessimistic view of the future of Oltu-stone products due to market conditions. Struggles in the local market and inefficient market strategies are causing the sector to be unprofitable and craftspeople to stop practicing their skills (Eymirli, Gürbüz, and Toy 2013).

Eymirli, Gürbüz, and Toy claim an NGO (Oltu Taşı Sanatını Geliştirme, Sanatkarlarını Koruma ve Kalkındırma Derneği) has withheld the brand registry for Oltu-stone even though this stone has been well-known in Anatolia for over 200 years (2013: 17). A competitive market, lack of quality standards, design incompetency, lack of after-sale service, and inadequate promotion devalue the brand's worth (Ibid.).

The large producers of Oltu-stone products are known to be targeting a middle-class market, while small enterprises do not have enough capital to adequately do so (Eymirli, Gürbüz, and Toy 2013). Kılıç (1996: 111) mentions that, as early as 1996, more technologically advanced workshops began to be offered. However, even today the old methods of processing the black amber are being practiced in Erzurum and Oltu (Figure 7.3). Eymirli, Gürbüz, and Toy claim the lack of technology integration and inadequate marketing strategies are reducing the potential for local competition of Oltu-stone products (2013).

Both craftspeople and local development agency officers who were interviewed for this research mentioned the Georgian stone, which has recently started to be imported. One of the craftspeople explains, "The challenge is the Georgian stone, it is a different type of Oltu-stone and the battle with that stone is hard because it is

FIGURE 7.3 An Oltu-stone master in his workshop, c. 2015. Courtesy Gümüş Çiftçi.
© Hazal Gümüş Çiftçi.

very cheap. Say we pay 300 Turkish Liras on average for 1 kg and it is 50 Turkish Liras per kg. That is the only problem, to be confused between the two."

Georgian (Russian) stone is very much like the Oltu stone and there is a possibility that they come from the same geological vein (Anon.). However, mass-produced prayer beads made of Georgian stone create unfair competition. The stone from Georgia is reported to be softer, and therefore, more suitable for mass-production (Kocaman 2013: 123). The stone is ground and liquefied with glues and then moulded into two thousand prayer beads each week (Ibid.). According to Alparslan (2009), the majority of craftspeople in Erzurum and Oltu are processing genuine Oltu-stone. However, Kocaman (2013) states that, in the last two decades, Georgian stone took over almost eighty-five percent of the market, thus affecting the excavation of Oltu-stone; in the 1990s there were 152 familes working in the quarries, whereas recently only eighty-nine families were found to be operating (2013: 125).

There are no regulations about imports and consequently no labeling for genuine Oltu-stone. One of the masters carving Georgian stone explains his reasons for using it; simply that it is cheaper but similar to Oltu-stone. As well as low costs, there are concerns about health issues since there are no quality control mechanisms for how the mass-produced Georgian stone prayer beads are made (Kocaman 2013: 125).

The struggle to distinguish between the two stones results in mistrust between end-user and retailers (Eymirli, Gürbüz, and Toy 2013: 17). Some of the vendors may not be able to tell the difference between the original, handmade Oltu-stone prayer beads and the mass-produced Georgian-stone prayer beads. Together with the unfair competition, the sector also faces a lack of governmental support and this clearly makes them feel isolated and abandoned. Masters and their apprentices interviewed were not sure if it is worth being a member of the jewelers' guild and do not know if any other such organizations exist.

Oltu prayer bead making is considered to be fine work of a genuine craft. The stone is quite well known in the region and throughout Turkey. However, the unfair competition posed by the Georgian stone should clearly be taken under control. Since the makers are not well organized, control of the Georgian mass-produced stone is almost impossible. Customers question the authenticity of the prayer beads and rumors put the craftspeople's work at risk.

Oltu-stone carving is one of the few traditional handicrafts that evolved over time and is still being conducted by master craftspeople in Eastern Turkey (Alparslan 2010). Therefore, incentives for young people are required for this invaluable craft to be passed on to future generations (2010: 189). Eymirli, Gürbüz, and Toy suggest that an organization for the producers and retailers of Oltu-stone would be a way forward to create a reliable national brand (2013).

Considering each step that one stone has to go through demonstrates the difficulty of creating a product by hand. There are plain stones that are processed by eight different pairs of hands and there are the silver ornamented ones that require even more work for additional patterning. One of the interviewees said that customers often make comments about this as they visit the workshop and experience the long path a stone must travel. This delicate work is closely associated with Erzurum and the city has a potential for growth in tourism, especially during the wintertime. Since the 1990s, the Palandöken Ski Centre attracts many tourists and the locally produced Oltu-stone souvenirs are the tourist market's most attractive merchandise (Kocaman 2013: 117).

The workshops have been described as being dark and dusty, where craftspeople sit for up to 10–12 hours during the day to fashion the products (Alparslan 2009; McKanna 2011). Visits to three workshops showed that the workshops are indeed a somber and unhealthy place for the craftspeople to work and the craftspeople themselves are also concerned about their working conditions. One of the junior craftsmen described their work as painful since they have to sit down all day for long hours. He also believes that the use of glues affects their eyes. The apprentice then added: "Maybe it is not important for one day but doing it for years might affect health. The workplace is also important, if there is no sun coming in; then you get sick."

A recent study conducted among the Oltu-stone carvers states that half the craftspeople think their occupation might disappear, whereas forty percent are hopeful for a better future, and the rest think they could preserve what they have as of today (Alparslan 2009). However, the need to adapt to market demands and raise the value of authentic Oltu-stone is generally recognized.

A pathway for visibility

Oltu-stone carving is struggling to survive due to numerous local and global reasons: Şişman, Ünlü, and Kaygan (2009) suggest that crafts are not regulated and need to become accustomed to contemporary market conditions; designers are seen as bridges for crafts, especially in keeping up to date (Vencatachellum 2005); and Risatti claims that after the Industrial Revolution, crafts became diminished by design due to machine production (2007: 153). However, Shiner says that craft and design are "historical partners" (2012) and Julier also acknowledges that designers contribute to cultural development (cited in Akbulut 2013).

There are a number of studies suggesting different approaches for the survival of traditional handicrafts. Although McGuirk defines this comeback as a "post-industrial nostalgia for the pre-industrial" and argues that designers are benefiting from crafts because there are not enough manufacturers supporting them (2011), there are others who state the opposite (Chick and Micklethwaite 2011; Tung 2012). This counterargument may vary from "playing a catalytic role in facilitating the propagation of local craft knowledge into other industries" (Tung 2012: 12) to being "exposed to international market trends that will hopefully inspire new marketable products" (Chick and Micklethwaite 2011: 150). The Craft Revival Trust's book, *Designers Meet Artisans*, is one of the studies with several suggestions of such rejuvenation. It states that ritual crafts should be evaluated from a different perspective, by asking questions like:

> Does the craft remain a "ritual" craft if people begin using it for decorative purposes that are not relevant to the context? Does the craft remain relevant if the cultural and ritual context that initially underlay it changes organically (the change may not be fostered by external intervention or be the fallout of an external intervention), making the craft irrelevant in the new context? (Vencatachellum 2005: 10)

"Product differentiation and adopting new market strategies" are the two main propositions for Oltu-stone made by the researches done in the sector (Eymirli, Gürbüz, and Toy 2013). However, findings of this research point out that developing a brand identity, which tells the story of Oltu-stone prayer beads and includes all the stakeholders involved in the process, to reveal the genuine value of these exquisite artifacts will help build a viable and robust future.

Propositions for Oltu-stone prayer beads' future

Story crafting through brand identity

According to a piece of research done by KUDAKA (North Eastern Anatolia Development Agency), although the users claimed they were not satisfied with the designs of the Oltu-stone products, half the users named their reasons for selecting the Oltu-stone prayer beads as being local and handmade and twenty percent because the stone is semi-precious (Eymirli, Gürbüz, and Toy 2013: 15). During the interviews, KUDAKA officers claimed that Oltu-stone producers lack any interest in developing strategies for innovation/market differentiation.

Traditional handicrafts are learned through apprenticeship and evolve over time through practicing the craft. Thus, documenting the craft happens "in craftspeople's minds and at their fingertips" (Vencatachellum 2005: 6). A study about Oltu-stone reveals that 77.1 percent of the craftspeople use a catalog and only 16.7 percent take photographs of their products (Alparslan 2009: 113). The literature about Oltu-stone prayer beads is very limited and needs to be conveyed to end-users. Therefore, one of the design interventions might be telling the stories of these time-consuming and delicate prayer beads.

The terms "unique and authentic" are on the rise as globalization and monoculture have resulted in a search for more customized, creative products (Vencatachellum 2005). Certification for the authentic Oltu-stone products to label their quality and regulate prices is seen as one of the solutions to overcome this issue (Eymirli, Gürbüz, and Toy 2013). Although the brand registry of Oltu-stone exists, the original Oltu-stone products are not yet certified (Ibid.). The use of a certificate stating the authenticity of products would guarantee end-users' trust and enable a stronger brand for Oltu-stone prayer beads to be built globally.

Inclusive crafts

The Oltu-stone crafters are reported to start working at an early age and the craft is transferred from generation to generation, especially within families (Alparslan 2009). Only men were observed to be involved in the making of Oltu-stone during the field trips; nevertheless, women do produce objects in their homes (Yol Arkadasim Oltu Bolumu 2014). However, it is said that women's involvement in the production of Oltu-stone accessories has decreased over time (Ibid.). According to Merriam, craft-related businesses empower women and reduce the need to migrate to bigger cities (cited in Chick and Micklethwaite 2011: 150).

Occupational safety is another important issue this sector faces. A considerable number of the mines are illegal (Menteşeli cited in Kocaman 2013: 117-118) and therefore the safety measures are questionable (Eymirli, Gürbüz, and Toy 2013). Health and safety issues do exist for the makers, as stated in Alparslan's research conducted among forty-eight Oltu-stone masters (2009: 113-116).

Suggestions of policy makers and local authorities for the development of the sector seem rather weak, and although there are a few reports on sectoral problems, craftspeople complain about lack of support and limited resources. The mines are still not mapped and the potential capacity of the reserves is unknown (Devlet Planlama Teşkilatı Müsteşarlığı 2000); consequently, the sector is forced to import Georgian stone. A report prepared by local universities suggests that these mines would generate jobs for thousands of people (Ibid.). Vencatachellum (2005: 5) writes,

> Several craft activists and interventionists also see design intervention as a "problem solving methodology" to be applied as a tool for development, essentially as a means of removing bottlenecks to viability and of easing the move from tradition to modernity.

The lack of dialogue between craftspeople, local authorities and non-governmental organizations has been recognized during this research. KUDAKA officers seem rather uninformed about the sector's issues and believe that craftspeople are not involved in their studies, whereas prayer bead makers claim there is a lack of support from the local authorities. Therefore, creating a synergy between those parties is required. Design interventions to enhance relationships and bring the stakeholders together for a deeper understanding about the challenges and potential opportunities would open a reliable and sustainable path for Oltu-stone prayer beads. In such a scenario, inclusion of all interested parties might be ensured.

Conclusion

Indeed, the loss of traditional handicrafts cannot solely be related to migration and is linked to transitional problems encountered in the move from the traditional, predominantly rural production methods that were prevalent during the Ottoman Empire to the modern Turkish Republic with its development of more up-to-date, technologically sophisticated, "modern" fabrication sites (Şişman, Ünlü, and Kaygan 2009). A large number of recent studies on traditional crafts in Turkey demonstrate that traditional skills and artisans are decreasing day by day (Ibid.).

Although there have been attempts to overcome divisions among the regions, it is seen that those efforts were not successful and most of the economic growth initiatives have favored the western part of Turkey (Türkiye Kalkınma Bankası 2012). As a result, investments in industrialization were made in the west and the socioeconomic gap between the west and east of the country increased (Ibid.).

Traditional handicrafts are products that arose from the needs of the people and are practiced over long periods of time. With so-called technological and scientific advancements, handicrafts started to fade away due to competitive global markets. Consequently, there are other reasons why traditional handicrafts are being diminished day by day such as keeping up-to-date, since contemporary taste in clothing, furnishings and lifestyle changes so quickly and the traditionally handcrafted goods are viewed as old-fashioned.

Although the aforementioned reasons are the main obstacle in the evolution of traditional handicrafts, there is also a lack of understanding and a devaluing of these striking and attractive pieces. Hirszowicz says:

> I do not know why people have a low opinion of what this word implies; for we depend on the crafts for all the necessary things of life. Anyone who has taken the trouble to visit casually the workshops will see in all places utility applied with the greatest evidence of intelligence (cited in McCullough 1996: 12).

In light of these findings, the Oltu-stone prayer bead sector requires an intervention for its revival and development. Reasons for design interventions in similar contexts are listed as, "designers being a bridge between tradition and modernity, a tool for development and a way for preserving cultural resources" (Vencatachellum 2005: 4). On a positive note, there are various attempts to develop traditional handicrafts and the socio-economic prosperity of craftspeople around the world. However, diverse applications are required for different domains. Fundamentally, Oltu-stone prayer beads' sectoral development demands the highlighting of cultural significance, awareness of social implications, and the inclusion of all stakeholders.

References

Akbulut, D. (2013), "İnanç ve Üretim Bağlamında Hacıbektaş Taş İşçiliği," *Türk Kültürü Ve Hacı Bektaş Velî Araştırma Dergisi*, 68.

Alparslan, E. (2009), *Oltu Taşı İşlemeciliği ve Yörede Üretilen Ürünlerin Bazı Özellikleri*, Ankara: Ankara Universitesi.

Alparslan, E. (2010), "Oltu Taşı, Altın Ve Gümüş Kullanılarak Üretilen Kol Düğmesi Ve
    Kravat İğnesi Örneklerinin İncelenmesi," *Journal of World of Turks*, 2 (2): 179–89.
Anadolu Ajansı (2013), "Oltu taşının zorlu yolculuğu," s.l.: Anadolu Ajansı.
Bağlı, H. (2015), "Material Culture of Religion: New Approaches to Functionality in Islamic
    Objects," *The Design Journal*, 18 (3): 305–25.
Bonanni, L. and A. Parkes (2010), "Virtual Guilds: Collective Intelligence and the Future of
    Craft," *The Journal of Modern Craft*, 3 (2): 179–90.
Chick, A. and P. Micklethwaite (2011), *Design for Sustainable Change: How Design and
    Designers Can Drive the Sustainability Agenda?* Lausanne: AVA Publishing SA.
Devlet Planlama Teşkilatı Müsteşarlığı (2000), "Doğu Anadolu Projesi Ana Plan," s.l.:
    Atatürk Ünversitesi, Fırat Ünversitesi,İnönü Ünversitesi, Kafkas Ünversitesi, Yüzüncüyıl
    Ünversitesi.
Eymirli, E. B., G. Gürbüz, and S. Toy (2013), "Oltu Taşı Sektörü Değer Zinciri Analizi," s.l.:
    KUDAKA.
Kalkan, E., Ö. Bilici, and H. Kolaylı (2012), "Evaluation of Turkish Black Amber: A Case
    Study of Oltu (Erzurum), NE Turkey," *International Journal of Physical Sciences*, April
    12, 7 (15): 2387–97.
Kılıç, E. (1996), "Erzurum'da Geçmişten Günümüze Devam Edegelen Ve Kaybolmaya Yüz
    Tutan El Sanatları," *Journal of Turkish Research Institute*, 5: 99–114.
Kocaman, S. (2013), "Russian Stone as an Touristic Product (Georgian Black Amber) and Its
    Effects to Erzurum Oltu Stone Sector," *Eastern Geographical Review*, 18 (30): 115–34.
McCullough, M. (1996), *Abstracting Craft: The Practiced Digital Hand*, Cambridge, MA:
    The MIT Press.
McGuirk, J. (2011), "The Art of Craft: The Rise of the Designer-Maker," *The Guardian*,
    August 1.
McKanna, B. (2011), "Mountain Treasure: EthnoTraveler Magazine." Available at: http://
    www.ethnotraveler.com/ 2011/02/mountain-treasures/ (accessed June 2015).
Özkan Taği, S. and Z. Erdoğan (2008), "The Changes that The Handicrafts of Turkey have
    Gone Through," *The Social Sciences*, 3 (1): 41–4.
Risatti, H. (2007), *A Theory of Craft:Function and Aesthetic Expression*, Chapel Hill, NC:
    The University of North Carolina Press.
Shiner, L. (2012). ``Blurred Boundaries"? Rethinking the Concept of Craft and its Relation
    to Art and Design. *Philosophy Compass*, 230–44.
Smith, C. B. (2009), "Sustaining Tradition." Available at: http://www.handeyemagazine.com/
    content/sustaining-tradition (accessed April 2015).
Şişman, O., C.Ünlü, and H. Kaygan (2009), "Fate of Turkish Traditional Crafts: A Case of
    Economic, Legal and Political Marginalisation," Making Futures: The crafts in the context
    of emerging global sustainability agendas, Plymouth College of Art, September 17–18.
Tekin, K. H. (2014), "Türk-İslam Sanatinda Tesbih Üzerine Notlar," Turkish Studies—
    International Periodical for The Languages, Literature and History of Turkish or Turkic,
    Fall, 9/10: 1009–18.
Tung, F. W. (2012), "Weaving with Rush: Exploring Craft-Design Collaborations in
    Revitalizing a Local Craft," *International Journal of Design*, 6 (3): 71–84.
Vencatachellum, I. (2005), *Designers Meet Artisans: A Practical Guide*, New Delhi: Craft
    Revival Trust, Artesanías de Colombia SA. and UNESCO.
Walker, S. (2006), *Sustainable by Design: Explorations in Theory and Practice*, London:
    Earthscan.
Wiley, E. and M. O. Shannon (2002), *How to Make and Use Prayer Beads*, York Beach, ME:
    Red Wheel/Weiser, LLC.
Yol Arkadaşım Oltu Episode (2014) [Film] Dir. Neşe Uğur Nohutçu, Turkey: TRT.

8

The Miān-Sarā

Traditional Iranian Homes and Sustainability

Poone Yazdanpanah and Stuart Walker

Introduction

The Miān-Sarā is the name given to the central open courtyard of the traditional Iranian home. This domestic architectural form existed in Iran for at least 8,000 years but, since the coming of modernity at the end of the nineteenth century—known in Iran as *The Change*—the Miān-Sarā has fallen into decline and, today, these types of homes are rarely built. This relatively recent decline can be understood in terms of two primary concepts: (1) *The Container and the Contents*, which refers to the house and the lifestyle it allows and (2) *Form follows Meaning*, which refers to the symbolism of our built environment. Together, these two concepts constitute critical aspects of the fundamental transformation in the Iranian worldview over the past century and a half. Today, other forms of domestic architecture, modelled on Western prototypes, represent a very different Iranian identity. Even so, the Miān-Sarā can be understood as an architectural feature that symbolizes many aspects related to contemporary understandings of sustainability. By investigating the physical, functional, and symbolic features of the Miān-Sarā, we can begin to understand its important role in the traditional Iranian home and why it lasted for thousands of years. The *Quadruple Bottom Line of Design for Sustainability* (Walker 2011: 127, 190) is used here as the framework for this understanding in order to draw lessons for contemporary domestic design.

The Miān-Sarā in Iranian homes

The Miān-Sarā or central courtyard was an essential part of the traditional Iranian house. And this courtyard house was an element within an urban milieu that had a distinct hierarchical spatial structure. This structure was ordered through a series of architectural forms arranged through a physical sequence of *path*, *portal* and *enclosure*, which corresponded to and allowed the dynamic actions of *movement*, *passage*, and *arrival* (Carruthers 1984: 17–23). This hierarchy afforded different levels of public, semi-private, and private space—culminating in the domestic courtyard, which was the most private spatial domain for family members (Ramezani and Hamidi 2010: 502).

The courtyard house, with a central space that was open to the sky, was the prototypical architectural form not only in Iran and the Islamic world but in almost all traditional cultures (see Sarkis 2010: 191–202). Archaeological excavations in the Ghazvin region, to the north-west of Tehran, (Hosseini et al,. 2015: 12) show that courtyard housing has existed in Iran for some 8,000 years. The traditional domestic courtyard house still can be found in historic parts of Iranian cities and towns. Some have new functions such as museums, galleries, offices or hotels. However, most are in poor condition, providing housing for low-income tenants.

Traditionally, a domestic courtyard house has a plain, bare exterior, often entirely free of windows, and an intimate interior in which the courtyard is its centerpiece. According to Schadl (2010: 47–64) the Miān-Sarā serves as the connector between the various rooms situated around it; allows light and fresh air into the heart of the residence; provides a space for interaction; and is a stage for hosting many domestic activities. In studying the typical Miān-Sarā, it is useful to consider it in terms of its (a) physical, (b) functional, and (c) symbolic features. Here, we show how these features represent holistic thinking that brings together a broad range of human needs (Maslow 1968: 149–66), meanings (Hick 1989: 12), and higher values within a single architectural form.

Physical features

Physical features include the facades around the courtyard, greenery, a water pool, material types and the landscape design of the courtyard. The *facades* separate the open courtyard from the surrounding rooms and are arranged according to a prototypical design that includes symmetrical ordering of windows, doors, and frames. This creates a peaceful tranquility within the courtyard (Salingaros 2010: 169). This basic design allows variations in arrangement and decoration that give each courtyard a unique character and displays the taste and status of its residents. *Greenery* consists of flowers and shrubs as well as trees for shade; these vary according to location and climate. In hot, dry zones, common trees are figs, palms, pomegranates, and mulberries (Ghezelbash and Abolzia 1985: 33). In cooler zones, cedars and pines are common. Shrubs include oleander, acacia, and jasmine, and flowers such as geranium, zinnia, and damask rose can be found. *Water pools* vary in form and location—they can be central or placed to the north of the courtyard—depending on geographical and climatic conditions. *Material types* again vary according to geography—in central

Iran, for example, the most common materials are those that are available locally, such as adobe, baked brick, stone, and wood (Ardalan 1986). *Landscape design* includes the arrangement of the flower beds, the water pool, flooring, and vegetation. Usually there is a predominant pattern in each city.

Functional features

Functional features include *physical* and *socio-ethical* functions. The former includes the ways in which the architecture provides for the residents' physical and environmental needs, such as bringing light into the rooms around the courtyard, and creating a microclimate for a comfortable living environment. The latter are related to the ways in which the architecture allows residents to interact among themselves via the courtyard and the surrounding rooms and—according to varying levels of privacy/familiarity—with visitors.

Physical: The Miān-Sarā creates a microclimate within the house to make it liveable. This is critical in the harsh, arid climate of the Iranian plateau, which covers one fifth of the country. The orientation of the courtyard differs according to its specific geographical region. It is always oriented with regard to the passage of the sun, to provide one comfortable room in terms of temperature within the house in both summer and winter, which helps promote peace of mind (Day 2002: 220–1). The Miān-Sarā also provides water storage in the pool for daily use such as washing and irrigation.

Social/ethical: The courtyard is a place for interaction among family members. It provides privacy, which is important in traditional Iranian culture and Islamic teaching. Another important aspect in traditional Islamic architecture is the avoidance of futility and absurdity (Pirnia 1989, 1991). There should be no improper grandeur and splendor in the architecture because it increases the cost of construction and wastes materials. Righteousness/appropriateness is a traditional value in Iranian culture that has an impact on architecture, and these values are expressed in the spatial order and functional arrangement of the rooms around the courtyard. The social functions provided by the courtyard include: a safe play area for children in the open air but within the home and under the supervision of adults; preparing and cooking food for special occasions such as weddings and ritual ceremonies; washing and drying dishes and clothes; heating water in the sun or over a small fire; bathing children; daily family gathering and dining; sleeping outside on hot summer nights. It also serves as a central hub for social gatherings and ceremonies as, in conjunction with the surrounding rooms, it allows for separation between men and women—a cultural norm and religious recommendation within Islam.

Symbolic features

The physical and mental effects associated with the open space of the traditional Iranian courtyard are also important, as are its philosophical and spiritual meanings. Lad (2010: 3–28) describes the courtyard as "the home's window to the sky." It is also the core that integrates the different spaces of the house, linking them into a whole. Its symbolic features can be considered as: the creative *archetype*; the earthly *paradise garden* within the house—related to religion and spirituality; the *void*—as symbol of the presence of the divine in all things (Nasr 1987: 185–6); a "place" of *permanence and change* that represents essential aspects of life based on Iranian pre-Islamic mythology; and *nature* in the center of the home.

The Miān-Sarā and contemporary understandings of sustainability

The Miān-Sarā will be considered here through the framework of Walker's meaning-based *Quadruple Bottom Line of Design for Sustainability*, QBL (2011: 127, 190; 2014: 118–19). This extends Elkington's *Triple Bottom Line* (1998: 2) to include inner values and spirituality, and prioritizes fundamental aspects of being human that align with human needs (Maslow 1968: 149–66) and philosophical understandings of human meaning (Hick 1989: 12). The QBL comprises: **practical meaning,** providing for physical needs while recognizing environmental consequences; **social meaning**, ethical behavior, and concern for others; **personal meaning**, inner values, and spirituality; and **economic means**, financial considerations as a means rather than an end in itself.

Practical meaning

The Miān-Sarā is a practically meaningful design because it provides for people's physical needs and activities in a manner that is environmentally responsible. The environmental aspects of this architectural form are very impressive, relatively straightforward to investigate and, historically, vital for survival in the regional climate. By surrounding a small plot with high walls and adding some natural elements such as a water pool and greenery, a pleasant, tranquil atmosphere can be created. Through this means, with orientation to the path of the sun, a courtyard house is naturally cooled in summer and naturally heated or supplemented with relatively low use of energy consumption in cold winters. Residents move to different parts of the house seasonally and daily to achieve comfortable living conditions— thus heating and cooling occur relatively passively, with little need for use of other energy sources. Use of natural, local building materials has many advantages. Local workers are familiar with the necessary building skills. The materials are readily available and affordable, with little or no additional costs for transportation to the site. Local materials are also well understood, easily maintained and repaired, and therefore suited to extended use. Thus, there was, traditionally, a strong integration of technique, materials, architecture, and construction in Iran for many centuries.

Traditional techniques: These became well adapted over time to materials, climate and human needs, and provided skilled work that was uniquely suited to place (Van der Ryn and Cowan 1996: 63–4; Salingaros 2010: 169). Moreover, traditional local techniques had their own variations and displayed differences from town to town and city to city, helping to create a sense of cultural identity and belonging. The Miān-Sarā fulfils its residents' basic needs, i.e. *shelter, comfort,* and *safety.* With regard to the latter, the Iranian plateau has always faced many invasions. Safety measures include an inward-looking design with high, blank exterior walls. Houses are approached via narrow, low, dead-end alleys and passages, which in some parts are covered. Inside the house, after entering the vestibule, there is usually a narrow dark corridor, which is angled to hinder a direct view of, and immediate access to, the rooms and courtyard. Another aspect of the embodiment of practical meaning is the way traditional living *engaged with nature*, where people could benefit from being part of, rather being disconnected from, nature (Van der Ryn and Cowan 1996: 163; Salingaros 2010: 169); this comes from their belief system and is manifested through the architecture.

Social meaning

The following three considerations show how the Miān-Sarā accords with the social issues of design for sustainability:

"Houses within a house": The traditional family lifestyle in Iran was to live as an extended family in a courtyard house. Each individual family unit would have exclusive use of one or two private rooms, while sharing common spaces with others. Residents who had the same occupation or the same employer meant these family units had much in common; their income was from the same source, their levels of income would be about the same and they had more or less equal social status. This notion of equality is one of the main considerations in creating social sustainability (Wilkinson and Pickett 2009: 215–28) and was provided by traditional Iranian housing design not only inside the house but also in the neighborhood. In addition to safety considerations, discussed above, the blank exterior wall revealed nothing of the financial status of the residents.

Sense of community among extended family members: As residents shared the domestic open space, social activities center around this area. Close living meant that there tended to be mutual trust and honesty among family members, and they would help and support each other in many aspects of life. Cooperation, collaboration, and mutual support were among the social virtues fostered by this lifestyle. Not only did these virtues exist among the residents in one house but also among neighbors, who were often relatives.

Social mediation: Due to its design, the Miān-Sarā was a very private space; strangers would be unable to see directly into the courtyard from the entrance door, street or neighboring houses. Visitors experienced varying degrees of "closeness" and the journey from the doorway to the Miān-Sarā served as a filtering space. If visitors were not considered to be close enough to be invited inside the rooms or if they didn't want to stay long, then the Miān-Sarā provided a place to host visitors. Also, from time to time the Miān-Sarā was used for more formal social gatherings— to celebrate family events, and traditional and religious ceremonies. At these times, neighbors often shared their own Miān-Sarā and provided lighting, floor coverings, chairs and tables, and would help with the decorations.

Privacy and *hospitality* norms help demonstrate how the Miān-Sarā accords with important ethical considerations. Traditionally, Iranian families are very private. History had taught them to keep themselves to themselves. Islam taught people to take seriously the protection of the family. In those times, the design of the home and the extended family lifestyle worked in conjunction to fulfil this need. The inward-facing courtyard design, where physical boundaries limited intrusion of sound and visual distractions, helped create an atmosphere of safety, privacy, and serenity. A courtyard house proved to be the best means of creating unrestricted freedom in an enclosed private area. However, the need to provide hospitality is an equally important aspect of traditional and contemporary Iranian lifestyles. Residents have to be ready to serve guests to the best of their ability. Traditionally, there was a balance between *privacy* and *hospitality* and there were different degrees of serving visitors. The host would choose the appropriate place depending on the length and the degree of importance of a visit, and according to the kind of relationship between the visitor and the host. Short, informal visits might be hosted near the door whereas longer, more formal visits were hosted in the heart of the house.

Life in the courtyard house was in accord with social, religious, and cultural norms but it was the Miān-Sarā, the heart of the home, that integrated social needs, cultural values, and natural elements.

Personal meaning

The Miān-Sarā also had very important symbolic and sacred meanings that relate to the inner, spiritual person. In the traditional, pre-modern worldview, every element associated with the Miān-Sarā had a higher symbolic meaning. Sun, water, light, and earth were seen not only as being vital to human biological life but also had symbolic significance. On the Iranian plateau, the sun is a dominant presence. Typically, the Miān-Sarā had a rectangular plan oriented according to the direction and position of the sun. The rooms of the house surrounded it on all sides and it was open to the sky. Hence, symbolically, the Iranian sun god Mithrā, the most powerful divinity in Pre-Zoroastrian times, was present in the very heart of the home. Water, a permanent element in the Miān-Sarā, has always been a precious resource in this region and residents stored it in the courtyard pool. Its presence was, of course, functional, but it also symbolized Anahita, the goddess of water. In Islamic times, water has always been associated with ritual ablutions before prayer—the prophet Mohammad placed a basin of water in the center of the first mosque. Light has always been an important factor in the physical arrangement of rooms. One of the most significant benefits of the courtyard was that it brought light into the center of the house. Light also symbolizes God. Although in Islam, God is a very abstract notion, the only verse in the Quran that gives a tangible sense of God, is, "Allah is the light of the skies and the earth" (the Quran 24:75). Earth, a natural element in the Miān-Sarā, is not only the main construction material for the house, it is also one of the four basic natural elements. Symbolically, earth creates the sense of place.

As a whole, the Miān-Sarā has both symbolic and functional meanings. First, the Miān-Sarā can be understood as a physical absence that symbolizes something that is intangible and invisible to the eye but has deep sacred meaning. The void represents transcendent meaning that is beyond words and explanation. The manifestation of the void arises in music, as in John Cage's 4′33″; in calligraphy with the white spaces between black letters; in Islamic religious practice with a month's fasting. The void is also a symbolic form in contemporary spiritual architecture such as the 9/11 memorial in New York. The presence of a void can be understood as being symbolic of higher thoughts—beyond "doing." The void in the spatial core of the home is a significant representation of what people believed in the past—symbolizing what they couldn't see but intuitively knew. Second, it is a common belief among traditional Iranian Muslims that the green open space at the heart of the home represents the *Lost Paradise* (Ardalan 2002: 9–18; Memarian and Brown 2003: 181–98). Traditionally, Iranians living near or in deserts have tried to recreate this promised, beautiful place in accord with descriptions in the Quran, as a constant reminder of the *Lost Paradise*. Its wide spectrum of meanings contrast with the "hell" that can be felt just beyond the walls in the searing days of summer.

Economic means

In traditional Persian society, house design was an economically viable architectural form that enabled a comfortable way of living for an extended family. This was achieved through three interrelated factors: local materials, usually earth that was readily available, with little or no transportation costs; local designers and local workers who had the necessary skills and experience, thus creating local employment; and designs that were adapted, over many generations, to local conditions and within the financial limits of the owner. These designs were able to provide passive cooling, which did not impose any extra financial costs on residents. In winter, residents used the warmer rooms that were penetrated by the rays of the sun, and this was sometimes supplemented by a low-cost traditional heating system, the *kors*, that burns coal to heat a limited area.

Economies associated with traditional lifestyles included a sharing of certain domestic spaces as well as the facilities and tools of the household, accommodation for newly married couples, and annual and daily repairs by residents and local workers. Traditional design combined with the communal lifestyle made these small communities almost self-sufficient. Traditional life was usually based on farming, and people usually produced more than they consumed, allowing them to share or sell any excess produce. The distance between home and workplace was usually short, so people could walk or cycle; thus daily travel incurred no cost. In addition to the housework, women would usually weave carpets to bring in extra income. The modern mantra of "Reduce, Reuse, Repair, and Recycle" was represented in almost every aspect of the traditional Iranian life. Consumption was reduced due to sharing, and spaces such as the Miān-Sarā and the kitchen were shared, along with the utensils and tools. Residents also shared activities, such as bread making, cooking, and childcare. A principle of self-sufficiency and living with minimal needs fostered a culture of repair, rather than one of consumption and disposal. Re-using clothes for younger children was another way of being economically self-sufficient; even when the clothes finally wore out, the material was used to make rough rugs and mats. Traditionally, Iranians were very creative in using everything to its ultimate capacity. The traditional courtyard was the "container" for this kind of lifestyle.

It can be concluded from this that, traditionaly, economic considerations were an integral factor in a way of life, manifested in the architecture and other tangible artifacts produced within that culture. This way of life endured for thousands of years and was, by any standards, sustainable. However, in Iran today, contemporary living is more Western in style, with people living as nuclear families, which has put an end to many of these cultural values and practices.

The decline of the Miān-Sarā

The transition from traditional domestic architecture to contemporary housing for nuclear families was a striking transformation in Iranian culture and is known as "The Change." It was an invisible but fundamental upheaval that resulted in social, economic, and environmental reforms. We will consider this change in terms of the two themes discussed earlier: (1) The Container and the Contents, and (2) Form follows Meaning:

(1) **The Container and the Contents:** The container here is the Iranian house, and the contents refers to the lifestyles of the residents. It is a very natural and basic notion for a house to be suited to and reflect the lifestyle of its residents. The container can acquire different levels of meaning according to the expectations of its residents. On the level of practical meaning, the container would generally be a place for the *protection* of inhabitants from the elements and a place to be comfortable. On the level of social meaning, it is a *home*, a place for social interaction, a place for the expression of love among family members and kindness between family and guests, and a place for cooperation and collaboration with neighbors. On the level of personal meaning, a home transcends to a *temple*, a place for contemplation and *reflection*, and a place where the beliefs of its residents are made manifest.

(2) **Form follows Meaning:** On each of the levels discussed above—house, home, and temple—the home can be understood in terms of Walker's "Form follows Meaning" (2011: 192). The normal life for many contemporary families tends to be characterized by residents being out of the house for many hours of the day. The main thing they need is comfortable, clean, and safe accommodation to have a restful sleep in order to be able to start the next busy day. The contemporary nuclear family home with its convenient, modern appliances, serves this need well. However, as is the case elsewhere, it also depends on a highly consumptive lifestyle. The result is that the holistic way of living that used to be found in traditional homes no longer suits modern families. There is no holistic approach to the design of the home, as the residents tend to think about their accommodation in purely functional terms.

Changes in the Iranian worldview—from traditional to modern—resulted in changes in values and the Iranian identity. In turn, these became visible in Iranian domestic architecture. These changes began in the mid- to late-nineteenth century, following a visit of the Qajar king, Nasser al-Din Shah, to Europe. Iranians became exposed to European modernity and they began to lose their national pride and confidence. The result, which was initially not very evident, was a gradual losing of their awareness of, and respect for, the natural world and living in harmony with it.

Iranians were also slowly but steadily losing their faith in deeper values—such as mutual trust, honesty, and social collaboration. All this started to become manifest in the tangible world, especially in architecture and housing design. The resulting instability in thought and belief meant there was no longer a secure sense of self and so a narrative unity that seamlessly integrated practical, social, and personal meaning was lost in the transition to modernity (MacIntyre 2007: 218–27). Iranian identity could no longer be recognized in architecture and housing design.

Thus, the Change was part of a collective loss in national confidence (Yazdanpanah 2014). In this unstable context, Western consumerist export strategies and the rapid introduction of modern technologies caused major changes in Iranian socio-cultural and economic policies. These are linked to the loss of tradition and subsequent environmental degradation. Modern technological facilities and new materials help create a more comfortable, convenient lifestyle, but also mean that contemporary homes no longer reflect or support a clear sense of Iranian culture and identity.

Economic changes: When Iranian thought changed, the primary motivation behind housing design and construction changed too—from one of bringing comfort, tranquility and safety to a family to a means of making a profit for landowners and contractors. Profit-making has now become a dominant force in Iranian culture. Whoever decides to build or buy a house considers it as an investment for the future, rather than as a home for living in the present.

Social changes: Along with technological and economic changes, there was also the transition to nuclear family homes and the phenomenon of social mobility. Generational differences meant siblings no longer wished to live in extended family homes with shared facilities; they no longer had enough in common to be able to live harmoniously. Consequently, the father of the family was no longer able to maintain the dual role of being the family's main employer in the workplace and the head of the family at home. Each smaller family unit started a new life as a nuclear family in independent accommodation. In this milieu, the influx of modern technologies and products occurred, and people began to develop a more materialistic outlook—an outlook that continues to the present.

Comparing the Miān-Sarā home with its modern alternative

Table 8.1 shows the traditional functions of the Miān-Sarā home together with modern alternatives for the same function. These are grouped in four categories: environmental, social, economic and symbolic, following the practical, social, personal meanings and economic means of the Quadruple Bottom Line.

The style of contemporary living, in both traditional and contemporary houses, shows that the symbolic meanings of the Miān-Sarā have become neglected and its social and environmental meanings have been replaced by compact modern technologies. The Hayāt, which is equivalent to a front or back yard, does not provide the privacy, tranquility, sense of safety or opportunities for sharing and cooperation offered by the Miān-Sarā. With land becoming ever more expensive, even the Hayāt has become rare, and residential architecture is now often high-rise apartments.

TABLE 8.1 The Physical, Functional and Symbolic Features of the Miān-Sarā. © Poone Yazdanpanah and Stuart Walker

	Traditional way ...	Replaced by
Environmental role	Passive natural cooling system: the whole system of wind-catcher, Miān-Sarā, basement, greenery, the pool of water (almost the whole form of the house)	The electro-mechanical air conditioner that works with just a push of a button
	The pool of water: The main water storage facility Washing dishes Washing clothes	A useless ceramic or concrete basin or nothing A hose connected to the plumbing system Electric dish washer Electric washing machine and dryer
Social role	A Playground for Children	Public parks in towns or neighborhoods, Electronic gadgets and digital games.
	Family gathering	A busy family doesn't have time to sit together
	Wedding and family parties	Rented halls in towns, or gardens in the countryside
	Religious and traditional ceremonies	In local streets or neighborhood mosques and shrines
	Traditional inward-looking housing style	Contemporary outward-looking housing style
Functional role	Traditional local material	New materials
	Traditional local architects	A common plan used in all cities in Iran despite the local climate, copying Western styles of housing, readymade blue-prints
	By having a new plumbing system there wasn't any need to store water, then there was no need to dig the plot enough to make adobe for construction	
	Narrow, shaded, cool passages to protect passers-by in hot summers	Wide, asphalt, Western type streets for cars that also need their own 'room' in the house A place to park the car
Symbolic role	Miān-Sarā as a reminder of the lost paradise, the void, the connection between the sky and the earth etc.	Facts (see Walker 2014, Chapter 5, *Design and Spirituality*)

Conclusions

The Miān-Sarā was an example of environmentally and socially sustainable design as well as an economically viable architectural form. It was a design that was tried and tested over millennia. However, while it may have been a sustainable architecture form, it is no longer a part of today's housing form.

Its environmentally sustainable design has been replaced by new technological facilities. Its socially sustainable design benefits are ineffective since the structure of modern Iranian families has changed from an extended to a nuclear family. In this context, having a Miān-Sarā is neither affordable nor efficient. Moreover, the symbolic language of the Miān-Sarā is no longer understood by people—its symbolism is now largely lost.

Consequently, this archetype is no longer the core of the home, nor is it part of contemporary domestic design. However, this does not make it meaningless or worthless. While it may not be feasible to reintroduce the Miān-Sarā as a building form, the overall cultural and practical significance associated with the features of the Miān-Sarā can be respected and carried forward into the design of modern dwellings in Iran.

References

Ardalan, N. (1986), "Architecture: viii. Pahlavi, after World War II—Encyclopaedia Iranica." Available online: http://www.iranicaonline.org/articles/architecture-viii (accessed September 23, 2013).

Ardalan, N. (2002), "'Simultaneous Perplexity': The Paradise Garden as the Quintessential Visual Paradigm of Islamic Architecture and Beyond," in A. Petruccioli and K. Piriani (eds.), *Understanding Islamic Architecture*, 9–18, New York, NY: Routledge.

Carruthers, K. (1984), "Architecture Is Space: The Space-Positive Tradition," *Journal of Architectural Education*, 39 (3): 17–23.

Day, C. (2002), *Spirit and Place*, Amsterdam: Elsevier.

Elkington, J. (1998), *Cannibals with Forks: The Triple Bottom Line of 21st Century Business*, Gabriola Island, BC: New Society Publishers.

Ghezelbash, M. and F. Abolzia (1985), *The Alphabet of the Traditional House in Yazd* (in Persian), Tehran: Budget and Programming Organization Publications.

Hick, J. (1989), *An Interpretation of Religion: Human Responses to the Transcendent*, London: MacMillan Academic and Professional Ltd.

Hosseini, S. R., A. Nik Ethegad, E. Uson Guardiona, and A. Armesto Aira (2015) "Iranian courtyard housing: The role of social and cultural patterns to reach the spatial formation in the light of an accentuated privacy," *ACE: Architecture, City and Environment*, Universitat Politècnica de Catalunya, Barcelona, 10 (29): 11–30.

Lad, J. (2010), "A House Divided: The Harem Courtyards of the Topkapi Palace," in N. O. Rabbat (ed.), *The Courtyard House, From Cultural Reference to Universal Relevance*, 3–28, Farnham: Ashgate Publishing Limited.

MacIntyre, A. (2007), *After Virtue*, 3rd edn, London: Bloomsbury Academic.

Maslow, A. H. (1968), *Towards a Psychology of Being*, New York, NY: Wiley and Sons.

Memarian, G. and F. E. Brown (2003), "Climate, Culture and Religion: Aspects of the Traditional Courtyard House in Iran," *Journal of Architecture and Planning Research*, 20 (3): 181–98.

Nasr, S. H. (1987), *Islamic Art and Spirituality*, Ipswich: Golgonooza Press.

Pirnia, M. K. (1989), *Shivehaei Memari Irani* (in Persian), Tehran: Nashr-I Honar Islami.

Pirnia, M. K. (1991), *Ashnaii ba Menari Islami Irani* (in Persian), Tehran: Iran University of Science and Technology.

Ramezani, S. and S. Hamidi (2010), "Privacy and Social Interaction in Traditional Towns to Contemporary Urban Design in Iran," *American Journal of Engineering and Applied Sciences* 3 (3): 501–8.

Salingaros, N. A. (2010), *Twelve Lectures on Architecture, Algorithmic Sustainable Design*, Solingen: Umbau-Verlag.

Sarkis, H. (2010) "One Thousand Courtyards: Observations on the Courtyard as a Recurring Design Element," in N. O. Rabbat (ed.), *The Courtyard House, From Cultural Reference to Universal Relevance*, 191–202, Farnham, UK: Ashgate Publishing Limited.

Schadl, M. (2010), "Tradition and Transformation of the Kabuli Courtyard House," in N. O. Rabbat (ed.), *The Courtyard House, From Cultural Reference to Universal Relevance*, 47–64, Farnham, UK: Ashgate Publishing Limited.

Van der Ryn, S. and S. Cowan (1996), *Ecological Design*, Washington, DC: Island Press.

Walker, S. (2011), *The Spirit of Design, Objects, Environment and Meaning*, London: Earthscan.

Walker, S. (2014) *Designing Sustainability*, London: Routledge.

Wilkinson, R. and K. Pickett (2009), *The Spirit Level: Why More Equal Societies Almost Always Do Better*, London: Penguin Books.

Yazdanpanah, P. (2014), "Architecture, Sustainability and Substantive Values: A Case Study—The Traditional Iranian Domestic Courtyard (Miān-Sarā)," Ph.D. thesis, Lancaster University, Lancaster.

9

IKEA

Mass-Produced National Design Identity

Sara Kristoffersson

Introduction

It would be difficult to envisage a company that is more "Swedish" than IKEA. With its network of furnishing stores, it has turned Swedishness into a virtue and an important part of the firm's branding strategy. The yellow and blue logotype alludes to the colors of the Swedish flag, while all products have Nordic-sounding names and IKEA's restaurants serve Swedish food: "A Taste of Sweden."

Making use of a national identity in a marketing strategy is neither unique to IKEA nor, indeed, particularly noteworthy. Everything from governments to commercial branding have long used national markers in order to position and give themselves a unique profile. Underlying these narratives are commercial forces but it would be an oversimplification to dismiss them as harmless or of no interest. Those responsible for the narrative do not need to have political, cultural or ideological aims but the narratives can, nevertheless, be of importance beyond the purely commercial sphere.

IKEA is a global brand that serves as Sweden's face on the world. Naturally it does not represent Sweden at a formal level, but very much so at an informal one. It helps to create ideas about Sweden and is even important with regard to the way that the Swedes see themselves. This role is by no means only something that IKEA has adopted. In Sweden the firm is seen as a sort of national symbol, and even though there is little in the structure of the company that has to do with anything Swedish, IKEA receives a helping hand from the Swedish government.

Few companies have such a pronounced national identity as IKEA. The firm's visual images, symbols and written materials are the same everywhere but they can, of course, be interpreted in different ways. The fact that a product has the same name and appearance all over the world does not mean it necessarily signifies the same thing. Like other global brands, IKEA arouses different associations in different parts of the world. When meanings and symbols travel the world they are uprooted from their original context and are bedded down in the places they end up, which results in a regional creation of meaning (Giddens 1991).

Looking at how IKEA is perceived in different countries is undoubtedly an interesting subject but is a gigantic task in itself and is not considered in this chapter. The question this chapter addresses is how IKEA has created a profile for itself using "Swedishness." What are these Swedish ideals and norms in IKEA's case? Where do the narratives come from? How are they expressed and how credible are they?

The intention is not to pierce the myths, nor to falsify or demolish IKEA's claims, but the chapter aims to give a more balanced account of the myths and to make the company's narratives of Swedishness, its impact and effectiveness more comprehensible. Simply put, to give visibility to the major reasons for IKEA's success (Kristoffersson 2014).

IKEA was founded in 1943 by Ingvar Kamprad when he was only seventeen years old. Over the course of several decades, the firm grew into one of the world's largest furniture retailers. Initially Kamprad sold all sorts of products, including matches and pencils, but he soon came to specialize in home furnishings. IKEA started selling furniture for self-assembly in 1956 and two years later the firm opened its first store in Älmhult, in the south of Sweden. During the 1970s IKEA opened a succession of stores outside Scandinavia and the international expansion continued throughout the 1980s. By 2013 there were 298 stores in more than thirty-eight countries and, according to the company, IKEA had a turnover of 27.7 billion euros (www.IKEA.com).

This remarkable success is often explained in terms of low prices, well-developed logistics, and a strong corporate sense. A point of departure, on the other hand, is the idea noted above that narratives have been of major importance in the company's success. That companies and organizations use narratives—true or false in themselves—in order to create a profile as well as encouraging a sense of community in the workforce is not uncommon (Boje 1995; Gabriel 2000), but the question is why IKEA's storytelling has proved to be so powerful.

The spotlight is focused on narratives about IKEA's design rather than the products themselves. The framework, discourse, and rhetoric pertaining to the company's products as well as to Swedish design in general are considered meaningful. This approach differs from a more product-oriented history of design with its emphasis on form, material, and production methods.

In spite of the importance of the company and its global presence, interest in its cultural significance is limited and there are surprisingly few studies from a history of design angle; instead, research into IKEA is concerned with financial and organizational aspects (Bartlett and Nanda 1990; Salzer 1994). This does not mean that the matter is totally unexplored and there is research based on a more cultural orientation. The American, French, British and Irish perceptions of IKEA have been considered (Andersson 2009b; Garvey 2010: 142–53; Hartman 2007: 483–98; Werner 2008: 249–69).

IKEA goes Swede

IKEA has been working with something that the firm terms as "Swedishness" for a long time (Markgren 2011). But what is typically Swedish? Does "Swedishness" actually exist and if it does, what does it consist of? Gloomy figures from a Bergman film, Vikings, elk, blue-eyed and blonde Swedish girls? These are just a few of many different phenomena that are associated with Sweden as a nation. Basically there is no checklist that determines what is Swedish or what defines the particularities of the national character. What we perceive as Swedish—or French, English or German for that matter—is determined by a whole succession of notions, traditions, histories, and fictions (Anderson 1983; O'Dell 1998: 20–37).[1]

The urge to project a homogenous and attractive national character can be seen in many contexts but IKEA's national identity is unusually distinct and it is, of course, a matter of financial interest. Such a profile was not in place in its initial stages but is a construction that grew as the company expanded internationally. Up until 1961, IKEA was pronounced to sound like a French word and was spelt with an accent: Ikéa. Product names gave rise to associations with Italy and the USA rather than with Sweden: "Piccolo," "Verona," and "Figaro," or "Tender," "Cowboy," and "Swing" (IKEA Catalogue 1955).

During the 1970s, when the company was opening ever more stores outside Scandinavia, there was an increasing need for a clearer profile. The new strategy was to present IKEA as an essentially different and innovative type of furniture store in a rather conservative industry. The German slogan was "Das unmögliche Möbelhaus aus Schweden" (The impossible furniture store from Sweden), while in France the slogan was "Ils sont fous ces suédois" (The Swedes are a bit crazy). National markers such as elks and Vikings were strewn around the stores to emphasize the company's Swedish heritage, but it was in connection with the international expansion in the 1980s that the Swedish profile was seriously cultivated.

The elks and Vikings disappeared, and the national identity was strengthened and charged with new content and new symbols. Swedishness became the core of the brand's narrative and the corporate profile became increasingly homogenous and formalized. A sort of filtered Swedishness was applied to all of the stores all over the world, with concrete markers and comprehensive images—both visual and linguistic—including relatively abstract notions about Sweden and Swedishness. The stores became increasingly identical and the sales pitch, products, and interiors were the same everywhere (Atle Bjarnestam 2009: 205–9; Ekmark and Kumpulainen 2009).[2]

IKEA's most concrete national marker, the blue and yellow logotype, was introduced in connection with the company's first branding manual from 1984, and replaced a red and white variation. In due course the stores were repainted blue with a yellow logotype on the facade. Staff uniforms match these colors as do shopping bags that are offered to customers when they enter the stores.[3] The blue and yellow aesthetic is accompanied by Nordic-sounding product names that include the letters å, ä, and ö: a "Hästveda" armchair is a Hästveda whether it is for sale in Stockholm, Los Angeles or Riyadh.

The food that is served in the restaurants and sold in the stores is another significant marker. Some stores serve local specialities but large parts of the menus are identical all over the world. The food shops—known as "Swedish Food Markets"—sell lingonberries, Swedish rusks, and pickled herrings (Figure 9.1). Since 2006 the product names have been based on the Swedish name for the ingredient: *Dryck Fläder* (Elderflower drink) and *Knäckebröd* (Crispbread) (Pettersson 2011).[4]

IKEA's first restaurant opened in 1959 but it was not until 1983, in connection with the introduction of a more considered Swedish profile, that the symbol-laden signature dish of meatballs, potatoes, and lingonberries was added to the menu (Pettersson 2011). It was all the more Swedish when ordered as a large portion that came with a Swedish flag ornamenting the dish.

In order to reinforce the Swedishness, more abstract notions about Sweden are also used. An important example is "IKEA's själ" (Soul of IKEA) from 1981. This can be seen as a powerful starting point for the company's process of "Swedification" (Atle Bjarnestam 2009: 104; Salzer 1994: 2–3). A photo shows a rolling rural landscape. The sky is blue and a long stone wall stretches out through the landscape. There are no products or price tags to be seen but the picture is intended to give an impression of the company's roots in the southern Swedish province of Småland.

This photograph is just one of numerous romantic images of the countryside that are employed to relate to what seems specifically Swedish. Simultaneously, the impression is communicated of the Swedes as a people who love the countryside and whose country is particularly beautiful (*Marketing Communication. The IKEA Way* 2010: 46). The idea of Swedes as a people with a passionate involvement in the countryside was formulated in connection with the late-nineteenth-century's ideal of romantic nationalism. In the construction of a Swedish identity, a calm and often melancholy landscape plays an important role with an almost metaphorical

FIGURE 9.1 IKEA food packaging. Courtesy Kusoffsky. © Bjorn Kusoffsky.

significance. The Swedish countryside began to be portrayed as something different, more attractive and more beautiful than the natural surroundings of other countries (Sundbärg 1911). The concept that a love of nature was deeply embedded among the Swedes is a classic notion and a stereotype that IKEA has embraced and continues to reproduce.

There is an evident regional element to the company's allusions to all things Swedish. Ingvar Kamprad's background in Småland has been raised to the status of a virtue and the claimed characteristics of the region are now part of the corporate identity. IKEA's definition of the province of Småland and its inhabitants could not be more stereotypical. Beneath the photograph in "IKEA's själ" the caption explains that the relatively barren earth of Småland forces people there to be thrifty, strong-minded, and humble, and that it is precisely here that the company has found its cultural heritage: "The dry-stone walls of Småland run through our hearts."

The stone wall in the photo is symbolically important. Farms that have drystone walls, in which fields are created by piling up the stones to create walls, are common in southern Sweden. They were originally constructed for fencing in animals as well as for marking boundaries between owners, villages, and different usages. Stone walls thus promote associations with grazing lands as well as with hard and strenuous work. In IKEA's narrative the company was built up in the same way as the drystone walls: through diligence and thrift. In connection with the "IKEA's själ" advertisement the drystone wall began to be used as one of the company's symbols, equivalent to such notions as hard work and persistence (*The Stone Wall—A Symbol of the IKEA Culture* 2012: 9).

Just as frequently as romantic images of the countryside are used for indicating what is essentially Swedish, IKEA appeals to modernity, democracy, and social justice. The company claims to share the values, ideals, and principles of Sweden's welfare system, with the focus on solidarity and equality. Essentially, IKEA and the Swedish welfare system are presented as synonymous, and the company seems to have grown out of this commitment to society (*Democratic Design. A Book about Form, Function and Price—Three Dimensions at IKEA* 1995: 9).

The notion of Sweden as a harmonious, exemplary country free from poverty and injustice has long been established in people's minds. An important contribution to this positive image was the book, *Sweden: The Middle Way* (1936), by Marquis Childs who described a middle way between American capitalism and Soviet socialism. The description of Swedish society as a model has been questioned by both the right and the left but the image has a foundation in the real world.

Between the years 1920 and 1965, Sweden was transformed from a poor country into a welfare state with an advanced standard of living. The Social Democrats, who effectively governed between the 1930s and the 1970s, introduced a succession of reforms that ensured financial and social security to an extent that few other countries could match. Thus, in Sweden the term "welfare" has a more extended meaning than the English language definition suggests. While in English the welfare state is associated with benefit cheques from the government, the Swedish equivalent stands for an idea about human welfare being a central aspect of organized society.[5] The Social Democrats' focus on social security played an important role in what came to be known as the "Swedish model." In Sweden the term *folkhem* (roughly meaning "people's home") is employed. The term is associated with Per Albin Hansson, the long-term leader of Sweden's Social Democrats. As early as the 1920s he used "home" as a metaphor for the nation, which would be inclusive of all and in which equality, concern, cooperation and helpfulness would reign.[6]

The modernization of Swedish society from the 1930s onwards can also be regarded as the construction of an identity. It was a matter of collective progress and of creating material security, but welfare policy also had more abstract and metaphorical elements: the right to belong, which denoted a sort of emotional security. Modernization went hand in hand with national pride and, in turn, welfare became something central in the process of creating a modern Swedish identity. Social and financial security linked up with a sense of national community and affinity, and was considered to be something specifically Swedish (Andersson 2009a; Hirdman, Björkman, and Lundberg 2012). It is here that IKEA claims to have its roots.

The image of Sweden as a golden mean between socialism and capitalism has had market value for Swedish design. The epithet "Swedish Modern" was minted as early as the 1930s to describe a less angular version of a modernist aesthetic. The style fitted very well with the "middle way" and from this it was only a short step to "Scandinavian Design." This term is a construction of the Nordic countries, which joined forces and launched the concept onto the American market during the 1950s (Halén and Wickman 2003).

Since the post-war period, Swedish design has been incorporated into the concept of "Scandinavian Design" and IKEA has, like many other companies, capitalized on this denotation (Brunnström 2010: 14; Werner 2008: 343–6). True, IKEA has a Swedish profile but it has also launched a sort of budget version of "Scandinavian Design." The range of products on offer is more or less the same all over the world. The size of the store naturally limits the range but, in principle, there is a uniform assortment of products and a homogenous company. Design is heavily influenced by price. The guiding light has involved limiting manufacturing costs by reducing the amount of materials used by means of clever solutions and constructions in which not a millimeter is wasted (Brunnström 2010: 352).

Since the mid-1990s IKEA's range has amounted to some 10,000 articles with varying life spans according to a special system. Naturally the range is not static. A number of new designs are added each year while others are withdrawn (Atle Bjarnestam 2009: 205–9; Dahlvig 2011: 94–7; Ekmark and Kumpulainen 2009). The aim is that the range should be understood as typically IKEA in Scandinavia and typically Swedish beyond Scandinavia (Dahlvig 2011: 94–7; *The IKEA Concept The Testament of a Furniture Dealer, A Little IKEA Dictionary* 2011: 24).

Alongside the principal range, IKEA has launched special collections in order to strengthen the national profile. Internally these ranges are classed as "Scandinavian Collections" (*Scandinavian Collections 1996–97* 1997). One example is "PS," which was first presented in 1995 accompanied by slogans such as "Design for the People!" and "Democratic Design."[7] The idea was that the name of the collection would be understood as a postscript to the main product range, but the name was also seen as an abbreviation for "Products of Sweden" (Howe 1999: 94–105).

"PS" consisted of a number of items of furniture and various furnishing products by a variety of designers but, taken as a whole, the collection was characterized by a common style of design. The range definitely lived up to its stereotype: blond, pared down, and socially responsible. The fact that "PS" was part of a proud Swedish tradition of design was underlined by a rather exclusive publication being produced to accompany the launch. In the catalog, each product was presented by itself as unique. At intervals there were evocative photographs of becalmed lakes and delicate copses of birch trees accompanied by a text about Swedish design and its history in which a well-established and straightforward narrative about how a modernist vision of cheap but well-designed products has been transformed into reality (*IKEA PS. Forum för design* 1995). This account of Swedish design corresponds to the success story about how, during a brief period, Sweden was transformed from a poor country to a democratic and socially just society. The story is, like the definition of Swedish design as blond and functional, a commercially viable concept. But success stories do not need to be true. Behind the national facade of normality and harmony and the tastefully furnished homes there is a miscolored narrative that testifies to a different reality.

Beyond the myth

There have long been other views about Sweden than the established one of a harmonious and sheltered welfare state. During the 1980s, the positive perception of Swedish society began to be seriously questioned and the success story was gradually rewritten (Andersson and Hilson 2009: 219–28; Andersson and Östberg 2013: 14–21). As well as the fact that the welfare state was considered economically inefficient and ideologically mistaken, this model of society was attacked as being collectivist and paternalistic. The notion of the "people's home" was linked to the image of a "nanny" state and with the exercise of government power, and was seen as preventing the individual's own freedom of choice. The disapproval did not come exclusively from the right wing; the Social Democrats in Sweden, the architects of the welfare state, were also critical (Demokrati och makt i Sverige 1990: 44).[8]

The Swedish economy also changed radically. In September 1992 the Swedish *krona* [SEK] fell dramatically and, at one point, the bank rate rose to an unimaginable 500 percent. This rate of interest was short-lived but the ensuing financial crisis had repercussions and was followed by pressure to reform the Swedish economic model. Important aspects of the social model that had been built up during the post-war period were abandoned and the mantra became the deconstruction of the welfare system (Andersson and Östberg 2013: 358, 366, 408–12).

Today, people speak of the Swedish welfare model as though it is just as it once was; however, welfare policy nowadays differs greatly from that of previous decades. It is now the market, rather than the government, that is expected to solve problems in the economy. The Social Democrats no longer have a special place as the governing party and, while Sweden was formerly relatively homogenous from an ethnic point of view, in the third millennium it appears as a multicultural society. Some people regard the changes as granting greater freedom from an autocratic state and welcome the dynamics of free-market forces, while others see growing social divisions and segregation (Andersson and Östberg 2013: 16–20; Larsson, Letell, and Thörn 2012).

During the 1990s Sweden changed from being a model society into a welfare state in crisis. It is interesting to note that, at the same time that the welfare state was being dismantled, IKEA's identity as a "people's home" was achieving an ever more prominent position.

Nor has IKEA taken changes in Swedish design into account. Towards the end of the 1990s and at the beginning of the new millennium, the understanding of Swedish design changed.[9] Was Swedish design really as blond, blue-eyed and functional as people claimed? Was it solely concerned with simple and practical everyday products? Who had written the historic narrative and for what purpose? Another important question was the extent to which a more or less hidden agenda regarding taste had a preferential right of interpretation.

The historic narrative has taken the side of the norms and can be characterized as a lack of diversity and excessive homogeneity (Brunnström 2010: 16–17; Kristoffersson and Zetterlund 2012). As a rule, people claim that Swedish design is functional in spirit and is shaped by critics concerned with society and with social issues. Norms and ideals that have not been in agreement with Sweden's design identity—industrially manufactured items, standardized everyday wares for the common man—have thus been marginalized.

The critical discussion of Swedish design is hardly focused on IKEA but is more a general review of cemented opinions. What is interesting, in this context, is the fact that IKEA has basically avoided the discussion and has defended the traditional view of Swedish design in establishing its specific profile. Like IKEA's use of established notions about the Swedish welfare state, the framework for Swedish design references are obsolete.

Sweden and IKEA—a love story

As we have noted, IKEA defines what is typically Swedish, using classical markers that, in an international perspective, stand for something exotic: rural environments but also modern welfare policies as stereotypical images of Swedish design. Briefly, it is a matter of established, positive images that the company uses and seeks to associate with the brand at the same time that the images are adapted for commercial use.

IKEA's idealization may seem attractive but it is constructed largely on timeworn or questionable notions: nostalgic flashbacks to a romanticized idyll. IKEA's Swedish profile is certainly neither static nor exclusively blond and blue-eyed, but is subject to change. During the new millennium there have been both internal and external references to diversity, not least through the campaign entitled "Long Live Diversity" and mottos like "Everyone is Different" (Wigerfeldt 2012). The strategies involving diversity can be seen as updated narratives on Swedishness. Many of IKEA's other stories about Sweden are, nevertheless, very dated and controversial.

IKEA has long marketed home furnishings under the blue and yellow banner. Now, in the third millennium, the roles seem to have been reversed. The company's smartly packaged narratives are particularly popular among Swedish ambassadors and consuls abroad, which largely consider IKEA as Sweden's face on the world. There is a general understanding that the company stands for values that Sweden wishes to be associated with and so IKEA is seen as playing an important role in creating an image of Sweden (Kristoffersson 2014: 84–7). The fact that the company's products are not manufactured in Sweden and that the IKEA concept is owned by a foundation in the Netherlands is of less importance in this context. IKEA plays an important role for "Sweden," that is to say, the country's national brand. Whether IKEA's profits contribute to the tax-financed welfare system that is praised in the company's marketing campaigns and to what extent the company's stories conform to the truth is another matter altogether.

Notes

1   Starting from the work of Benedict Anderson, researchers have maintained that the sense of being a nation relies on a feeling of community. There are numerous Swedish studies of Swedish mentality. O'Dell is a survey in English.

2   In spite of global guidelines, there are local variations.

3   The red and white logotype was used in Scandinavia until 1997.

4   Almost all of the products are sold under the brand name IKEA Food Service.

5   At that time, a people's temperament was considered as something inherited in a nation or a geographical district in Sweden. The book, *Det svenska folklynnet,* was widely circulated and important in maintaining that a love of nature was inherent to the Swedish people.

6   Per Albin Hansson used the term in a famous speech in 1928, in the Swedish parliament's second chamber.

7   Lennart Ekmark was in charge of the project together with consultant Stefan Ytterborn.

8   The inquiry into political power in Sweden was a government study and a social-science research project ordered by Deputy Prime Minister Ingvar Carlsson in 1985. The final report was issued in 1990.

9   As early as the 1960s there was discussion of the dominant approach and the norms of taste in Swedish design but there was renewed focus in the 1990s.

References

Anderson, B. (1983), *Imagined Communities. Reflections on the Origin and Spread of Nationalism*, London: Verso.

Andersson, F. (2009a), *Performing Co-Production. On the Logic and Practice of Shopping at IKEA*, diss., Department of Social and Economic Geography, Uppsala University, Uppsala.

Andersson, J. (2009b), *När framtiden redan hänt. Socialdemokratin och folkhemsnostalgin*, Stockholm: Ordfront.

Andersson, J. and M. Hilson (2009), "Images of Sweden and the Nordic Countries," *Scandinavian Journal of History*, 34 (3): 219–28.

Andersson, J. and K. Östberg (eds.) (2013), *Sveriges historia 1965–2012*, Stockholm: Norstedts.

Atle Bjarnestam, E. (2009), *IKEA. Design och identitet*, Malmö: Arena.

Bartlett, C. A. and A. Nanda (1990), *Ingvar Kamprad and IKEA*, Boston, MA: Harvard Business Publishing.

Boje, D. M. (1995), "Stories of the Storytelling Organization: A Postmodern Analysis of Disney as 'Tamara-Land'," *Academy of Management Journal*, 38 (4): 997–1035.

Brunnström, L. (2010), *Svensk designhistoria*, Stockholm: Raster.

Childs, M. (1936), *Sweden: The Middle Way*, New Haven, CT: Yale.

Dahlvig, A. (2011), *Med uppdrag att växa. Om ansvarsfullt företagande*, Lund: Studentlitteratur.

Demokrati och makt i Sverige (1990), Stockholm: Allmänna förlaget, Statens offentliga utredningar, SOU, 44.

Democratic Design. A book about form, function and price—Three dimensions at IKEA (1995), Älmhult: IKEA.

Gabriel, Y. (2000), *Storytelling in Organizations: Facts, Fictions, and Fantasies*, Oxford: Oxford University Press.

Ekmark, L. and L. Kumpulainen (2009), Interview, Stockholm, June 12.

Garvey, P. (2010), "Consuming IKEA. Inspiration as Material Form," in A. J. Clarke (ed.), *Design Anthropology*, 142–153, New York, NY: Springer Verlag.

Giddens, A. (1991), *Modernity and Self-Identity: Self and Society in the Late Modern Age*, Cambridge: Polity Press.

Halén, W. and K. Wickman (eds.) (2003), *Scandinavian Design Beyond the Myth. Fifty years of Design from the Nordic Countries*, Stockholm: Arvinius.

Hartman, T. (2007), "On the Ikeaization of France," *Public Culture*, 19 (3): 483–98.

Hirdman, Y., J. Björkman, and U. Lundberg (eds.) (2012), *Sveriges Historia 1920–1965*, Stockholm: Nordstedts.

Howe, S. (1999), "Untangling the Scandinavian Blonde. Modernity and the IKEA PS Range Catalogue 1995," *Scandinavian Journal of Design*, 9: 94–105.

IKEA Catalogue (1955), Älmhult: IKEA Historical Archive.

IKEA PS. Forum för design (1995), Älmhult: IKEA of Sweden.

Kristoffersson, S. (2014), *Design of IKEA. A Cultural History*, London: Bloomsbury Academic.

Kristoffersson, S. and C. Zetterlund (2012), "A Historiography of Scandinavian Design," in F. Fallan (ed.), *Scandinavian Design. Alternative Histories*, 13–31, Oxford: Berg.

Larsson, B., M. Letell, and H. Thörn (eds.) (2012), *Transformations of the Swedish Welfare State. From Social Engineering to Governance?* New York, NY: Palgrave.

Marketing Communication. The IKEA Way (2010), Inter IKEA Systems B.V., Leiden, Netherlands: IKEA Historical Archive.

Markgren, L. (2011), Interview, Waterloo, January 4.

O'Dell, T. (1998), "Junctures of Swedishness. Reconsidering Representations of the National," in B. Svensson (ed.), *Ethnologia Scandinavica*, 20–37, Lund: Folklivsarkivet.

Pettersson, T. (2011), "Så spred IKEA den svenska köttbullen över världen," *Expressen*, February 21.

Salzer, M. (1994), *Identity Across Borders: A Study in the 'IKEA-World'*, Ph.D., Linköping University, Linköping.

Scandinavian Collections 1996–97 (1997), Inter IKEA Systems, Leiden, Netherlands: IKEA Historical Archive.

Sundbärg, G. (1911), *Det svenska folklynnet*, Stockholm: Norstedts.

Werner, J. (2008), *Medelvägens estetik. Sverigebilder i USA Del 2*, Hedemora/Möklinta: Gidlunds.

The IKEA Concept The Testament of A Furniture Dealer, A Little IKEA Dictionary (2011), Inter IKEA Systems B.V., Leiden, Netherlands: IKEA Historical Archive.

The Stone Wall—a Symbol of the IKEA Culture (2012), Inter IKEA Systems B.V., Leiden, Netherlands: IKEA Historical Archive.

Wigerfeldt, A. (2012), "Mångfald och svenskhet: en paradox inom IKEA," Malmö: Malmö Institute for Studies of Migration, Diversity and Welfare. Available online: www.IKEA. com (accessed October 29, 2013).

PART THREE

Revitalization by Design

Editorial Introduction

Tom Cassidy

In this section, five examples of revitalization of culturally significant designs, products, and practices are provided. Perhaps we can consider these as three targets for design researchers and designers. The examples given will include the work of individual design researchers and groups of design researchers. The term "revitalization" has been carefully chosen to mean that one or more of the targets have been addressed in order to maintain/sustain its existence or perhaps to transform the application of the selected target into one or both of the other two targets.

Throughout this book, the social and ethical responsibility of the designer is made clear and its importance is emphasized. However, it also has to be understood that professional designers, and/or the agencies they may be employed by, have to make a living and, if possible, a healthy profit. Revitalization can offer designers and their agencies sound commercial opportunities. A cursory examination of the successful careers of a number of fashion and textile designers and product designers will demonstrate this.

Approaching revitalization from the point of view of designers who come from the culture to which the designs, products, and places belong, we have to consider pride as a motivating factor. Most of us have grown up within a community that takes pride in and values the creativity of our ancestors. In a European context, we can use the example of Celtic designs to particularly evidence the aspect of pride. It is very difficult to place-point the origin and development of Celtic culture and design, and yet it is recognized, claimed, and considered culturally significant by a wide range of European peoples and countries or areas within countries.

Each of the five chapters provided in this section addresses one or more of the three design/design research targets belonging to different cultures, and having different original meanings and uses within these cultures. The stage of transition of the designs, products, and practices from local and often spiritual meanings and uses to commodities and thence tourist products or even to mass production also differs. Related design elements such as colors and how their meaning and preferences may have changed with the effect of globalization are discussed. Such areas will offer further study opportunities for researchers and designers.

In *Culture as a Resource for a Sustainable Future in Indigenous Communities,* Anne Marchand and her colleagues report on their work aimed at enhancing the cultural identity and financial position of the Atikamekw Nation of Canada, who have suffered, in terms of maintaining their cultural heritage, through the often well-meaning assimilation policies of the Canadian government. A participatory action research approach has allowed the team of non-indigenous designers and researchers to interact and collaborate successfully with intergenerational groups of native Atikamekw people in a project titled *Tapiskwan*. The chapter includes many photographs illustrating the strong participatory nature of the research.

Indonesia is a country that is putting a great deal of effort into the revitalization of its native craft-making industries. Adhi Nugraha, in his chapter *Transforming Tradition in Indonesia*, discusses a tool he has developed to facilitate the important process of transforming tradition to sit comfortably with contemporary society. Indonesia is a good example of where a government is supporting efforts to make changes to craft-making processes to improve quality and productivity while maintaining cultural meanings and significance.

The work described by Meong Jin Shin in *New Translations of South Korean Patterns* describes how the patterns traditionally employed in the creation of *bojagi* wrapping fabrics have been reinvented into patterns that can be employed in contemporary global fashion markets. In order to carry out this type of project, it was necessary to examine many facets and therefore the multi-faceted or bricolage research approach was used. Meong Jin begins by looking at the cultural origin of *bojagi* and the meaning, use and importance of color, and how these would affect the translation into fashion products. She goes on to look at technical aspects and produces a marketing tool to support the penetration of the patterns into fashion garments.

Sebastian Cox's chapter *Revitalization by Design* helps to emphasize that the moral and ethical responsibilities of the designer must always be of great importance and business owners can use these sensibilities to provide a sustainable future for the business as well as for the craft-making tradition. He provides us with the excellent example of how, as a child, he observed the care, skill, and pride with which medieval timber-framed houses were restored by his parents. He describes how he is able to employ the lessons he learned to allow him to guide the direction of traditional crafts towards the creation of modern products. He offers the interesting concept of "traditional as radical" as a way of allowing the craft makers to fight back against the degrading of "craft" by the big brands.

The final chapter in this section, *New Caribbean Design* by Patty Johnson, offers an introduction into a very exciting concept and again illustrates how traditional communities have to find ways of defending their way of life against mass-produced products. Patty describes how design has been used to develop "hybrid" products that reflect the melting pot of cultures that makes up the Caribbean region. The use of a soft systems approach in the future might add to this already exciting and valuable study, and offer insights into the etymological challenges of developing "hybrid" designs, products, and practices.

10

Culture as a Resource for a Sustainable Future in Indigenous Communities

Strengthening Atikamekw Identity and Economics through Design

Anne Marchand, Karine Awashish, Christian Coocoo, Solen Roth, Renata Marques Leitão, Cédric Sportes, and Caoimhe Isha Beaulé

Introduction: Rootedness and creativity

The Atikamekw people, as most First Nations groups in Canada, face a number of challenges in relation to the perpetuation of their identity. Members of the Atikamekw Nation and a team of Université de Montréal designers have been working together since 2011 to enhance the preservation and valuation of tangible and intangible Atikamekw heritage. This project, named *Tapiskwan* after the Atikamekw name of the Saint-Maurice River, seeks to foster productive connections between the past and the future by revisiting ancestral Atikamekw iconography through the development of contemporary products.

The Atikamekw are one of the ten First Nations whose traditional territories are located in the Province of Québec, Canada. Although up to fifteen percent of the

Atikamekw live in urban areas, the remaining eighty-five percent reside in one of the three communities of Wemotaci, Manawan, and Opitciwan. With close to seventy percent of the nation's 7,500 community members under the age of thirty-five, and only four percent over the age of sixty, the Atikamekw are a particularly young population (Aboriginal Affairs and Northern Development Canada (AANDC) 2015; Statistics Canada 2006, 2011).

Atikamekw identity is in large part defined in relation to land and territory. The latter has been radically transformed over the course of the twentieth century. Atikamekw society was also severely disrupted in the 1950s when the creation of reserves meant having to settle on a tiny portion of their ancestral territory. This resulted in a much more dense and sedentary population, thereby imposing drastic reformulations of Atikamekw ways of life and social relations. Furthermore, the government sent several generations of children to residential schools located far away from their home, against their family's wishes. The explicit assimilationist objective of this policy has had a deep and lasting effect on the intergenerational transmission of knowledge, practices, and skills. It is in this context that *Tapiskwan* was directed toward the development of intergenerational workshops designed to favor knowledge sharing and re-appropriation through creative activities.

This chapter is comprised of five sections. First, it discusses the historical context that motivates many First Peoples to actively nourish and, in some cases, reconnect with their cultural roots. It also briefly presents the social and economic situation of the Atikamekw. Second, it argues that culture is a central feature of sustainable development, both as a valuable resource and as an aspirational project. Third, it discusses several issues relative to cultural sustainability, in particular with respect to the effects of territorial transformations on culture. Fourth, it describes the principles and practices of *Tapiskwan*, a series of intergenerational design workshops led by the Atikamekw Nation and the Design School of Université de Montréal. Fifth, it presents some findings that have emerged from our experience so far, as well as possible next steps.

Historical context: Towards self-determination

Since the 1900s, due to intensive industrialization, the *Nitaskinan* (Atikamekw territory) has been subjected to intensive natural resource extraction and exploitation. During the same period, the Atikamekw were forcibly displaced several times due to the construction of hydro-electric dams that flooded much of their traditional territory. Since the 1960s and the sedentarization of many Atikamekw due to the reserve system, the community has seen its population grow just as its access to resources was being substantially diminished (Awashish 2013).

According to various social indicators of development (Tremblay 2006), the Atikamekw currently face a very challenging socio-economic reality, with particularly low levels of income, education, and employment (Statistics Canada 2006, 2011). Over seventy percent of the population of more than fifteen years of age does not hold a recognized degree, and approximately fifty percent of this age group is considered "inactive." While the nation's youth have great potential, many of them feel they have a limited future, and face serious social problems such as substance abuse, dropping out of school, and suicide epidemics.

There are direct links between these issues and Canada's governmental policies, and the devastating legacy of Canada's Indian Residential School policy (1820–1996) in particular. In general, the policies associated with the Indian Act have created, maintained, and worsened the social and economic gap that exists between the country's Indigenous and non-Indigenous population. As noted by First Nations' health officials, "The Indian Act is a specific juridical regime that unequivocally aims to place First Nations under the tutelage of the federal government" (Commission de la Santé et des Services Sociaux des Premières Nations du Québec et du Labrador (CSSSPNQL) 2013: 7). In 2008, the Canadian government presented an official apology regarding Residential Schools. The government acknowledged that "the consequences of the Indian Residential Schools policy were profoundly negative and that this policy has had a lasting and damaging impact on Aboriginal culture, heritage and language" (AANDC 2008). The following excerpts of then Prime Minister Stephen Harper's apology highlight the deep wounds the policy caused and their lasting effects on Indigenous people and Canadian society to this day.

> For more than a century, Indian residential schools separated over 150,000 Aboriginal children from their families and communities.
>
> … Two primary objectives of the residential schools system were to remove and isolate children from the influence of their homes, families, traditions and cultures, and to assimilate them into the dominant culture. These objectives were based on the assumption Aboriginal cultures and spiritual beliefs were inferior and unequal. Indeed, some sought, as it was infamously said, "to kill the Indian in the child." Today, we recognize that this policy of assimilation was wrong, has caused great harm, and has no place in our country.
>
> … The Government of Canada built an educational system in which very young children were often forcibly removed from their homes, often taken far from their communities. Many were inadequately fed, clothed and housed. All were deprived of the care and nurturing of their parents, grandparents and communities. First Nations, Inuit and Métis languages and cultural practices were prohibited in these schools. Tragically, some of these children died while attending residential schools and others never returned home.

The government's formal apology elicited ambivalent reactions and unfortunately did little to assuage the concern that it could do much more to address the consequences of its policies. Six years later, a 2014 United Nations report by special rapporteur James Anaya concluded that the gap between the quality of life of Indigenous peoples and non-Indigenous peoples in Canada continues to be alarming (UN 2014). Wanting to take things into their own hands, the Atikamekw Nation has been asking that the provincial and federal governments both recognize its ancestral territorial rights, as well as its right to self-government and well-being.

Culture: A resource and a project

Arguably, culture is an invaluable resource and a powerful leveraging point for sustainable development in vulnerable communities (UNESCO 2012). Culture can be defined as the complex assemblage of knowledge, values, customs, and resources a community inherits, adopts, and creates in order to flourish in its social and natural environment (Verhelst and Tyndale 2002). Culture also refers to the processes through which a society solves its problems and projects itself into the future (UNESCO 2009). As such, it is a key component of economic, social, and environmental sustainability (UNESCO 2012). Sustainable development aims to perpetually improve quality of life through reasoned and responsible uses of each community's tangible and intangible resources, protecting them against depletion, renewing them, as well as revealing new ones (Orr 2002; UNESCO 2009). As argued by anthropologists, cultures are alive and dynamic: "culture" is not something people "have" or inherit passively; rather, it is a project that is in a perpetual state of production (Sahlins 1999). Cultural heritage is the resources, meaning, and identity that each generation transfers to the next so that it can face new challenges equipped with a specific cultural matrix. In this sense, cultures are future-oriented projects that help humans draw on their past to imagine new aspirations and strive towards them (Appadurai 2004).

Prospering through protection, transmission, and innovation

Since 2011, the Atikamekw Nation Council (Conseil de la Nation Atikamekw, ANC) and the Design and Material Culture research group (Design et culture matérielle (DCM), Université du Québec à Chicoutimi and Université de Montréal) have been exploring how contemporary creation and innovation can be used to support cultural transmission and promotion. The DCM group uses design as a tool to reinterpret and re-appropriate culture (Kaine and Dubuc 2010). Founded in 1982, the ANC provides all three Atikamekw communities with administration, education, and culture services. In addition to these services, its mandate includes the protection of the rights and interests of the Atikamekw Nation, in particular in the context of negotiations with various representatives of the Federal and Provincial governments (ANC 2015).

Early on in the project, the ANC identified four main concerning issues, which are presented below. These were used to define *Tapiskwan*'s objectives, which were later refined during the participatory action research activities that were led in the field.

Intergenerational transmission

Elders are the holders of precious knowledge and know-how. They are an aging population and represent a small proportion of the Atikamekw population. In addition, many of those in the generation situated between the elders and the youth have a strained relationship to their cultural roots. Although there certainly are exceptions, most of those of the residential school generation have found it very difficult to partake in the process of intergenerational transmission, whether it is regarding familial responsibilities or cultural knowledge. Given this situation, how could the nation's living heritage continue to be perpetuated? What would help facilitate the re-appropriation of their culture by community members, including by the youth?

Heritage protection

All around the world, Indigenous communities rely on their culture in order to support their economic development. While such a strategy can have positive repercussions, including from the perspective of promoting local prosperity and identity in a globalized context, it also raises a number of questions. It is very common for Indigenous heritage to be exploited with neither the consent nor the participation of the community in question and its artists. In such cases, not only do they not receive any tangible benefits, they also see their culture being disrespected and folklorized. In this context, there is a real stake in Indigenous people being able to take part in the market and assert control over how their culture is represented. Under what conditions is it possible for Indigenous communities to foster economic development without feeling they have to "sell out" by way of cultural commodification? When only some cultural elements can be shared with outsiders, what are appropriate ways to safeguard the knowledge that should only circulate within the community? Whose responsibility is it to do so, and what means do they have in order to achieve this goal?

Imposed transformation vs. innovation

Territorial transformations and governmental policies have placed limitations on the Atikamekw's access to the raw materials necessary for the production of their material culture. And yet, collecting and preparing these materials are crucial activities for intergenerational transmission between elders and youth. These activities are also a means of identity formation and affirmation. The Atikamekw have been called the "people of the bark," celebrated for their exceptionally well-crafted birch bark canoes and baskets. However, wide-scale deforestation has turned birch bark into a scarce resource. Getting an appropriate supply of moose hide, another crucial material for Atikamekw art, poses a similar challenge. Not only does the Nitaskinan's transformation have an impact on culture, identity, and ways of life, it also has economic repercussions for the nation's artists and artisans. Indeed, access to raw materials has a direct effect on their ability to secure steady income from the items they produce. Furthermore, they often find themselves with little choice but to purchase materials they once harvested from their territory. In the face of such limitations, which stem from imposed territorial transformations, how can voluntary innovation processes help the Atikamekw identify and develop viable alternatives? Indigenous people have always been innovating in order to adapt to their ever-evolving circumstances and environments. How can this ability to innovate be used as leverage by the Atikamekw in order to address the challenges they face today?

The weight of consumer expectations

Many consumers who have an interest in products coming from other cultures than their own are looking for quality, affordable products. In Québec's Indigenous art market, however, these kinds of items are hard to find. While the Indigenous fine art market is on the rise, most inexpensive Indigenous-themed products are made off shore. This leaves an opening for middle-range Indigenous-made products that are able to convey meaning and identity (Christen 2006). Elsewhere in Canada, much of this market is dominated by non-Indigenous companies who draw on stereotypical images of indigeneity (Hill 2011). This tends to reinforce misrepresentations of Indigenous people, leading some consumers to wrongly associate "authentic traditions" to static production processes and meanings, and to expect the repetition of certain forms instead of seeking out innovative products (Bousquet 2008). Such expectations can compromise Indigenous artists and artisans' sense of rooted but continuously renewed identity (Kaine, De Coninck, and Bellemare 2010). How can the Atikamekw innovate in a way that effectively makes consumers revisit their expectations of Indigenous art?

Tapiskwan: Intertwining past and future

Based on the needs identified by the ANC and the expertise of the DCM research group, the project partners developed a model for intergenerational workshops that are focused on the creation by Atikamekw participants of products inspired by their cultural heritage (Marchand and Leitão 2014). Lasting anywhere between a few days to several weeks, the primary focus of these workshops is to help participants draw on their nation's cultural heritage to design new products by exploring different materials, mediums, and techniques.

This model was collaboratively developed based on exchanges between experienced Atikamekw artists, youth, cultural stewards, entrepreneurs, and Université de Montréal's non-Indigenous designers. A common vision of existing problems and opportunities came to light through their joint activities in the field. This process eventually led the team to focus the workshops more specifically on the intergenerational transmission and promotion of the nation's rich visual heritage through the creation of contemporary products based on Atikamekw iconography.

The Atikamekw's rich graphic heritage was clearly identified as a powerful vehicle for the transmission of knowledge, the affirmation of identity, and economic development. Atikamekw visual culture encompasses an elaborate system of symbols and adornments that convey meaning and elements of identity that are specific to the Atikamekw and to the families that make up the nation. This graphic heritage was found to be in and of itself a resource that could be exploited in new ways, using techniques and technologies that circumvent the issue of increasingly unavailable materials.

The first two editions of the *Tapiskwan* workshops took place in the summers of 2013 and 2014, each lasting approximately two weeks (see Figs 10.1–10.7). Around two dozen community members participated, most of them youth working under the guidance of Atikamekw knowledge holders and experienced artists, and two Université de Montréal designers. Taking inspiration from the iconography present on

FIGURE 10.1 Birch bark basket (unknown author and year), piece 0079–02. Courtesy Atikamekw Nation Council. © Conseil de la National Atikamekw.

the nation's material culture as well as stories told by elders, they designed bandanas, T-shirts, tote bags, and greeting cards. These were sold during special events and online.

Based on these two experiences, it became clear to all partners involved that, in order to have measurable cultural and economic impacts, future workshops would have to (1) put a stronger emphasis on cultural immersion, (2) include the development of a collective entrepreneurship model based on Atikamekw values, and (3) lead to more in-depth professional training opportunities. The following

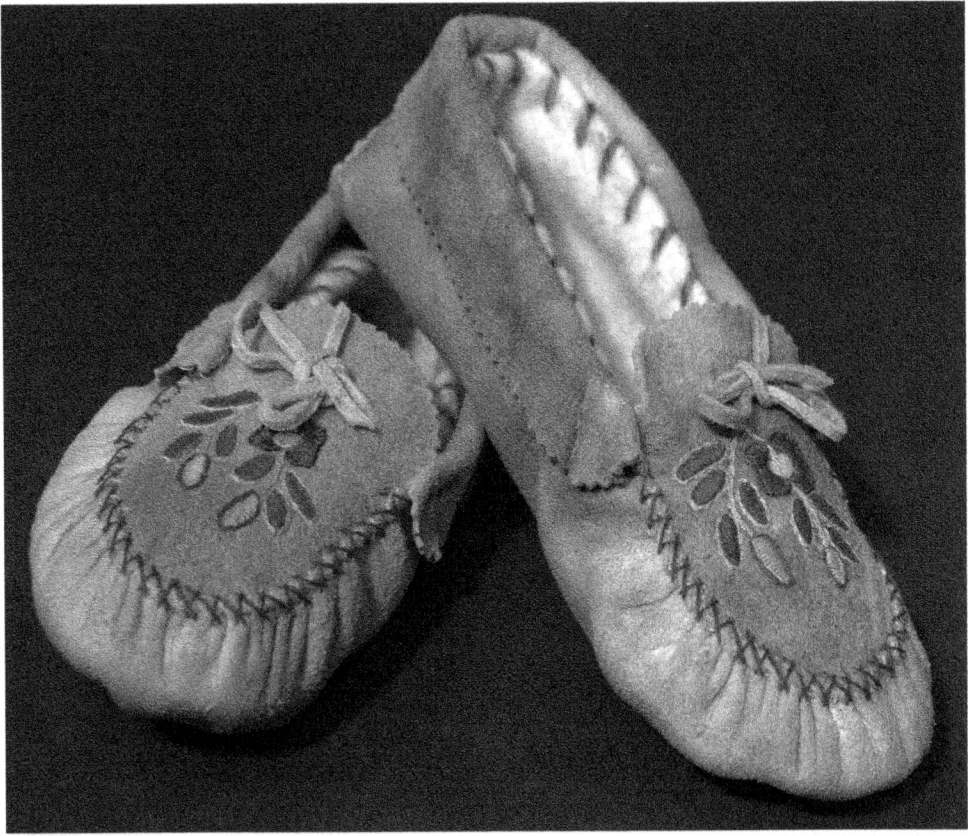

FIGURE 10.2 Moccasin (CHACHAI, Juliette, 2011), piece 0045–03. Courtesy Atikamekw
Nation Council. © Conseil de la National Atikamekw.

year's workshop program was created with these findings in mind, leading to two
additional partnerships. Montreal's foremost textile design school, the Centre
Design et Impression Textile de Montréal, was brought into the partnership for its
expertise in textile and printing techniques; the Nitaskinan Cooperative also joined
the partnership to assist with socio-economic development initiatives. Founded in
2015, the Co-op's objective is to provide a structure that supports initiatives in which
work, creativity, and development are used to foster cultural, social, environmental,
and economic well-being in First Nations' communities and beyond.

The third series of *Tapiskwan* workshops took place in the summer and fall of
2015, in the community of Wemotaci. This time, participants were introduced to a
variety of artisanal printing techniques, including block printing, stencil printing, and
silk-screening. Using these techniques, they (1) created finished products such as bags,
cushion covers, and booklets adorned with motifs directly inspired by Atikamekw
iconography and stories, and (2) designed fabric that could be distributed and sold
as a material for the creation of various products.

This 2015 workshop mobilized a little over a dozen Atikamekw community
members, including the participants (youth and adults), two experienced artists who

FIGURE 10.3 Youths draw images inspired by Atikamekw iconography during the Tapisk-wan workshops in Wemotaci, 2004. Courtesy Renata Marques Leitão. © Anne Marchand.

acted as mentors and coordinators (Jacques Newashish and Christiane Biroté), the nation's cultural services coordinator (Christian Coocoo), and one entrepreneur (Karine Awashish, co-founder of the Nitaskinan Co-op). In addition, the Montréal-based team, led by designer and professor Anne Marchand, was comprised of three designers (Renata Marques Leitão, Cédric Sportes, and Lucie Leroux, specializing in graphic, product, and textile design respectively), as well as one cultural anthropologist (Solen Roth). As explained in more detail below, the program was divided into four phases.

Phase 1: Cultural immersion—three days

The focus of this first phase was to share Atikamekw knowledge with those participants who did not possess it already, most notably some of the young people. The objective was to ensure they could immediately reinvest this knowledge in their artistic practice, and therefore each discussion was followed by a creative activity. Cultural stewards presented Atikamekw history and heritage through images of ancestral iconography and stories about their meaning and significance in Atikamekw culture. Immediately afterwards the participants were invited to partake in drawing exercises during which they were asked to select and reinterpret elements of Atikamekw iconography based on what had just been shared with them.

FIGURE 10.4 Participants listen carefully to cultural steward Christian Coocoo sharing knowledge on the foundations of Atikamekw visual culture, 2005. Courtesy Renata Marques Leitão. © Anne Marchand.

Phase 2: Visual composition—two days

During the second phase, the participants learned about the principles of visual composition, which they applied in a variety of exercises. The objective was that they use their nation's and family's iconography in order to create original and meaningful compositions and patterns. These creative activities were also an opportunity for the participants to become increasingly familiar with the motifs by experimenting with them.

Phase 3: Creation and printing—four days

The third phase focused on various printing and serigraphy techniques. The patterns and compositions developed in the previous phase were printed on fabric and paper so that these could serve as a new source of material for future artistic production. The participants used these samples to create several product prototypes, encouraging them to think about the commercial potential of their creations. Interspersed in these production activities were discussions about

FIGURE 10.5 Workshop participant and experienced seamstress Jeannette Boivin creating a composition with her drawings of the partridge, an animal of particular significance to the Atikamekw, 2015. Courtesy Renata Marques Leitão. © Anne Marchand.

community-based entrepreneurship, including an introduction to social economy by the Co-op Nitaskinan and a presentation about a successful co-op in an Algonquin community.

Phase 4: Collaborative production session—three days

While phases 1 to 3 took place back-to-back over the course of two weeks in the summer, phase 4 took place in the fall several weeks later. In an effort to maintain the project's momentum and capitalize on the participants' growing enthusiasm, it was decided to hold a three-day production workshop so that the participants could apply what they had learned to the creation of a small line of products. Several participants had indeed expressed the desire to use their newly acquired skills to create products for sale as soon as possible. Thus, a smaller group came together for an intensive three days of work. Using the motifs and patterns developed over the summer and reproduced in silk screening frames, they produced a series of cushion covers, bags, and booklets, with the intention of selling them as gifts during the holiday season.

FIGURE 10.6 Artist and coordinator Jacques Newashish showing off one of his textile creations, 2015. Courtesy Renata Marques Leitão. © Anne Marchand.

Findings and perspectives

The work accomplished so far has shed light on the opportunities and limitations of using design as a tool for the sustainable cultural and economic development of the Atikamekw Nation. As discussed below, diverse perspectives shared by the project's participants, elders, coordinators, cultural stewards, designers, and university researchers serve as the basis for the planning of future initiatives. After three consecutive years of workshops focused primarily on training, the partners now see *Tapiskwan* as a possible starting point for the creation of a local Indigenous business. However, interviews conducted with the participants during an internal evaluation of the 2015 workshop revealed several important issues.

Remarking that Atikamekw life is generally organized around the activities that take place during each of the region's six distinct seasons, it was pointed out that this rhythm ought to be taken into consideration when planning the next phases of the project. It became clear that taking part in *Tapiskwan*'s activities should not come into conflict with hunting, hide tanning, blueberry picking, or birch bark gathering, for instance. These activities, once crucial for survival, are more difficult to maintain today, but remain central to the Atikamekw way of life and represent privileged moments of cultural transmission and expression. Furthermore, while the

FIGURE 10.7 Examples of cushion cover (hand-printed on fabric and hand-sewn) and booklets (hand-printed on paper and assembled manually) that were created during the Phase 4 production workshop, 2015. Courtesy Lucie Leroux. © Anne Marchand.

Atikamekw are no strangers to collective and intensive work, chain production does not resonate particularly well with the project's partners and participants. The need for a collective organization of the production process that meshes well with the specifics of Atikamekw ways of life and values was strongly felt. A "bottom-up" approach that will help imagine a new model of Indigenous entrepreneurship is indispensable to turning *Tapiskwan* into a sustainable community initiative. At the same time, it is desirable to make professional training become more integral to the project, as studies show that traditional know-how tends to disappear when youth are unable to associate them with real professional perspectives (Leite 2005).

Serigraphic reproduction techniques were selected as a way to ensure the workshops could provide a sufficient volume of handmade, middle-range products that could reach other First Nations' communities as well as non-Indigenous consumers, all the while increasing the reputation of Atikamekw art. Artisanal printing techniques are less time-consuming than the beadwork and bark etching techniques that the Atikamekw use to create their artworks, which are usually expensive one-of-a-kind items. The ability to serially reproduce the same pattern represents an important advantage when aiming for the middle-range market that was identified in the early stages of the project. However, it is crucial to the success of the project overall that the workshops also continue to be used to facilitate intergenerational exchanges and cultural transmission. The social dimension of these activities will also help ensure the products created remain culturally relevant and meaningful. In order to avoid the pitfalls of cultural folklorization, it is essential to maintain cultural transmission as one of the project's central objectives, lest it be overshadowed by strictly economic considerations. This can only be done if due emphasis is placed on the role played in the project by elders and cultural stewards, as well as other reliable sources regarding the community's iconographic heritage, stories, and oral histories.

Conclusion

In summary, *Tapiskwan* is a community-based response to the threat of cultural assimilation posed by territorial transformations and their effects on Atikamekw material culture. The workshops place creativity at the heart of an approach to cultural and economic sustainability that aims to (1) further sensitize community members, and youth in particular, to their culture's important creative potential, (2) facilitate intergenerational transmission between elders and youth, and (3) support the community's efforts to lead the charge of their own future.

The participatory action research project presented in this chapter is based in an approach that favors social innovation as a way to find new answers to a dissatisfactory situation and improve individual and collective well-being (Cloutier 2003). It uses design as a tool to initiate and support social innovation processes (Brown and Wyatt 2010; Janzer and Weinstein 2014). The design process is informed by concrete situations and utilizes creative means to identify what needs to be done to improve a situation, and imagine ways to create a new reality (Nelson and Stolterman 2012). It is in this perspective that *Tapiskwan* draws on the Atikamekw

Nation's existing resources—the creative power of its youth and artists, as well as its rich visual heritage—to create a positive path forward.

In order for this initiative to become sustainable, it is important to continue developing an Indigenous model of collective entrepreneurship. This model should be based in ancestral Atikamekw values and principles, and foster the latter's transmission in a way that is adapted to their current lived reality. There is reason to believe that a collective approach to entrepreneurship would work well in an Atikamekw context because it offers a structure and a management dynamic that is already reflected in the community's values (Awashish and Verrier 2012). However, it is important to also realize that putting this model in place could prove challenging if the approach isn't carefully devised. Deciding exactly how resources will be used, members mobilized, and leadership shared will require careful consideration.

References

AANDC (2008), "Statement of Apology to Former Students of Indian Residential Schools," June 11. Available online: https://www.aadnc-aandc.gc.ca/eng/1100100015644/1100100015649 (accessed September 25, 2015).

AANDC (2015), "Tribal Council Details," January 23. Available online: http://pse5-esd5.ainc-inac.gc.ca/fnp/Main/Search/TCMain.aspx?TC_NUMBER=1064&lang=eng (accessed September 25, 2015).

ANC (2015), "Son Mandat." Available online: http://www.atikamekwsipi.com/son_mandat (accessed November 28, 2015).

Appadurai, A. (2004), "The Capacity to Aspire: Culture and the Terms of Recognition," in V. Rao and M. Walton (eds.), *Culture and Public Action*, 59–84, Palo Alto, CA: Stanford University Press.

Awashish, K. (2013), "Economie Sociale en Contexte Autochtone: La Création d'une Coopérative d'Artisanat Atikamekw," MA diss., Université du Québec à Trois Rivières, Trois Rivières.

Awashish, K. and J. Verrier (2012), "Mamo Otamirotan/Travallons Ensemble," *Les Cahiers du CIÉRA*, 9: 25–42.

Bousquet, M. P. (2008), "Tourisme, Patrimoine et Culture, ou que Montrer de Soi-Même aux Autres: Des Exemples Anicinabek (Algonquins) au Québec," in K. Iankova (ed.), *Le Tourisme Indigène en Amérique du Nord*, 17–42, Paris: Harmattan.

Brown, T. and J. Wyatt (2010), "Design Thinking for Social Innovation," *Stanford Social Innovation Review*, Winter 2010: 31–5.

Christen, K. (2006), "Tracking Properness: Repackaging Culture in a Remote Australian Town," *Cultural Anthropology*, 21 (3): 416–46.

Cloutier, J. (2003), "Qu'est-ce que l'Innovation Sociale?" *Cahier du CRISES—Collection Études théoriques*, ET0314 Montréal: CRISES.

Cole, D. (1985), *Captured Heritage. The Scramble for Northwest Coast Artifacts*, Vancouver: Douglas & McIntyre.

CSSSPNQL (2013), *Racisme et Discrimination envers les Premières Nations: Portrait Sommaire et Recommandations*, Wendake: CSSSPNQL/FNQLHSSC Publications.

Hill, L. L. (2011), "Indigenous Culture: Both Malleable and Valuable," *Journal of Cultural Heritage Management and Sustainable Development*, 1 (2): 122–34.

Janzer, C. L. and L. S. Weinstein (2014), "Social Design and Neocolonialism," *Design and Culture*, 6 (3): 327–43.

Kaine, E., P. De Coninck, and D. Bellemare (2010), "Pour un Développement Social Durable des Individus et des Communautés Autochtones par la Recherche Action/Création: le Design et la Création Comme Leviers de Développement," *Nouvelles Pratiques Sociales*, 23 (1): 33–52.

Kaine, E. and E. Dubuc (2010), *Passages Migratoires. Valoriser et Transmettre les Cultures Autochtones*, Sainte-Foy: Presses de l'Université Laval.

Leite, R. P. (2005), "Modos de Vida e Produção Artesanal: Entre Preservar e Consumir," in ArteSol (ed.), *Olhares Itinerantes—Reflexões Sobre Artesanato e Consumo da Tradição*, 27–41, São Paulo: Cadernos ArteSol.

Marchand, A. and R. Marques Leitão (2014), "Innovative Atikamekw Products Dedicated to the Global Marketplace," *The International Journal of Design in Society*, 7 (2): 87–101.

Nelson, H. G. and E. Stolterman (2012), *The Design Way: Intentional Change in an Unpredictable World*, 2nd edn, Englewood Cliffs, NJ: Educational Technology Publications.

Orr, D. W. (2002), *The Nature of Design: Ecology, Culture, and Human Intention*, New York: Oxford University Press.

Sahlins, M. (1999), "What is Anthropological Enlightenment? Some Lessons of the Twentieth Century," *Annual Review of Anthropology*, 28: i–xxiii.

Statistics Canada (2006), "Aboriginal Population Profile," December 6. Available online: http://www12.statcan.ca/census-recensement/2006/dp-pd/prof/92-594/index.cfm?Lang=E (accessed October 14, 2015).

Statistics Canada (2011), "Aboriginal People," October 15. Available online: http://www5.statcan.gc.ca/subject-sujet/theme-theme.action?pid=10000&lang=fra&more=0 (accessed October 15, 2015).

Tremblay, S. (2006), "Hétéronomie ou Coproduction du Développement Social: Réflexion sur l'Usage du Concept de Développement Social," in P. A. Tremblay, M. Roche, and S. Tremblay (eds.), *Le Développement Social, un Enjeu pour l'Économie Sociale*, 37–65, Québec: Presses de l'Université du Québec.

UNESCO (2009), *Investing in Cultural Diversity and Intercultural Dialogue*, UNESCO World Report, Paris: UNESCO.

UNESCO (2012), *Culture: A Driver and an Enabler of Sustainable Development*, UN System Task Team on the Post-2015 UN Development Agenda, Thematic Think Piece, Paris: UNESCO.

UN (2014), "The Situation of Indigenous Peoples in Canada," report of the special rapporteur on the rights of indigenous peoples, James Anaya, July 4. Available online: http://unsr.jamesanaya.org/docs/countries/2014-report-canada-a-hrc-27-52-add-2-en.pdf (accessed September 16, 2015).

Verhelst, T. and W. Tyndale (2002), "Cultures, Spirituality and Development," in D. Eade (ed.), *Development and Culture*, 1–24, Oxford: Oxfam.

11

Transforming Tradition in Indonesia

A Method for Maintaining Tradition in a Craft and Design Context

Adhi Nugraha

Introduction

Preserving, revitalizing, and transforming

There are three important issues for artists and designers when they work with traditional items: preserving, revitalizing, and transforming.

Preserving: Focuses on efforts to protect specific traditions that today are in rapid decline and in danger of becoming lost. The aim of preservation is to protect the original tradition as a whole, without any changes. For example, to preserve the boat building tradition, a particular traditional dance, or basket making within the aboriginal tribes.

Revitalizing: Focuses on traditions that are no longer practiced. It deals with reviving traditional practices and securing their future in contemporary society. An example is revitalizing the knowledge of using herbs in medical practice, which has gradually disappeared in modern society.

Transforming: Aims to reinvent an old form of tradition so that it fits into and suits contemporary lifestyles. The main difference between this activity and the two others is its goal, which is to create *a new form* from a particular tradition, whereas the aim of preserving and revitalizing is to *maintain* the tradition in its original form.

Some examples of transforming are: redesign of traditional woodworking tools for use with modern carpentry equipment; adapting traditional knowledge of house-building to create contemporary eco-friendly houses. There will be a more detailed discussion of these three issues later in this chapter. In the discussion, the three terms are often used in association with some specific idea, depending on the context of the discussion.

Examples from Indonesia

Indonesia is a country of diversity. As the largest archipelago in the world, it is home to a large variety of natural resources, peoples, cultures, traditions, tribes, and ethnicities, as well as creative expressions and art-craft traditions. This richness has made Indonesia a paradise for artists and designers whose work focuses on developing objects that are based on old traditions. Throughout the islands, a variety of traditional arts and handicrafts are still practiced and are available to artists and designers as sources of ideas and inspiration.

Until recently, in many parts of Indonesia, making art and handicrafts was regarded as a meaningful way of sustaining and strengthening social life, rather than just to make a living. Today, however, the traditional arts in Indonesia constitute a complex phenomenon that reflects a number of different developments. In some places, the method of making traditional objects is a direct continuation of old modes of work, reflecting practices that have been handed down over generations in communities in relatively isolated areas. In other places, the current generation of makers seems comfortable producing work for both ritual and commercial purposes, as is the case in Tana Toraja, Sulawesi. Elsewhere, some of the traditional arts survive because of the efforts of academic institutions to preserve old practices and train new generations of practitioners. And in other cases, traditions thrive because they are set in a contemporary commercial setting (Jaszy 2009: 5).

This former "paradise" is now endangered. As in many parts of the world, folk theaters shut down every year; traditional techniques of weaving, jewelry making, boatbuilding and basket making vanish; and many traditional children's games and toys disappear from everyday life. According to National Geographic, "about every two weeks another language disappears from everyday use, taking millennia of human knowledge and history with it" (Williams 2007: 26). Similarly, in Indonesia, some traditional art and handicraft productions have declined, and knowledge of techniques is at risk of being lost (Jaszy 2009: 6).

In such situations, projects that deal with the preservation, revitalization and transformation of traditions in Indonesia are valuable because they can help keep these traditions alive. However, an appropriate strategy and suitable method are needed, not only for the purpose of preservation, but also to make sure that traditions are kept alive in appropriate ways. It is important for a country like Indonesia to pay significant attention to this issue or its heritage will be lost. Moreover, many principles emerge from vernacular designs, old techniques and traditional knowledge, all of which are valuable for our contemporary ways of life, especially in today's context where sustainability is such an important issue (see

Howes 1980; Papanek 1984; Reason and Bradbury 2001; Benyus 2002; Walker 2006; Snell and Callahan 2009). In this regard, it is important to recognize that some valuable folk arts and traditional crafts vanish because they are not developed to suit the changing needs of contemporary lives (Steadman 1979; Williams 1981). Traditions have to constantly change and adapt in order to stay relevant—otherwise they die.

Fortunately, there is a growing awareness among artists, craftspeople, designers, and art-design educational institutions of the loss of traditional knowledge and practices, and the importance of preserving them. This contribution plays a large role in transforming various traditional objects and making them available for today, as well as for the future. In particular cases, however, there is a limited number of local artisans and craft communities able to design and produce the type of objects that would suit contemporary needs. Some attempts at redeveloping and reproducing traditional items, such as souvenirs for tourists, seem futile as long as they continue to be of very poor quality, whether in the materials used, their design, their intended use, the making techniques employed, or any combination of these. On the other hand, artists, designers or students from outside the region who aim to help, often do not have a clear understanding of context or clear strategies, methods or tools to guide the creative process of reviving the particularities and developing the potential of a tradition. To do this more effectively, they need a specific model, an appropriate tool to be used in the creative process of the transformation of tradition.

Transforming tradition

"Tradition": In this chapter, the term is associated mainly with words such as old, past times, outdated, pre-industrial, simple, handmade, indigenous, vernacular, and less-integrated economies. This is in contrast to the words such as up-to-date, novel, innovative, dynamic, new, hi-tech, industrial, machine-made, technological, and progressive.

Furthermore, "tradition" in this discussion refers to any kind of "valuable" old practice, method, object or product that is disappearing or being gradually replaced by the new. This occurs because such traditional practices and products tend to be considered impractical, old fashioned, or out-of-date, and no longer relevant.

Why tradition?

Tradition is regarded with interest today for several reasons. First, it can strengthen cultural identity. According to Alver (1992: 66), tradition has become important to many nations as a "counter-culture" to the dominant culture of globalization. Giving tradition a new life has become a national pursuit; in local communities across the globe there is a strong sense of need to assert one's identity. The second factor is concern over the loss of valuable knowledge. Most traditional knowledge and practice is silent or "tacit." As Dormer (1994: 148) argues, if the practitioners fail to pass on their knowledge, there is a risk of losing it. Reconstructing lost knowledge can be very difficult and time consuming.

Third, tradition gives us many lessons in balancing life and living in harmony with nature. Scientific studies have shown that much traditional knowledge and many traditional practices and artifacts often reflect a harmonious balance between aesthetics and function, and physical and ideological purposes, integrated with economic and ecological concerns. Such a quality is the result of thousands of years of accumulated practices, experiences, and collective wisdom, handed down over many generations (Papanek 1984; Williams 1981). Different studies of traditional knowledge systems have also shown that traditional and indigenous knowledge, practices and artifacts that have been passed on from one generation to another, are of excellent quality in both use and design; many of them are still in use today.

Social anthropologist Michael Howes (1980) has shown that various indigenous knowledge bases and practices often have a comparative advantage for sustainable improvements in the environment and in people's lives, especially in relation to their ability and empirical understanding of localized ecosystems. In Howes's opinion, it is necessary to explore the use of such knowledge so it might be assimilated with existing science and technology.

Some studies confirm that the majority of indigenous practices tend to function within, and correspond to, nature. Cultures that depend directly on hunting, gathering, and fishing, as Janine Benyus (2002: 294) notes, tend to work out codes of behavior that honor both product and source. It is considered strictly taboo, for example, to kill more animals than one needs, or to waste any part of an animal. According to the laws of nature, nothing is waste, and an organism uses only the energy it needs.

In the field of architecture, we can learn valuable lessons from the traditional practices of house building. What makes most vernacular buildings a good model is that they are predominantly made of local materials and fit ecologically with the local climate, flora, fauna, and ways of life (Papanek 1995: 118). In Papanek's view, all these aspects of ecological suitability, human scale, craftsmanship, and commitment to quality, combine very effectively to give a true elegance to vernacular architecture.

It is not simply a romantic idea that modern societies should, perhaps, look back and learn from the past: traditional practices took into consideration nature, climate, and the environment. Our entire world needs, as Papanek says, "a great spiritual rebirth or reawakening, a desire to re-establish closer links between nature and humankind. Deeply embedded in our collective unconscious is the intuitive awareness of our relationship to the environment" (1995: 9).

To maintain tradition is to keep developing it

"What does it mean to maintain tradition in a craft, and to design context?" To answer this philosophical question, it is important to first understand the fundamental difference between preservation and transformation. Both terms are used frequently to express the meaning of maintaining tradition:

Preservation is concerned with *protecting* buildings and objects, and keeping them in their original state. The aim is to maximize the amount of the original material, in as unaltered a condition as possible, that is preserved (Bjorneberg 2016). Preservation refers to an act of carefully protecting a tradition, preventing any exploitation or destruction, and maintaining the practice and/or the product in its original form.

Transformation deals with reviving and revitalizing through change. Abdul Wahab (2008: 9) defines the term as changing, altering, or transferring. In the case of batik, for example, transformation means to alter and reinterpret batik, and it may mean going beyond conventional ideas of batik to improve or update it for modern needs or tastes. (Batik is a traditional technique of applying motif and color to a fabric using wax-resist dyeing. Wax drawings are made using a spouted tool called a "canting.") In contrast to preservation, transformation means continuous development and change. It is based on the philosophy that in the real-world situation, there is no stability; nothing is stagnant; everything changes; everything is connected to everything else; and everything works together in a never-ending process (McNiff and Whitehead 2010). Based on this principle, therefore, to be sustainable, things have to be constantly revived, revitalized, restored, and transformed (Steadman 1979; Williams 1981).

Among craft and design activities, it is rare to find cases that are representative purely of preservation. It is evident that the essence of maintaining tradition in a craft and design context fits more readily with the idea of transformation. Most curricula in the art, craft, and design education worldwide emphasize exploring and developing new ideas, not purely preserving existing objects. Typically, artists' and designers' curiosity drives their creativity and proposals for fresh ideas. The main task of the artist and designer is to consider "how to develop things," not "how to preserve things." They aim not to violate an esteemed tradition, but instead, to give it fresh possibilities for a new existence. For example, jewelry designers may have a great deal of interest in traditional jewelry. They will then carefully study the original meanings of ornaments that have emerged through tradition and document through text, images, and objects. However, they do not stop here. Employing their creative imagination and skills, they will often create new forms of jewelry, inspired by their collected knowledge of form, ornament, technique, and symbol, all of which are based in the tradition they studied. This is what a designer means by reviving or maintaining tradition.

Nevertheless, there certainly are a number of artists and designers around the globe who are greatly interested in preservation and conservation work. Some are happy to produce traditional designs using traditional methods that are exactly the same as in the past, such as forged metal objects, jewelry, baskets, or even old houses. Others may work for various institutions concerned with heritage conservation. It is important to respect both "preservers" and "transformers" because they are both contributing to making different traditions available and easily accessible today and in the future.

Consequently we can say that, viewed within a craft and design context, the appropriate interpretation of "maintaining tradition" is to keep developing it. In other words, to maintain tradition is to constantly update it to keep it relevant. Hence, the key to maintaining tradition lies in the "transformation of tradition." Transforming tradition means connecting it to modernity. By linking tradition with modernity, we update it and give it new possibilities for living and working within contemporary contexts.

The "ATUMICS" method: A tool for transforming tradition

In 2012, as a key goal of the author's doctoral dissertation at Aalto University in Finland, a method for transforming tradition was proposed, which was termed the ATUMICS method (see Figure 11.1). ATUMICS is an acronym for **Artifact, Technique, Utility, Material, Icon, Concept and Shape**; these are the six fundamental elements related to an artifact. They result from an analysis of various conceptions of artifact and product design, as taught in most art and design schools and proposed by many design scholars. The main aim of creating ATUMICS was to propose a method that can be used as a tool for artisans, craft communities, designers, students and design practitioners when carrying out work that deals with maintaining tradition.

Practically, one can use the ATUMICS model as a guide in the process of creating a new object or system. When designing a new object inspired from tradition, the ATUMICS method is used to inform the designer which factors should be considered; which elements of tradition or contemporaneousness can be used in producing new objects/products; and how to combine these traditions with contemporary elements. The ATUMICS was created to help artists and designers to conceptualize ideas systematically, by providing a clear scheme and "step by step" ideation process.

Six fundamental elements of an artifact

The "A" in the model refers to **Artifact** or object, which acts as the centerpiece of the activity of transformation of tradition. The other elements to be considered in the transformation process are described below:

Technique (T)—suggests any kind of technical knowledge or technology, such as a production process, way of making or producing things, skills, tools, and other facilities. Each type of technical processing brings its own consequences. Application of new tools and technologies can offer new possibilities for traditional forms, and, at the same time, can simplify the work process. It is important to know that, as tacit knowledge, traditional technical skills will survive only by keeping the practice alive. If not handed on to other people, it will disappear when the artist or craftsperson who holds that knowledge dies. Unfortunately, the loss of traditional, technical skills often also results in the loss of the specialized tools. For example, if the hand drawn process of making traditional batik in Java were to vanish completely, no more "*canting*" would be produced and developed (*canting* is a small brass jug with a wooden handle that is used as a pen for drawing on the fabric).

Utility (U)—refers to the functionality and usability of a product. It relates to Aristotle's term "purpose," and Papanek's (1995: 34) term "use." Utility or functionality has always been connected with form. A valuable lesson one could learn from nature about functionality is that "nature fits form to function" (Benyus 2002: 7). Many traditional cultures have created locally specific artifacts, which in their materials and idioms of form and function were an integral part of the harmonious environment as a whole. Utility is also correlated with the concepts of need, fear, desire, and demand (Joedawinata 2005; Mänty 1985; Papanek 1995), in relation to nature and the cultural system that the community supports. A bamboo basket may represent not only functionality, but also the availability of local resources, the skill of the maker, and the desire, hopes, and fears of the community.

Material (M)—refers to "any physical matter from which things can be made or which can be used for a specific purpose" (Fulton 1992: 1). Material has been classified in many ways. Grenier (2006) divides all materials into three categories: natural, synthetic, and composite. However, it is also common for people to classify materials into two main groups: natural and synthetic, or traditional and new. In general, most traditional materials are classified—but not always—as natural. They include wood, bamboo, clay, stone, rubber, glass or metal. Some materials, such as natural fiber, rice straw, leaf, rattan, coconut shell and stone might be strongly associated with their locale. Many are specific to a particular geographic area. Products that use a specific local material often express a strong relationship to the place where they originated.

Icon (I)—can be any form of local images that emerge from nature, color, myth, people, or artifacts. In the ATUMICS method, the role of "icon" is to give a distinctive image and symbolic meaning to an object. To a certain extent, Buddhist and Hindu temples, rice fields, noodles and woks seem to be strong images throughout Asia. On a smaller scale, each culture has its own specific images, which are often used as icons or identifiers to distinguish objects from those made elsewhere. It is important to note here that the term "icon" in this paper refers mainly to 2D ornamentation or object decoration.

Concept (C)—refers to hidden factors that exist beyond objects and forms. These factors deal mostly with things that can be understood qualitatively, such as customs, norms, beliefs, characteristics, feelings, emotions, spirituality, values, ideology, and culture. Concept is what Papanek (1995: 136) means by "social needs, status, or religion morality that all influence the existence of the object." In an object, "concept" or hidden factors are best understood through its visual performance, whether emerging in its shape, icon or utility.

Shape (S)—refers to 3-dimensional form, performance, and visual and physical properties of an object. It also involves the notions of *Gestalt*, size, structure, and proportion. The most commonly substituted word for shape is "form." Many shapes of traditional artifacts have been taken as inspiration by artists, craftspeople, and designers for their creations. Today, for example, ceramic artists continually produce new teapots that are often inspired by previous designs. Old shapes of cooking utensils give inspiration for craftspeople and designers to make new kitchenware. Different shapes in traditional architecture have inspired architects to create contemporary, neo-traditional, buildings.

Motivation background

Figure 11.1 shows that there are an additional six components of the ATUMICS method. These are: cultural, social, ecological, economic, survival, and self-expression, and they are closely related to the six fundamental elements of an artifact. When creating new objects, a harmonious balance must be established between these components. At this stage, it should be noted that the creation of an object may vary in emphasis and motivation. Whether pursued for cultural or commercial reasons, or driven by ecological concerns, the process of transformation starts with the identification of certain features of tradition that have the potential to be developed. These can be a specific material, a fascinating shape, an old ornament, or a particular production technique. The next task is to explore the new elements of today that might work well with specific characteristics of the tradition we plan to develop. Here we are questioning, for instance, which new technology can be applied to the traditional elements in question, or which new materials can be combined with the particular traditional form and technique.

As shown in Figure 11.1, the process of merging tradition and newness occurs on the platform, which is drawn as a pyramid form. This pyramid represents the volume of the production of objects we are aiming or willing to produce. The higher up, the fewer will be produced, and the lower down, the greater volume of production. So the pyramid shows that its peak is the most appropriate position for art-craft objects because these items are usually made as single pieces or in a very limited numbers. This scheme also correlates with the type of field and the person creating the object. For example, the art located at the peak of the triangle indicates a small production volume and is related to independent artists, craftspeople, or studio arts and crafts, while the design located at the bottom of the pyramid indicates large production volumes corresponding to industrial scale manufacture (Nugraha 2012: 208).

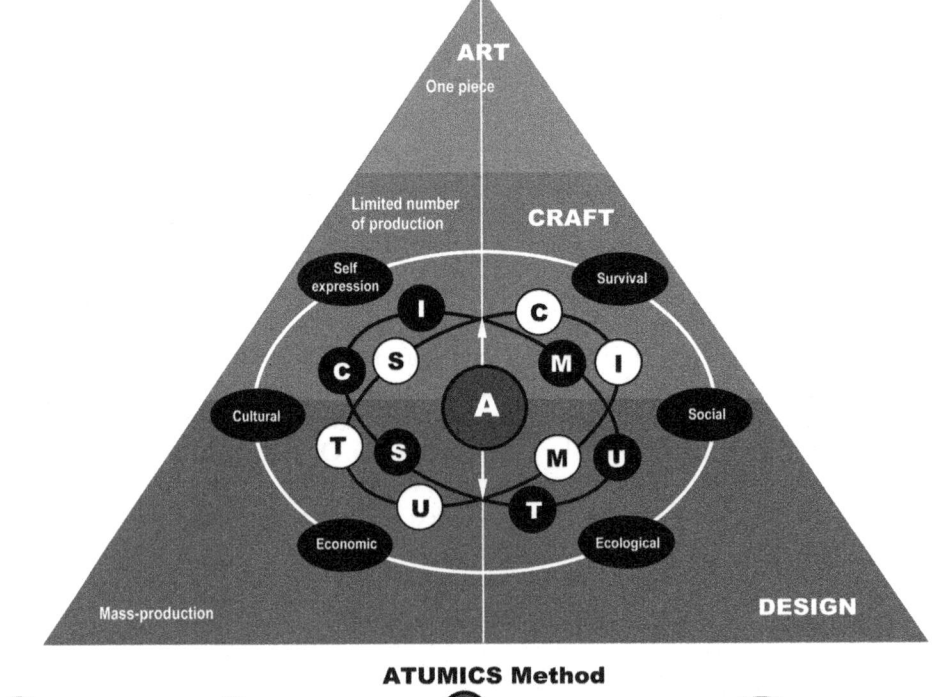

FIGURE 11.1 The ATUMICS Method. © Adhi Nugraha.

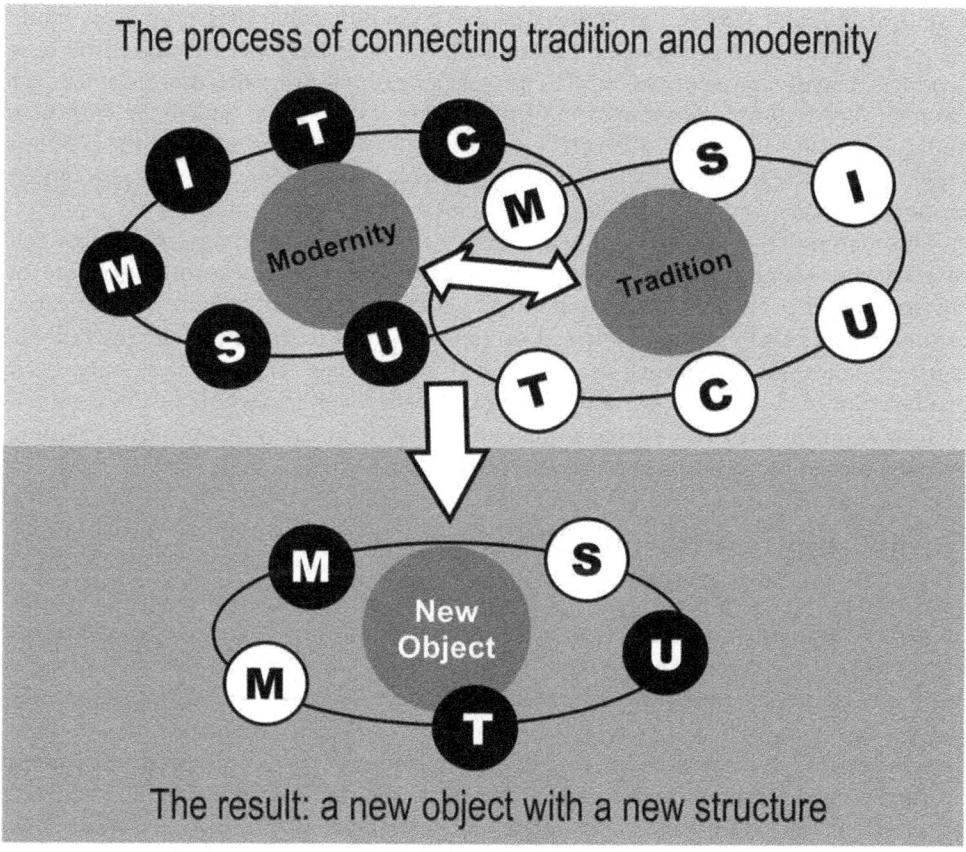

FIGURE 11.2 The Process of Transforming Tradition. © Adhi Nugraha.

The transformation process, i.e. "the integration of tradition and newness," works by connecting six fundamental elements from both tradition and newness. As shown in Figure 11.1, two distinct colors are used to differentiate between the elements; tradition in white, and newness in black. When the elements of tradition and newness are connected, they will produce a specific structure that reflects the new object we want to create: a blend of the old and the new, which can be craft or design. Figure 11.2 shows the process of transforming tradition that has achieved a particular structure for a new product, which combines elements of traditional material and shape with new material, technique, and utility.

Examples of transforming tradition

Coconization

The "Coconization" project is an example of the process of transforming tradition shown in Figure 11.2. The project was one of author's research projects that aimed to redesign traditional utensils made of coconut shell. Many utensils made of coconut shell have disappeared from daily use and have been replaced by new products, usually made of plastic. The project's result shows a new development for the utensils based on a combination of the traditional material and shape with new material (laminated wood), a new technical solution to join the wood to the coconut bowl, and a new function. "Coconization," which has ecological issues as its main motivation, has given a traditional material—coconut shell—a new life.

This material, re-born through new design, offers many advantages. Coconut shell as a natural material is readily available, inexpensive, and does not contribute to environmental problems. The production of utensils does not require sophisticated technology. It can be optimally based on existing local technology that is available in the villages, so it sustains local technical knowledge. The products have been produced in medium-scale workshops in Java. Moreover, the whole business model of Coconization provides an economic contribution to many people by providing employment in the creative industry sector (see Fig 11.3).

Animal figure—Jewelry box

The jewelry box project aimed to demonstrate another way of creating a new object by transforming traditional materials, techniques, and ornamentations into a new form and a new function. The design was meant to be used as a template, which can be adopted anywhere using different techniques, materials, shapes, and ornamentations, according to local regional conditions. The benefit of this strategy is that each society can keep developing designs that are rooted in their own culture and environment, so there will be different products created by different communities. For example, one village may produce a jewelry box made of bamboo with additional ornaments adopted from its textile products, while another village may create a similar box but using wood carved with figures that are transformed from the decorative patterns on local boats. This could then allow local people to contribute to sustainable development by making effective use of their own local resources. As with the Coconization project, this jewelry box project contributes to the local economy by generating income in the creative economy (tourism) sector.

Java Cutlery

Java Cutlery shows a specific approach where the "concept" or "hidden factor" is central. This cutlery aims to symbolize the value and function of Indonesian eating culture. Its language of shape and form demonstrate the dominant role of the right hand in society and also the function of the implement: a knife is not used for eating, instead, people use a spoon in the right hand and a fork in the left (see Fig 11.4).

Wok cooking set

The wok cooking set represents a design approach that is inspired by the image, shape, and function of a traditional wok. It uses both traditional and new materials

FIGURE 11.3 Coconization. Courtesy Nugraha. © Adhi Nugraha.

FIGURE 11.4 Java Cutlery. Courtesy Nugraha. © Adhi Nugraha.

FIGURE 11.5 Wok cooking set. Courtesy Nugraha. © Adhi Nugraha.

(wood, bamboo, and stainless steel) and new production techniques. The set is designed to serve a traditional Asian type of cooking that suits the contemporary lifestyle (see Fig 11.5).

The cases above are examples of how ATUMICS works in different settings, with a variety of motivations and intentions. By mixing the six elements of tradition and the six elements of newness, combined with the six aspects of motivation, the application of the ATUMICS method can result in a rich diversity of new objects. Since 2012, it has been tested and applied in a range of applications and practices. The "Revitalization of Tradition" lecture series has been delivered to Master's students of the Design Department at Bandung Institute of Technology (ITB), which uses ATUMICS as one of its key teaching methods. It is interesting to see that there have been many fresh ideas and exciting results emerging from this course for developing traditional artifacts and practices in Indonesia.

The results of experiments conducted by students over three years vary in the focus of interest and the scale of product category. Some students have focused on redesigning traditional artifacts or products, while others have been concerned with the system, traditional technical knowledge and practices. In the product category, one group of students proposed a redesign of a traditional Javanese toy that was in danger of disappearing. Another group revitalized a traditional textile in Bali called *Gringsing* and developed it as a raw material for the fashion market. Others took the significant role of the traditional puppet show and transformed it into the main role, or icon, of a new web game and applications for mobile phones (see Fig 11.6).

Within the focus of interest category, there has been a proposal to re-brand a traditional herbal drink called *Jamu* for it to be re-accepted into society, especially by the younger generation. One working group proposed an event for transforming a traditional barter system for the use of hobby-based communities, such as book

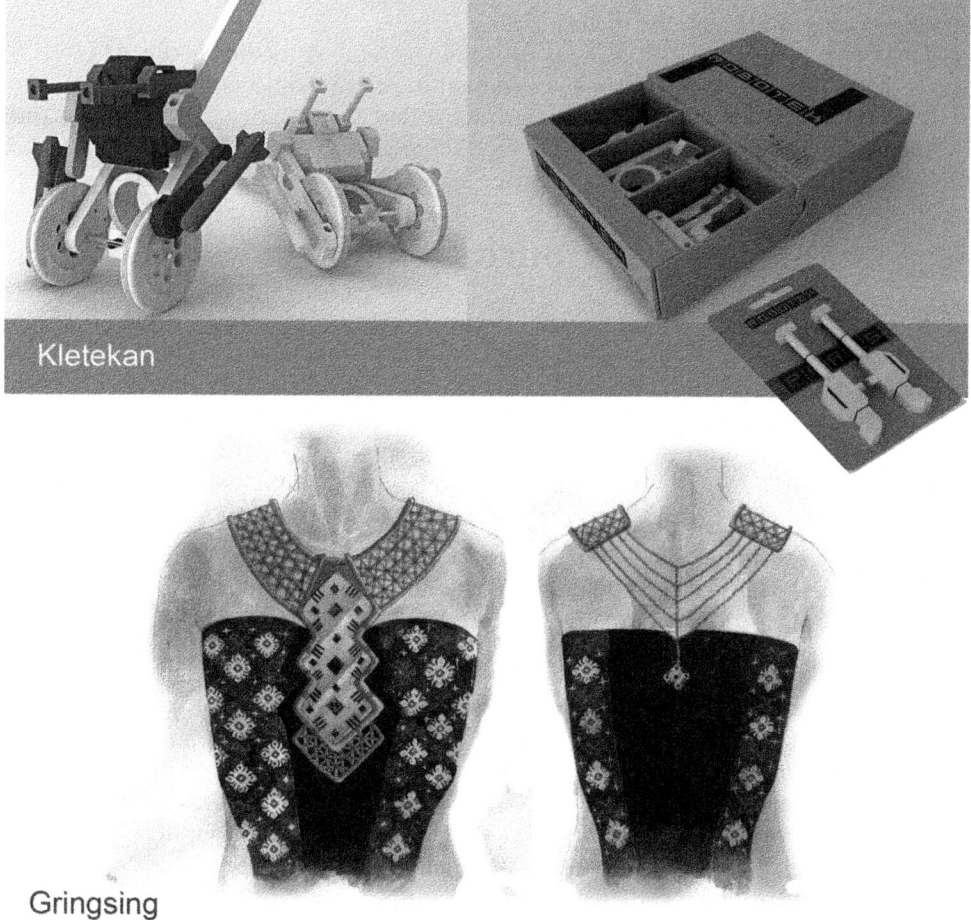

Kletekan

Gringsing

FIGURE 11.6 Student works: transforming the traditional Javanese toy *kletekan*, and the traditional Balinese textile *Gringsing* for the fashion market. Courtesy Nugraha. © Adhi Nugraha.

lovers, vintage motorcycle collectors and music clubs, using modern technology applications. Another group developed game applications, education tools, and an outdoor theme park for learning how to write old Sundanese script in new and enjoyable ways.

These various and interesting student projects have been a success in many ways. Primarily, they showed deep concern about issues of locality, cultural roots, and cultural identity in relation to the continuing pressure of globalization. Through interdisciplinary teamwork, they have proposed creative solutions to a diversity of problems by using the newest technology but without losing their traditional roots and identity. Some projects have demonstrated models of products or systems that address the balance between nurturing culture and preserving the environment; maintaining local handicrafts and developing community; or strengthening cultural identity and applying new technologies. Altogether, the results reflect a wide-ranging exploration of the use of the ATUMICS method and, in the process, they have contributed to improving the method.

As well as being presented in many seminars and workshops, the ATUMICS method has also been applied in the production of craft objects in Indonesia. The results are a diverse selection of new products that maintain rich expressions and features of tradition.

Conclusion

This chapter asserts that the true meaning of maintaining tradition is to continuously develop it. It also suggests that traditional and contemporary can, and should, go hand-in-hand. Traditions should be regarded as constituents of a life worth living. No element of contemporary technology could exist without a long tradition behind it that has made it possible. It is, therefore, critical to maintain tradition, as expressed in the old Javanese saying, "we need to preserve tradition, not only as a heritage of our ancestors, but also as a valuable gift and lesson to live."

In contemporary society, where "newness" is rapidly and constantly accelerating, the fundamental role of tradition is to make these new inventions and innovations more "humane," down-to-earth, and have meaning for societies. In this scenario, tradition can be very useful for the contemporary setting, in ways that will keep all aspects of our contemporary lives connected to their roots.

The ATUMICS method is intended to be used as a tool to keep tradition updated, through a transformation and integration process of six fundamental elements of tradition and newness. As long as at least one element of a particular tradition is transformed in the creation of new objects, a part of that tradition will be kept alive and sustainable. By bridging tradition and contemporary settings, we connect the past and our history with the present and the future.

The ATUMICS method has been developed based on the belief that every culture and every society should continue to flourish based on their own roots, their unique natural resources, their history, and their choices. It shows "how to be up-to-date without losing our own roots, our own tradition."

References

Abdul Wahab, F. (2008), "Transforming Tradition for Contemporary Context towards Shaping of Identity," *National Art Gallery Malaysia*. Available online: http://www.artgallery.gov.my/html/themes/bsln/artikel/kpkkk.pdf (accessed December 12, 2011).

Alver, B. (1992), "The Making of Traditions and the Problem of Revitalization," in R. Kvideland (ed.), *Tradition and Modernization*, 66–9, Turku: Nordic Institute of Folklore.

Benyus, J. M. (2002), *Biomimicry: Innovation Inspired by Nature*, New York, NY: Harper Collins Publishers Inc.

Bjorneberg, B. (2016), "Renovation, Restoration, Preservation, Conservation," Conservation and Design International, A publication of DPR Art Resque, March. Available online: http://www.conservation-design.com/newsletter1_BA.html (accessed April 24, 2017).

Dormer, P. (1994), *The Art of the Maker: Skill and Its Meaning in Art, Craft, and Design*, London: Thames and Hudson Ltd.

Fulton, J (1992), *Materials in Design and Technology*, London: The Design Council.

Grenier, J. (2006), "From Materials to Design," in R. Guidot (ed.), *Industrial Design Techniques and Materials*, 88–263, Paris: Flammarion.

Howes, M. (1980), "The Uses of Indigenous Technical Knowledge in Development," in D. Brokensha, D. M. Warren, and O. Werner (eds), *Indigenous Knowledge Systems and Development*, 102–23, Washington, DC: University Press of America.

Jaszy, P. A. (2009), *Traditional Culture: A Step Forward for Protection in Indonesia, A Research Report*, Jakarta, Indonesia: Institute for Press and Development Studies.

Joedawinata, A. (2005), "Unsur-unsur Pemandu dan Kontribusinya Dalam Perwujudan Sosok Artefak Tradisional Dengan Indikasi-indikasi Lokal yang Dikandung dan Dipancarkannya," Ph.D. thesis, Institut Teknologi Bandung, Bandung.

McNiff, J. and J. Whitehead (2010), *You and Your Action Research Project*, London: Routledge.

Mänty, J. (1985), *Principles of Architecture*, Tampere: Datutop-Department of Architecture Tampere University of Technology Occasional Papers.

Nugraha, A. (2012), *Transforming Tradition: A Method for Maintaining Tradition in a Craft and Design Context*, Helsinki: Aalto University Publication Series.

Papanek, V. (1984), *Design for the Real World: Human Ecology and Social Change*, London: Thames and Hudson.

Papanek, V. (1995), *The Green Imperative: Ecology and Ethics in Design and Architecture*, London: Thames and Hudson.

Reason, P. and H. Bradbury (2001), "Introduction: Inquiry and Participation in Search of a World Worthy of Human Aspiration," in P. Reason and H. Bradbury (eds), *Handbook of Action Research: Participative Inquiry & Practice*, 1–14, London: Sage Publications Ltd.

Snell, C. and Callahan, T. (2009), *Building Green: A Complete How to Guide to Alternative Building Methods*, New York: Lark Books, A Division of Sterling Publishing Co., Inc.

Steadman, P. (1979), *The Evolution of Designs: Biological Analogy in Architecture and the Applied Arts*, London: Cambridge University Press.

Walker, S. (2006), *Sustainable by Design: Exploration in Theory and Practice*, London: Earthscan.

Williams, A. R. (2007), "A World Loses Its Tongue," *National Geographic Magazine*, October, 212 (4): 26.

Williams, C. (1981), *Origin of Form*, London: Intermediate Technology Publications Ltd.

12

New Translations of South Korean Patterns

Meong Jin Shin

Introduction

Traditional products express cultural values as a symbol of a certain time and to certain members of a society (Shweder and LeVine 1984: 88). Those things of which there is common understanding, such as textiles, clothing, music, furniture, and the totality of our symbolic universe, can be perceived as cultural (Davis 1992: 13).

Culturally influenced design, as a strategic marketing perspective, can be employed as the basis for competitive advantage or product differentiation (Farr 1966: 6). It is important for businesses to have the skill of storytelling and knowledge of cultural understanding as they try to create products and brand identities that have meaning—functional, cultural, mythical, symbolic, and ethical meaning—around the world (Munnecke and Van der Lugt 2006: 8).

Traditional textile patterns express historical and cultural values that reflect native cultures through national values and shared history (Hyun and Bae 2007: 140). Design elements used in traditional textiles—patterns, colors, forms, materials, constructions, and functions—can reflect cultural identity and national image. In the textile and fashion industries it can be important to develop culturally influenced products that are distinct in terms of cultural identity and stylish in their design (Hyun and Bae 2007: 139).

Textile designs and concepts that are culturally influenced incorporate the significance of their textile history as a mean of creating, producing and marketing new innovative designs. Harnessing the power of modern technical design capabilities (e.g. computer-aided design, graphic programs etc.) with the creative heritage of traditional textiles can facilitate the development of commercial possibilities within the textile and fashion areas (Perivoliotis 2005: 1). Creating a product with a cultural style can also enhance existing product lines leading to new market opportunities (Power and Scott 2004). For these reasons, textile designers should be encouraged to consider design processes that can convey traditional values as well as the new values through their textile designs.

The aim of this chapter is to introduce the design reinvention process as applied to the Korean cultural textile *bojagi*. Historically, these were cloths used for wrapping as well as for covering, storing, and carrying everyday objects. To apply the process, a computer-based design tool has been developed that enables digital manipulation of the traditional design components to create fashion *bojagi* patterns suitable for a specified market. A model of design reinvention for traditional Korean *bojagi* is proposed and a process to develop the computer-based *bojagi* design tool is illustrated. New fashion *bojagi* designs have been created with the design tool and textile samples of the design prototypes have been produced using digital printing. Findings from in-depth interviews conducted with UK fashion retailers and designers to evaluate design values and commercial values of the generated *bojagi* design prototypes and the textile samples are also provided.

The concept of design reinvention for traditional textiles

Design reinvention is a way to translate traditional cultural products into modern products, presenting something entirely new while maintaining a story or a message that involves the development of an existing product (Shin, Cassidy, and Moore 2015).

The first step of the design reinvention of traditional textiles is the identification of the cultural values in its traditional textiles, e.g. patterns, colors, forms, materials, constructions, and functions. The second step is the understanding of the design business, which is based on product development with the involvement of marketing. The last step is reinvention, which is considered to be an important element of the design process for producing commercially successful cultural products. Here, two principal ways to reinvent traditional textiles are suggested: (1) through modernization or contemporizing and (2) through popularization or globalization (see Figure 12.1).

These processes of modernization and contemporizing are connected with design strategies for translating traditional textile products into offerings adapted for contemporary markets. The concept of modernization and its desire to exploit the latest materials, technology and construction methods are expressed through new forms and designs of traditional textile products (Bhaskaran 2005: 122; Holder 1990: 123). Technological innovation drives modernization of traditional textile designs; the success of technological innovation resides in the marketplace (Gaynor 2002: 17).

The other route to reinvention is the popularizing and globalizing of traditional textile products worldwide. These processes are more related to marketing strategies;

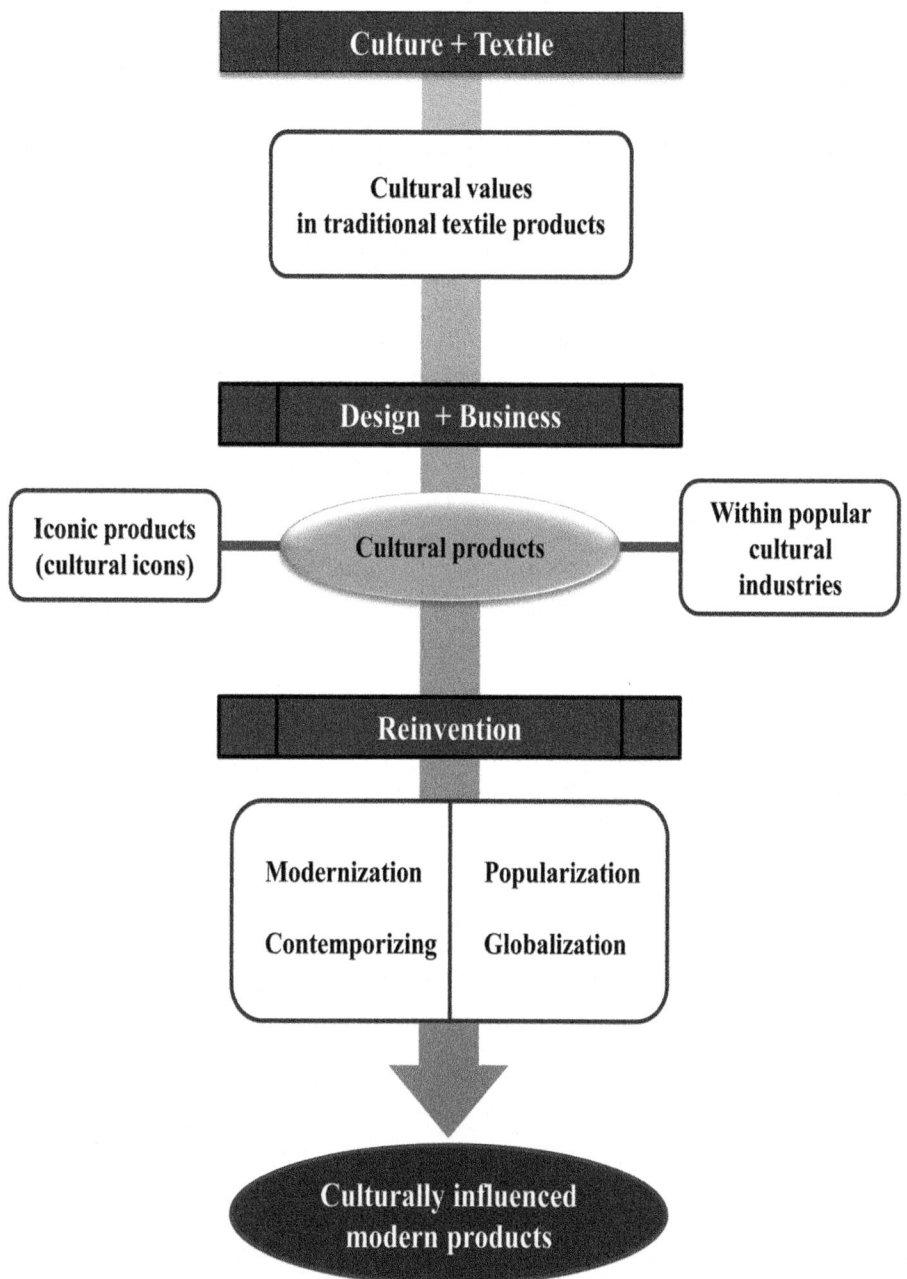

FIGURE 12.1 A design reinvention model for traditional textiles. © Meong Jin Shin.

how business can meet the needs and wants of potential global consumers. Mass media brings together people from varying geographic areas around the world (Hofstede 2001: 453).

The design reinvention of Korean *bojagi* textiles

Through exploration of traditional Korean textile products, *bojagi* have been identified as the strongest category of Korean cultural textiles for design reinvention. The Korean *bojagi* textiles are a category of textile products that incorporates formative characteristics—the use of pattern, color, fabric, and style—to convey meaning and aesthetic value. The manipulation of these characteristics became the basis for the reinvention of *bojagi* textiles within contemporary fashion items; the aesthetics of *bojagi* textiles have the potential to be modified and applied to modern fashion textile designs (Shin, Cassidy, and Moore 2015).

Essentially, reinvention is a translation process of the past into the present to design contemporized traditional *bojagi* textiles. The process includes design strategies and a marketing strategy for a specific market sector. A web-based interface was chosen to communicate with the target consumers. This is similar to the case of Scottish tartan, which has been successfully reinvented globally as a fashion textile (Shin, Cassidy, and Moore 2011).

A computer-based *bojagi* textile design tool has been programmed for designing modern fashion *bojagi* textiles as an effective translation from traditional iconic features into modern fashion products. Also, a website for the popularization/globalization of Korean *bojagi* has been developed to communicate with the target consumers. Three potential target markets that can be applied to future Korean cultural products have been identified by Shin, Cassidy, and Moore (2011); the young trendy generation group, the tourist group, and the business market for designers. The young trendy generation group (Korean/Western) has been selected as the primary target consumer group due to their expected interest and familiarity with the interactive components of the mass customization aspect of the design tool. They are also aware of global fashion designs and are early adopters of innovative fashion apparel. This group also overlaps with the tourist and the business market for designers. Therefore, it could disseminate the global interest in *bojagi* more rapidly than any other group. As can be seen in Figure 12.2, the design reinvention process for the traditional Korean textile products known as *bojagi* is progressive and iterative.

The traditional *bojagi* textiles

Wrapping cloths (*bojagi*) occupied a prominent place in the daily lives of Koreans of all classes during the Joseon dynasty (1392–1910). They have been passed down through generations of women. The Confucian social structure was predominant in this period so that a woman's life was very restricted; women would rarely step beyond the gates of the family compound (Lee 2014: 1). It was impossible for women to receive any formal education and they were treated as secondary to men. Gender inequality was exceptionally severe and rigid in this dynasty (Yi 1998: 22).

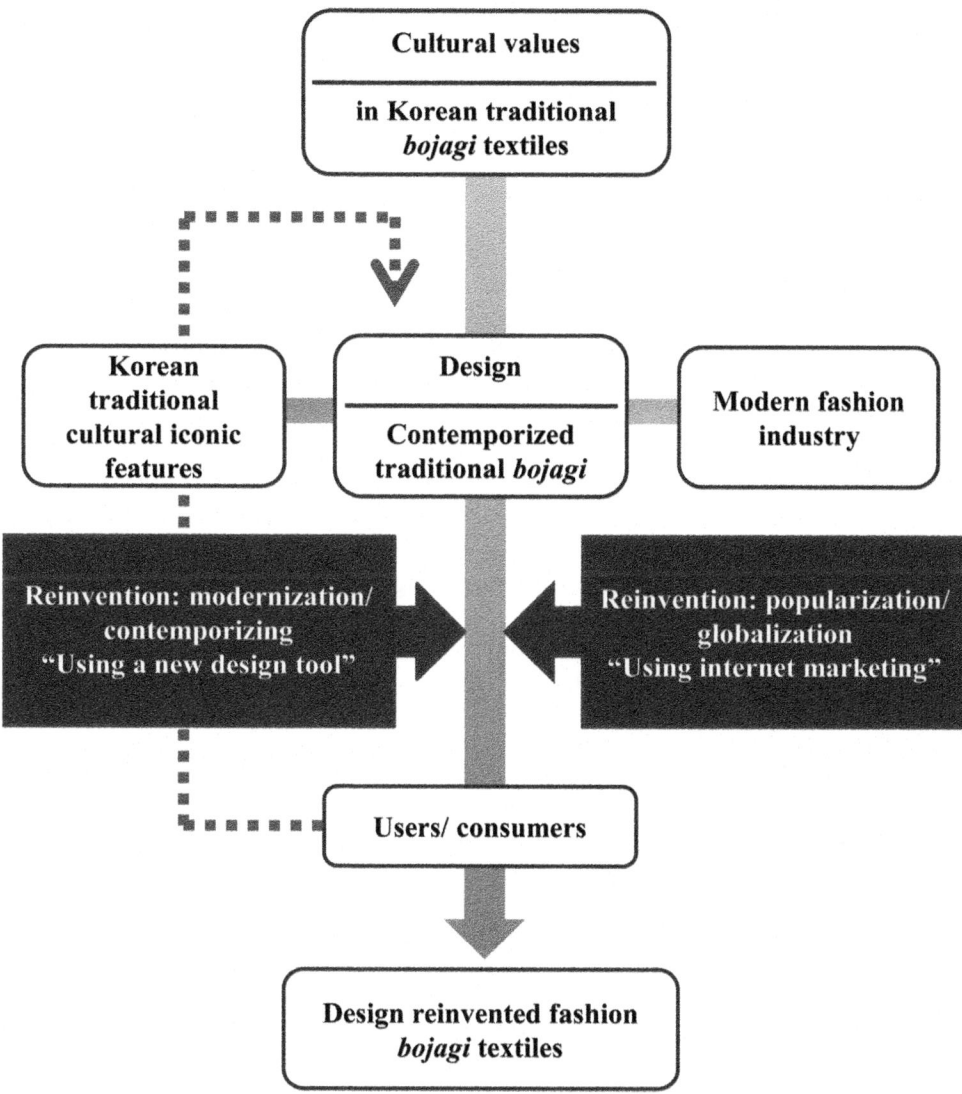

FIGURE 12.2 A design reinvention process for traditional *bojagi*. © Meong Jin Shin.

Designing and making *bojagi* was an opportunity to express creative ideas, channel their feelings of unhappiness, and cherish their hope for the afterlife as a free human being (Hur 2004: 20).

Bojagi have decorative, religious, and symbolic uses. They can cover a dining table; be used as the cloth for a Confucian or Buddhist altar; to wrap a wedding document; serve as a bedsheet; or be used as body ornaments. The use as a table cover or altar cloth signifies the importance of the occasion, the wrapping of objects represents the individual's concern for that which is being wrapped and respect for the person to whom it is given. There was an unspoken Korean folk belief that to

TABLE 12.1 Different types of *bojagi*

Name	Feature	Meaning
Gyeop-bo	Lined	*Gyeop*: double
Hot-bo	Unlined	*Hot*: single
Som-bo	Padded	*Som*: cotton
Nubi-bo	Quilted	*Nubi*: to quilt
Jogak-bo	Patchwork	*Jogak*: small segments
Su-bo	Embroidered	*Su*: embroidery
Jikmun-bo	Woven pattern	*Jikmun*: woven patterns
Geumbak-bo	Pressed gold	*Geum*: gold
Chaesaek-bo	Colored	*Chaesaek*: coloring

wrap an object meant capturing and enclosing good luck within a *bojagi*. Special events such as weddings required that an entirely new *bojagi* be used (Hur 2001: 35; Kim 1998: 13). The traditional Korean *bojagi* was made from many pieces of fabric, which was much easier and cheaper than making wooden boxes. It also had the advantage of taking up a small amount of room in living spaces; the *bojagi* can be folded for compact storage (Lee 2014: 1).

The different types of *bojagi* are classified both by the users and their uses. According to the users it is divided into two groups: *gung-bo* (wrapping cloths used by the upper class) were usually not pieced together but made from sheer silk that was lined; *min-bo* (wrapping cloths used by the lower classes) were mainly of a patchwork style and often decorated with embroidery, block printing, or painting (Lee 2014: 3; Roberts and Hur 1998: 13). They can be further classified according to their construction, design, and the purpose they serve (see Table 12.1). *Jogak-bo* are the most popular wrapping cloths and are used exclusively by ordinary people. These are wrapping cloths with patchwork designs made from small pieces of leftover scraps of silk, ramie, and hemp, and they embodied a wish for longevity (Lee 2014: 5; Roberts and Hur 1998: 14). The figures and designs portrayed in embroidered *bojagi* also represent a deep symbolic significance. The layers of complicated stitching portray motifs that express the desire for happiness and good fortune as well as a belief in the spiritual power of objects and creatures found in nature (Hur 2003: 23). In the case of *su-bo*, the embroidered motifs are based on trees, flowers, birds, clouds, fruits, dragons, phoenixes, and ideographs (written symbols such as Chinese characters of luck, longevity, prosperity, and other good wishes) (Kim 2003: 12). *Bojagi* decorated with designs in pressed gold are called *geumbak-bo* (*geum* means "gold") and wrapping cloths with colored designs drawn onto the fabrics are called *chaesaek–bo* (*chaesaek* means "coloring"). *Geumbak-bo* and *chaesaek–bo* are only used by the upper classes.

The computer-based *bojagi* application

The development of the computer-based *bojagi* in this research allows users and consumers to become involved in the design process, and it can also be an effective research and communication tool, not only for promotional activity but also as an educational interface. Use of this *bojagi* design tool allows the users to learn about the history and design characteristics and cultural meanings of the Korean *bojagi* in an entertaining as well as an educational way. Interactions within the web interface are not simply between the sender and receiver of information, but with the medium itself. Thus, companies can interact and communicate with consumers (Chaffey et al. 2006: 22).

Designing the *bojagi* interactive website

An interactive website was considered to be the most appropriate for promotion and for use as a design tool to communicate with target consumers. The Korean *bojagi* web-based application was developed with Adobe Dreamweaver CS4. The content is divided into six categories—1. History, 2. Styles, 3. Patterns, 4. Colors, 5. Fabrics of the traditional *bojagi*, and 6. "Design your own *bojagi*". This final section was developed using MATLAB 7.0.4 (see Figure 12.3). The development of the application will achieve the primary marketing aims of effectively identifying, anticipating, and satisfying user requirements through the application of digital technologies (Chaffey et al. 2006: 9). Further, if this application can be utilized by manufacturers, consumers' designs will be manufactured and sold online. This could possibly co-create and increase value

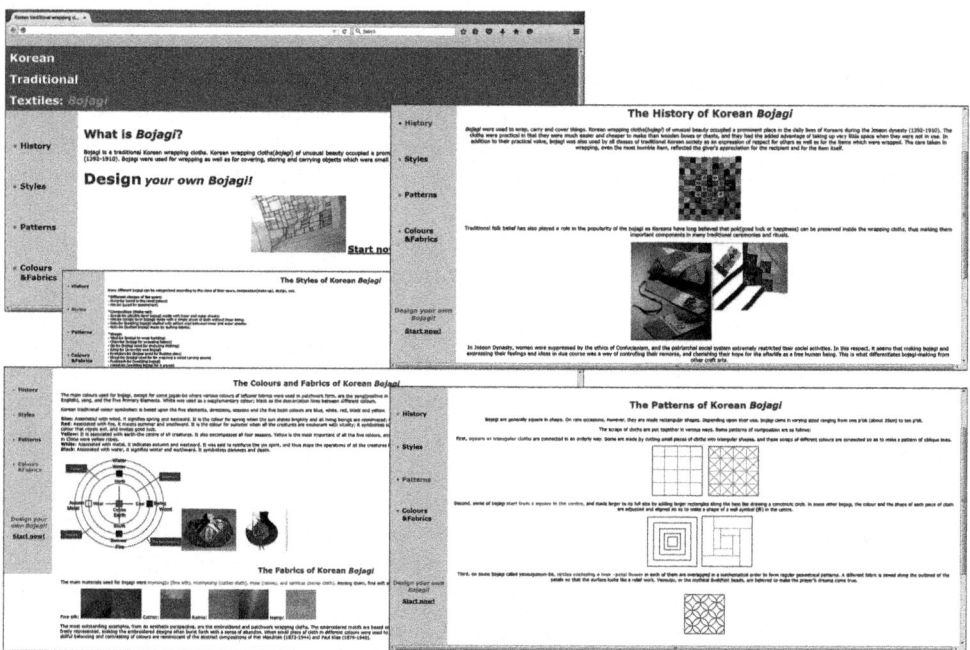

FIGURE 12.3 The Korean *bojagi* web-based application. Courtesy Shin. © Meong Jin Shin.

through design choices of patterns, colors and textures for the design of new *bojagi* by consumers (Shin, Cassidy, and Moore 2011).

Developing the fashion *bojagi* design tool

The "design your own *bojagi*" section of the application includes the interactive fashion *bojagi* design tool, which offers a selection between six pattern types, five color choices and six textures, all based on traditional *bojagi* textiles. From this, users can generate their own combination of *bojagi* designs.

Pattern types

In general, *bojagi* cloths are square but, on rare occasions, some are rectangular. Depending on the use of the *bojagi*, the size varies from one *p'ok* (about 35 cm) to ten *p'ok* (Kim 2003: 12). The scraps of cloths are put together in a variety of ways. Square or triangular scraps of material are connected in a regular pattern. Some are made by cutting small pieces of cloth into triangular shapes, and different colors are combined to make a pattern of oblique lines (Hur 2004: 37). Some start from a square in the center, and are made larger by adding rectangles of increasing size along the outer edge. In others, the color and shape of each piece of cloth are adjusted and aligned to create a symbol (井) in the center (Hur 2004: 38).

In a different type of *bojagi* called *yeoeuijumun-bo*, circles, each enclosing a four-petalled flower, overlap to form geometrical patterns. A different fabric is sewn along the outer edge of the petals, creating a surface that looks like relief work. *Yeoeuiju* (Cintamani), or the mythical Buddhist beads, are believed to make the prayer's wishes come true (Hur 2004: 38).

Bojagi can also be made in irregular patterns without specific rules. These wrapping cloths with their patchwork design are called *jogak-bo*. Numerous pieces of different size, shape and color are put together randomly, but still fit harmoniously with each other on the *bojagi* (Hur 2004: 38).

The irregular pattern type feature on the majority of *bojagi* patterns with the square type and the *bojagi* starting from a square in the center are next in popularity. Only very few are based on circles enclosing a four-petal design (Choi and Eun 2004: 268). Consequently, six types of pattern were selected to produce *bojagi* patterns in this interactive textile design tool: Square, triangular, two different styles starting from a square in the center, circles enclosing a four-petal flower, and irregular are generated in patterns A, B, C, D, E and F respectively (see Figure 12.4).

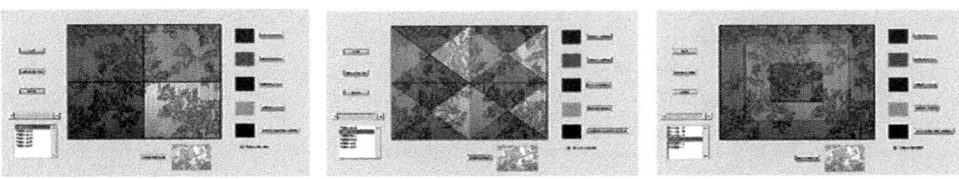

FIGURE 12.4 Pattern types of fashion *bojagi* design tool. Courtesy Shin. © Meong Jin Shin.

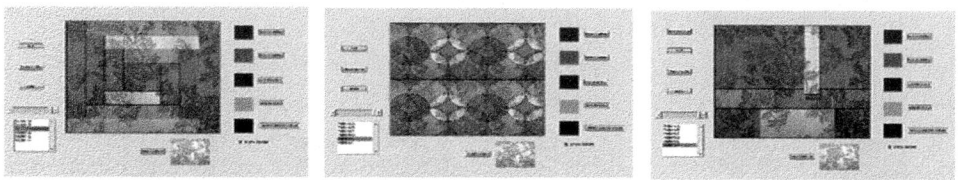

FIGURE 12.4 (*Continued*)

Color selection

In general, five different colors were used for traditional *bojagi* designs, except for some *jogak-bo* where diverse colors of leftover fabrics were used in a patchwork form. These five colors were based on the principle of *yin* and *yang* and the five primary elements. White was used as a supplementary color and black as the demarcation lines between colors. Traditional color symbolism in Korea is based on the five elements, compass points, and seasons; the five basic colors are blue, red, yellow, white, and black (Hur 2003: 23).

Blue is associated with wood, it signifies spring and the east. It is the color of spring, when the sun shines brightly and all of nature is revived; therefore, it symbolizes life and vitality. Red is associated with fire; it means summer and looking to the south. It is the color of summer when all the creatures are full of life and vitality; it symbolizes sunshine, flames, and other things that are full of life. Like blue, it is a representative *yang* color that repels evil and invites good luck. Yellow is associated with earth—the substance of all creatures. It also encompasses all four seasons. Yellow is the most important of the five colors, and it symbolizes the brightest light in the world. White is associated with metal, and indicates autumn and a westward view. It reinforces the *yin* spirit, thus puts an end to the activities of all the creatures in the world. Black is associated with water, signifying winter and northwards. It symbolizes darkness and death (Hur 2004: 22).

Thus, five color selections are provided for users to create their new *bojagi* designs. However, a variety of other colors can be selected by users as the tool also provides colors with HSB/RGB values similar to Adobe Photoshop. Specifically, the users can choose four of the main colors for the key design part and the last color selection is a border color, as the border was an integral part of the original *bojagi* designs. Traditionally, *bojagi* products are handmade and a wide range of borders can be created depending on the makers' individual style or preference in combining the pieces (see Figure 12.5).

Texture selection

Most *bojagi* are made of silk, gossamer, cotton, and ramie (a fabric made from the nettle plant family), and in colors ranging between red, purple, blue, green, yellow and pink, dark-blue, and white. The main materials were *myeongju* (fine silk woven in patterns), *mumyeong* (cotton), *mosi* (ramie), and *sambae* (hemp); fine soft silk was especially favored. In particular, *jogak-bo*, made of loosely woven silk, fine silk,

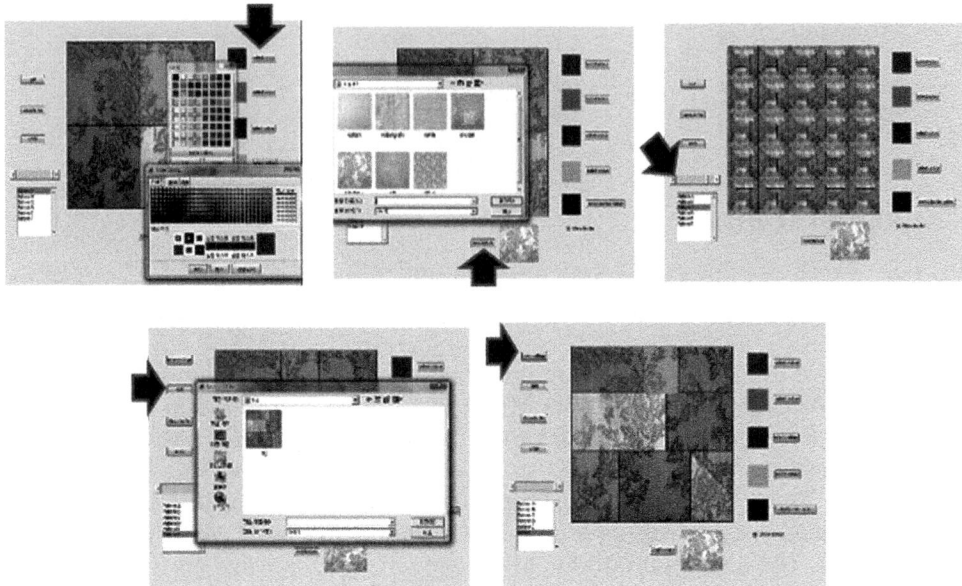

FIGURE 12.5 The fashion *bojagi* design tool. © Meong Jin Shin.

ramie or hemp, was used in the summer months to protect food from flies and dust while permitting the circulation of air (Hur 2003: 22).

When using the application, the images of the various materials are displayed once the user selects a texture image by clicking the "load texture" button. It would be helpful for the users, in deciding their design choices, to visualize the end fabric with the incorporated texture images. Therefore, the tool offers a section for choosing texture images that were mainly used for traditional *bojagi*; five different types of silk, one ramie, and one cotton texture (see Figure 12.5).

Scaling bar, "undo," "save to file," "quit," and "new settings" button

One of the important parts of designing textile patterns is the repeating or scaling of patterns. To this end, a scaling bar has been developed within the design tool to produce a repeated pattern between four and thirty-six times.

By incorporating an "undo" button, the users and consumers can see their previous design when they are designing their own *bojagi* patterns. After finishing the design process, the designs can be saved in TIFF file format simply by clicking the "save to file" button. A "quit" button allows the user to exit the design tool.

A "new settings" button is activated for pattern F only, as it is not needed for the other patterns, which are fixed. Pattern F is developed to generate the irregular pattern type of the *bojagi* so it is programmed to randomly change the portion of each block of pattern F by clicking the "new settings" button (see Figure 12.5).

Producing and evaluating fashion *bojagi* prototypes

Using the *bojagi* design tool, a range of fashion *bojagi* prototypes were designed and these were digitally printed on five different types of fabrics; coated stretch twill classic cotton, coated plain cotton, coated linen, coated heavy twill silk, and coated medium viscose-satin silk. The textures of all these fabrics are similar to the fabrics that were traditionally used for *bojagi*. Apart from silk, all of them are washable so consumers can handle them more easily than traditional *bojagi*, which are delicate and need careful handling due to the materials and hand sewing.

The majority of prototypes were designed using pattern F, which was programmed to change the portion of each block by clicking the "new settings" button. The colors were selected from both the S/S 2011 women's wear trend colors in the WGSN trend report and from the results of a psychophysical experiment on color among the target consumer groups in both Korea and the UK (Shin et al. 2012: 55).

To visualize fashion products using these prototypes, it was essential to put illustrations of the fashion *bojagi* applications and fabric samples of the design prototypes in a *bojagi* fabric sample book. Adobe Photoshop 7.0 was used to produce the illustrations of the fashion applications, which is a simple method of superimposing a design image over an existing photograph of a garment or room to illustrate a potential end use of the design. Four examples of fashion *bojagi* design prototypes consisting of fashion garments and home-textiles are shown in Figure 12.6.

For evaluation of these fashion *bojagi* prototypes using printed fabric samples, four fashion retail companies (Cohen & Wilks, Next, Mother of Pearl, and Hawick Cashmere) were selected because they target the global young consumer market. In-depth interviews were conducted with designers, fabric-sourcing managers, and quality assurance managers. The evaluation criteria considered: their opinions of the fabric samples (design values of patterns, colors, texture images and fabrics, and

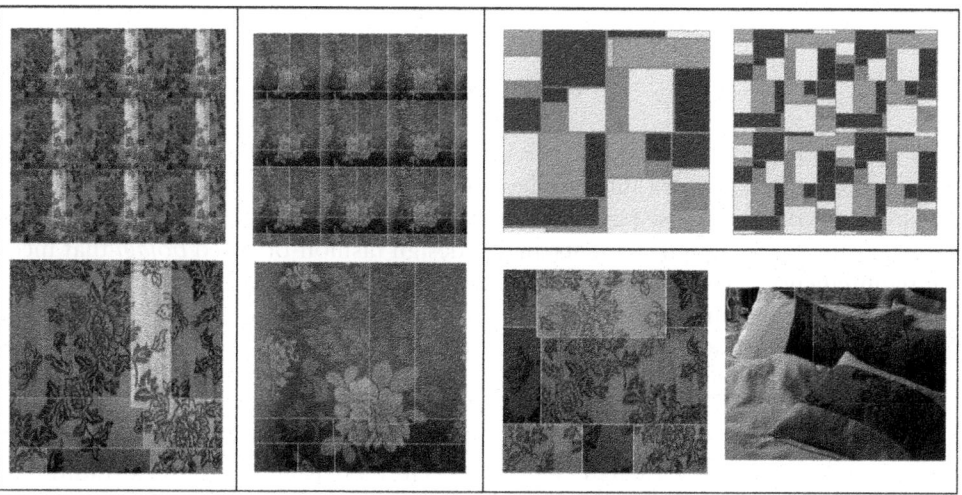

FIGURE 12.6 Examples of fashion *bojagi* prototypes. Courtesy Shin. © Meong Jin Shin.

commercial values of the designs); the interest of these designs to their company; suggestions of other relevant companies or brands; other types of fashion products that would be suitable for these designs; and any thoughts on the adoption of cultural textiles into mainstream fashion.

According to the interviews, the design value of patterns was highly rated, and block patterns and geometric designs were of interest to all of them. Color combinations and choices were also highly valued; however it was recommended that the black be changed to dark-indigo or dark-blue. The floral texture images were preferred for fashion products and the coated linen fabrics were recommended for homeware products (e.g. tableware, bedding, cushions, and curtains). The cotton samples could work for T-shirts, and the silk design samples would suit scarves or dresses. The interviewees suggested Laura Ashley, Zara and Pierre Frey as suitable brands for home textiles and Zara, Monsoon, Topshop, John Lewis and Jonathan Saunders as suitable brands for fashion garments. They also pointed out that cultural values are a very important added value in the fashion industry. They become fashion trends and each fashion brand then itself interprets the main trend to match their own brand images. This happens ever more frequently these days, especially in the high-end fashion market. Commercial values of the prototypes were assessed and they commented that although the cost of production and the price of products could be an issue, they could enter the fashion industry as fashion garments or home textiles if they were effectively commercialized.

It appears, therefore, that there is much potential for a translation from the Korean traditional *bojagi* textiles into contemporary fashion products. The four fashion retail companies interviewed ranged from high street and middle market to high-end fashion companies in the UK. Thus, the evaluation results of the fashion *bojagi* applications by these companies have highlighted that these design prototypes and fabric samples could be successfully commercialized across a wide range of current fashion markets.

Conclusion

This chapter has introduced design reinvention models for the transformation of traditional cultural textiles into modern products. The focus has been on how to develop new computer-based applications for translating Korea's traditional *bojagi*'s cultural values into design elements and to design fashion-oriented *bojagi* that meet the requirements of today's markets.

Design reinvention begins with cultural values, which are developed into a contemporary product within a popular cultural industry. It then undergoes some forms of reinvention (modernization/contemporizing or popularization/globalization), and is finally manufactured and commercialized (Shin, Cassidy, and Moore 2015) (see Figure 12.1). The process of design reinvention for traditional *bojagi* was proposed, as shown in Figure 12.2. The models illustrated how traditional *bojagi* textiles could be translated into contemporary fashion products by using modern technologies. The interactive web interface (fashion *bojagi* design tool) was developed to communicate with target consumers. This tool can be used for determining consumer preferences, product development and the early promotion of Korean *bojagi* as fashion fabrics. It also opens up an opportunity as an educational, web-based interface to learn about the historical background and aesthetics of traditional *bojagi*. Cultural references to the traditional *bojagi* designs were utilized to develop the fashion *bojagi* design tool.

To evaluate fashion *bojagi* prototypes and fabric samples produced by the *bojagi* design tool, it was essential to have them examined by fashion industry experts who target global young consumers. Participants from four UK-based fashion retailers were interviewed to evaluate the prototypes and fabric samples, which were provided as a fabric sample book. The conclusion from the interviews was that there is potential for traditional *bojagi* textiles to enter contemporary fashion markets. The industry experts agreed that cultural factors are becoming more important than product differentiation in fashion trends. However, cost is very important for fashion suppliers and retailers, and the move towards mass customization has had a significant effect. Also, scaling for repetition is an important issue in the fashion design process in the generation of different pattern designs. According to the evaluation results, it was suggested that the fashion *bojagi* designs and fabric samples could be successfully commercialized for the global young consumers market and the designers showed a great deal of interest in the fashion *bojagi* design tool.

As with all research, there will be many aspects that can be addressed in future research. Application of the concept of design reinvention to another country's cultural products and other product categories (industrial products, artworks, toys, and graphic design) is of considerable value to the design of commercially reinvented products. In taking advantage of new opportunities to develop innovative ways of using and interpreting traditional heritage (emerging within the creative industries), it will be helpful to maintain a balance between tradition, current needs, and the benefit to future generations. Developing a design-marketing model for translating cultural factors and developing applications by using digital technology are also areas for possible future research. Furthermore, digital application designs for cultural products could be an educational and promotional marketing tool for a global society. They could offer new opportunities to designers and global consumers, thus having huge potential for the consumer-led design market. An understanding of this concept as an aspect of design management could be a bridge to connect designers, marketers, and technicians. Although this would require close collaboration, it is potentially of great value across numerous subject fields in the future.

References

Bhaskaran, L. (2005), *Designs of the Times*, Mies: Roto Vision SA.

Chaffey, D., F. Ellis-Chadwick, K. Johnston, and R. Mayer (2006), *Internet Marketing: Strategy, Implementation and Practice*, Harlow: Prentice Hall/Financial Times.

Choi, Y. H. and Y. J. Eun (2004), "A Study of the Sensitive Image of Pattern Applied Colour and Formative Types of the Traditional Jogakbo," *Journal of Korean Society for Clothing Industry*, 6 (3), 266–74.

Davis, F. (1992), *Fashion, Culture, and Identity*, Chicago, IL: The University of Chicago Press.

Farr, M. (1966), *Design Management*, London: Hodder and Stoughton.

Gaynor, G. H. (2002), *Innovation by Design*, New York, NY: AMACOM.

Hofstede, G. (2001), *Culture's Consequences*, London: Sage.

Holder, J. (1990), "Promoting Modernism in Britain," in P. Greenhalgh (eds.), *Modernism in Design*, 122–43, London: Reaktion Books.

Hur, D. H. (2001), *The World of Colourful Delight*, Seoul: Young-In Process.

Hur, D. H. (2003), "History and Art in Traditional Wrapping Cloths," in J. M. White and D. H. Huh (eds.), *Wrapping of Happiness*, 20–4, Honolulu, HI: Honolulu Academy of Arts.

Hur, D. H. (2004), *Bojagi's Simple Elegance*, Seoul: The Museum of Korean Embroidery.

Hyun, S. H. and S. J. Bae (2007), "Aesthetic Characteristics of Traditional Korean Patterns Expressed on Contemporary Fashion Design—from 1990 to 2005," *Journal of Fashion Business*, 11 (6): 139–56.

Kim, K. P. (1998), "Profusion of Colour: Korean Costumes and Wrapping Cloths of the Choson Dynasty," in C. Roberts and D. H. Huh (eds.), *Rapt in Colour*, 10–18, Sydney: Powerhouse Publishing.

Kim, K. P. (2003), "Korean Costumes and Wrapping Cloths of the Choson Dynasty," in J. M. White and D. H. Huh (eds.), 10–19, *Wrapping of Happiness*, Honolulu, HI: Honolulu Academy of Arts.

Lee, C. H. (2014), *Bojagi & Beyond II*, Rhode Island: Beyond & Above.

Munnecke, M. and R. Van der Lugt (2006), "Bottom-up Strategies in Consumer-led Markets," *Second International Seville Seminar on Future-Oriented Technology Analysis*, September 28–29.

Perivoliotis, M. C. (2005), "The Role of Textile History in Design Innovation: A Case Study Using Hellenic Textile History," *Textile History*, 36 (1): 1–19.

Power, D. and A. J. Scott (2004), *Cultural Industries and the Production of Culture*, New York, NY: Routledge.

Roberts, C. and D. H. Hur (1998), *Rapt in Colour*, Sydney: Powerhouse Publishing.

Shin, M. J., T. Cassidy, and E. M. Moore (2011), "Cultural Reinvention for Traditional Korean Bojagi," *International Journal of Fashion Design, Technology and Education*, 4 (3): 213–23.

Shin, M. J., T. Cassidy, and E. M. Moore (2015), "Design Reinvention for Culturally Influenced Textile Products: Focused on Traditional Korean bojagi Textiles," *Fashion Practice*, 7 (2): 175–98.

Shin, M. J., S. Westland, E. M. Moore, and T. L. V. Cheung (2012), "Colour Preferences for Traditional Korean Colours," *Journal of the International Colour Association*, 9: 48–59.

Shweder, R. A. and R. A. LeVine (1984), *Culture Theory*, Cambridge: Cambridge University Press.

Yi, S. M. (1998), "Women in Korean History and Art," in C. Roberts and D. H. Huh (eds.), *Rapt in Colour*, 22–7, Sydney: Powerhouse Publishing.

13

Revitalization by Design

Sebastian Cox

My personal design roots

My introduction to the world of craft and design was informal. My parents started a business restoring medieval buildings the same year I was born and I was exposed to wattle and daub, tie beams, and crown posts from birth. The smell of green oak shavings is highly evocative of my youth and transports me back to being seven or eight on a building site, watching carpenters shave scarf joints with electric chainsaws. I use the word informal because although I was surrounded by exposed construction and honest materials at home, my grammar school education largely overlooked the value of these experiences. Students were instead channeled into Oxbridge via "core subjects," with little acknowledgement or nurturing of any desire we may have had to *make* things.

Despite this largely uncreative academic environment, after much research I found a degree course at Lincoln University that seemed to suit my desire to make– with the promise of fifty percent workshop time, fifty percent desk time. For me, the start of my course was very much "make first, write essays later," but as I progressed through the academic year I realized that I was simultaneously becoming a conscious consumer concerned with issues like waste and sustainability, and yet embarking on a career to make more stuff with which to fill the world. I turned to books and my academic tutors to seek guidance as to how to navigate these conflicting ideas.

University is a hugely important time for young makers to develop their practice. Personally, I used the time, expertise, and workshop afforded me by my course to gain making skills based upon traditional techniques. I learned how to cut joints by hand and how to master machinery. "Dovetail Wednesdays" were a comical but important part of my first year, racing against the more experienced third-year students to hand cut the quickest, neatest dovetail joints. I was immersed within a strong culture of making.

Outside the workshop, I learned to question and interrogate things around me. I have always had a curious mind but I learned how to convert that curiosity into research, and that research into an object. At the top of my personal FAQs was the query, "Where does that come from?" I understood the basic principle of carbon footprints, particularly in the food I was now buying for myself as a student living away from home, and applied this same responsibility to the materials I was using in my projects. Driving past acres of woodland to arrive at a timber yard that was selling mostly imported timber struck me as being somewhat counterproductive. As I started to explore the possibilities of sourcing UK grown timber, I faced a number of hurdles that combined to create the design brief that formed my Master's degree and the foundations of my furniture design business.

Turning a by-product into a product

Having completed my undergraduate degree course and about to embark upon a Master's to passionately and doggedly explore sustainable design, my tutor casually asked me, "Seb, if you really care about sustainability, why make anything at all?"

As well as being a really good question, it was a hugely problematic one that required a great deal of time and reading to answer. Most notably and most usefully I began with *Sustainable by Design: Explorations in Theory and Practice* (Walker 2006) and came to understand that sustainability wasn't just about lowering carbon footprints and using degradable materials; true sustainability is about developing a new material culture that is more engaging and aesthetically or emotionally durable.

This meant that I had a purpose and an answer for my tutor. Through my Master's I would design and make a collection destined not for landfill but as encouragement towards an infinitely more engaging material culture.

As I began to tackle the task I had set myself and struggled to find British grown timber, I became aware of new "super materials" sourced from overseas. Bamboo was being celebrated as the material of the future with its fast growing, straight poles that are self-replenishing when harvested. As a country boy, hailing from Kent, I was quite certain we had our own fast growing, self-replenishing super material growing across the UK unnoticed: coppiced hazel.

Upon further investigation, it became clear that coppicing was not only a great way to grow a self-replenishing resource but was also a process many woodland sites needed in order to encourage biodiversity. This was not so much a means of deforestation but rather a form of simple and essential woodland management. I got in touch with my local Forestry Commission site who laughed when asked, "Would you happen to have any hazel?" They were based within a mile-long ride through a mixed woodland where huge amounts of hazel were being thinned out from under the standard oaks as part of their biodiversity program. Hazel was the main attraction for me but to them it was a mere by-product of the process. I asked what would happen to the hazel that had been cut only to hear it would be, at best, burned.

To me, as a student in need of a Master's project, the discovery of a fast-growing, self-replenishing material growing abundantly in the UK, as a by-product of a biodiversity program yet being hugely underused was almost mouthwatering. Equally juicy, but at that point unrealized, was the vast heritage of craft that came along too, embedded in this material. Through my studies it became clear how coppiced hazel and its associated crafts have been completely ingrained into our material culture for centuries; the objects made from coppiced material simply had not been archived, and had not survived in the same way that mahogany dressers had.

The crafts associated with coppiced wood are to this day generally practiced by people who are passionate about the lifestyle that comes with it, often living rurally and well-connected with their resource. On the whole, the products they produce are traditional in style with a rustic aesthetic, superbly made and true to their origins. Very little is designed in a modern but respectful way, leaving me with the opportunity within my Master's to use design to create a new commercial market for this material and its rich cultural heritage.

Material-driven design

In order to design anything using this material, I needed to understand it. I started with a process that almost all green woodworking activities begin with: cleaving. This is the controlled splitting of a piece of wood along its grain. This skill is traditionally executed to reduce the size of a rod or pole (usually 15–35 mm in diameter) to something that's workable, and to remove the pith (the unstable center of the tree). It's also much quicker to split a piece of wood than saw it without access to machines, and splitting the wood follows the fibers of the tree's growth, giving a much stronger section of timber than something sawn. Quite how long people have been cleaving wood is unknown, the oldest known example in the UK are hurdles in the peat bogs of the Somerset Levels that are 6,000 years old (Tabour 1994: 77) and it was used widely in construction and crafts up until the mid-twentieth century; so it is a process that unarguably has underpinned our material culture.

"What an excellent place to start a making and design project," I thought as I excitedly unwrapped my newly bought Froe, the ancient tool most commonly used to cleave. Cleaving sounds simple, like splitting logs, right? It's not. To learn to cleave accurately took me around six weeks, and even then I was still wasting considerably more material than a skilled hurdle maker. What this repeated activity taught me was a tacit understanding of the material. I spent six weeks feeling the material literally come apart in my hands; something you just don't get with machinery. I learned the exact limitation of its strength and flexibility, and acquired an understanding of its structure. I developed a connection with the material and an insight into how I might learn to make and therefore *design* sympathetically with it.

I was becoming aware that sustainable design isn't just about careful material specification, but about developing objects that are more engaging and last aesthetically, and that the heritage of craft and textures available in coppiced (or green wood) products is a huge pool of inspiration to draw from. What became apparent was that coppiced hazel wasn't just a renewable and self-replenishing resource, but an opportunity to connect to a more meaningful material culture.

Cleaving acted as a textural catalyst for my creative imagination. I realized that cleft wood had a certain honest beauty and efficiency about it, and had superb properties of strength with minimal material. Harnessing the split fibers of the tree reflects the tree's response to its environmental conditions, giving it a great deal of textural integrity, as well as allowing you to use the least amount of usable fiber to create a length of wood, which to me is a kind of perfect minimalism. A cleft surface is also quite a difficult one to finish or polish, proving the perfect opportunity to introduce a deliberate canvas for patina to accumulate on. Unlike the perfect sheen of a highly lacquered table, there is no immediate degradation with use and any marks made only add to the existing, highly textured surface.

There is also something about the global connection of the material too, cleft material is found in many cultural heritages from around the world, because it is a way of working wood or plant material that pre-dates metal tools (Tabour 1994: 77). The type of cleft wood I use is most relevant to the UK and northern Europe, but this process has a tactile appeal in Asia and the Americas too. Cleaving led to weaving, and I was eventually able to make up surfaces and panels using young coppiced hazel by weaving thin cleft strips together in a pattern that resembles traditional wattle hurdles. Weaving too has ubiquitous appeal and is another opportunity to move away from the short-lived aesthetic pleasure of glassy-finished furniture.

From a position of respectful understanding of the origins of coppiced hazel, I felt ready to put the material through its paces with some machinery, drawing on my skills as a furniture maker rather than a novice green woodworker. An essential part of the success of my first collection was the combination of crisp, accurately machined faces with rougher, more textural surfaces. I played with steaming, boiling, beating, shredding, knotting and turning, and found that the ways you can use green wood are very diverse. This cross-over point between green wood skills and tools, and machinery and knowledge normally applied to kiln-dried wood, was an exciting way to discover new ideas. One particular process I developed was one I named "kerfing." This involves repeatedly sawing a piece of green hazel into slices, cutting square holes through the slices and sliding them on to square dowel that has been dried. As the green slices dry, they shrink and grip the dowel, forming a strong and rigid panel that looks like exploded hazel poles. This technique came from green wood chairmakers, who, instead of using pegs, would fit dry spindles into greener legs, which, as the leg material dried, would grip firmly onto the spindles, making a strong glue-less joint. It was clear that there were so many traditional processes to draw from.

Inspiration, not nostalgia

The Heritage Crafts Association is an advocacy body for traditional heritage crafts. It represents approximately 169,000 people working in heritage crafts businesses from wheelwrights to weavers. Their recent *Manifesto for Making Report* concludes: "If craft skills are to survive we urgently need to take direct action now" (Reynolds 2014). This sounds bleak and while I support their work I believe we should view this as a collaborative opportunity for designers. In those scores of near-forgotten crafts are textures, skills, proportions, colors, materials, sounds, smells, and aesthetics that can provide a rich starting point for so many projects or objects, which could simultaneously keep those skills and materials alive and contribute to a richer material culture that will appeal to the modern consumer. It's important that we save our heritage crafts, but not for reasons of nostalgia or sentimentality, but because there is so much in those traditional activities that could be applied to our current material culture in order to improve it. To me, it's not a bleak list of endangered species, but a hugely exciting list of inspiration.

The boundaries of what I was able to explore during my Master's degree and the vast pool of inspiration were seemingly endless because of the depth of skills and processes buried in the history of coppiced hazel. This is not at all exclusive to green wood, or cleaving, but can, and arguably should, be successfully applied to many other disciplines.

The General Conference of the United Nations Educational, Scientific and Cultural Organization (UNESCO 2003) *Text of the Convention for the Safeguarding of the Intangible Cultural Heritage* recognizes the importance of heritage crafts globally, with its ability among other things to "enrich cultural diversity and human creativity." If there are 169,000 people working in the UK in various heritage crafts, imagine how many there might be globally and therefore the potential to adapt that skill and knowledge into meaningful objects that will resonate with their part of the world.

Swill is the perfect example of this process of inspiration rather than preservation (see Fig. 13.1). Swill is a collection I created two years after graduating from my Master's degree and two years into my business, in collaboration with swiller Lorna Singleton, following an introduction from the National Coppice Federation. Swill is boiled cleft oak, split with a knife down to around two millimeters thick. It is then woven into a basket, which is normally strong enough to stand on when turned upside-down. Swill baskets originate from Cumbria and were used for carrying everything from bread to babies, coal and cockles; now, however, there are only a handful of swillers left.

Having had some experience of cleaving wood (and learning how difficult it is), I'm sure you can imagine the level of intrigue and near disbelief I felt at the prospect of working with two millimeter cleft oak that you could wrap around your finger. My role in our collaboration was to take Lorna's skills and materials to the contemporary design market and broaden the understanding of the ancient art of swilling. As a designer you cannot ask for a better brief—reviving a craft, supporting rural employment, and developing a product, which has bags of appeal through texture and a fantastic story of heritage. All you need to do is to make the material and skill desirable to a contemporary market by developing products that modern consumers want and are willing to pay for—in this case lighting and seating instead of baskets.

There is a greater purpose to collaborations like this than simply preserving skills and materials. Ingrained in this heritage craft is a tangible language of honesty that connects directly to the theories of sustainable design that I learned from the books I was reading to inform my Master's. Because of their often relatively simple composition, objects of craft heritage are easy to read and understand. You may not have the skills to throw a pot or turn a bowl by hand, but you can see in the clay pot or wooden bowl the rings of the direction of travel on the wheel or lathe, which gives a comforting explanation as to its origin. This therefore makes the object engaging—a key theme explored in *Emotionally Durable Design* (Chapman 2005). If we can begin to evolve our material culture to possess these explanatory

FIGURE 13.1 Swill Bench by Sebastian Cox and Lorna Singleton, 2013. Courtesy S. Cox.
© Sebastian Cox.

features, we will have engaging objects and will help to preserve our traditional crafts through consumer demand, rather than charity or subsidy.

The rise of the designer-maker

An Office for National Statistics (ONS 2014) report announced that self-employment in 2014, in the depths of an economic recession, was higher than at any other point during the last forty years. In the face of bleak employment opportunities where securing a graduate job in industry seemed impossible, the internet made freelance or entrepreneurial careers an appealing prospect. Many of my peers found themselves as sole-traders, developing products to make and sell from small workshops or studios around the country. And despite the dystopian setting, this ingenuity is something to be celebrated.

Speaking from my own experience, we have a handful of good manufacturers in the UK who are willing to realize a young designer's project but it can be tricky to connect with them. A small workshop equipped with second-hand tools and machinery where you can manufacture for yourself is a worthy alternative. Many designer-makers have a feeling of being secondary to "proper," well-established manufacturers or design studios, and perhaps that their small workshop is a stopgap until they have a proper studio or factory. I have always felt rather empowered by the agility my business has by virtue of being "small."

I often partner with companies or brands much larger than mine and I believe it gives me the advantageous and unique position of being able to move quickly and experiment using my diverse, adaptable workshop. As well as developing products, a designer-maker can develop their own methods of production and realize ideas with startling immediacy. If you have an idea in the shower that morning, you can have a prototype made by the afternoon. The designer-maker can also set and take control of the standards to which they want to work, be they environmental, ethical, or regarding customer service. These standards are what make designer-makers appealing to potential collaborators. Companies often want to work with me because our collaboration allows them to highlight their own sustainable values through mine. The independent designer-maker also has the freedom to communicate what they do and how they do it through a vast array of channels that creative behemoths may not have the time to consider. As well as allowing us to sell our products direct to customers, the internet also allows us to tell our story directly to customers.

The graduate designer-maker is lucky to occupy that unique territory between academia and industry. It is difficult to imagine how we might literally inject the very experimental objects in sustainable design textbooks and academic thinking into the world of commerce. I remember chewing over the idea that perhaps we need to do away with capitalism in order to reset our material culture and fill our lives with much more meaningful products. I concluded that there might be a gentler way, and this is to design and make objects that bridge the two schools of thought. We must design objects that are proportioned and familiar, but that bring in ideas of local meaning, patina and wear, turning these qualities into positive attributes, and designing objects that grow old gracefully.

This space between academia and commerce is fertile ground for new and innovative ideas, and I think an exhibition like *Tent London*, which takes place each year during the London Design Festival, illustrates this well. It has a diverse range of experimental design conceived in a commercial environment and is where I presented my first collection, created during my Master's degree, *Products of Silviculture*. The products I had produced proved not to be particularly commercially viable but people were excited by the idea of what I was showing. Thinking of that relationship between what is commercially appealing and what is meaningful and artisan, *Products of Silviculture* was at the crafted end of the scale and afforded me opportunities to develop them into less-experimental products. The challenge I had to overcome was to keep the essence of good sustainable design that I had captured, and develop it in a more commercially viable manner. This is a fine line I continue to tread five years on.

My main focus is to design things that I believe are a part of the positive bit-by-bit evolution to a more sustainable world of objects, and I won't design anything I can't defend as being that. And (not but) at the same time I want to earn a living. An example of striking this tricky balance lies in my *Chestnut and Ash* range, designed with Benchmark, which was, we felt, a triumph of amalgamating coppiced material with clean lines and CNC (computer-numerical controlled) production. The reason these pieces have been successful is because we struck that center ground between tradition and modern, craft and manufacture, and the whole collection was focused wholly on sustainability (see Fig. 13.2).

FIGURE 13.2 Shake Cabinet by Sebastian Cox and Benchmark, 2014. Courtesy Benchmark Furniture. © Sebastian Cox.

The now and the next

It is indisputable that we are in an age where craft is cool, and heading for (if not already in) the mainstream. *Viewpoint* predicted in 2010 that the consumers of tomorrow (i.e. the consumers of today) would be in search of a greater sense of meaning in the things they buy:

> [Consumers] are looking for more products embedded with provenance and longevity … Reviving, reinterpreting and reinventing old crafts, these rich and beautiful pieces strike an emotional chord, because we know they have been created with passion—made from the heart and for the love of a skill. Whether these products appear with a polished perfection or take on a cruder, rougher aesthetic … each has a story about the way it has been made while promoting the survival of crafts (Franklin and Till 2010).

Design has been a huge enabler or cause of this, offering an appealing modern perspective on the traditional, slower pace of life, which in turn has captured the attention of the everyday consumer. Subsequently, big brands have pricked up their ears and manufacturers of crisps claim their snacks are "hand cooked." Discussion is rife among the "original" artisans and the small designer-makers, who would consider themselves the real craftsmen and women, that large brands encroaching on their territory risk devaluing the word "craft." There is no doubt that my practice has benefited from this growing interest in that which is crafted but I hold my breath and hope that as the trend washes away, people will continue to see a degree of authenticity in what I do and my business will continue to thrive. I am often comforted by the words of my colleague, collaborator and friend, Sean Sutcliffe, of one of our only "proper" remaining woodworking manufacturers, workshop of dreams and powerhouse of craft, Benchmark:

> I was a craftsman in business for twenty-five years before craft was the zeitgeist, and I'm confident we'll still be in business after the "trend" has calmed because the core value of what we do doesn't disappear (2016).

My intentions upon setting up my business were never to target a hipster market, interested in spoon carving and splitting logs, but part of a wider (or indeed greater) mission to make forgotten materials and the associated crafts desirable. And to a degree, regardless of who my customer may be, I have done that. And I believe that if your work genuinely explores a craft or traditional process with a great deal of depth and respect, you will end up with a body of work that will remain relevant once the marketeers' lexicon has moved on from "artisanal."

I also believe that Sean is absolutely right; his business will be fine and others with making at their core will be too, mine included. As Daniela Walker of The Future Laboratory explains, the reason there has been such a strong pull towards the handmade is not arbitrary:

> The rise of the internet and the information age means that a majority of people in developed countries spend much of their days staring at screens … the reaction to our enslavement to computers and smartphones is a mass search for what is "real"—a quest for authenticity (2016).

People are now craving the "real" and increasingly want to have objects that momentarily offer them an escape from the screen-based world. I believe if used correctly, this is an enabler of that richer and more engaging material culture that is required for a more sustainable material culture—one that is full of objects that are designed through craft to avoid landfill. However, we need to be aware that "trends" can end up creating landfill. I am hopeful that the reaction to a mainstream appetite for craft will lead to a deeper inquiry and understanding of that subject. It is vital now that those who are exploring craft do so in a genuine and respectful way and avoid marketing clichés at all costs. Design has played a critical role in the popularization of craft, and designers must not turn their back on it as it enters the mainstream consciousness.

As well as negotiating the rather flattering problem of popularity, the future of the designer-maker is set against a changing landscape. As the digital world provided e-commerce and self-retail, it is now bringing to bear new kinds of digital manufacture—most notably 3D printing. I maintain that machines are tools, regardless of how autonomous, and can be used with the same degree of skill and thought of process as any hand tool demands. By this definition I also believe that CNC manufacture or 3D printing can be considered craft, and should be considered as tools of the designer-maker. Although we haven't seen uptake of these tools by designer-makers in the way that many had predicted, I see a new type of industrial activity on the horizon that harnesses both a handmade and machine-made approach: "The Third Industrial Revolution is best seen as the combination of digital manufacturing and personal manufacturing: the industrialization of the Maker Movement" (Anderson 2012: 40). The prospect of not relying on factories or large workshops to get products made, and items being printed or assembled in kitchens and spare bedrooms up and down the country is so exciting, and today's designer-makers are casting the mould for this future.

I would like to draw this chapter to a close with an example that gives me optimism about the future of the relationship between design and craft. A former intern of mine, Joel Haran, explored the relationship between coppiced hazel and 3D printing at university (notably studying on one of the few remaining designer-maker courses). He developed a simple component that allowed straight rods of hazel to be connected at right angles in order to build structures. The standardized component is 3D printed in bio-resin and fits three hazel rods that have been sized to fit on each end. The natural straightness of the hazel and the exact replication provided by the 3D printing make this a very beautiful amalgamation of traditional and future making. As with all projects, this still needs development before it can be a commercial product, but it is rich in possibility and the thinking is, in my view, exactly right (see Fig. 13.3).

The new tools available to the designer-maker bring a wealth of opportunity of scalability within the small workshop and with that, access to genuinely democratic products. The old tools and processes offer an anchor to hold an idea or product in the right place through trends that come and go. In the not too distant past, craft relied on design to bring it to contemporary consciousness, now design needs craft to keep it on the straight and narrow in an exciting future that will not just be considered a trend of the post-recession twenty-first century, but a lasting movement that will nudge us, product by product, into a sustainable material culture.

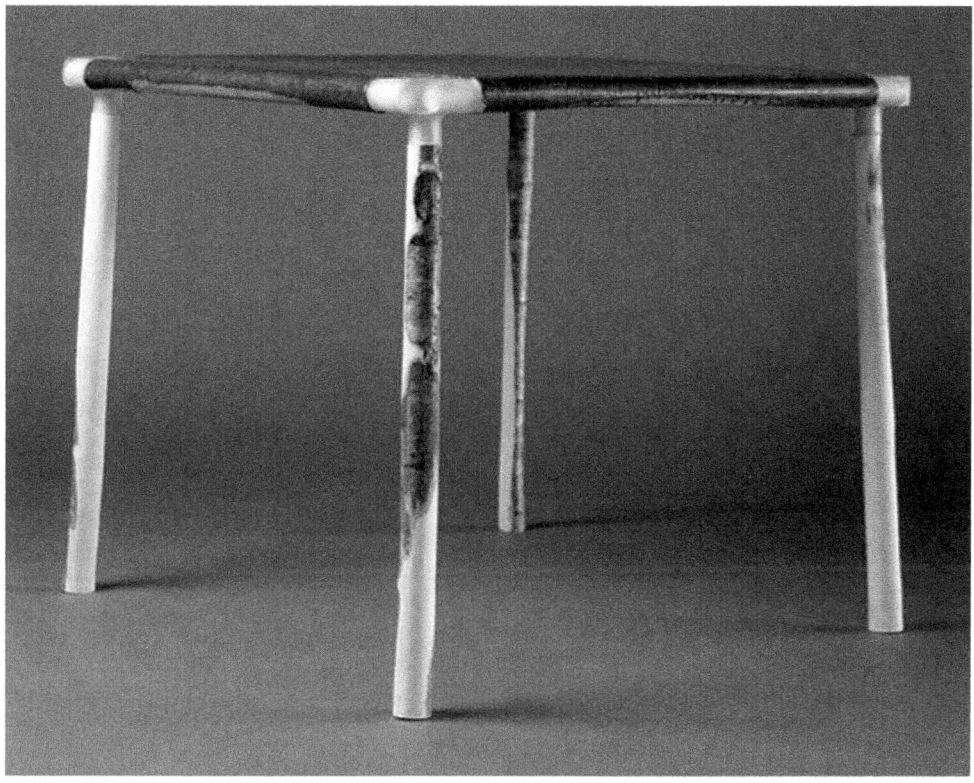

FIGURE 13.3 Coppiced Hazel Table by Joel Haran, 2013. Courtesy Joel Haran. © Joel David Christian Haran.

References

Anderson, C. (2012), *Makers, The New Industrial Revolution*, London: Random House.

Chapman, J. (2005), *Emotionally Durable Design: Objects, Experiences & Empathy*, London: Erthscan.

Franklin, K. and C. Till (2010), "Beyond Endurance," *Viewpoint*, 25: 103.

ONS (2014), *Self-employed Workers in the UK*. Available online: http://www.ons.gov.uk/ons/dcp171776_374941.pdf (accessed August 3, 2016).

Reynolds, P. (2014), "Crafts in the English Countryside: Dark Reflections from the Future," in *Manifesto for Making Report*, Appendix 9a, Oundle: Heritage Crafts Association.

Sutcliffe, S. (2016), Personal interview, January 27.

Tabour, R. (1994), *Traditional Woodland Crafts*, London: B.T. Batsford Ltd.

UNESCO (2003), *Text of the Convention for the Safeguarding of the Intangible Cultural Heritage*. Available online: http://portal.unesco.org/en/ev.php-URL_ID=17716&URL_DO=DO_TOPIC&URL_SECTION=201.html,(accessed August 3, 2016).

Walker, D. (2016), "Craft's Identity Crisis," *Crafts Magazine*, 258: 42–5.

Walker, S. (2006), *Sustainable by Design*, London: Earthscan.

14

New Caribbean Design

Revitalizing Place-based Products

Patty Johnson

Introduction

Design practice is rapidly changing in response to new technologies, global marketing, environmental concerns, and the internationalization of commodity flows and channels of production. Design practitioners need to address how these social, economic, and political shifts will affect the conditions of innovative production and distribution and how the "life histories or biography" (Appadurai 1986) of the objects they design will be received by consumers, who are becoming increasingly aware of the ethics of manufacture. Design and making need to be developed and promoted as positive engines of change in the context of contemporary cultural and social concerns.

Paul Greenhalgh writes in *The Persistence of Craft* that,

> The best products of the next decades will be the result of a reconciliation of what have previously been understood to be opposition: specialization and generalization: the individual and the collective; globality and locality; the avant-garde and the popular. Everything relates to everything. Accepting this without losing ourselves or sacrificing the quality of the things we make will be the great challenge (2002: 207).

This poetic rally for the future of design and making has appeal for a designer working in the developing world. It provides a context for creation and, at the same time, a rationale for cross-cultural collaborations.

A contrasting view comes from Ivan Illich in his 1968 address to the Conference on Inter-American Student Projects in Cuernavaca, Mexico,

> you might have invited me here hoping that you would be able to agree with most of what I say, and then go ahead in good faith and work this summer in Mexican villages. This last possibility is only open to those who do not listen, or who cannot understand me. I did not come here to argue. I am here to tell you, if possible to convince you, and hopefully, to stop you, from pretentiously imposing yourselves on Mexicans.

Although Greenhalgh understands and articulates broader issues in contemporary design and craft practice, Illich speaks directly about a very real problem. This ground is more frequently investigated in anthropology and development literature by authors ranging from the popular, Dambisa Moya in *Dead Aid: Why Aid is Not Working and How There is a Better Way for Africa* (2009), to Robert Chambers, a theorist and practitioner who pioneered a participatory approach to development (1983).

But recently, design academics and thinkers have been exploring similar topics and critiques on design practice. In a paper for the *Design Principles and Practices Journal* titled "Engaged Design," James Fathers asks, "In 2016 many people across the world are asking similar questions—about the pace of life, the environment, food production, etc. and about the unassailable power of trans-national companies. In light of this damning critique, what role can designers play?" (2016: 2).

So, how do we prioritize the elements of design practice in different situations? Why do we need design intervention? What should be the role of the designer in the global marketplace? How can interventions mediate between traditions and change, and should they be attempting to do so? What is the nature of design in this collaborative process or is it antithetical to design? Is design intervention a short-term intrusion into an artisan's sensibility and life or can it develop sustainable livelihood options?

This chapter engages these questions and debates through a view into the successes and failures of two product development programs in the Caribbean—New Caribbean Design and Vodunuvo—that put into action the circumstance of contemporary artisan production and design practice in global contexts.

Historically in the West, design education has trained practitioners to operate autocratically as key decision-makers in the development of products. Many designers have assumed that the nature of "first world" design practice and problem solving is appropriate for all situations (MacHenry 2000). This attitude is frequently and repeatedly brought into the "developing" southern countries. For example, super factories and high volume outputs in Southeast Asia have reassured the design industry that "first world" design can continue to use developing countries as part of a vast outsourcing system of product manufacture. This has had long-term detrimental economic impacts on micro-economies and artisan trades in the region; it has influenced policy formation and implementation of development agencies and NGOs, both foreign and local, who work in these areas and who have continued to struggle with the challenges of supporting local, sustainable craft and design practices (McComb 2007).

Current design approaches and systems are, to a very great extent, dissociated or disengaged from the needs of "people-on-the-ground" and from the capacities of local production processes (Greenhalgh 2002). I believe that contemporary product aesthetics that fail to capture consumers' attention are a result and reflection of this sense of detachment and ill-advised development (Dormer 1997). In order to create products that are at once sustainable, locally meaningful, and globally marketable, it is imperative to begin developing, or perhaps retrieving, these integral connections.

Fathers suggests an engaged, self-reflexive, context-centered approach to design process. "The more we choose to engage in co-production and give up our control of the creative process, the more we will encounter and be able to learn from the unexpected. In my limited experience, this has resulted in a richer, more creative and more rewarding process" (2016: 6).

The key here is that Fathers' methodology is immersive and flexible, "there is no formulae for engaging in contexts as an outsider. In my experience being authentic and self-reflective is the best way to begin to understand the realities of the context in which you are intervening" (2016: 7). Within this relationship, if design principles are applied in informed practice it can be a perennial asset to artisan communities. And I agree with Fathers; in my experience it is equally beneficial for both designer and artisan to share creativity about the production of integral goods.

At the same time, regional organizations like the Caribbean Export Development Agency and the Barbados Investment and Development Corporation have identified that there is a critical need for quality production and good design to raise the positioning of craft producers in the Caribbean so that they can compete effectively in local, regional, and international markets, and differentiate their products from low-cost competition from highly industrialized manufacturers in Asia and elsewhere.

Local agencies, NGOs, and government organizations have increasingly been taking a leading role in defining criteria for competitiveness as applied to traditional craft practices. In 2007, a summary report on a mapping exercise for handicraft projects in Latin America and the Caribbean was published by the Inter-American Development Bank (2007). It outlined a series of collective best practices for design interventions in handicraft sectors to address development challenges including: begin and end with the market and diversify risk by promoting access to multiple markets (local, national, regional, global, tourist, luxury etc.) and channels (large chains, independent stores, direct-purchase retailers, traditional wholesale distributors); work collectively with groups and associations; build local capacity rather than establish a reliance on outside assistance; and emphasize innovation, continual product development, and improvement in general business skills.

During a seminar at Central Saint Martins College of Art and Design in 2006, John Ballyn, an industrial designer and engineer with long experience working in development contexts, analyzed his work on the Fair Trade program with Oxfam (Ballyn 2007). His conclusion was that by emphasizing social "good" over product quality, the organization had had a detrimental impact on the long-term economic development of many of the micro-enterprises they served. This assessment has been validated by my own experiences and observations, and has had a lasting influence on my work with artisan communities.

As regional stakeholders in development contexts and the international donor agencies who fund them focus on building economic capacity through collective action and design inputs, the most challenging issue "on the ground" that remains for me is balancing socially and culturally informed practice with sustainable economic outcomes.

Product design differs from traditional crafting practices, mainly in that it is an iterative process that is generally *separate from* the actual making of the object. Although designers create visual models, mock-ups and prototypes, the finished products are usually manufactured in number by industrial processes. As with good architecture and advertising, good product design is self-explanatory and logical in hindsight; aiming to communicate and evoke a reaction from the potential user that inspires enjoyment and intangible value; and outlasting the commercial value of the initial purchase. It is a critical link in the value chain of manufactured objects and has been used in developed countries as a tool for creation of wealth and to drive the process of innovation.

In contrast, the "descriptive" accounts of craft production and culture in the Caribbean are well-established as documents that primarily identify particular types of crafts with production in specific locales. Within the broader, and more "Western"-based, art history scholarship, the study of craft and functionally designed objects, especially those of countries, was often restricted to "decorative art" studies, thereby marginalizing their place in the design domain (Kangas 2006; Kuspit 1996). Scholarship on the social, political, and economic conditions of craft production and design processes in Southern countries is still lacking. More urgently, the impact of a changing global design culture on micro-manufacturers demarcates a contemporary frontier of design practice.

If "Western" designers are disassociated from the "people on the ground," merging craft-based design with product design techniques and processes offers both opportunities and challenges to Caribbean producers. It provides inspiration for the use of traditional practices and indigenous raw materials in ways that communicate new ideas about culture, history, and identity to receptive audiences in new markets. It also has the potential to overcome a history of low-value-added primary production for limited markets, particularly in rural areas of the Caribbean. For a long time, design in these places has been restricted to handicrafts and regional products.

Therefore, producing unique regional hybrids that combine craft tradition and contemporary design process was the aim of the New Caribbean Design program. Caribbean culture is a confluence of African, European and Amerindian heritage, and these complex and mixed histories have tremendous value to the peoples in the region. They are often expressed through material culture and making is often tied to the politics of oppression and resilience. The Coal Pot Bottles in Figure 14.1 are made in Chalky Mount, Barbados, at a centuries-old pottery works originally founded to supply basic tableware to the families of slaves and indentured servants.

Through the push and pull of cross-cultural collaboration, the group of designers, companies, indigenous communities, and enterprises that made up New Caribbean Design tried to balance traditional cultural practice in the Caribbean with forward-looking design solutions; seeking to develop new methods and a new vernacular that respected and elevated local traditions.

A design-led approach enables producers to position their products in higher end segments of the market. The fusing of traditional craft with product design

FIGURE 14.1 Coal Pot Bottles, terracotta, Hamilton Pottery, Barbados, 2010. Courtesy Johnson. © Patricia Johnson.

has proven potential in increasing the competitiveness of micro and small-sized enterprises in the Caribbean region. Ideally, new product collections, along with a constant framework for innovation to sustain them, can provide a passport for non-traditional market entry opportunities and increased longer term market access.

However, producers and artisans are confronted with numerous challenges in the Caribbean. One of the major constraints faced by the communities on the New Caribbean Design project was the inadequacy of reliable infrastructure. For example, poor availability of standardized and properly dried timber and complementary industries like metal fabricators and plastics manufacturers, as well as a lack of government support for business development. Such factors created difficulties in securing and creating new networks and distribution channels. A lack of information about market demands and benchmarks was one of the most commonly cited problems by the participants on the project. And, design-driven iterative product development and capital investment, even for small machinery, is an economic risk that most producers cannot afford to take.

As one of the key connections between the factory floor (or micro-enterprise workshop) and the market, designers have a pivotal role to play. They are in a unique position to move between cultures and to facilitate an exchange of information. By acting as receptive information gatherers, designers are able to engage as instigators rather than key decision-makers.

The revised model of work that emerged via the analysis of the final results of the New Caribbean Design project was that of a contemporary design laboratory. This was achieved through the adoption of dynamic locally-sensitive processes, and efficient and effective methodologies.

The Vodunuvo project, which was implemented in Haiti two years later, followed the anthropological model of reflexive ethnographic fieldwork to inform and generate the design work. Akin to Fathers' model of participatory development, all issues were evaluated jointly by the design team, members of craft-skilled communities, and the manufacturers, and more broadly with community members and stakeholders.

Anthropologist Nancy Munn argues that "to understand what is being created when Gawans make a canoe, we have to consider the total canoe fabrication cycle which begins ... with the conversion of raw materials into a canoe, and continues in exchange with the conversion of the canoe into other objects" (1977).

In a sense, Munn's argument became central to product creation on the project. Vodunuvo was inspired by the tribulation, struggle and survival of one of the world's oldest religions. As the Vodu artist transforms space to open the doors to imagination, historical and contemporary artifacts were re-examined and transformed; reimagined as products and objects that carried the essential culture of Haiti in a new form. These potent collisions produced more fluid and complex conceptualizations that better represented the dynamism of the relationship between craft and design, and between making and manufacture, in both the Caribbean and the global contexts; see Figure 14.2.

Through this experimental process I realized that beyond traditional design skills, market intuitions and strategic foresight, there was tacit knowledge gained through education and experience providing multiple perspectives on the intimate and intangible relationships between material, process, objects, and transformation.

Some of the biggest obstacles to the sustained commercial success of the New Caribbean Design project were ameliorated by a retail partner, Selfridges, on the Vodunuvo project. The company committed to buying the entire product line, launching in store during London Design Week, and, then stocking inventory. This "built-in" network and distribution channel also allowed for much greater latitude on the range of products in the collection. In addition to new product development, the collection also included temple artifacts and contemporary work by Vodu artists like flags (Figure 14.3) and *pakes* (see below) as well as domestic tools made by Haitians for Haitians sold in the Iron Market in Port au Prince.

At the core of Vodu is the belief in Iwa, spirits who exert influence over all spheres of life and death. There is no separation of body and soul in the religion and priests and priestesses preside over rituals that use rhythm, music, dance, and magic

FIGURE 14.2 Vodu Metal Bowl Series, hand-hammered recycled oil drum, Croix des Bouquet, Haiti, 2012. Courtesy Johnson. © Patricia Johnson.

FIGURE 14.3 Vodu Flag, date and artist unknown, Vodunuvo, 2012. Courtesy Jason Gordon Photography. © Kimon Kaketsis.

substances to expand spiritual consciousness. *Pakes* (from the French word *paquet*) are decorated sealed jars that contain these magic substances made from plants and animals; they are preserved by the priests and priestesses to capture natural forces.

The result of the Vodunuvo project was a more culturally complex body of artistic work as well as multiple frameworks for understanding contemporary design practice within ethical and sustainable production in the Caribbean. It makes a case for Haiti as an evolving, dynamic culture with a critical place in a contemporary design milieu.

The relationship between traditional crafting practice and design interventions in action is more complex than commonly understood. The application of business and design thinking and the power of collective design engagement along with generous development funding did not ensure the long-term success of either of these projects. Driven by multiple stakeholders, including activist artisan groups, micro-enterprise workshops, NGOs, government agencies and individuals with competing interests for donor dollars, programs, and projects are often fraught with the politics of conflicting goals. The results are too often a compromise, no matter how capable the players or how good the intentions.

These endeavours should be collaborative and engaging but not necessarily always equal. Above all else they must, as the Inter-American Development Bank summary report suggested, begin and end with the market. Among the most controversial choices a designer can make on these projects are creative decisions based on merit rather than need, even though most of the original proposals are written to appeal to the inclusive objectives of donor countries like the USA, Canada, and the European Union. By taking the long view and attempting to create a culture of quality rather than focusing on short-term gain, the designer and the artisan both have a better opportunity to ensure sustainable economic development.

I think there is both humility and truth in Henry Dreyfus's statement, "Industrial designers are employed primarily for one simple reason: to increase the profits of the client's company" (Whiteley 1993: 161), especially when this idea is applied to artisan communities. I also know that designing with these manufacturers, agencies, producers, and creative communities is one of the most enriching experiences of my life and has profoundly changed the way I think about design.

It has allowed me to challenge the common exclusion of things on the edge and to strike a new balance between redundancy and relevance; exploring the friction between the "preservationist" view of craft as intangible heritage and its status as living tradition, and therefore, inherently and constantly changing and adapting.

References

Appadurai, A. (ed.) (1986), *The Social Life of Things: Commodities in Cultural Perspective*, Cambridge, MA: Cambridge University Press.

Ballyn, J. (2007), *Innate Design Skills: Looking for Origins*, New Delhi: Craft Revival Trust.

Chambers, R. (1983), *Rural Development: Putting the Last First*, London: IT.

Dormer, P. (1997), *The Culture of Craft: Status and Future*, Manchester and New York, NY: Manchester University Press.

Fathers, J. (2016), "Engaged Design," *Design Principles and Practices Journal*, 10: 1/6/7.

Greenhalgh, P. (2002), *The Persistence of Craft*, London: A & C Black Ltd.

Inter-American Development Bank (2007), "Handicraft Mapping Exercise Abridged." Available online: https://www.scribd.com/document/34680004/IDB-Handicraft-Mapping-Exercise-Abridged-Version (accessed August 3, 2016).

Illich, I. (1968), "To Hell with Good Intentions" from an address to the Conference on Inter-American Student Projects (CIASP) in Cuernavaca, Mexico, April 20.

Kangas, M. (2006), *Craft and Concept: The Rematerialization of the Art Object,* New York, NY: Midmarch Arts Press.

Kuspit, D. (1996), "Craft in Art, Art as Craft," *The New Art Examiner*, April: (53) 14–18, 53.

MacHenry, R. (2000), "Building on Local Strengths," in K. Grimes and B. L. Milgram (eds.), *Artisans and Cooperatives: Developing Alternative Trade for the Global Economy*, 25–44, Tucson, AZ: University of Arizona Press.

McComb, J. F. (2007), *The Effects of Modernity and Postmodernity on the Significance of Craft in the Process of Globalization*, New Delhi: Craft Revival Trust.

Moya, D. (2009), *Dead Aid: Why Aid is Not Working and How There is a Better Way for Africa,*

Munn, N. (1977), "The Spatiotemporal Transformation of Gawa Canoes," *Journal de la Société des Océanistes*, 33: 54.

Whiteley, N. (1993), *Design for Society*. London: Reaktion Books Ltd.

PART FOUR

Enterprise, Policy and Education for Positive Development

Editorial Introduction

Jeyon Jung

The preceding sections explored key concepts and examples of culturally significant artifacts, as well as the role of design in their revitalization. Part 4 takes a broader approach to consider the factors that support revitalization through design, including sustainable enterprise models, policy dimensions, and education. Understanding the role of these factors and their interrelationships is crucial to ensure positive development and sustain cultural significance attached to designs, products, and practices. The chapters in this section provide a range of in-depth case studies and international examples detailing contemporary approaches to development centered around traditional arts and crafts.

In *Sustaining Culturally Significant Designs, Products, and Practices: Lessons from the Hohokam,* Jacques Giard provides an overview of the Hohokam culture and their artifacts in order to draw lessons for design and design education today. The Hohokam people lived in the American Southwest from 300 BCE to 1500 CE. They not only became master potters but also engaged in the quantity production of pots for the purpose of trade, which made them the first industrial designers in the American Southwest, if not all of North America. This chapter describes the evolution of Hohokam pottery production and provides reflections for contemporary designers about ways to sustain cultural significance in the design and making of everyday things.

Steven Marotta, Austin Cummings, and Charles Heying, in *Accidents, Intentions, Movements, and Makers: Artisan Economy in Portland, Oregon, USA,* examine craft brewing, handmade bicycles, and street food carts. In discussing these examples, the authors apply the concept of over-determination, the idea that the causality of social phenomena is complex, sometimes contradictory, and results from multiple points of intersection. While identifying seemingly important policy interventions, they also show that unique local conditions as well as changing values and markets helped make Portland a place where these artisan enterprises took root and prospered. The authors' insistence on a deeply contextual reading of the development of Portland's artisan economy initially seems to yield no transferable lessons for other cities. However, the opposite is the case. Transferable lessons include: sensitivity to local conditions; an understanding of the actor/ecology interface; and the encouragement of policy makers to creatively respond to the situation as it develops.

In the next chapter, Sirpa Kokko considers *The Role of Higher Education in Sustaining Culturally Significant Crafts in Estonia*. Since gaining independence from the Soviet Union in 1991, Estonia has progressed enormously in terms of its technological development, and today it is a very modern country. Yet, despite the pressures of globalization, crafts remain an important aspect of Estonian cultural heritage and national identity. The Department of Estonian Native Crafts of Viljandi Culture Academy (University of Tartu) is devoted to the mission of researching and making visible Estonian craft traditions and to developing them further. This case study focuses on the role of this unique institution of higher education in sustaining culturally significant crafts. Participatory observation was used during several short visits between 2012 and 2015, and teachers and former students were interviewed in 2014. The findings suggest a need for similar institutions in other countries. Furthermore, cultural and social well-being deserve attention alongside economic considerations in education and research on crafts.

The Challenge of Intellectual Property Rights for Culturally Significant Patterns, Products, and Processes is based on the realization that Intellectual Property Rights (IPR) for design have challenged society for centuries. Tom Cassidy and Tracy Diane Cassidy acknowledge that there was little or no chance of being prescriptive about IPR in the context of culturally significant designs, products, and processes, but that it was necessary to make readers aware of the problems in defining and protecting design rights in their various forms. The chapter begins by looking at the law as it exists in the UK and highlights some of the difficulties and complexities that confront those who wish to try to use the system to protect designs or to obtain compensation for their abuse. Case studies are considered where culturally significant designs, products, and processes are involved. The chapter does not offer a complete understanding of the problem as it is unlikely that this exists, but rather it invites the reader to be aware of the complexities and suggests that a sound research approach may help avoid some of the pitfalls.

This section concludes with a chapter about Santa Fe, New Mexico, the second oldest city in the United States. Today, it consistently ranks among the top five cities in the US to visit by *Travel + Leisure* magazine, a ranking based in large part on the vibrancy of the traditional arts and crafts that continue to be made by the local Native American and Hispanic communities. In *The Case of the City Different: The Intersection of the Museum, the Artist, and the Marketplace*, Marsha C. Bol discusses how, when the traditional arts were under duress and disruption, and facing decline in so many other locales, the community of Santa Fe recognized the value of these arts as an asset to be fostered. In the past 100+ years, the Museum of New Mexico and other local cultural institutions have played a pivotal role, and continue to do so, in the conscious effort to sustain the health and economic viability of these unbroken traditional arts practices.

15

Sustaining Culturally Significant Designs, Products, and Practices

Lessons from the Hohokam

Jacques Giard

Introduction

Native cultures have forever designed and made artifacts. The now extinct Hohokam, a Native American people of southern Arizona, were no exception. They lived in the Sonoran desert for nearly 1,500 years. Despite the formidable challenges posed by the inhospitable climate and minimal natural resources, the Hohokam became master potters. This was not only the case for individual ceramic pieces made for personal use but also with pieces that were mass produced for trade. In some ways the Hohokam were the early industrial designers of the American Southwest. And like so many designers today, they created objects with attention to place, people, and process, or what I have come to call the 3 Ps of designing.

Are the designing activities of the Hohokam relevant to contemporary designers? That is, are there lessons of design and sustainability for industrial design in the twenty-first century? More specifically, can design educators and design professionals borrow from the Hohokam experience? The answer to all of these questions is yes, most definitely.

The chapter begins with a short description of place, people, and process, or the 3 Ps of designing. This trilogy provides the framework for the understanding of the cultural significance of designs, products, and practices. This is followed by an equally short description of the American Southwest, the people who originally inhabited the area in the millennium beginning around 1 CE, and the designing and making processes most commonly practiced. A more detailed description of what is known about the Hohokam people follows, with a focus on designing and making of ceramic artifacts over a period of a millennium and a half. This not only provides historical facts and evidence of the Hohokam culture but also applies the framework of place, people, and process as a means of understanding the overall impact on designing and making. The chapter ends with reflections on the designing and making of ceramic pots by the Hohokam and the relevance to contemporary industrial design practice and education.

Understanding designing using the 3 Ps

In most ways, contemporary design practice is based on a phenomenon that incorporates place, people, and process. That is, Place—era, location, and culture; People, whether as designers, makers or users, or in combination; and Process—how everyday things went from a concept imagined by people to physical realities in their world.

The 3 Ps of designing is not a stand-alone framework divorced from other definitions of design. Herbert Simon's definition is a case in point. In his book, *The Sciences of the Artificial*, Simon stated that, "Everyone designs who devises courses of action aimed at changing existing situations to preferred ones" (1996: 111). Implicit in his definition are elements that connect to people (e.g. everyone), process (e.g. courses of action), and place (e.g. "preferred" connects to place by way of the unique cultural values of place). All three need to be explained in more detail.

Place

The designing of artifacts always occurs in context. Context is a combination of place, era, and culture. It can be explicit or implicit but either way context is reflected in all artifacts. At a basic level, place is about geographical location, where factors such as climate and topography have measurable impact on designing and artifacts. Context is also about era, or the historical setting for an artifact. Culture is the last factor embedded in context. It is the value set of a group or society, and it permeates the artifact.

People

People are an intrinsic part of designing. After all, what reason is there to design other than for a human need or want? Admittedly, most early artifacts were strictly utilitarian and served a direct human need for subsistence. Inevitably, there is always a human dimension to an artifact, much like there is to designing.

Different people play different roles in the designing process. Generally speaking, they can be the designer, the maker, or the user—either separately or in combination. For instance, most consumers in today's developed world are users only; that is, they mostly acquire artifacts designed and made by others. Craftspeople, such as potters and weavers, are designer/makers. Less frequently, there are designer/maker/users, such as individuals who design and build furniture for their homes.

Process

Process is the third factor in the 3 Ps. It has always been part of designing, and occurs as the result of human intention. Furthermore, the designing process is either explicit (i.e. a well-intentioned plan executed properly) or implicit (i.e. an accidental discovery or unintended consequence). The *Post-it Note* was an accidental discovery, much like the suburb is considered an unintended consequence because of Henry Ford's Model T and the mobility that it provided to its owners.

As self-evident as the 3 Ps of designing are, they nevertheless provide an effective framework for understanding the presence of artifacts or everyday things, both past and present, including the ceramic pottery of the Hohokam. A study of Hohokam pottery follows, but not without first gaining an appreciation of the 3Ps in the American Southwest.

The American Southwest: Place, people, and process

This section examines the 3 Ps of designing and the American Southwest. It provides a macro perspective of the conditions that affected the designing and making activities of the people who inhabited this region. This initial information is general; details are provided in the section on the Hohokam, which follows on.

The American Southwest is a vast area. It includes the American states of Arizona and New Mexico as well as the southern parts of Colorado and Utah (Figure 15.1). In the context of early Native American culture, parts of northern Mexico are often included because national boundaries did not exist in pre-colonial time, i.e. prior to the arrival of the Spaniards in 1540, the first Europeans to set foot in the area (Reid and Whittlesey 1997: 3). In earlier geological eras, a great deal of the American Southwest was totally under water. The calcified tree trunks in the petrified forest of northern Arizona clearly show the results of this sea. There is also evidence of volcanic activity as late as 1040 CE with Sunset Crater near Flagstaff, Arizona. The topography is varied, from the low-altitude river valleys in the Salt River Basin of Arizona, at around 1,100 feet above sea level, to the higher elevations of the Colorado Plateau, with elevations of well over 7,000 feet (Plog 2008: 26–27). The Ancestral Puebloan cliff dwellings found at Mesa Verde in Colorado, for example, are situated at elevations that range from 7,000 to 8,500 feet. The vistas are high, long and wide and the sheer vastness of the place has led to it being known as "big-sky country."

As is to be expected, the climate and temperature varies between these topographical extremes. In the summer, the temperature in the Sonoran Desert can easily reach 110° F or more whereas the foothills of Colorado and New Mexico can

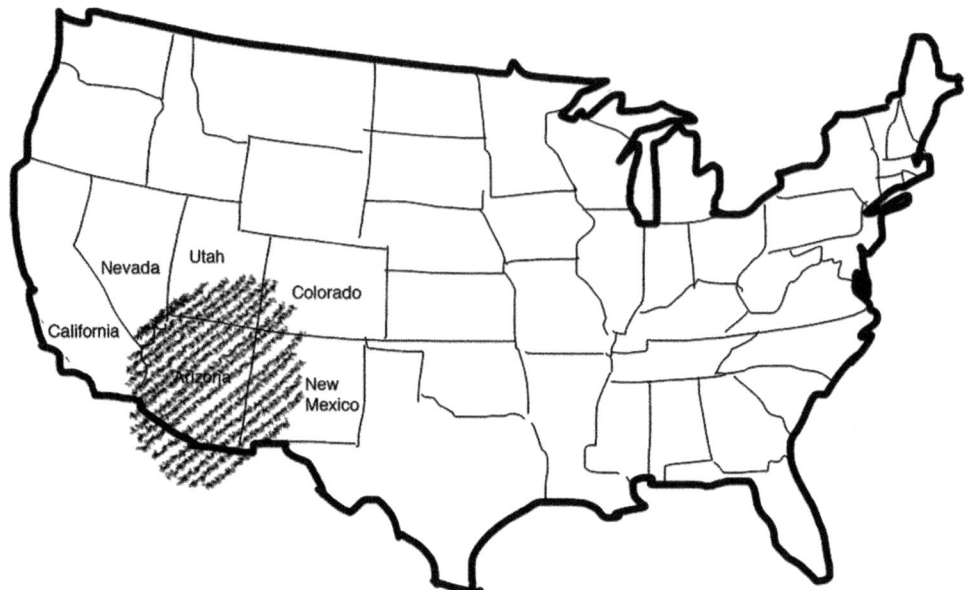

FIGURE 15.1 Arizona and New Mexico as well as the southern parts of Colorado and Utah are generally considered to be the American Southwest. Courtesy Giard. © Jacques Giard.

experience temperatures below freezing on a regular basis and for extended periods during the winters. Precipitation also poses unique challenges for human habitation. Many parts of the American Southwest get as few as 7–9 inches of rain a year. More significant is the fact that the rain is most often sporadic and comes as a deluge with sudden summer storms. Additionally, the soil does not absorb moisture quickly. Flooding is therefore a recurring problem. Furthermore, the rainfall in the area alone cannot be relied upon to sustain sufficient agriculture, which, in part, explains the building of canals by the Hohokam in both the Salt and Gila River Basins.

The land in many parts of the American Southwest is barren, with little or no vegetation. It does not appear to be habitable, and yet it was. Early natives found edible plants such as nuts from piñon pine and fruit of certain cactus (Plog 2008: 25). Plants also provided sustenance for a variety of birds and mammals, which became yet another food source (Plog 2008: 25). Cottonwood and pine provided the materials for construction of *kivas*, the ceremonial building (Sagstetter and Sagstetter 2010: 191) and larger trees, perhaps Ponderosa pine, provided the beams for the pueblo construction at Chaco Canyon in New Mexico (Strutin 2014: 19). In addition, mesquite and cottonwood were often used as uprights for the construction of *ramadas* (roofed shelters without walls) and round houses (Andrews and Bostwick 2000: 19). Even the woody ribs of the saguaro cactus, which is endemic to the Sonoran desert, were used as roofing material for round houses (Andrews and Bostwick 2000: 20).

Most archeologists agree that the early natives of the American Southwest, in the period prior to 1 CE, were hunter-gatherers. They are referred to as the Archaic people. Because of their nomadic lifestyle there is scant evidence of who these people were, their tools or their rituals (Reid and Whittlesey 1997: 42–68). The physical evidence that does exist begins to appear after 1 CE, when these same people became more sedentary and built permanent settlements. These settlements were basic and evidence shows that agriculture, as primitive as it was, now began to complement hunting and gathering (Reid and Whittlesey 1997: 43).

The overall population in the years after 1 CE grew, but slowly. Dispersion over such a large territory was neither equal nor evenly distributed. The transition from hunter-gatherer to agrarian culture led to a more stable lifestyle with a consequential growth in population. The ability to not only grow food but also to store it provided a level of predictability in food supply not typically possible as hunter-gatherers (Plog 2008: 57).

A sedentary lifestyle brought other changes to these early native residents of the American Southwest. There was the construction of simple quasi-permanent shelters such as pithouses (Figure 15.2). Later would come the cliff dwellings, which, by their very nature, created permanent communities in specific places principally because these provided protection as well as a dependable source of food. Staying in one place also meant more everyday things such as tools for agriculture and pots for the storage of the surplus (Plog 2008: 56–70).

The Hohokam: Place, people, and process

This section focuses on the Hohokam people, the place that they inhabited, and the process of ceramic production.

As is evident from the foregoing, the American Southwest poses almost insurmountable challenges for human survival. The Sonoran Desert, which is a specific area in the American Southwest, poses even greater challenges (Reid and Whittlesey 1997: 70). Yet this is where the Hohokam settled.

The Sonoran Desert occupies over 100,000 square miles of territory that spreads from southern Arizona and northern Mexico to parts of western California and south into Baja California (Figure 15.3). Despite being considered one of the most ecologically diverse deserts in the world, the Sonoran desert is arid; temperatures can exceed 120° F in summer yet drop to freezing or near freezing at night in the winter. The topography is generally flat with some mountains such as the McDowells (4,000 feet) and Four Peaks (7,600 feet) in the Salt River Basin and the Santa Catalinas (9,000 feet) in the Tucson area. The distinguishing feature of this part of the Sonoran Desert is the Gila and Salt Rivers, both of which had a perennial flow of water at the time of the Hohokam. Over the millennia, plants, mammals, birds, insects and reptiles have inhabited this desert region. Despite the harsh conditions and by using their ingenuity and knowledge of place, the native peoples were not only able to survive, they were also able to thrive (Reid and Whittlesey 1997: 70).

The Hohokam people lived in a specific part of the Sonoran Desert, an area bounded by the Salt River and Gila River Basins, in what is now Phoenix and Coolidge in Arizona. Because of the regular flow of water, the two rivers made this place a logical choice for habitation. Water, because of its use in agriculture, its transportation via canal building and perhaps because of its scarcity, would become a significant part of Hohokam culture and provide it with a distinct tribal identity.

a

b

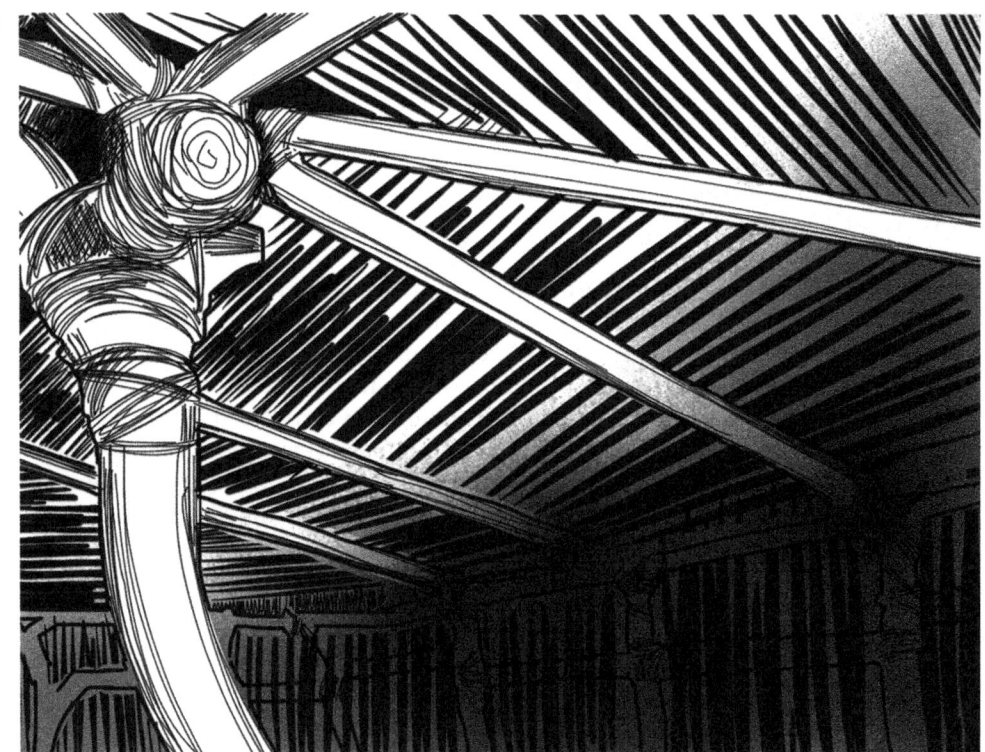

FIGURE 15.2 (a) Replicas of Hohokam pithouses, including a *ramada*; and (b) Internal structure and construction of a pithouse. *Source:* Pueblo Grande Museum, Phoenix, Arizona. Courtesy Giard. © Jacques Giard.

FIGURE 15.3 The Sonoran Desert spans parts of Arizona and California and stretches south into Mexico and Baja California. Courtesy Giard. © Jacques Giard.

An amazing people in an amazing place

People are affected by place and this was certainly true for the Hohokam, "To understand the Hohokam, one must understand the desert setting in which they lived" (Andrews and Bostwick 2000: 7). In the 1,500 years of Hohokam presence in the Gila and Salt River Basins, archeologists have identified five distinct periods of cultural development.

300 BCE–300 CE: Archeologists are divided on the origins of the Hohokam (Reid and Whittlesey 1997: 86). Consequently, they have not given a name to the earliest period of Hohokam culture. Nevertheless, it is a period when the first villages were established. These consisted mostly of pithouses and storage pits. It was also a period when local agriculture began, although the Hohokam continued to be hunter-gatherers. Little physical evidence remains from these sites, except for a few grinding tools, baskets, and pottery (Reid and Whittlesey 1997: 86–7).

Pioneer Period (300 CE–775 CE): This is regarded as the earliest period of Hohokam culture. It was a time when more permanent and larger settlements were created, some of them with lodges and plazas. It is also the beginning of early canal construction, which led to improved agriculture including the growing of cotton (Reid and Whittlesey 1997: 88–9).

Colonial Period (775 CE–975 CE): In this period there was an increase in population and a subsequent expansion of territory. The settlements were more numerous; some had platform mounds and ball courts, both of which are indicative of specific Hohokam rituals. The canal systems also became more extensive. There was also a general refinement of artistic work, which, in part, encouraged the development of a trade network with other indigenous tribes (Reid and Whittlesey 1997: 91–6).

Sedentary Period (975 CE–1150 CE): In this period, archaeologists begin to detect major changes in the Hohokam culture. For example, many ancestral sites were abandoned and the ball-court system ended. It also appears that the Hohokam were undergoing certain sociocultural changes, especially in the hierarchy within individual settlements. Evidence of such changes include novel building types such as new above-ground structures, as found in the Casa Grande in Coolidge, Arizona, which is a four-story adobe building believed to be for the leaders of the village (Reid and Whittlesey 1997: 96–100).

Classic Period (1150 CE–1500 CE): Archeologists divide the Classic Period into three separate eras. In the Early Classic Period, 1150 CE to 1300 CE, the canal systems became as extensive as they would ever be in Hohokam culture, as were the settlements and villages. In this time, two architectural types dominated the Hohokam villages: the platform mounds and the compounds, where individual groups within a settlement created a more private space often with walls (Reid and Whittlesey 1997: 100–7). The ruins found at Pueblo Grande in Phoenix, Arizona are a good example of this kind of settlement. The period 1300 CE to 1400 CE saw the continued development of communities based around large irrigation networks. These communities often had great houses as well as elevated structures on top of platform mounds, features that were exceptional in the past but that had now become more common (Reid and Whittlesey 1997: 103–4). The demise of the Hohokam culture began in the Late Classic Period, 400 and 1500 CE. For reasons not fully understood, large community settlements and canals were abandoned, and the Hohokam returned to living in small villages. Some archeologists believe that the place—the Gila and Salt River Basins—could no longer sustain what had become relatively large population centers. The water in the canals had not only become salinated, reduced quantities could no longer produce enough crops to sustain the population (Reid and Whittlesey 1997: 106–7).

Process: Designing and making of ceramics objects

The earliest evidence of Hohokam pottery dates back to the Pioneer Period (Barstad 1999: 8). By the time of the Civano phase in the Late Classic period, around 1300

CE, the Hohokam had become known as master potters; their pots could be found throughout the Southwest (Barstad 1999: 28).

The processes that underpinned the particular skills and production methods over a period of 1,500 years provides insight into the designing and making of everyday things, initially as objects of utility and personal use but eventually leading to quantity production and trade.

The Pioneer Period (300 CE) had some of the earliest examples and production of ceramic artifacts in the form of clay figurines, plain ware, red ware, and red-on-buff decorated pottery. Plain buff/brown and a polished red ware were among the earliest forms of Hohokam pottery; most pieces were utilitarian in design. Applied decoration began to appear around 500 CE, but was limited to red chevrons and spirals painted on gray backgrounds. The quality of the ceramic pottery improved over time with details such as the incising of bowl interiors, and the applied decoration became more refined with the use of fine red lines, at times covering the entire vessel (Barstad 1999: 14).

In the Colonial Period (775 CE–975 CE), Hohokam pottery became more distinctive and intricate (Barstad 1999: 22). It is not unusual to find flared bowls and straight-sided jars, all showing a design direction that goes beyond mere utility. Decoration also became more prevalent with details such as hatching, which replaced solid lines. There was also the increased use of geometric elements such as curvilinear scrolls and, for the first time, the use of human and animal figures. By

FIGURE 15.4 A ceramic bowl from the Santa Cruz era in the late Colonial period. *Source:* Pueblo Grande Museum, Phoenix, Arizona. Courtesy Giard. © Jacques Giard.

most accounts, painted decoration hit its peak in the period from 850 CE to 975 CE (Figure 15.4).

It is in the following era, the Sedentary Period from 975 CE to 1150 CE, where the making of ceramic artifacts appears to depart from small quantities for individual use to large quantities for trading purposes (Figure 15.5). Quantity also appears to have affected the quality. Wall thickness, for example, increased and the applied decoration became less refined. The design of the pottery—its shape and decoration—also took on a regional style, one that archeologists could more easily identify (Barstad 1999: 24).

For reasons that remain unclear, Hohokam pottery began to lose its variety of form and refinement of decoration beginning in the Early Classic period (1150 CE–1300 CE). Red-on-buff pottery continued to be made but forms appeared to be limited to jars and handled pitchers. Similarly, applied decoration became limited with a disappearance in human and animal shapes as well as repeated

FIGURE 15.5 A ceramic pot from the Sacaton era in the early Sedentary period. *Source:* Pueblo Grande Museum, Phoenix, Arizona. Courtesy Giard. © Jacques Giard.

geometric elements. Changes in pottery design became even more dramatic by the Late Classic period (1300 CE–1400 CE). For example, decorated pottery was replaced with slipped and red ware, which was highly polished. There was also the appearance of exceptional pieces, such as Salado Polychrome. Archeologists consider such pieces as clear departures from traditional Hohokam pottery of the era. No one is certain whether these pieces were made locally or traded (Barstad 1999: 26–8).

Sustaining culturally significant design: Lessons from the Hohokam

Despite the presence of artifacts going back millions of years in human history the birth of industrial design is most often associated with the Industrial Revolution. After all, this was the era when everyday things went from being made by hand to being mass produced by machines. With this came the concept of designing for industry or, as it is called today, industrial design. In the case of the Hohokam, mass production did not occur with machines but it was mass or quantity production nevertheless. Moreover, the quantity production of ceramic artifacts was for the purpose of trade and not strictly for personal use. The latter direction in artifact production is often identified with industrial design.

This brief exploration of culturally significant designs, products and practices in the context of the Hohokam allows us to identify lessons for contemporary designers. Six lessons are described below. However, the section begins with a brief overview of contemporary design education because it is in this setting where most designers today acquire their requisite skills and knowledge in design.

Contemporary design education

Contemporary design education in the developed world tends to mimic its professional counterpart, more or less. This is certainly the case for architecture, interior design, and graphic design; it is also the case for industrial design. It therefore comes as no surprise that the curricula of most design programs today, at least generally speaking, mirror the ethos of the design professions. As a consequence, today's designers are educated in a formal way and according to well-established practices mostly determined by their respective design professions.

Neither does it come as any surprise that the requisite skills and knowledge in contemporary design education reflect the overarching ethos of the developed world. This is the case for Europe, North America, and parts of Southeast Asia. This direction is often evident in a reflection of the broader context including national and international issues with industry, trade, and commerce. Despite the fact that many designers and design advocates continue to laud intrinsic values of artifacts via design awards and design collections in museums, the greater part of the design profession exists to serve the needs of industry, trade, and commerce. Consequently, design education has tended of late to become more interdisciplinary. It is not unusual, for example, for a program in industrial design to offer courses in engineering technology (industry), economics (trade), and marketing (commerce).

For the Hohokam, designing and making were quite different compared to the contemporary model just described. The links that connect design practices, significance of products, and the Hohokam begin with the transition from a society of hunter-gatherers to a culture based on agrarian practices and the surplus that ensued. It is at this point in history that we find the first lesson.

The age of surplus: An existential reason for everyday things

The Age of Surplus (Giard 2012: 73–93) occurred when our human ancestors began to settle in one location or another, some 10,000 years ago. Early agriculture and domestication of animals gradually put an end to an existence based solely on hunting and gathering. Agriculture and domestication of animals made people more sedentary, but also created the concept of surplus (Diamond 1999: 88–90), which became a catalyst for the evolution of most everyday things. A surplus of grain, for example, necessitated the need for vessels of one kind or another to contain, protect, and ship the grain. With these vessels came vessel makers, who also created a surplus of their own.

The Hohokam experience with ceramic pots closely followed this pattern. The first ceramic pots were meant for personal use. Pots were not made for the purpose of trade. With the development of tribal networks beginning in the Colonial Period, Hohokam pottery changed. Progressively, it became mass produced. Pottery became a surplus and a commodity to be traded.

Contemporary design practice and education is very much based on the concept of surplus. That is, contemporary design has roots in the fine and applied arts where, like fine and applied artists, production quantities were small and self-expression was most often the norm. Mass production, brought upon by the Machine Age of the nineteenth century, clearly amplified surplus production much like the more recent phenomenon of globalization, which has increased the amplification even more.

For the Hohokam, the concept of surplus and its impact on the production of pottery occurred incrementally. For contemporary designers, this same concept is both real and inevitable. It is the *raison d'être* for most everyday things. General population growth provides one reason for a surplus, as does the larger population base when societal groups interconnect. Nevertheless, the challenge of cultural identity remains a design factor that cannot be ignored. No one knows for certain how deliberate this factor may have been for the Hohokam, but it is an ongoing challenge for today's designers. By their very nature, artifacts contain the identity of a culture as well as the individual designers. This identity was evident in Hohokam pottery, a feature that today allows for the identification and cataloging of individual pieces. It appears that the challenge of identity is now greater than it has ever been.

On one hand, the pressures to conform to one homogenized global esthetic or other are real; on the other, conformity comes with the loss of cultural identity and self.

Place: More than location

Like culture, place too is reflected in the artifact. Consequently, place is a source of identity. The Hohokam understood the many and varied constraints of place. In several ways, place transformed the Hohokam. They may not have deliberately included place in an explicit way; nevertheless, there is a sense of locality in their artifacts. This was certainly the case with the clay used in the pottery, which of course came from the area. But it was also in the glyphs or pictograms that appeared on many of the pots. These represented local animals or characters from Hohokam myths and legends.

Artifacts, as mirrors of place, add a distinct identity. If anything, it is an antidote to the pressures of creating artifacts that not only lack an identity with place but that also strive to be global and not of one place or another. For contemporary designers, the question of location and identity via the artifact is perhaps a simple one: artifacts will reflect place with or without the intentional intervention of the designer. The choice to deliberately intervene or not therefore becomes the designer's to make, clearly.

The making process: The application of care and mindfulness

The Hohokam most likely had little choice about being efficient with the making of pottery. The latter underwent few processes other than removing the correct soil from the earth, doing whatever needed to be done to process the soil into clay, making the pots, and firing them. Overall, the making process was relatively simple. This is not the case for many of today's everyday things. The making processes can at times be highly complex. Efficiency may still be an issue, but efficiency can too often be limited narrowly to the making only. Issues that arise before making, such as the extraction of minerals at the front end of the making process, and the disposal of the everyday thing at the back end are rarely a significant part of contemporary design education.

Recognizing and acknowledging the full impact of the making process in product design—from extraction to disposal—becomes an important component in contemporary design education. The Hohokam were familiar with the full scope of the making process. To be ignorant of it today can easily place us in a position where many everyday things do very little but pay us a convenient visit on the way to the landfill (McDonough and Braungart 2002: 4).

Using and designing are interconnected

Unlike most contemporary designers, the Hohokam did not receive a formal design education. That is, they never attended design school. Instead, they learned the skills of pottery making—as well as associated knowledge—by making everyday things for which they had gained an in-depth knowledge by using these same everyday things every day. In other words, using and designing were interconnected.

Designers need to have this same in-depth knowledge of use if they are to design effectively. This approach of designing via using was quite common and even celebrated as a design direction of choice. Henry Dreyfuss, the American designer, was aware of this phenomenon and acknowledged as much with his advice posted on the wall of his New York office, which stated that " the object being worked on is going to be ridden in, sat upon, looked at, talked into, activated, operated, or in some other way be used by people individually or en masse" (1955: 23). Clearly, design was much more than visual appeal. Function was paramount. Today, many designers are confronted with a situation that allows them to at times experience product use vicariously because of digital technology. As enticing as this direction may be it no way replicates the actual use of the product.

Knowing your material makes a difference

The Hohokam developed an intimate knowledge of the material used in the making of their pottery. That knowledge was not theoretical. Rather, it came from a process that mingled heuristic knowledge of the material with a kinesthetic approach to making. The knowledge was hands-on and acquired by doing.

The situation with contemporary design is quite different. There are now more materials at the disposal of designers than there has ever been, and using them appropriately has become more complex. Nevertheless, designers cannot shirk their responsibility when it comes to having an intimate knowledge of materials. A great deal of this knowledge will necessarily be theoretical, at least to some degree. However, designers need to gain familiarity with materials well beyond the theory. Walter Gropius, in his role as director of the Bauhaus, was keenly aware of the advantage of material knowledge and encouraged students to develop the mindset of the craftsman by working with materials directly (Farmer 1971: 13). Contemporary designers must not forget this important lesson.

Learning by doing

There was no design school in Hohokam society. Learning to design occurred as a routine activity much like most other daily activities. Learning to design occurred by doing. In fact, a great deal of what we learn is often achieved by doing. That is how a person learns to swim or to paddle a canoe. Theoretical knowledge about such activities is not particularly useful in gaining proficiency. Knowing the theory of swimming when the canoe tips will not help you.

For the Hohokam, learning by doing was their only choice. However, that is not the case with contemporary designers. There are choices available. Digital and computer technologies are obvious ones. With the capacity to design with these aids the probability of designing by doing diminishes. The actual act of doing something—anything—far surpasses a doing experience that is strictly digital. No computer-aided design application can surpass the hands-on activity of visual thinking, something that I call PAD or pencil-aided design.

Conclusion

Scientists often make reference to standing on the shoulders of giants who came before them. They do so as a way of expressing that knowledge is cumulative and that contemporary scientists work from an existing foundation. To some degree, designers operate in a similar fashion. Like the scientists, there are giants of design who created a foundation for contemporary design. Most of these designers are relatively recent, and began laying the foundation some 200 years ago. Moreover, they mostly came from the developed world. Having said that, the Hohokam were also giants who came before us. And much like the other giants of design they too can teach us something about culturally significant designs, products, and practices.

References

Andrews, J. P. and T. W. Bostwick (2000), *Desert Farmers at the River's Edge: The Hohokam and Pueblo Grande*, Phoenix: Pueblo Grande Museum and Archaeological Park.

Barstad, J. (1999), *Hohokam Pottery*, Tucson: Western National Parks Association.

Diamond, J. (1999), *Guns, Germs and Steel*, New York, NY: W. W. Norton & Company.

Dreyfuss, H. (1955), *Designing for People*, New York, NY: Simon and Schuster.

Farmer, J. (1971), *Concepts of the Bauhaus: The Busch-Reisinger Museum Collection*, Cambridge, MA: Harvard University.

Giard, J. (2012), *Designing: A Journey Through Time*, Phoenix, AZ: The Dorset Group.

McDonough, W. and M. Braungart (2002), *Cradle to Cradle: Remaking the Way We Make Things*, New York, NY: North Point Press.

Plog, S. (2008), *Ancient Peoples of the American Southwest*, London: Thames & Hudson.

Reid, J. and S. Whittlesey (1997), *The Archaeology of Ancient Arizona*, Tucson, AZ: University of Arizona Press.

Sagstetter, B. and B. Sagstetter (2010), *The Cliff Dwellings Speak: Exploring the Ancient Ruins of the Greater American Southwest*, Denver, CO: Benchmark Publishing of Colorado.

Simon, H. (1996), *The Sciences of the Artificial*, Cambridge, MA: The MIT Press.

Strutin, M. (2014), *Chaco: A Cultural Legacy*, Tucson, AZ: Western National Parks Association.

16

Accidents, Intentions, Movements, and Makers

Artisan Economy in Portland, Oregon, USA

Steve Marotta, Austin Cummings, and Charles Heying

Introduction

It may be tempting for urban designers to look to cities that are having their moment in the spotlight in search of the policies, particularities, and dogmas that got them there. The idea, of course, is to convert these signposts into revitalization strategies in other cities. But the research that we have undertaken in Portland over the past decade was never meant to be a user's manual for how to remedy developmental conundrums in other cities, or even how to produce vibrancy or liveability in places that are doing just fine. We see Portland's artisan economy (Heying 2010) as locally distinctive, and although numerous other cities have similar artisanal characteristics, the economies of those cities have grown up in different ways. Some of the inputs, such as global capital and popular media, are indeed connected, which certainly gives the artisan milieus in these disparate cities a likeness. Other inputs, such as local history and regional *terroir*, are unique to each place. To attempt to show our insistence on complexity and nuance for urban design scholars, we will demonstrate the multitude of factors that have contributed to the development of Portland's artisan economy in three case studies below.

In discussing our cases, we consider the notion of overdetermination (Althusser 2005). Borrowed in part from Freud, overdetermination is the idea that determining the causality of a social phenomenon is complex and often contradictory, as causality is the result of an impossible number of points of intersection. For Althusser, determinants are everywhere, and most are superficially invisible. Some determinants are obvious—a directly influential piece of legislation, for example. Some determinants are less obvious but still as influential, such as the effects of the global economy on the local scale. Gibson-Graham interprets overdetermination as the "irreducible specificity of every determination" (1995: 27), a point that stresses the further need to explicate the determinants of each input into the phenomena in question. In other words, singling out a specific determinant does little to explain the conditions of that determinant. Gibson-Graham continues: "Every event is constituted by all the conditions existing in that moment (including the past and future)" (1995: 28).

A major implication of the idea of overdetermination is anti-essentialism. One way to think about essentialism is to say that one causal factor is essential while others are inessential (Gibson-Graham 1995); Althusser argues that there is no way to make such a claim. Instead, he is asking us to consider the totality of context: the conditions in which something is brought into existence are inseparable from the thing itself. In this chapter, we intend to show why determining causality for a particular social phenomenon—in our case, Portland's artisan economy—can better be understood through the lens of overdetermination. The three cases below will describe the overt causal factors in some detail while also pointing to various other social contexts that may have played a role in structuring each case.

Craft beer

In 1933, the US Congress passed the 21st Amendment, thus ending the Prohibition era in the US and making it legal for private citizens to make wine in their homes. Curiously, it would remain illegal to brew beer at home for the next forty years. This "clerical error" (Lenatti 2013) was eventually corrected, and this correction has led to the popular internet meme that credits the 39th American President Jimmy Carter with saving craft beer. In 1979, Carter signed HR 1337, a House of Representatives bill that corrected the 21st Amendment's omission (Alworth 2010; Carlson 2011), finally legalizing home brewing right at the historical moment when the global economy was starving for new entrepreneurs.

Of course it's not a far leap to assume that the legalization of home brewing would correlate to a rise in the number of craft brew brands, breweries, and brewpubs, as potential craft brew entrepreneurs could now legally buy supplies and market-test on their friends and family. But the legalization of home brewing does not explain the unevenness of craft brewing between various cities in the US. Craft brewing has set deep roots in certain cities around the US—Denver, San Francisco, and Brooklyn, for example—while not thriving (or perhaps just getting to the party late) in other cities. Portland, though, might be the vanguard of the craft brew resurgence, a hub for the craft brew industry. Two of Portland's favorite monikers are "brewtopia" and "beervana" (Heying 2010: 67–70), and the city was referred to as America's beer capital as early as 2001 (Jones 2001). As of June 1, 2015, Oregon had 234 craft breweries. It's a good thing there are so many options, as Oregonians consumed over 580,000 barrels of Oregon-brewed craft beer in 2014 (Oregon Brewers Guild 2016). Of Oregon's 234 brewing facilities, ninety-one are in the Portland metro area and sixty-one are within Portland's city limits, giving substance to Portland's claim to have more craft breweries than any other city in the world (Lefferts 2014).

Portland didn't get to be the "beer capital" of the US by accident, at least not completely by accident. While other west coast cities had been developing a craft beer culture around beer styles and variation, Portland's craft beer community was somewhat more focused on the social aspect of beer drinking—the brewpub. As in most states, Oregon law historically separated beer consumption from production, meaning that beer producers could not sell beer in the same building in which they produced it. This made no sense to Oregon's nascent crop of craft brewers, eventually motivating the McMenamin brothers—along with the owners of Portland Brewing, Bridgeport Brewery, and the Widmer brothers—to lobby for a law allowing beer to be brewed and consumed in the same place. The bill was finally passed in 1985; the number of brewpubs that have sprung up in Portland seems to testify to the bill's influence (Woodward and Bennett 2010).

While this policy shift directly influenced the establishment of a very important element of the craft beer culture in Portland, there are countless other policies that surely had indirect influence. Take, for example, Portland's industrial sanctuary policy, introduced in the city's 1980 comprehensive plan to reserve urban space specifically for manufacturing purposes. This was an interesting policy move considering Carl Abbott's claim that Portland had deindustrialized "before anyone had coined the term" (2000: 245). When the sanctuary policy came into effect, Portland was already reorienting its industrial buildings to fit the demands of the emerging service economy, well ahead of most other cities. The timing of the aforementioned homebrew bill and Portland's sanctuary policy played well to the craft brew industry, and it provided the space into which home brewers could gradually scale up production. And indeed, the central eastside neighborhood, one of the industrial sanctuary zones, is home to at least eight craft breweries today (Travel Portland 2016). To further reinforce the relationship between industrial zones and craft breweries, a swath of the Pearl District (also a former industrial site before rezoning) known as "Brewery Blocks" is home to another five breweries.

Policy alone, however, did not determine the shape of the craft brewing industry in Portland. The *terroir* of the Portland region creates special possibilities for craft beer production. First, the water Portland brewers use is classified by the City of Portland as very soft, with hardness in the 3–8 ppm range (hard water is usually thought of in the 180+ ppm range). Second, water is in ample supply, thanks to six-to-eight months a year of steady light rain (Portland Water Bureau 2016a,b). Third, the wet climate of Oregon's Willamette Valley is perfect for growing the hops that give many craft beers their hallmark bitterness. In fact, the Pacific Northwest states of Washington, Oregon, and Idaho together produce about ninety-nine percent of the United States' hops (George 2015: 4). Recently, a shift from commodity production to specialty hops production has given Portland brewers access to small batch growers (Cizmar 2012). Access to plentiful soft water and locally-sourced ingredients—malted barley and yeast are also easy to source locally—(Ransom 2011) has given brewers a level of flexibility that would be difficult to find in other cities.

The weather isn't the only competitive advantage Portland can claim. There are a handful of industrial resources—perhaps because of the craft-brewing explosion—that can't readily be found elsewhere. Three companies, MCF:Craft Brewing Systems, Portland Kettle Works, and JNVW, in metropolitan Portland make specialty equipment for the craft brewing industry, allowing local craft brewers quick and in-person access to the exact equipment they need. In terms of access to a competent labor force, there are education programs at major universities that offer degrees and certifications in brewing. The fermentation science concentration in the Food Science and Technology Degree Program at Oregon State University is a four-year degree that allows students to hone their brewing skills while studying the precise sciences of quality control, preservation, and even public health aspects of brewing. The University of Portland's business school has created a "Master Strategist" Certification specifically oriented to the craft beer business. Portland State University also offers a Business of Craft Brewing Certification. Instruction in both programs focuses on the specifics of marketing, operations management, and distribution for the craft brew industry.

An additional important determinant is Portland's social and political climate. Besides being one of the most politically progressive cities in the US, Portland has recently become a hub for all things DIY (Heying 2010). The resurgence of localism, community-based knowledge production (Heying and Marotta, 2016), and the increasingly large economic impact of Portland's maker movement (Heying and Marotta 2014) all show Portland as a place with a fiercely independent spirit. Perhaps it is this spirit that rejects "corporate" beer: according to Oregon Public Broadcasting, Portland is the only city in the United States that consistently spends more money on craft beers than on beers from the large beer conglomerates such as Miller-Coors and Anheuser-Busch/InBev (Anderson 2014). Portland's small businesses rely on this spirit of independence, but independence doesn't necessarily translate into fierce competition. Rather, what has materialized in the city's artisan economy is what Portland's New Deal Distillery has phrased "coopertition," a portmanteau of cooperation and competition (Heying 2010: 271). Coopertition is an apt neologism for why there seems to be enough room for almost 100 breweries in the metropolitan Portland area: breweries don't see themselves in competition with each other; rather, they collaborate on a regular basis. In fact, Base Camp Brewing has begun hosting an annual *Collabofest* (2016) to celebrate this convivial spirit among Portland's craft brewers.

Bikes

As gas prices soared in 2009, many Portland craft bike builders couldn't keep up with demand. So steep was the demand curve that Sacha White, owner of Vanilla Bicycles, had some customers waiting up to five years for a handmade bike (Jacklett 2009). Between 2006 and 2008 the handcrafted bicycle sector grew quickly from five to seventeen makers, with most of the new businesses being small, and locally owned (Alta Planning + Design 2008). By 2016, that number had more than doubled to thirty-seven bike builders (Portland Bike Links 2016). Portland has developed a national reputation as a bicyclist's nirvana: the city has over 4,000 annual races, rides, events and tours, more than 270 miles of bike paths, lanes, and boulevards, and is consistently ranked as one of the most bike-friendly cities in the nation (Alta Planning + Design 2008). Biking, like beer, has taken on mythological characteristics in Portland, becoming branded into the city's built environment, its history, and even the image it broadcasts to the world.

But Portland was not always synonymous with bicycles. It wasn't until the early 1970s that the first real push to legitimize bicycling as a form of commuter transportation occurred. These early efforts by the Bicycle Transportation Alliance, the Bike Lobby, the Oregon Environmental Council, and Portland State University students pushed to secure funding for bicycle facilities and publicly financed infrastructure. This advocacy culminated in House Bill 1700, known informally as the "bike bill." It was the first legislation in the US to designate state funding for bicycle infrastructure. The bill required cities and counties receiving state highway funds to designate one percent of tax revenues to the construction of new bicycle and pedestrian pathways. By the fall of 1971, the city of Portland started construction on new bike pathways, conducting bicycle studies for future pathways, and creating ways for bicycling advocates to be a part of the formal governmental structure (Johnson 2002).

Securing funding helped legitimize bicycling as a form of transportation rather than a form of recreation. Legitimacy helped incorporate bicycling into the city's planning process, further enhancing Portland's emerging image as a bicycling and environmental leader. After the passage of the bike bill in 1971, bicycling advocates became further entrenched in the planning process and gained roles in city government, including a full-time bicycle program manager position in 1978 (Johnson 2002). In 1981, bicycling was incorporated into Portland's Comprehensive Plan. In 1994, the city created its first Bicycling Master Plan, which administered projects by tapping into federal funding through the Inter-Modal Surface Transportation Efficiency Act of 1991. The cumulative legacy of these policy and planning decisions has been a sense of political legitimacy for Portland's bicycling community as well as some real grist for the media mill; Portland was recognized as America's most bicycle friendly city by *Bicycling Magazine* in 1995, and continues to be ranked among the world's best bicycle cities (Ibsen and Cunningham 2015: 7).

Portland's government agencies do more than just write policy documents: in some cases, they directly contribute to the expansion of the craft bicycle industry. The Portland Development Commission (PDC), for example, has worked closely with Portland's craft bike makers to encourage the growth of the industry through a variety of actions. They have sponsored "cyclocross" races, handmade exhibits in the Portland International Airport, and the North American Handmade Bicycle Show. PDC also hosted classes to teach frame builders basic business management and organization skills, and worked with the Urban Bicycle Institute, a well-known bike design school, to open a new campus location in Portland. PDC's explicit goal has been to improve cohesion and innovation within the industry and to solidify Portland's image as a bicycle design innovation hub (Haight 2006). This image has contributed to Portland's reputation as a bicycling destination, attracting new tourists, residents, and businesses that want the benefits of the lifestyle affiliated with bicycling culture.

Aside from policy-related determinants, the craft bicycle industry in Portland has been influenced by a host of contextual factors, not the least of which is a piece of geographical serendipity. Portland's flat topography, temperate climate, lush greenery, and clean air have all contributed to a climate conducive to bicycling. This is not to mention the fact that it rarely dips below 40°F (5°C) degrees, meaning infrequent snow and no threat of frostbite or icy streets. And although the city is known for its rainy climes, hard rain and severe weather are rare. These geographic factors together with the city's history of environmental activism have been crucial in making bicycling an important part of the DNA of Portland.

The internet, popular media, and the external image of Portland as a bicycling utopia also factor as determinants of the bicycling culture in Portland. According to Smith and Wineman (2010: 117): "Two key tools help market Portland's artisan bike goods: One is the Internet, which allows people from around the country and world to gain knowledge about the products. The other is Portland itself: the association of products with Portland, the 'platinum' bike city, makes builders more attractive to bike-savvy individuals beyond the region." The majority of Portland craft bicycle manufacturer's sales are outside of Portland, and it is e-commerce that has allowed craft bicycle makers to be profitable. The blogosphere has been crucial in the promotion and proliferation of Portland's bicycle culture. Most notable is Bike Portland (Maus 2016), a globally popular blog devoted to promoting races, rides, and reporting on planning and policy issues related to bicycling in Portland. In interviews we conducted with Portland's bicycle artisans, product features in blogs like Bike Portland are routinely credited as being indispensable to an enterprise's success.

Portland's bicycle culture is also nurtured by a variety of bicycle-related educational programs and nonprofits. The most prominent bicycle trade school in Portland is the aforementioned United Bicycle Institute, regarded by many as the bicycle industry's leading technical school. Portland State University students have won awards at the ASME Human Powered Vehicle Challenge (Lydgate 2008), and the university is home to the Initiative for Bicycle and Pedestrian Innovation research program. There are many nonprofits that help foster Portland's climate of innovation—Cycle Oregon, the Bicycle Transportation Alliance, and the Community Cycling Center, just to name a few. With so many resources, the bicycling industry in Portland has exploded over the past two decades. Portland has hundreds of small artisanal bicycle frame makers, high-end accessory makers, bike rack makers, gear makers, bike apparel makers, and bike bag makers. Other bicycle businesses include bicycle brew tours, a variety of ride-up bike bars, and a handful of messenger and delivery services (Portland Bike Links 2016); even the weekly alternative papers are often delivered by bike.

Food carts

With over five hundred of these wheel-bound eateries organized in parking lot "pods" or staking claim on sidewalks, food carts are a full-fledged urban phenomenon in Portland (Burmeister 2015; Rodgers and Roy 2010). Street food is relatively new to US cities, but Portland's food cart vendors take this culinary form to new levels.

Besides providing inspired food, the artisanal entrepreneurs complement other forms of pedestrian urbanism, and act as a viable form of interim or "pop-up" retail development. A number of unique contextual factors have contributed to the growth of Portland's food cart culture including: Portland's built environment; the city's light touch approach to food cart regulation and zoning; Portland's internationally renowned food and urban agriculture movement; low barriers to entry; the almost unexplainable lack of friction between food cart and brick and mortar restaurant owners; and the use of social media.

Portland has some of the shortest blocks in the nation, creating a city that is highly walkable and integrated with its surroundings. The success of food carts is partially due to their embeddedness in Portland's most walkable areas. For example, the pod at 9th and Alder in downtown Portland, which, having over sixty carts, is "the largest concentration of street food in America" (Urban Vitality Group 2010), thrives because of its access to downtown workers during lunch. Food cart pods also often locate close to areas with a vibrant nightlife; many of these carts stay open until 3:00 or 4:00 a.m. *Food Cartology* (Urban Vitality Group 2010), a study of Portland's food carts corroborates this observation with survey data, indicating that sixty-five percent of food cart customers walk to the food cart. The relationship between food carts and foot traffic is mutually constitutive, however, in that food carts generally increase foot traffic in an area, activate streetscapes that may not be initially "ripe" for development, and capture money spent in the community. From a development perspective, starting a food cart pod requires low upfront capital costs, with the potential to increase the desirability of tenant mix by rewarding food carts that achieve higher sales with longer leases, making it a viable and valid development strategy for land and property owners.

The City of Portland has also had a powerful impact on the food cart industry, but not necessarily in the ways we might imagine. In 1965, Portland's mayor allowed a food cart outside of City Hall in downtown Portland. Twenty years later, the same year the brewpub law was passed, the zoning and development of Pioneer Courthouse Square (a "public" space in central Portland) included dedicated space for food carts. Since then, however, the city has generally taken a hands-off, if sometimes ambivalent, stance towards regulating food carts. For example, there are loose definitions of what is considered a food cart in Portland and very little zoning regulation in place that delineates where food carts can locate, how long they can stay there, relevant permit structures, and regulating private property owner's rights to develop food cart pods. The proliferation of food carts is therefore somewhat determined by a *lack* of regulation and public sector involvement (Multnomah County Health Department 2016; OBM Team 2010; Rodgers and Roy 2010).

Establishing and running a food cart business is a form of artisanal entrepreneurialism emblematic of Portland's other artisanal sectors (Heying 2010). With low overhead and startup costs, food carts offer "recession-busting" business and encourage immigrants, chefs, and other entrepreneurs to start a food cart enterprise (OBM Team 2010). Additionally, the low capital costs and relatively unrestricted environment create incentives for brick and mortar restaurants to invest in developing their own food carts, thus contributing to the overall feeling of collaboration between Portland's food carts and traditional restaurants. This form of low capital expansion (Chastain 2010) also encourages food entrepreneurs to try new menu items and reach a larger clientele at a lower price point than is possible with a brick and mortar restaurant. Unlike some cities, the vast majority of restaurants have a good relationship with food cart vendors (Urban Vitality Group 2010). Lastly, the low barriers to entry have coincided with larger economic shifts and unemployment. They succeed because Portland has a recognized tradition supportive of local artisan enterprise; patrons in Portland seek out and support the adventurous and bohemian over the comfortable and corporate (Heying 2010).

Another major determinant is Portland's international reputation for having an innovative and vibrant culinary scene, and an equally influential local agriculture movement. Food blogs and bloggers play a major role in spreading Portland's foodie reputation; blogs like *Eating My Way Through Portland* and *The Spicy Bee* are widely read. Influential social media feeds, notably Portland foodie/photographer Eva Kosmas Flores, who has nearly 120,000 Instagram followers, have contributed to the rise of "food porn," the practice of curating and carefully photographing food scenes. Food carts both contribute to and benefit from these larger trends, and often feature experimental and rotating menus at far lower prices than a brick and mortar restaurant could. Portland-based food cart blogs such as *Food Carts Portland* and social media feeds act as a gateway through which consumers can follow the Portland food cart scene; additionally, they function as a conduit for setting up food cart tourism and hiring food carts for large events.

The many determinants of Portland's food cart culture also point to the tenuous ground on which that culture now rests. As there is increasing real estate development pressure, the spaces food carts inhabit—normally underused parking lots—are beginning to dwindle. The "highest and best use" of these urban spaces often turns out to be high-rise mixed-use development and market-rate housing rather than food cart pods, especially as Portland has entered a period of rapid population growth. Two prominent food cart pods have already closed and planned development in the downtown will eliminate the sixty carts in the city's largest cart pod and ultimately over one half of all food carts currently operating in the downtown (Burmeister 2014, 2016; Vincent 2016). Soon, the city may find itself in an interesting position in which it must rectify its hands-off approach to food carts, so as to prevent food cart pods from being displaced and seriously reduced in number. As mentioned above, the city created an industrial sanctuary to curb deindustrialization in the city; might we soon see food cart sanctuaries?

Conclusion

The original motivation for expanding Portland's bicycle infrastructure was rooted in promoting public health and creating a sustainable city, not creating a niche economic sector. This focus on sustainability has been a key transition. Portland's former mayor Sam Adams illustrates this transition: "Our intentions are to be as sustainable a city as possible … that means socially, that means environmentally and that means economically. The bike is great on all three of those factors" (Yardley 2007). The initial objective of making Portland a sustainable city laid the foundation for creating a strong bicycle culture, but the sustainability discourse also carved out space for increased pedestrian-friendly measures. The pedestrian- and bicycle-friendly spaces of the gentrified inner neighborhoods of the city have partially determined the proliferation of food carts, which now occupy places where cars used to live. These neighborhoods also host many of Portland's craft breweries, and many of these breweries build their brand around the image of sustainability: Hopworks Urban Brewery (2016) for example, claims that two-thirds of their staff gets to work via bicycle: "Everything we do at Hopworks is filtered through a lens of sustainability." Lucky Lab uses solar power to heat water for their brewing needs; Laurelwood Brewery was Portland's first certified organic brewery (Heying 2010: 69); and the beat goes on. So might we say that shifting toward sustainability determined the proliferation of these three cases?

At the local level, the craft beer milieu, the bicycle milieu, and the food cart milieu are all part of the same cultural moment in Portland—all contribute in some way to the mythological imaginary through which Portland is understood across the globe. And at the global level, the media construction of Portland as a sustainable, creative, vibrant, walkable, bike-friendly "brewtopia," by the likes of *The New York Times*, *Kinfolk* and numerous other lifestyle and travel websites and magazines, feeds back into the local level, especially in the collective and singular experiences of in-migration and tourism. Yet Portland is in the midst of another transformation: the industrial buildings that artisans have long occupied are being sold to investors, who in turn displace artisans as they convert these buildings to LEED-certified "creative" office space and eco-condominiums. Sustainability, then, might be a determinant of the artisan economy's creation and destruction. This aspect introduces even more uncertainty into describing causation, as the very things that appear to determine a social phenomenon are often also determinants in their undoing.

We hope that this chapter works toward the blurring of cause-effect relationships in the development of Portland's artisan economy. Although it has been influenced by more factors than we can account for here, Portland's artisan economy truly has no determined or replicable essence; rather that essence is dynamic, contested, and constantly renegotiated. We would hesitate to generalize any further, since our research expertise lies in this specific realm, but given Althusser's thesis, it seems unlikely that singular and direct determinants in any context would make sense. Each of our cases grew out of a specific social context, both local as well as global. On the global level, structural economic change has continued to put downward pressure on the local scale (Peck and Tickell 2002), forcing place-based actors and policymakers to examine new forms of creativity, labor, and innovation that fit the decentralized and networked trends of the so-called neoliberal era (Heying 2010). In Portland, some of these stresses have manifested in terms of the city's blooming artisan economy, but also as gentrification, insecurity, and precariousness.

With the notion of overdetermination in mind, we can think about the rise of the artisan economy in Portland in the context of the myriad intersections between deliberate multi-scale policy actions, individual and collective consumption patterns, global economic changes, geographical specificities, and the many inputs that can best be thought of as accidents or chance. We are occasionally asked to communicate some "best practices" for policy in terms of artisan economy development in other cities. But we have grown resistant to the idea that such a way of thinking about best practices is possible. We hope we have shown here that policy is an important input into social phenomena, but policies and culture are mutually determined within the contexts that created them. None of Portland's bicycle or craft brew policies would have mattered without other contextual realities such as land use policies like the industrial sanctuary being in place. Policy grows out of specific contexts, both global and local, both economic and cultural, and both intentional and accidental. We hope this chapter illustrates why we see Portland's artisan economy as a complex balance between all of these possible determinants, as well as the countless others that we have not thought of.

References

Abbott, C. (2000), "The Capital of Good Planning: Metropolitan Portland since 1970," in R. Fishman (ed.), *The American Planning Tradition: Culture and Policy*, 241–61, Washington, DC: Woodrow Wilson Center Press.

Alta Planning + Design (2008), "The Value of the Bicycle-Related Industry in Portland." Available online: http://bikeportland.org/wp-content/uploads/2008/09/2008-portland-bicycle-related-economy-report.pdf (accessed February 21, 2016).

Althusser, L. (2005), *For Marx*, London: Verso.

Alworth, J. (2010), "Beervana: No, Jimmy Carter Did Not Save Beer," Beervana.blogspot. com. Available online: http://beervana.blogspot.com/2010/08/no-jimmy-carter-did-not-save-beer.html (accessed February 17, 2016).

Anderson, J. (2014), "City Toasts 30 years of Craft Beer," *Portland Tribune*. Available online: http://pamplinmedia.com/pt/221417 (accessed February 20, 2016).

Burmeister, B. (2014), "Food Cart Pod Closures," Food Carts Portland—A Guide to Food Carts in Portland Oregon. [online] *Food Carts Portland*. Available online: http://www.foodcartsportland.com/ (accessed March 18, 2016).

Burmeister, B. (2015), "Portland Food Carts Year in Review—2015," Food Carts Portland—A Guide to Food Carts in Portland Oregon. [online] Food Carts Portland. Available online: http://www.foodcartsportland.com/ (accessed March 18, 2016).

Burmeister, B. (2016), "Portland's Downtown Food Cart Pods to Close," Food Carts Portland—A Guide to Food Carts in Portland Oregon. [online] *Food Carts Portland*. Available online: http://www.foodcartsportland.com/ (accessed March 18, 2016).

Carlson, R. (2011), "Micro-Brewing the Bioeconomy: Beer as an Example of Distributed Biological Manufacturing (Updated, and again)—synthesis," *Synthesis.cc*. Available online: http://www.synthesis.cc/2010/03/micro-brewing-the-bioeconomy-beer-as-an-example-of-distributed-biological-manufacturing.html (accessed February 17, 2016).

Chastain, A. (2010), "Food Carts as Retail Real Estate," *Quarterly & Urban Development Journal*, PSU Center for Real Estate 2nd Quarter: 61–70.

Cizmar, M. (2012), "Beer of the Future: A New Era of Oregon Hops will Better your Brew," *Willamette Week*, 15–19.

Collabofest (2016), "Base Camp's Collabofest 2016—Oregon Craft Beer," Oregoncraftbeer. org. Available online: http://oregoncraftbeer.org/base-camps-collabofest-2016/ (accessed February 20, 2016).

George, A. (2015), "USA Hops: Statistical Report 2014," *Hop Growers of America*. Available online: http://www.usahops.org/userfiles/image/1421356603_2014%20 Stat%20Pack.pdf (accessed February 18, 2016).

Gibson-Graham, J. (1995), *The End of Capitalism (as we knew it)*, Minneapolis: University of Minnesota Press.

Haight, A. (2006), "Hub of the Action, Portland's Cycling Culture has been a Magnet of Homegrown Bike Gear Manufacturing and Design, and It Keeps on Growing," *The Oregonian.*

Heying, C. (2010), *Brew to Bikes: Portland's Artisan Economy*, Portland, OR: Ooligan Press.

Heying, C. and S. Marotta (2014), "Portland Made Collective Survey Results," *Portland Made.* Available online: http://www.portlandmade.com/wp-content/uploads/2014/10/PMC-Survey-Report.pdf (accessed March 18, 2016).

Heying, C. and S. Marotta (2016), "Portland Made: Building Partnerships to Support the Local Artisan/Maker Community," in J. Allen, J. Sherman, and B. D. Wortham-Galvin (eds.), *Innovative Engagement: University-Community Partnerships for Sustainability*, 112–122, Sheffield, UK: Greenleaf Publishing.

Hopworks Urban Brewery (2016), "Environment: Hopworks Urban Brewery," *Hopworks Beer.* Available online: http://hopworksbeer.com/do-good/environment (accessed March 18, 2016).

Ibsen, M. and B. Cunningham (2015), "The Economic Impact of the Bicycle Industry in Portland," *City of Portland Bureau of Planning and Sustainability.* Available online: https://www.portlandoregon.gov/bps/article/555482 (accessed February 21, 2016).

Jacklett, B. (2009), "The Bicycle Industrial Complex: Bike Madness Fuels $150 Million Industry," *Oregon Business Magazine.*

Johnson, S. (2002), *The Transformation of Civic Institutions and Practices in Portland, Oregon, 1960–1999* Ph.D, Didd., Portland State University, Portland.

Jones, A. (2001), "Craft Brewing Defines Oregon as U.S. 'Beer Capital,'" *News, nationalgeographic.com.* Available online: http://news.nationalgeographic.com/news/2001/08/0808_oregonbrewing.html (accessed February 17, 2016).

Lefferts, D. (2014), "The 10 Best Cities for Beer Lovers: These Towns Know How to Brew," *Bustle.com.* Available online: http://www.bustle.com/articles/18032-the-10-best-cities-for-beer-lovers-these-towns-know-how-to-brew (accessed February 18, 2016).

Lenatti, C. (2013), "Craft Beer Week: It All Began with Home Brewing," *Examiner.com.* Available online: http://www.examiner.com/article/craft-beer-week-it-all-began-with-home-brewing (accessed February 17, 2016).

Lydgate, C. (2008), "Downwardly mobile," *Portland Tribune*, June 26 pp. A1, A5.

Maus, J. (2016), BikePortland.org—Portland Oregon Bicycle News, Events, Culture, Travel and Opinion," *BikePortland.org.* Available online: http://bikeportland.org/ (accessed February 21, 2016).

Multnomah County Health Department (2016), "Mobile Unit Playbook," *Multco.us.* Available online: https://multco.us/file/35485/download (accessed March 18, 2016).

OBM Team (2010), "Portland food carts push through recession," *Oregonbusiness*.com. Available online: http://www.oregonbusiness.com/article/archives-2006-2009/item/5639-cash-and-carry (accessed March 18, 2016).

Oregon Brewers Guild (2016), "Facts- Oregon Craft Beer," *Oregoncraftbeer.org.* Available online: http://oregoncraftbeer.org/facts/ (accessed February 18, 2016).

Peck, J. and A. Tickell (2002), "Neoliberalizing Space," *Antipode*, 34 (3), 380–404.

Portland Bike Links (2016), *bikeportland.org.* Available online: http://bikeportland.org/portland-bike-listings (accessed February 21, 2016).

Portland Water Bureau (2016a), "Discover Your Drinking Water," *Portlandoregon.gov.* Available online: https://www.portlandoregon.gov/water/article/225481 (accessed February 20, 2016).

Portland Water Bureau (2016b), "Frequently Asked Questions about Water Quality | Water Quality | The City of Portland, Oregon," *Portlandoregon.gov.* Available online: https://www.portlandoregon.gov/water/article/327613#hardness (accessed February 18, 2016).

Ransom, D. (2011), "Why Portland's Beer Economy Is 'Hoppy,' *Entrepreneur*. Available online: http://www.entrepreneur.com/article/220319 (accessed February 18, 2016).

Rodgers, K. and K. Roy (2010), *Cartopia: Portland's Food Cart Revolution*. Portland, OR: Roy Rodgers Press.

Smith, O. and B. Wineman (2010), "Bikes," in C. Heying (ed.), *Brew to Bikes: Portland's Artisan Economy*, 107–122, Portland, OR: Ooligan Press.

Travel Portland (2016), "Central Eastside brewery tour—Travel Portland," *Travelportland. com*. Available online: https://www.travelportland.com/itinerary/central-eastside-brewery-tour/ (accessed February 20, 2016).

Urban Vitality Group (2010), "Food Cartology: Rethinking Urban Spaces as People Places," *Portlandoregon.gov*. Available online: https://www.portlandoregon.gov/bps/article/200738 (accessed March 18, 2016).

Vincent, J. (2016), "A Legacy Project for Portland," *Portland Business Tribune*. Available online: http://pamplinmedia.com/but/239-news/297366-173866-a-legacy-project-for-portland (accessed March 18, 2016).

Woodward, B. and L. Bennett (2010), "Oregon Beer History," *1859oregonmagazine.com*. Available online: https://www.1859oregonmagazine.com/oregon-beer-history (accessed February 20, 2016).

Yardley, W. (2007), "In Portland, Cultivating a Culture of Two Wheels," *nytimes.com*. Available online: http://www.nytimes.com/2007/11/05/us/05bike.html?_r=0 (accessed March 18, 2016).

17

The Role of Higher Education in Sustaining Culturally Significant Crafts in Estonia

Sirpa Kokko

Introduction

In the present world of globalization, mass production, and consumerism, there is a danger that local craft traditions will be lost (Kokko and Kaipainen 2015). Often, the material representations of local craft traditions have been placed into museums and archives, where they represent the relics of the past. However, the counterforce of grassroots-level activism is keeping these traditions alive in various parts of the world (Hackney 2013). Crafts connect people across national boundaries in new ways, utilizing new forms of web-based media (Gauntlett 2011).

In Estonia, crafts still play an important role in local culture, with an abundance of craft galleries, workshops, and markets. There is also a wide range in terms of quality: from high-quality art and design crafts to quickly made hobby crafts. Although Estonian knitting and textiles are the most well known (e.g. Kabur, Pink, and Meriste 2011), others such as jewelry, bone-craft, wood, metal, and ceramics can also be found. During the recent Soviet rule (until 1991), there was a shortage of goods in the shops and Estonians needed to be capable of producing many things for their daily use themselves. Consequently, a living tradition of handmaking in Estonia continues today, and hobby crafts are widely practiced (Annist 2009; Parts 2015).

In many countries, craft has been removed from comprehensive school education but in Scandinavian and Baltic countries, craft has the status of a standard school subject (Kokko 2009; Müürsepp 2014). The focus of higher education on art, craft, and design is facing constant changes, as seen in the UK (Journeaux, Wade, and Bolton 2015). In higher education institutions, cultural and traditional aspects may be included in their arts, crafts, and design curricula (e.g. University of Leeds in the UK), but often the focus is on design, digitalization, and an industrial approach (e.g. Aalto University in Finland). In Estonia, Viljandi Culture Academy (VCA),[1] one of the four colleges of the University of Tartu, aims to sustain and develop the values of Estonian traditional culture. It offers graduate and undergraduate study programs in such fields as theater and dance arts, Estonian native crafts, music, sound engineering, leisure studies, and culture management. The Department of Estonian Native Crafts also provides higher education in the fields of Estonian native textiles, construction, and metalwork. The website of the department (UT, VCA 2016) explains that "The mission of the department is to represent the local and native traditions and values that strengthen the sense of identity. This is done by integrating traditional craft techniques into contemporary functional milieu." The institution claims to be unique in the world in concentrating on Estonian crafts.

The purpose of the case study presented in this chapter was to find out how the Department of Estonian Native Crafts is sustaining Estonian craft traditions. The analysis focuses on the role of higher education in sustaining culturally significant crafts.

Methods

According to Verschuren (2003: 121), "the object of a case study is one single case, temporally, physically or socially limited in size, complex in nature, unique and thus not comparable with other cases." This description applies very well to VCA, the object of this case study. As is typical of a case study, the research utilized a variety of qualitative data-collecting procedures (ibid.: 125). Participatory observation (e.g. Marvasti 2014) was used during the four visits to VCA, one week at a time: twice in 2012, and once in 2014 and 2015 respectively. The visits were part of a teacher and researcher exchange program, and included participation in activities at VCA. Craft exhibitions and museums were also explored widely; observations were documented via notes and photos.

To get an in-depth view, the department curriculum developer, three teachers and four former students were individually interviewed in 2014. The interviews were semi-structured, meaning that a list of questions was followed, although not rigidly (e.g. Kvale 1996). The interview questions concerned the background of the informants, how they had learned their craft, and how they made a living through craft. The role of VCA in their professional development was discussed. Further questions concerned their perceptions of the future of craft.

The interviewees were chosen to represent different aspects and study fields of VCA, and will be introduced later in the article. The interviews with the teachers were conducted in English; one of the teachers helped with the English translations of three of the student interviews.

The analysis here relies mainly on the interviews but is supported by the notes taken during participatory observation. The transcribed interviews were analyzed according to the basic ideas of qualitative data analysis (Flick 2014). Each interview was listened to several times to get an overall understanding. After that, the transcriptions were coded and clustered thematically according to the discussions related to the experiences of teaching and studying in VCA. This analysis forms the basis for exploring the role of VCA in sustaining culturally significant crafts.

Teaching and studying in VCA

The study program of VCA consists of theoretical and practical craft studies. In their theses, both the BA and MA students concentrate on a chosen field of Estonian craft tradition and study its background, materials, and technical variations. They search for the roots of their chosen Estonian craft in museums and archives. In addition, they conduct fieldwork to learn about the living practices that are still available. Based on these findings, they create designs, products, and practices that offer a better fit for present-day purposes.

The institution collects these BA and MA theses in online archives (Rahvuslik Käsitöö 2016) and some of the students present their findings in the VCA's publication, *Studia Vernacula* (2014). However, since the work is mainly in Estonian, it is not easily accessible to an international audience. In addition to their basic educational programs, VCA also educates the wider community in craft traditions and entrepreneurship (Summatavet 2012).

The informants had typically tried many different career paths before starting their studies in VCA. In fact, when they made their first career choice, they had not known about the possibility of academic craft studies. All of the informants had an earlier interest in making crafts as a hobby. They had learned these skills mainly at home and from relatives or neighbors. Crafts had also been taught at secondary school. Below, is a brief introduction of the interviewees using their full names. Later in the chapter, only their first names will be used.

Teachers

Anu Raud, a famous tapestry artist, was the person who first developed the craft curriculum for the department (see Reinholm 2013); she was interviewed to find out about the background of the department. She had studied textile arts at the Estonian State Art Institute. Before starting to work at VCA, she had a career as a designer at Folk Art Company "UKU" and as a lecturer at the Estonian Academy of Arts. She came to live in her family's country house near Viljandi in 1990 and became involved with VCA. She initiated a new curriculum, then called farm design and handicrafts. She also started to restore the Heimtali Museum and donated her vast collection of folk art (see Reinholm 2013). Since then, the museum has been used as part of the studies in VCA. Anu utilizes Estonian nature and traditions as a source of inspiration in her tapestries (see Figure 17.1).

Ave Matsin teaches in the Department of Estonian Native Crafts. When Ave had almost completed her MA in the Estonian Academy of Arts, she was asked to come to work at VCA, where she soon became head of department. She concentrates

FIGURE 17.1 Example of Anu Raud's tapestry. Courtesy Kokko. © Anu Raud.

mainly on administration but also teaches weaving, historical textiles, and the reconstruction of old crafts as well as giving seminars on craft research. Currently, Ave is working on a Ph.D. on archaeological textiles.

Kristi Jõeste is a teacher and program manager at VCA. She gained her first academic degree at VCA and then obtained her MA degree in Semiotics at the University of Tartu (Jõeste 2012). She teaches traditional crafts, knitting, patchwork and Tunisian crochet, and gives craft research seminars with Ave. Kristi has written books on Estonian knitting (Jõeste and Ehin 2012; Pink, Reimann, and Jõeste 2016). She is a well-known knitting master herself and has had several exhibitions in Estonia and internationally (see Figure 17.2). With the help of an award from the Estonian cultural endowment, she started her own company and sells knitted gloves, mainly to order. She also employs knitters who make the gloves she designs.

FIGURE 17.2 Examples of Kristi Jõeste's knitted mittens. Courtesy Kokko. © Kristi Jõeste.

Priit-Kalev Parts is a program manager of the Estonian native construction curriculum and a lecturer in Estonian native construction. His background is in Estonian philology and languages, and more recently in landscape architecture. He wants his students to "dream realistically." He felt students were motivated to study crafts but not to stay in the field, and has recently added more commercial aspects to the curriculum. He has just finished a Ph.D. on community development and management (Parts 2015).

Students

Veinika Västrik first studied history at the undergraduate level at the University of Tallinn, and learned weaving in a guild and through a number of courses. Because of the flexible study arrangements, studying in VCA gave Veinika the possibility to combine MA studies with her work as a weaving teacher and her family life in Tartu. She concentrated on rep mats in her MA thesis (Västrik 2014). This is a special type of warp-faced weave where the warp threads are put so close together that no weft is visible. As Västrik (2014) notes, the making of rep weave floor coverings had been widely practiced in northern Estonia between 1950 and 1970, but was later almost forgotten. Although she already worked as a teacher of weaving, she did not have any official qualification in crafts; studying at VCA gave her the possibility to achieve one.

Andres Rattasepp had previously obtained a BA in art and craft pedagogy at the University of Tallinn, and had worked as a woodwork teacher. He entered the MA program at VCA to learn more about the birch bark crafts that he had practiced. Birch bark crafts have long been an important part of traditional Estonian crafts but nowadays there is a danger of the skills being lost. During his studies, he found a master in Novgorod who taught him more about birch bark crafts, which helped in writing his thesis on the topic (Rattasepp 2014). Andres described the atmosphere of VCA as supportive and said that it was important for him to study there.

Kristina Libe first planned to study history, but changed her mind after hearing about the possibility to apply to VCA. She explained that she did not know exactly what she was going to study when she started her BA studies in textiles, but during the course she became interested in traditional crafts and ultimately based her diploma on traditional coats. Afterwards, she went to a vocational school to improve her skills in dressmaking.

Monika Hint was a self-employed farmer and artist before starting her BA and later MA studies at VCA. While she had always enjoyed practicing different forms of crafts, it was only at VCA that she had the opportunity to concentrate on bone crafts, which became her specialization. She explored archaeological findings in Estonia to reconstruct her own bone craft techniques, utilizing bones of agricultural animal by-products as her raw material (Hint 2013). For her, the positive learning community at VCA was important.

Living and making a living with crafts

After graduating from VCA, the former students had multiple sources of income. They all emphasized that they had gained a great deal from studying at VCA; they gained practical craftmaking skills, entrepreneurial skills, professional networks, self-confidence, and research skills. These students were characterized by their enthusiasm about their work. They had visions about the future and were not afraid of risk-taking. The question of making a living with crafts is a central topic for all practitioners, but within the market of a small country such as Estonia it is especially demanding.

When talking about the effect of studying at VCA, Veinika thought that her work as a weaving teacher had not changed considerably. However, she was now also teaching a special field of weaving, rep mat. Together with her brother's wife, Veinika has her own company selling equipment, raw material, and books about weaving. As part of running her company, she gives courses on weaving and helps weavers to put the warp into their looms. She also weaves rep mats herself, taking inspiration from old patterns and developing them into more up-to-date designs. She sells her products in fairs and to order.

Veinika appreciated the research skills she had learned during her studies at VCA. She was planning to make handbooks for weavers, having noticed they were needed in Estonia (Freienthal and Västrik 2012). She also felt that more people were starting to weave and do handicrafts, and she thought it was because cheap Chinese products did not satisfy everyone. Instead, many people wanted to make something with their own hands and needed guidance in doing so.

At the time of the interview, Andres was working as a craft teacher in a primary school. Together with his wife, he had continued to study crafts, this time through woodwork courses, and had also been teaching on various craft courses in Olustvere. When possible, he taught his special field of crafts, birch bark work, and made birch bark artifacts for sale, but only to order. Andres had many plans for the future, and was aiming to continue doing research on birch bark crafts. At the completion of this chapter in 2016, he had secured a position as head of a museum in Estonia.

Monica had run her own business as a bone artist for one year prior to the interview. However, during this time she had gained experience and self-confidence. She said that she could make a living together with the income of the farm she was running with her husband. During her studies at VCA, she had learned the commercial aspects of business work. She was selling her products mainly in Estonia by taking orders at markets and in the studios of other craftspeople (see Figure 17.3). She had realized that people either like or dislike her products and the idea of making something out of bones. She had also invested in a watermill to help in her work. Monica was planning to open an online shop and attend fairs. She aimed to put greater effort into advertising her work and was considering hiring someone to help with the marketing.

After finishing her studies in VCA, Kristina traveled for about a year. After returning to Viljandi, she opened her own tailoring studio within a business incubator. She also taught some courses on sewing at VCA. After the incubator period finished, she worked with two VCA graduates until they left on maternity leave. She made dresses to order and enjoyed the process of designing with the customers. Kristina intended to continue with her tailoring studio in Viljandi and was hoping to find partners to help run it. She did not want to make the business too big since she appreciated the calm lifestyle and having direct contact with her customers. She thought that the roots of crafts in Estonia were so deep that they would not die.

FIGURE 17.3 Examples of Monika Hint's bone crafts. Courtesy Kokko. © Monika Hint.

The interviewees shared the idea that crafts still play an important role in Estonian society, where there are many skilful craftspeople and hobbyists. Kristina pointed out that craftmaking skills may also be an obstacle for selling craft products; often people are not ready to buy something if they think that they would be capable of making it themselves. Yet Kristina could see a difference between the professional and a hobby craftsperson in terms of design and taste. Even though hobby craftmakers may reach a good level of technical quality, compared to educated professionals there is a difference in the quality of design. She remarked on the competition at markets between professional and hobby craftspeople; the latter often sell their products at a much cheaper price. Kristina stressed the importance of recognizing the variety and value of one's own traditional crafts.

Future of crafts in Estonia and VCA

During the discussions about the future of crafts, Ave thought that because making by hand is not a necessity anymore, people will lose their skills over time. She was worried about crafts being mainly connected to hobbies, rather than professional or artistic dimensions. In her mind, the mission and role of VCA is to highlight the richness of Estonian craft traditions and also help people to realize that craftmaking can be a profession. Ave thought that it was important to introduce the students to the vast variety of professional opportunities relating to crafts. She highlighted the importance of people who are role models, such as the Estonian, Reet Aus (2011), who uses waste textiles to create new work. Also, she noted the need to further develop existing craft research.

Kristi was very concerned about the fact that there are few living craft masters from whom people could learn craft traditions. She mentioned Kihnu Island as the best place for knitting traditions to thrive (Jõeste 2012; Summatavet 2010). She has explored the varieties of knitting traditions all around Estonia and utilized them in her contemporary knitting (Jõeste and Ehin 2012). Kristi thought that Estonian knitting has international importance due to its uniqueness and variety of techniques. She argued that it is important to be aware of these specialities, and to preserve them. She considered herself and others to be the "missionaries of knitting." Kristi is fulfilling this role with great success: her knitting courses are always full. Women of different ages attend her courses: older ones to get some help in making the complicated traditional patterns, the younger ones to learn techniques they have not learned anywhere else. She felt that crafts are important for the Estonian national identity, but fears there is a danger of craft skills disappearing over time. However, she believed that there are also counterforces to the globalizing tendencies and there will always be people who value handmade crafts. She had noticed that more small-scale craft entrepreneurs were starting up in Estonia, which she thought to be a sign of people choosing a certain lifestyle.

Kristi was happy that VCA has decided to establish research in craft, as this has helped them to develop their teaching and research work. For her, the mission of VCA was important in preserving and developing traditional Estonian crafts as part of the Estonian national identity. She raised the topic of education in cultural heritage and crafts (see Kokko and Dillon 2016) and would like to add aspects of Estonian traditional craft culture into the craft education of secondary schools.

When thinking about the possibilities to earn a living by making crafts, Priit-Kalev concluded that some possibilities exist, "if the craft person's demands are not high and he can build up a personal relationship with clients. This is what the clients miss: the clients want the story." According to him, Estonians appreciate their heritage and have a romantic view of the past. Priit-Kalev was interested in developing the aspect of spirituality in craft culture and researching the inner motivation of making crafts. He was talking about the interaction of cultures which would, on one hand, lead to global identities, and on the other, strengthen local identities as an opposing force.

Anu had noticed the abundance of quickly handmade crafts of poor quality being sold at local markets to tourists at a lower price than the high-quality crafts. For Anu, being over seventy years old, her main worry was to take care that her work would be continued. She did not approve of the globalizing effects and mixing of cultures. She was happy about the current state of things in VCA, but spoke about the importance of keeping a balance between theoretical and practical studies.

Discussion and conclusions

There is a growing interest in crafts and handmaking skills, which has arisen recently in academic research (Greenhalgh 2002; Charny 2011; Sennett 2008). The importance of education at all levels in recognizing the value of craft as both skilled and intellectual activity, and its relevance for cultural understanding, is also discussed more widely (Kokko and Dillon 2016; Niedderer and Townsend 2013). Drawing on the analysis of this study, VCA has an important role in sustaining culturally significant craft designs, products, and practices in Estonia, in carrying out research and in showing their importance to a wider society. For an institution of higher education, VCA is unique in the world with its mission of making Estonian crafts and their designs visible, and in developing them to adapt to present-day purposes. Evidently, opportunities should be given to similar institutions in other countries to sustain their cultural traditions. The work of the School of Design at the University of Leeds is a good example of similar approaches but with a wider global perspective and more extensive use of ICT (Shin, Cassidy, and Moore 2015). Since the Estonian language is only spoken within the population of 1.3 million Estonians, there is a need for efforts to reach a wider audience. In fact, VCA is making plans to open up an international study program on crafts and related fields. Furthermore, they have plans to place greater emphasis on international cooperation and research.

The history of Estonia has had an impact on the continuance of local craft traditions. Compared to many other countries, Estonia is still culturally homogenous; this makes it easy to explore native craft traditions. For a small country that has gained independence relatively recently, to survive as a nation it is important to preserve various forms of tradition, including crafts. Annist (2009) notes that the Estonian cultural sphere was already highly formalized in the nineteenth century and that Soviet cultural hegemony was never properly established; instead it enabled the perseverance of nationalist cultural counter-hegemony. "Especially in the later years of the Soviet rule, there were hobby-groups that appeared apolitical but would spread nationalist mentality" (Annist 2009: 119). Accordingly, the Estonians actually never lost their cultural heritage and identity under the occupation and thus, after their second independence from the Soviet Union in 1991, they had good foundations on which to construct their nation and revive their traditions.

Crafts and their studies play an important role in the interaction of global and local cultures and identity construction. In the present global society of ever-growing consumption, it is necessary to pay serious attention to sustainable design (Walker and Giard 2013). The economic sustainability of practicing crafts is a topic that concerns craft professionals all around the world. Education on entrepreneurship skills is important for all higher education on art, craft, and design (Hjelde 2015); this topic has demanded growing attention in the study programs of VCA. Apparently, a successful craft entrepreneurship requires enthusiasm and risk-taking from the practitioners: the qualities possessed by the informants of this study. They have found a way of surviving by using multiple means of earning a living. For them, craft making was a choice of lifestyle that allowed them to work on the things that gave them pleasure and inner satisfaction; this outweighed the low income that was provided (see also Parts et al. 2011). The follow-up of the students' careers after they had left VCA is encouraging in showing that most of them have found or created a working place in their craft or a related field.

For the informants of this study, crafts held very important personal meanings. They talked about the inner need for making crafts, which gave them pleasure and satisfaction. Crafts provided them a means for expressing creativity and the possibility to relax. The aspect of crafts as an important part of the well-being of people is becoming more topical, not only in Western countries. Looking at the Indian context, Kasturi (2005: 75–7) notes that thinking of design only as a contributor to the economics of crafts offers design a rather limited role. Instead, its relevance to overall well-being and its role as an integrator between customers and craftspeople needs attention; this issue was raised by the informants of this study. When thinking about the sustainable future of crafts, these aspects require attention in the study programs of crafts and design in higher education.

Note

1   The Academy has offered specialized culture education since 1952. The former Viljandi Culture School was recognized as a college providing applied higher education in 1991, and it joined the University of Tartu in 2005. MA level studies were introduced in 2011 (UT, VCA 2016).

References

Annist, A. (2009), "Outsourcing Culture: Establishing Heritage Hegemony by Funding Cultural Life in South Eastern Estonia," *Lietuvos Etnologija: socialinés antropologijos ir etnologijos studijos*, 9 (18): 117–38.

Aus, R. (2011), *Trash to Trend—Using Upcycling in Fashion Design*, Tallinn: Estonian Academy of Arts.

Charny, D. (ed.) (2011), *Power of Making: The Importance of Being Skilled*, London: V & A Publishing and the Crafts Council.

Flick, U. (ed.) (2014), *The SAGE Handbook of Qualitative Data Analysis*, London: SAGE.

Freienthal, M. and V. Västrik (2012), *Lapilised Vööd* (Lapilised Belts), Tallinn: Saara Kirjastus.

Gauntlett, D. (2011), *Making is Connecting: The Social Meaning of Creativity, from DIY and Knitting to YouTube and Web 2.0*, Cambridge: Polity Press. Available online: http://www.makingisconnecting.org (accessed June 1, 2016).

Greenhalgh, P. (ed.) (2002), *The Persistence of Craft*, London: A&C Black.

Hackney, F. (2013), "Quiet Activism and the New Amateur: The Power of Home and Hobby Crafts," *Design and Culture*, 5 (2): 169–93.

Hint, M. (2013), "Luu töötlemine lamba sääreluust vilepilli näitel," *Lugusid materjalidest. Stories about materials. Studia Vernacula*, 3: 58–72.

Hjelde, K. (2015), "Paradox and Potential: Fine Art Employability and Enterprise Perspectives," *Art, Design & Communication in Higher Education*, 14 (2): 175–88.

Jõeste, K. (2012), *Kihnu kördid eile ja täna.* (Book about Folk Skirts of Kihnu Island) *Semiootiline esemeuurimus*, Studia Vernacula, Viljandi: Eesti Loomeagentuur.

Jõeste, K. and K. Ehin (2012), *Ornamented Journey*, Turi: Saara Publishing House.

Journeaux, J., S. Wade, and T. Bolton (2015), "Controversy and Conformity—25 Years of Transforming the Academy," *Art, Design & Communication in Higher Education*, 14 (2): 107–10.

Kabur, A., A. Pink, and M. Meriste (2011), *Designs and Patterns from Muhu Island. A Needlework Tradition from Estonia*, Estonia: Saara Publishers.

Kasturi, P. B. (2005), "Designing Freedom," *Design Issues*, 21 (4): 68–77.

Kokko, S. (2009), "Learning Practices of Femininity through Gendered Craft Education in Finland," *Gender and Education*, 6 (21): 721–34.

Kokko, S. and P. Dillon (2016), "Engaging Trainee Teachers with Crafts and Cultural Heritage," *International Journal of Education through Art*, 12 (1): 21–37.

Kokko, S. and M. Kaipainen (2015), "The Changing Role of Cultural Heritage in Traditional Textile Crafts from Cyprus," *Craft Research*, 6 (1): 9–31.

Kvale, S. (1996), *InterViews: An Introduction to Qualitative Research Interviewing*, Thousand Oaks, CA: SAGE.

Marvasti, A. B. (2014), "Analysing Observations," in U. Flick (ed.), *The SAGE Handbook of Qualitative Data Analysis*, 354–66, London: SAGE.

Müürsepp, M. (2014), "Cooking and Hammering: Primary School Pupils' Concepts of Their Craft Skills," *International Electronic Journal of Elementary Education*, 6 (3): 371–84.

Niedderer, K. and K. Townsend (2013), "Craft, Society and the State," *Craft Research*, 4 (2): 153–9.

Parts, P.-K. (2015), *Sustainable Community Management in Estonia: Reflections on Heritage Projects on Kihnu Island, in Viljandi County, and in Various Protected Areas*, Tartu: Eesti Maaülikool/Estonian University of Life Sciences.

Parts, P.-K., M. Rennu, L. Jääts, A. Matsin, J. Metslang (2011), "Developing Sustainable Heritage-Based Livelihoods: an Initial Study of Artisans and Their Crafts in Viljandi County, Estonia," *International Journal of Heritage Studies*, 17 (5): 401–25.

Pink, A., S. Reimann, and K. Jõeste (2016), *Estonian Knitting: Customs and Techniques*, Vol 1, Türi: Saara Publishing House.

Rahvuslik Käsitöö (2016), *The Online Archive of Thesis of the Department of Native Crafts*, VCA. Available online: http://kultuur.edu.ee/rahvuslik/?dir= (accessed June 1, 2016).

Rattasepp, A. (2014), "Kasetohust punutud Eesti ala märsid: eripärad ja valmistamine," (Estonian Birch Bark Pouches: Particularities and Weaving Techniques), *Käegakatsutav. The Tangible. Studia Vernacula*, 5: 69–93.

Reinholm, V. (2013), *Anu Raud. Estonian Textile Artist*, Tallinn: Valgus.

Sennett, R. (2008), *The Craftsman*, London: Penguin Books.

Shin, M. J., T. Cassidy, and E. M. Moore (2015), "Design Reinvention for Culturally Influenced Textile Products: Focused on Traditional Korean Bojagi Textiles," *Fashion Practice*, 7 (2): 175–98.

Studia Vernacula (2014), 5, *Käegakatsutav. The tangible.* Tartu: University of Tartu Viljandi Culture Academy.

Summatavet, K. (2010), *My History. The letters of Kihnu Roosi*, Viljandi: Viljandi Culture Academy and Varrak Publishers.

Summatavet, K. (2012), *Käsitöögä tööle 2. Handicraft for Job 2*, Tartu: University of Tartu Viljandi Culture Academy.

UT, VCA (2016), *University of Tartu Viljandi Culture Academy*. Available online: http://www.kultuur.ut.ee/en/departments/crafts (accessed June 1, 2016).

Verschuren, P. J. M. (2003), "Case Study as a Research Strategy: Some Ambiguities and Opportunities," *International Journal of Social Research Methodology*, 6 (2): 121–39.

Västrik, V. (2014), "Lõimeripstehnikas põrandakatete kudumine Avinurmes 1950–1970 aastatel kui piirkondlik pärandoskus" (Production of Rep Weave Floor Coverings in Avinurme in the 1950s to the 1970s as a Regional Inherited Skill), *Käegakatsutav. The Tangible. Studia Vernacula*, 5: 47–68.

Walker, S. and J. Giard (eds.) (2013), *The Handbook of Design for Sustainability*, London: Bloomsbury.

18

The Challenge of Intellectual Property Rights for Culturally Significant Patterns, Products, and Processes

Tom Cassidy and Tracy Diane Cassidy

Introduction

Intellectual Property Rights (IPR) in the UK has been a topic of controversy, frustration, and complexity for design and designers for many years, and this continues to be the case. The situation is further complicated by the different laws affecting IPR in different countries and, often, a lack of knowledge about IPR, especially among young designers. Indeed, there are significant differences in knowledge and understanding of IPR among designers in both economically developed and developing countries. To understand IPR, we must first alter or augment our perception of property.

We grow up to consider property as a material entity: a car, a house, a television etc., something tangible that an individual has paid to take possession of or has manufactured themselves and therefore has the right to charge another individual for or even to give away; the last three words are important and may become more important as we begin to discuss IPR in relation to culturally significant patterns, products, and practices. For example, many of us will give away our personal property to charity shops or another non-profit organization because we believe that, in doing so, we are contributing towards the good of our national and global society.

The concept of design knowledge as a property is covered in depth and breadth by Mwendapole (2005) in her Ph.D. thesis. She explains that, although property is probably not semantically the right word to cover design knowledge, it is used because, as MacPherson (1978: 11) stated, "property must be grounded in a public belief that it is morally right; if it is not so justified it does not remain an enforceable claim. If it is not justified, it does not remain property." Design knowledge can be placed into one of two groups (Rodgers and Clarkson 1998): tacit or explicit. To put this simply, tacit knowledge is what is in the designer's brain; it has been put there by training, education, practice, and experience. It is how the designer collects and interprets previous knowledge. The knowledge will remain tacit throughout most of the idea generation stage and even up to the stages of early sketches. Once the designer moves on to technical drawings, models, computer simulations and so on (i.e. they become explicit) the ideas can be tested, viewed, used, and enjoyed in the public domain, and therefore should be protected and a value placed on them. How this value is arrived at and whether it is purely temporal or spiritual or both is difficult enough in contemporary society; when the designer is an individual or corporate entity, when the designer is part of a cultural group or ecology that has existed for decades, centuries or even longer, the situation is highly complex.

The protection of design

Mwendapole's research (2005) primarily considered the protection of modern individual designers or design agencies/groups. She proposed a model (Figure 18.1) and her evaluation tests of this model showed that designers appreciated it as a checklist and awareness tool to remind them when the explicit stage(s) of design had been reached.

In 2012, a substantive report was produced by the UK Intellectual Property Office (IPO). It was reported that designs are protected in the UK by five legal rights:

- EU registered design rights;
- EU unregistered design rights;
- UK registered design rights;
- UK unregistered design rights;
- artistic copyright.

This report goes on to show that the protection of design rights presents a maze that designers and companies have to try to navigate, and in which most feel unlikely to succeed and/or that even success would be more costly than it is worth. The cost of failure when attempting to protect design rights is more or less prohibitive to small and medium enterprises (SMEs), which make up the majority of design agencies. Across Europe there has been an effort through the Community Design Regulation introduced in 2001 (Intellectual Property Office 2012) to bring about a unitary system and approach but this has had limited success.

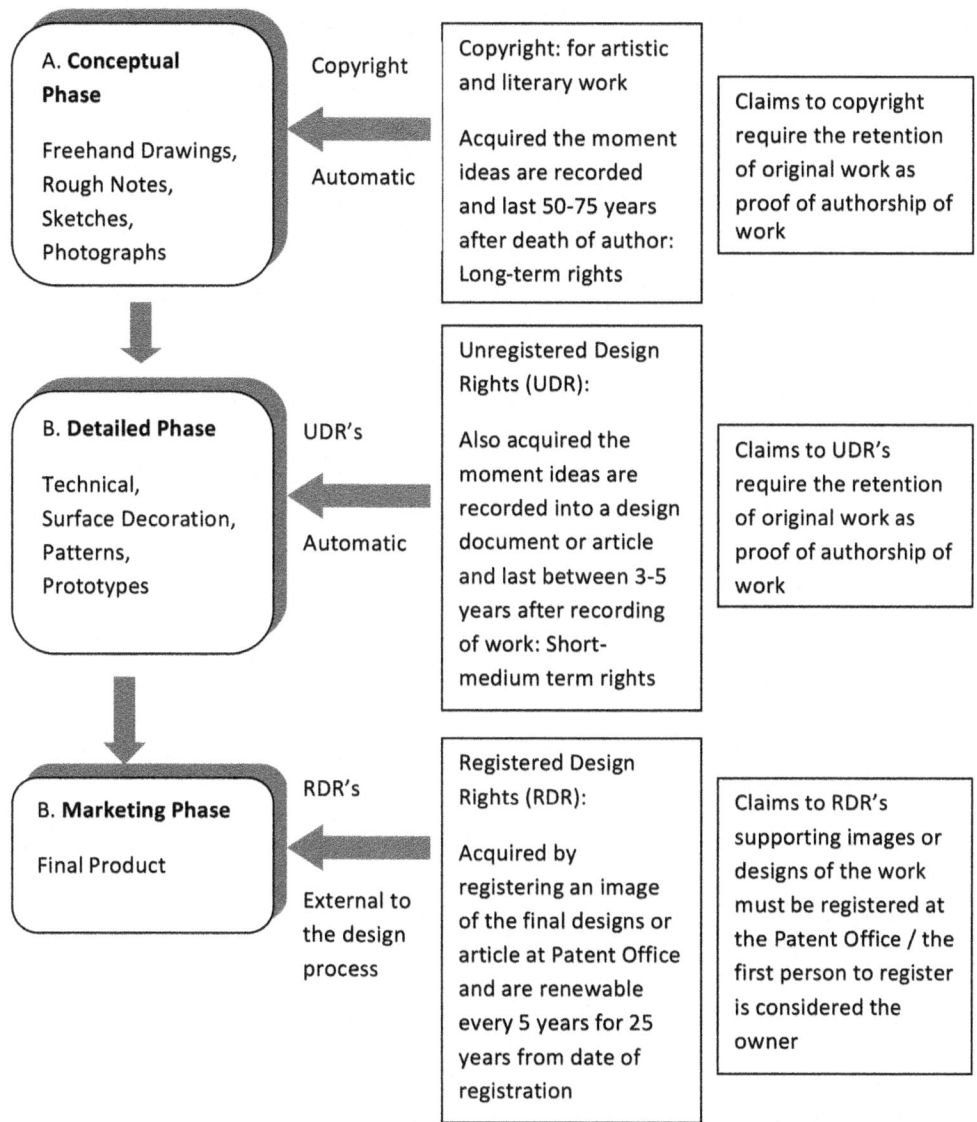

FIGURE 18.1 Model illustrating the allocation of property rights to design knowledge. Adapted from Mwendapole (2005). © Tom Cassidy and Tracy Diane Cassidy.

A section of the report that may be considered of significant interest to individuals, agencies, companies, and cultures is the "Effect of Design Rights on Motivation and Innovation." Many companies will quote their number of patents in promotional materials but very few quote their design rights/copyrights etc., in the same manner. Are they missing a trick or is it simply that product/design lifecycles are so short that it is not worthwhile? For many years, Taiwanese product/industrial design agencies have used the award of a patent to an individual designer's work as a mark of esteem and as a motivational tool. Perhaps in the West we need to consider this more thoroughly. Might it also be that cultures would be inspired, motivated, and feel important if their patterns, products, and practices were considered valuable enough to be legally protected?

It was reported that most designers, agencies, and companies were most comfortable with the concept and reality of copyright and would normally revert to that as a first choice.

Recommendations from the development of design law report

The recommendations of the report are briefly outlined as follows:

- The IPO could offer design rights as an insurance policy for which companies/individuals would have to pay a registration fee. The IPO should then make the information related to the protection of registered designs more accessible and clear.

- The IPO could give clear guidelines as to the likelihood of success in litigation cases brought about due to perceived design right infringement. Information regarding costs, time, and benefits of such action should be made available.

- Among the main problems perceived in the current system are time and cost. In order to alleviate this, it is recommended that a superfast track be considered that would be available to small value design claims. The associated cost would then also be limited but no precise figure is suggested. Extra expense could be attributed to any party wishing to step outside the superfast process.

- Problems can arise due to the judiciary having a different value perception from that of the design community. In order to obviate or at least lessen the likelihood of this occurring, "lay assessors" or "informed users" could be appointed to be on the bench and advise the judge.

- The time taken for and cost of bringing about a judgement on IPR infringements may be reduced by introducing an IPO tribunal system. This would hear cases only where registered design rights exist and last up to a maximum of three hours. One final recommendation is for the formation of a design list to help accommodate an expedited process. This list would comprise cases where it was considered by the judiciary that decisions could be reasonably achieved in three hours or less.

These recommendations are much more expansively described in the report. The above outline gives the reader some flavor of what could be done. At this time, these recommendations remain just that, "recommendations," and the law with regard to Design Intellectual Property Rights in the UK is still difficult to comprehend and/or to ensure firm expectations.

As stated before, the extant literature on Design IPR is mainly aimed at individuals, agencies (SMEs) or companies. In order to begin to consider culturally significant patterns, products, and processes it is necessary to look at some case studies and, while trying to relate back to the current IPR situation, we can make some comments on the deeper complexities therein. Five case studies are considered: Harris Tweed; American Hopi designs; the Paisley pattern; an Inuit design; and Fair Isle patterns. Let us begin with the recognized best protected process and product(s) of Harris Tweed.

The Harris Tweed Act 1993

The history of tweed fabric weaving in the Outer Hebrides in Scotland is checkered and clouded in mystery. At times, and up to the mid-1960s, spun yarn from the Scottish mainland was used in large quantities, but then the islanders on Harris, Lewis, Uist and Barra decided that they would only use yarn spun on the islands, albeit from wool that originated anywhere in Scotland. This in itself raises many interesting questions; anyone who has a knowledge of the wool industry knows that wool brokers have to source and use wools from every part of the world in order to produce economic blends of the right quality. No other fabric/garment styles produced around Scotland and Ireland (e.g. Fair Isle or Aran jumpers) enjoy the protection of an Act of Parliament in the way Harris Tweed does (Harris Tweed Act 1993). So the question could be asked—was this an acquired privilege, as was the case with all protection rights in the seventeenth and up to the mid-eighteenth century? It is also strange that no pattern types are protected by the Act and conversely this means that the designers can appropriate any other culturally significant patterns— or does it? The definition of Harris Tweed given in the Act is one any textile designer or technologist could easily challenge and navigate around. Perhaps this supports the recommendation of the UK IPO report, discussed earlier, that informed users be present on the bench to advise the judges. Let us have a close look at the first part of the definition as stated:

In this Act "Harris Tweed" means a tweed which:

> has been handwoven by the islanders at their homes in the Outer Hebrides, finished in the Outer Hebrides, and made from pure virgin wool dyed and spun in the Outer Hebrides.

The handwoven part has attracted sceptics down through many years but a more interesting question would be to wonder why, as often reported, they use large fiber preparation and spinning machinery, which, in order to run economically, would produce a volume of yarn far higher than could be coped with by the relatively small number of weavers available from the population of the islands. The pure virgin wool does not specify where that wool comes from and what quality (in terms of fineness, length, kemp content etc.) it should be. "Spun in the Outer Hebrides," but what kind of spinning, to what counts (thicknesses and plies), and what twist content and directions should be used? It would appear that, as long as the fabric is handwoven and finished in the Outer Hebrides it can be made from any fiber or yarn. This would surprise any customer of tweed fabrics as there is always a small amount of kemp (dead fibers) that gives these fabrics part of their character but must be carefully controlled, as many people find it can irritate the skin.

Interestingly, no patterns are mentioned either as surface design or as weave structure. Most textile designers would expect tweed to be herringbone or houndstooth weave but this is not mentioned. According to newspaper reports (Hollingworth 2012; Moss 2015), Japanese visitors will often buy the traditional weaves but sometimes ask for special designs, which the islanders are happy to accommodate. Thus it would appear that they require protection for their process and product but are able to use any patterns or weave structures asked for by the consumers. The Act also covers the right to use the Orb symbol as a logo by Harris Tweed producers.

A search for cases brought to the judiciary under the terms of the 1993 Act will show little activity. The most well known one was that between Vivienne Westwood and the Harris Tweed Association. It was suggested that Westwood had used a version similar to the Harris Tweed Orb for garments not conforming to the specifications of the 1993 Act. However, Westwood, who has always been a great supporter and user of Harris Tweed and tartan in her designs, was able to show that her Orb included three variations of the original Orb design and won the case.

There is no doubt that the intent of the 1993 Act was, and is, laudable and that the protection of the livelihoods of islanders living in isolated regions is important. However, let us examine what has been protected from the perspective of IPR:

- There can be no protection of the processes as they exist in many parts of the world and there is little or no evidence of trade secrets.
- There is no protection of the wool type being used.
- There is no protection of patterns.

Therefore, what we have is protection of the place where a part of the design and processing takes place and no requirement for the islanders to adhere to the protection or desired protection of other culturally significant patterns, places, or processes. These are the views of the authors; others may disagree with this interpretation.

Appropriation of Hopi design and culture

This particular case was reported in the interesting chapter by David Howes (1996) in the book he edited called *Cross-Cultural Consumption*. He explains how "Indianness" had become, and remains, a particular target of exploiters in the American Southwest. He goes on to discuss how one of the most marketable cultures was that of the Hopi of Arizona. He describes the various ways that this tribe's culture had been, what can only be described as, abused, such as: the use of Hopi words to describe commercial products; the production and sale of Hopi "fakelore" products, which had no foundation in Hopi culture; the copying of Hopi motifs on cheap tourist consumables; annual ceremonial events by people emulating Hopi culture but having no real connection to it; teaching of spiritually related Hopi crafts by people with no right to do so; the production of children's comics with characters drawn from Hopi spiritual stories and portraying them as American anti-heroes.

Eventually, the Hopi people had taken enough of these abuses and wanted to call a halt to them, and therefore a series of incidents and law cases arose. Howes goes on to explain how it was hoped that the concept of "a right to cultural integrity" could be integrated into Anglo-American Law. He examines how various extant rights might be applied, namely:

- *The Right to Privacy*: This had been mainly used to protect the privacy of private life and, after much consideration, it was decided that this would not cover many of the transgressions of cultural integrity that were taking place.

- *Ordinary Sensibilities*: It was found that most cases considered under this concept, which lies within the right of privacy, had failed to reach a conclusion on the degree of offensiveness and tended to consider this from the point of view of the majority/dominant culture.

- *Copyright*: As stated earlier, this is the oft-used fall back of designers as it is the most widely understood outside the judicial community. Once again, although there have been many examples of successful litigation by designers using this right (e.g. Walt Disney v. Air Pirates 1978), it was realized that the law of copyright pertained more to the commodification of knowledge, rather than to its conservation, and so would have limited use in the protection of culturally significant issues.

- *The Right of Publicity:* At its core, this right is aimed at enabling persons to control and profit from the use of their name and likeness. Howes decided that this right may have some use in the protection of Hopi culture but ends by being somewhat doubtful as to the real value the people would obtain while fully supporting the need for an end to exploitative abuse.

It seems that the primary component in any use of culturally significant patterns, products, and processes is that of ensuring the participation of the culture in the design or exploitation process. Of course, there can be situations where the culture involved may be difficult to identify, as with the next case study.

The Paisley pattern

The teardrop shape known by many in contemporary society as the Paisley pattern (Figure 18.2) is called many other names by a variety of nationalities. How has this come about? Let us look at the case of the town of Paisley in Scotland, which has been associated with this pattern by many people over the last one hundred and fifty years.

At the middle of the nineteenth century, the British Raj in India was still strong but beginning to feel pressure from Indian nationalists, and therefore the influx of British soldiers was at its highest. At the same time, many of these soldiers came from towns where the biggest sources of employment were involved in the weaving of fabric that had flourished since the Industrial Revolution. The soldiers, while mindful of their duties, were also mindful of the time when they would return to their hometowns and, hopefully, to jobs in the local industries. It was therefore natural that when they saw beautiful surface and structural decoration on sale in Indian markets they were quick to capture these patterns and take them back to their local weavers. The Paisley pattern was one such design and could just as easily

FIGURE 18.2 Paisley pattern. Courtesy M. Evans. © Martyn Evans.

have been called the Bolton pattern or the Norwich pattern; it would seem that the
Paisley weavers were a larger and perhaps more organized or vociferous group and
so the pattern became known as the Paisley pattern in much of the Western world.
This is one version of the story; there may be others.

It is also generally accepted that the pattern may not have originated in India and
there are suggestions that it is evidenced in archaeological findings from Babylon
(Reilly 1987: 10). The question, therefore, is to which culture does this pattern
belong and who would ask for protection? The pattern has gone through many
metamorphoses and some of its reincarnations could hardly be called revitalizations;
by revitalization, we mean bringing again into use, prominence, and sustainability.
In the course of the Design Routes project, designers have been asked to carry out
a revitalization exercise on the Paisley pattern with particular consumer markets in
mind. If the output of one such exercise were to be successfully used in the fashion
market, who would hold the IPR? Perhaps this is the answer to the future of design
in the global market. We no longer exist as separate cultural entities and design ideas
should be shared as long as we respect the culture(s) and do not cause spiritual or
temporal offense to those cultures.

Possible appropriation of Inuit design

A case study of considerable interest and one that challenges various aspects of IPR
was reported in the *Toronto Star* in 2015 (Kestler-D'Amours 2015). A Nunavut
woman, Salome Awa, accused a UK fashion label of using a design that had been on
a parka (coat) worn by her great-grandfather, and which had been photographed by

Knud Rasmussen, a Danish explorer, in 1922. She said that she was particularly upset because the design was of great spiritual meaning and importance. She explained that her great-grandfather had been a Shaman and that he had asked his wife to make the parka with a design that emphasized two large hands pushing out from the parka to protect him from anyone who might wish to do him harm. The fashion label stated that their clothes were known for "raw energy and contemporary urban edge, but also for embracing ethnographic references and multiculturalism." The Nunavut woman told the newspaper that she was consulting a lawyer about possible Intellectual Property infringement by the fashion label but would consult with her family before making any decision. This case raises a number of questions/ issues that lawyers and the general public would have to consider:

- Is it possible that the great-grandfather would have been proud that his wife's design had been introduced to and appreciated by the world?
- Did the company consider that any copyright ownership (even if it had been registered) would have now run out, in the same way that music/song copyright does?
- How can one measure the level of spirituality assigned to the design?
- Who would the lawyer fight for: the great-granddaughter and her family, the great-grandfather and his wife, the Nunavut people?
- Consequently, to whom would any compensation be paid?
- Are the great-granddaughter and her family concerned with cultural outrage or the compensation that might be obtained?
- Could the company simply claim, as in other cases, that showing the design on the catwalk did not provide monetary gain and that they would produce no articles for sale?

We await the result, if the case is ever brought to trial.

Fair Isle

The Fair Isle patterns produced on Shetland and surrounding small islands (a subarctic archipelago of Scotland that lies off the northeast coast of Great Britain) have never enjoyed the level of protection of Harris Tweed, and many famous designers have used typical Fair Isle patterns (see Figure 18.3) in their collections. Perhaps one of the reasons why protection has been difficult to obtain is the generally accepted knowledge that the patterns are Moorish in style and were possibly transferred to the already well-skilled knitters of Shetland from one or more Spanish Armada shipwrecks.

In late 2015, it was reported that a knitwear designer from the Shetland Islands had accused Chanel of copying her Fair Isle jumper patterns for a fashion show (Bobila 2015). This case is made all the more interesting in that the designer concerned is Venezuelan and has only lived on Shetland for a relatively short time. However, she felt that the incidence of two Chanel employees visiting in the summer

FIGURE 18.3 Fair Isle pattern scarves. Courtesy Elizabeth Gaston, University of Leeds. © Elizabeth Gaston.

of 2015, buying some of her stock garments and then the very close copies appearing on the catwalk, was not coincidental. The designer and Chanel have come to an out-of-court agreement by which the original designer was credited for the design patterns used.

Questions to consider include:

- Was this a culturally related issue or that of an individual, and therefore covered by design rights as described at the beginning of the chapter?

- Could Chanel have used the defense that showing designs on the catwalk does not constitute making money from them as has been used by fashion houses in the past?

- Does the settlement out-of-court mean that Chanel accept they have done wrong and what will be the implications of this in the future?

Because of this case, there has been talk of the need for better protection of Fair Isle patterns. Does this mean that the designer living on Shetland, though not a native, should be compensated for the use of her own designs or should the Shetland Islands or some affiliation have a case of their own to prosecute?

Conclusion

The complex nature of Design Intellectual Property Rights has been outlined here but the reader will have to refer to the texts cited to go into greater detail on the plethora of issues involved. Examples have been given of possible misappropriations of culturally significant patterns, products, and processes. Outcomes have been given, though there are few actual settlements, and, as the reader will have discovered, these can be cloaked in secrecy. The questions then remain; can the revitalization of culturally significant patterns, products, and processes be protected? Should they be protected? And who should be protected?

Perhaps the answers lie in chapters where it is made clear that the people of the culture concerned must participate in the revitalization process at every stage and be allowed to collaborate with the designer(s) to avoid the temporal and spiritual pitfalls that surround the subject. The authors would like to suggest that protection should be available against exploitation, spiritual, and/ or temporal misuse, abuse or mockery of culturally significant manifestations, but that sharing and revitalization of such is an inevitable part of our global community and should be prudently encouraged. Since 2003, an EU community design rights regulation has been in force and it will be interesting to see what effect this will have; but it will not affect culturally significant patterns, products, and processes as dealt with in this book. This is not an easy subject and never will be. The chapter does not claim to provide definitive solutions but rather to pose questions and to continue raising awareness among readers and the design community generally.

References

Bobila, M. (2015), "Chanel Accused of Copying Knitwear Designer Mati Ventrillon," *Fashionista*, December 7. Available online: http://fashionista.com/2015/12/mati-ventrillon-chanel-metiers (accessed November 1, 2016).

Harris Tweed Act 1993 (c.xi) London: HMSO.

Hollingworth, W. (2012), "Traditional Tweed finds a new life in Japan," *Japanese Times*, March 30. Available online: http://www.japantimes.co.jp/news/2012/03/30/national/traditional-tweed-finds-a-new-life-in-japan/#.WBjDZYXXJMs (accessed November 1, 2016).

Howes, D. (1996), *Cultural Appropriation and Resistance in the American Southwest in Cross Cultural Consumption*, New York, NY: Routledge.

Intellectual Property Office (2012), "The Development of Design Law—Past and Future," July 24. Available online: https://www.gov.uk/government/publications/the-development-of-design-law-past-and-future (accessed August 1, 2016).

Kestler-D'Amours, J. (2015), "Nunavut Woman Accuses U.K. Fashion Label of Appropriating Inuit Design," *Toronto Star*, November 26. Available online: https://www.thestar.com/news/canada/2015/11/26/nunavut-woman-accuses-uk-fashion-label-of-appropriating-inuit-design.html (accessed August 1, 2016).

MacPherson, C. B. (1978), *Property, Mainstream and Critical Positions*, Oxford: Basil Blackwell.

Moss, V. (2015), "The Wool to Succeed," *The Telegraph*, April 25. Available at: http://www.telegraph.co.uk/luxury/womens-style/69209/harris-tweed-the-wool-to-succeed.html (accessed November 1, 2016).

Mwendapole, C. (2005), "Design Knowledge and Intellectual Property Rules," Ph.D. thesis, De Montfort University, Leicester.

Reilly, V. (1987), *The Paisley Pattern*, Glasgow: Richard Drew Publishing.

Rodgers, P. A. and P. J. Clarkson (1998), "An Investigation and Review of the Knowledge Needs of Designers in SMEs," *The Design Journal*, 1 (3): 16–29.

Walt Disney Productions v. Air Pirates (1978), 581 F.2d 751.

19

The Case of the City Different

The Intersection of the Museum, the Artist, and the Marketplace

Marsha C. Bol

Introduction

Tiny Santa Fe, New Mexico, consistently ranks among the top five cities in the United States to visit by *Travel + Leisure* magazine. In 2004, this small city was the first in the United States to be designated a UNESCO Creative City (in folk arts and design). This level of recognition for "The City Different" did not happen by accident. It was an intentional recalibration of a city, destined for modernization in the early twentieth century, principally by anthropologists, artists, writers, and historians, with the leadership of the Museum of New Mexico staff as the nexus of a series of events leading to a road map for creating a cultural center.

With the founding of the state Museum of New Mexico in 1909 "a new breed of cultural worker arrived in Santa Fe" (Wilson 1997: 94). The new museum Director, Edgar Lee Hewett, and his professional staff of three (Kenneth Chapman, Sylvanus Morley, and Jesse Nusbaum) took as their mandate the preservation and revival of local artistic and cultural traditions. "For the future cultural development of Santa Fe, the creation of the Museum of New Mexico and its residence in the Palace [of the Governors] may well have been the most important decision of the twentieth century" (Tobias and Woodhouse 2001: 73).

The development of an "Authentic" Santa Fe architectural style

In 1912, both Edgar Hewett and Sylvanus Morley (archaeologist of the new Museum of New Mexico and the School of American Archaeology [now the School for Advanced Research]) were appointed by the Mayor of Santa Fe to the newly formed City Planning Board with the task of developing a strategy to reverse a badly sagging city economy, resulting from having been bypassed by the main line of the Santa Fe Railroad in 1880. The revival of local Hispanic and Pueblo architectural traditions was the course of action advanced by Sylvanus Morley as the pathway leading to the city's rightful authentic architectural image, which in turn would promote tourism as a solution to Santa Fe's economic woes.

Sylvanus Morley became the principal spokesman for the move to identify and preserve the architectural traditions of Santa Fe's past, as he defined them based on a widespread photographic survey of local vernacular buildings by Jesse Nusbaum, the museum photographer. Morley worked feverishly to save "the old," speaking to all who would listen: "Part of the Battle will have been won if we can convince … that this city can acquire greater fame and more lasting prosperity by maintaining intact famous and important buildings rather than replacing them with new buildings such as one can see in any American city" (Nusbaum 1950:165).

At the center of Morley's plan was a formula of architectural ingredients for the ideal Santa Fe dwelling, synthesized from New Mexico's Spanish Colonial and Pueblo Indian past:

1st. The general effect is low and long. One story is the rule, two stories the exception …

2nd. All prominent façade lines are horizontal. Gable or pointed roofs are never seen … The uniform use of flat … roofs … is one of the most distinctive characteristics of Santa Fe Architecture, and greatly enhances the low and long effect.

3rd. The façade is broken by a number of architectural devices which relieve the monotony of the otherwise blank adobe walls, such as: inset porches (*portales*), balconies (*balcones*), projecting roof-beams and water-spouts (*vigas* and *canales*) …

4th. The color preferably should be one of the numerous shades of adobe … This "protective coloration" of the Santa Fe Style harmonizes admirably with its environment, and is one of its chief charms.

5th. Carved wood members are extensively and effectively utilized in façade decoration … carved wood capitals, columns, architraves, balustrades, cornices, and doors (Morley 1915: 283–4).

In an effort to promote the planning board's proposal by Morley, the city, the Chamber of Commerce, and the School of American Archaeology sponsored an exhibition in the fall of 1912, with Morley as the exhibition director. *The New-Old Santa Fe Exhibition* was installed in the Palace of the Governors, the oldest continuously occupied public building in the United States and home to the Museum of New Mexico. Artists, architects, archaeologists, writers, and members of the Santa Fe Planning Board and Chamber of Commerce were present to provide information, answer questions, and promote the objectives of civic planning "to preserve its character as the most ancient city of America" (Nusbaum 1950: 164, 166–70).[1]

In an effort to imprint their ideas for preserving and perpetuating the historic into the new era, Sylvanus Morley and several other supporters purchased old adobe homes and renovated them, thereby demonstrating the merits of preserving old Santa Fe style buildings while remodeling them to meet current needs. "By mid-summer of 1913, the Old Santa Fe renaissance movement was slowly gaining momentum, and the lag in the rate of starting construction of new modern and non-conforming structures was becoming widely apparent. The majority of potential builders and renovators were literally sitting on the fence watching and considering trends before reaching final decisions" (Nusbaum 1950: 171).

The impact and importance of the planning for a unified architectural image based upon heritage cannot be overestimated in the successful fashioning of a cultural identity for Santa Fe. The continued success of this identity is exemplified in the extraordinarily high volume of sales for the book, *Santa Fe Style*, first published in 1986 and now in its 13th printing (Mather and Woods 1986).

The newly minted Santa Fe architectural style figured in the upcoming World's Fair in San Diego, the Panama-California Exposition of 1915, with museum director Edgar Hewett in charge of the New Mexico exhibits for the fair. The New Mexico Pavilion provided the opportunity to draw upon the stylistic elements of Morley's plan and arouse public interest in New Mexico's unique architectural heritage. Hewett intended that the New Mexico Building design would serve a dual purpose, planning to replicate the same building back in Santa Fe after the fair as the state Museum of Art. Given this challenge, the architects (Rapp, Rapp and Hendrickson) rose to the occasion, designing and building a structure back home in Santa Fe in 1917 that ultimately became recognized as the iconic progenitor of the Santa Fe Style, the New Mexico Museum of Art, located at the northwest corner of the city's public plaza (Figure 19.1).

Jesse Nusbaum, museum photographer, observed:

It has long been the general consensus that the Art Museum, more than any other structure, turned the public trend firmly in favor of the Santa Fe style, and promoted the city-wide and public interest which has since not only dominantly characterized home, business, and public building architecture in Santa Fe, but influenced architectural trends elsewhere in New Mexico, and more widely. (1950: 173)

A surprising lesson that the Museum of New Mexico staff took away from the San Diego World's Fair was the observation that the fair tourists, whom they hoped to attract to Santa Fe, were more interested in Pueblo Indian cultures than in Hispanic culture (Wilson 1997: 129). At the Santa Fe Railway's *Painted Desert* exhibit, Edgar Hewett and his museum staff supervised the design and building of the exhibit including a life-sized "Indian Village." To add authenticity, the village was populated with families from San Ildefonso Pueblo, including the Pueblo potter couple, Maria and Julian Martinez. Hewett knew this couple well having previously worked with them when he excavated an archaeological site near their village.

FIGURE 19.1 New Mexico Museum of Art, built in 1917. Photograph by Wesley Bradfield.
Courtesy Palace of the Governors Photo Archives 12986.

The Pueblo pottery improvement project

Maria Montoya Martinez (c. 1887–1980) began making pottery as a young girl
growing up in the Tewa-speaking Rio Grande Pueblo of San Ildefonso. Like all
young Pueblo girls, she learned skills from a female relative, observing her aunt,
Nicolasa Montoya, as she worked the clay. Then Martinez experimented with the
clay by herself, receiving instructive feedback on her initial efforts from her aunt. She
made her pots for use at home: for cooking, food storage, and to wash hair, and mix
bread dough (Spivey 2003: 172).

The same day that Maria married Julian Martinez, they left on a train to travel to
the 1904 St. Louis World's Fair, where they were contracted to do performances in
the Midway. There Martinez had her first experience demonstrating and selling her
pottery to non-Indian people, spending her days making small bowls and jars to sell
to the crowds of fair visitors. She noted the buyers' preference, remarking that they
selected her plain polished red bowls over other types that she had for sale (Marriott
1948: 120).

Beginning in 1907, archaeologists from the School of American Archaeology,
under the directorship of Edgar Hewett, excavated a site on the Pajarito Plateau.
They employed workers from San Ildefonso Pueblo to assist. One of those workers

was Julian Martinez. During the second field season, Hewett encouraged Julian and Maria to reproduce the old pottery type from potsherds found at the site.

Maria Martinez's obvious skill as a potter came to Hewett's attention. Thus began a long relationship between the Museum of New Mexico as patron and Maria and Julian Martinez as artists. As Maria recalled, "He [Edgar Hewett] was the one that we know first, and he was the one that start us in pottery [*sic*]" (Spivey 2003: 178).

From 1909 to 1912, the wife and husband team became a living exhibit at the Museum of New Mexico, where they lived in the Palace of the Governors. Maria Martinez formed and polished pots daily, while her husband painted the designs, firing them in the courtyard of the Palace (Figure 19.2).

Even though Maria and Julian Martinez produced their pottery together, Maria is the recognized potter, based on the Pueblo traditional gender division of labor. Pueblo people said that the women were the potters. Even though men could be seen painting and helping, sometimes even making an entire pot, it would still only be considered "helping out" (J. J. Brody 1991, Personal communication).

Visitors to the museum purchased pottery directly from the artists, while the museum collected selected works as well. The museum officials made their preferences known to Martinez, as an excerpt from a letter written by curator Olive Wilson indicates: "[The museum staff] consider [Maria] the best of the pottery makers here-

FIGURE 19.2 Maria and Julian Martinez making pottery in the courtyard of the Palace of the Governors, 1912. Photograph by Jesse Nusbaum. Courtesy Palace of the Governors Photo Archives 40814.

about, and she knows that we expect her work always to reach a certain standard, so she brings us only good pieces" (Batkin 1987: 31–2).

In 1920, the intentional exertion of influence by Museum of New Mexico officials on Pueblo pottery-making standards developed into a formalized project, the Pottery Improvement Project. The intent of the project was to stimulate a high grade Pueblo pottery-making industry to counter the pottery curios made for the tourist trade, which they were witnessing. Hewett appointed two museum staff, Kenneth Chapman and Wesley Bradfield, to undertake the project. Chapman and Bradfield developed the following criteria for effecting this quality improvement:

1. Inviting the potters to submit their wares to us at the Museum before offering them for sale elsewhere.
2. Asking each potter to set her price, piece by piece.
3. Selecting a few outstanding pieces, if any, and explaining why they were chosen (for form, finish, decoration etc.).
4. Adding at least twenty-five percent to the price named by the potter for those selected, and promising still higher prices for further improvement. (Chapman 1970: 28)

Chapman tells the story of the first application of their quality improvement formula:

Julian and Maria Martinez of San Ildefonso appeared with a wagonload of pottery. Here was an unexpected problem. They were the last we would have picked for our experiment, for they were accomplished craft workers who might resent our suggestions for improvement of their wares. However, we knew they were forced to limit the time expended on each piece, for they had learned that the dealers would not pay higher prices for a more finished product. So, in hopes of finding one or more outstanding pieces in the lot, we decided to test our plan. It worked wonders! We set aside four unusually well-formed and finished pieces and asked their prices. Then we commended the couple for the attractive qualities of their pottery and paid 25 percent more than they had asked. That concluded, we told them of our plan and promised even more for others in their next lot if they showed further improvement (1970: 29–30).

Alfred Kidder, an archaeologist who witnessed this experiment, described the actions of the Museum:

The authorities of the Museum of New Mexico and the School of American Research threw themselves heartily into the task of stimulating the industry … The undertaking was not an easy one, however, for it was difficult to get most of the women to go to the trouble of making good pieces when the tourists, who were still the principal purchasers, were equally or even better pleased with imitations of china water-pitchers, ill-made rain gods, and candlesticks. The problem thus resolved itself into one of supplying a market. The Museum bought many good pieces and Mr. Chapman, who from the beginning had been a leading spirit in the attempt at rehabilitating the art, himself purchased large amounts of pottery, never refusing a creditable piece, never accepting a bad one ...

Maria especially shone. By 1915 she had far surpassed all others, her pots were in great demand, and at the present time she has a ready market, at prices which ten years ago would have seemed fantastic, for everything she can find time to make (1925: 14).

As Chapman reported, the Museum of New Mexico officials intentionally initiated a consumer standard, which they determined would be the desirable direction for the development of quality Pueblo pottery and the growth of a thriving market, encouraging Martinez to strive toward greater and greater technical perfection in her pottery making. Martinez responded to the market-driven call for perfection by making pots that were increasingly technical marvels, with seemingly mechanical precision of shape, sure-handed painting that belied the human touch and lustrous, unblemished polish. She remarked, "That's what people like, when I [make] the edge straight and perfect" (Spivey 2003: 175). Paradoxically, Martinez recognized that although her customers greatly admired her mechanical-like precision, they would not tolerate it if her pots were indeed mechanically produced. When asked if she would use the potter's wheel, Martinez replied, "Oh, if I try the wheel maybe the museum people will not like it" (Spivey 2003: 181).

Martinez took a risk investing her materials, time, and energy in making a single piece, when the same investment could be used to make multiple simpler, less accomplished pieces whose sales were assured. However her risk paid off. The buyers showed up to purchase every piece that she produced.

The lionization of Maria Martinez by the outside world was a first in the history of San Ildefonso Pueblo. Singling out of an individual genius artist for fame is a distinctly Western European concept, in all ways in opposition to the Pueblo concept of the primacy of the group. Martinez, as a traditional Pueblo woman, faced the dilemma of coping with individual fame within her culture that valued the welfare of the entire community over the importance of the individual. Repeatedly, when dealers wanted to purchase only Martinez's pottery, she professed, "It all comes from San Ildefonso ... It's the pueblo that make the difference, not the woman who makes the pottery" (Marriott 1948: 200). When other potters of their village wanted to learn how to make the black pottery, the Martinezes shared the firing method with them so that everyone could benefit from its popularity.

In 1923, the superintendent of the Santa Fe Indian School proposed that Martinez sign her pots like Euro-American artists. Thus buyers could be assured they were purchasing her original work. Martinez, again confronted with the Western European reverence for the individual named artist, negotiated this conflict with Pueblo group values by sharing her signature with other San Ildefonso potters. She signed their pots along with hers, so that all the pots would have an equal chance to sell. The signature exposes another basic difference between Western and Pueblo processes of artistic production. In Pueblo pottery making, several members of the family usually collaborate in making a pot, from collecting and preparing the clay to molding, sanding, painting, and firing. Thus most of Martinez's signed pots bear more than one name—hers plus another collaborating family member. Even so, it is

Maria Martinez singly who remains the most famous Native American artist of the twentieth century (Marriott 1948: 233–5; Bernstein 2012: 40).

"As the economic importance of pottery making grew, income from pottery began to exceed income from farm products. A dramatic rise in the standard of living became evident ... By 1931 Maria's annual income exceeded $5,000. She hired Spanish household help so that she could devote more time to pottery making" (Spivey 2003: 44).

The development of the Indian Market

The Native arts of the Southwest have been bought, sold, traded, and distributed as gifts—in other words, actively involved in economic and social transactions for millennia. "The reality is that art is a special type of commodity that has economic value and is sold in markets ... Artists, like consumers and collectors, do not work in social vacuums," observes anthropologist Nancy Parezo (1990: 563). Thus, in 1922 when the Museum of New Mexico spearheaded yet another project destined to offer economic and educational opportunities for Pueblo and other regional Native artists to exhibit and market their traditional arts, the artists quickly recognized the value of this project.

The Indian Fair, as it was called in the beginning, became an event at the Santa Fe Fiesta, an annual event to commemorate the re-entry of the Spanish into New Mexico in 1692. The principle criterion for entry into the Indian Fair was that Native artists must use the "traditional" methods of manufacture, which continues as a criterion today in certain categories. All entries were juried by assistant director Kenneth Chapman and two other museum curators to assure that only pieces of "quality" gained entry. Cash prizes were awarded to the "best" in various categories, thus rewarding excellence as judged by the museum jury. Maria Martinez consistently won the top awards for many years.

The Museum of New Mexico continued to manage the Indian Fair until 1926. Throughout its history, the fair went through a number of guises, moving outdoors under the Palace of the Governors' portal and ultimately taking over the entire city plaza and all adjacent streets fanning out from the plaza. For many years, Chapman remained the head judge.

During the 1960s, the American anti-Vietnam war generation of youth seized upon American Indian cultures as the "ideal" model for lifestyle, and Native American worldviews and systems of values received wide exposure within the American populace. As a part of this enthusiasm, from coast to coast, Americans' desire for Southwestern Native arts to wear and to decorate their homes burgeoned. Santa Fe's Indian Market, now sponsored by the Southwestern Association for Indian Arts (SWAIA), thrived within this tide of interest. The mission of the market changed from the original museum's Indian Fair mission "to preserve and revive old arts, to keep the arts of each tribe as distinctive as possible, to help to authenticate, to locate markets, and to obtain fair prices" to SWAIA's mission to "develop, sponsor, and promote the Santa Fe Indian Market and other educational programs and events that encourage cultural preservation, inter-cultural understanding, and economic opportunities for American Indians through excellence in the arts, with an emphasis on Indians in the Southwest" (SWAIA 2014: 3).

FIGURE 19.3 Indian Market vendor Margaret Tafoya displays her pottery, 1971. Unknown photographer. Courtesy Palace of the Governors Photo Archives 190688.

Some ninety years later, on the third weekend of August, the Indian Market hosts more than one thousand artists from more than four hundred Indian nations across the US and Canada (Figure 19.3). The artists sell directly to their customers without any intermediary, taking home their direct earnings. More than one hundred and fifty thousand visitors attend the Market annually, some flying into Santa Fe from long distances in their private planes. Over $80 million in revenue is generated for the city and the state annually in this, the largest juried Native art show in the world.

The influx of Euro-American artists and intellectuals as patrons of Hispanic arts

On yet another front, Edgar Hewett promoted Santa Fe as a desirable destination for Euro-American artists, living in New York and other American major arts centers, to come to Santa Fe and paint. To add to the attraction, he offered well-known painters the use of studio space in the Palace of the Governors, home to the Museum of New Mexico. While organizing the exhibitions for the San Diego World's Fair, Hewett became acquainted with Robert Henri, a well-known New York painter. Henri accepted Hewett's invitation to visit Santa Fe and ultimately proved to be a pivotal figure in attracting other talented painters to Santa Fe. Henri recommended that Hewett introduce an "open door" policy for the new art museum, which essentially offered any artist working in New Mexico the opportunity to exhibit their work free from the approval of a jury or a curator, a radical idea in the era of the academy system.

As word spread of the Museum of Fine Arts' (New Mexico Museum of Art) receptivity to radical aesthetic ideas, Santa Fe attracted modernist artists, intellectuals, poets, and writers to its growing arts community. The establishment of a progressive artistic milieu in Santa Fe set the stage for the expansion of the arts, efforts at cultural preservation, and social activism with Native American and Hispanic residents. After the opening of the museum, Henri wrote to a friend that the new museum "is a wonder." The museum signified the beginning of Santa Fe's evolution into a serious cultural destination. The new institution embodied Hewett's concept of cultural preservation in the service of tourism (Traugott 2007: 19).

These transplanted artists, plus artists and writers who came to the Sunmount Sanitorium seeking a cure for tuberculosis, formed a group of activists seeking to preserve and/or revive the traditional arts of the northern New Mexico Hispanic villages.

Three cycles of preservation of Hispanic arts transpired during the twentieth century, all initiated by Euro-American artists, writers, and arts patrons. The first initiative was spearheaded by writer Mary Austin and artist Frank Applegate, who formed the Spanish Colonial Arts Society in 1925 (incorporated in 1929). The Society took as its mission to revive the northern New Mexico Hispanic arts, never considering that most of these arts were still in practice, although often by a diminishing number of artisans (Wroth 1977: 5). What the artisans were in need of, with the loss of their local community clientele who were turning to new commercially-manufactured products, were new markets to supplement the villagers' meager income.

Santa Fe's artist-intellectual colony desired Spanish decorative arts to furnish their Santa Fe style homes. For the first time in over three hundred years, non-Hispanic outsiders became a major audience for the traditional Hispanic arts of weaving, furniture-making and carving, ironwork, tinwork, and even carved and painted religious saints. The *New Mexico Magazine* reported in 1938, "as New Mexico style homes grow in popularity the use of New Mexico style furnishings is coming into greater use" (1938: 48) (Figure 19.4).

The Spanish Colonial Arts Society opened a shop in 1930, the only shop to focus exclusively on Hispanic handmade items, such as *colcha* embroidered textiles, rugs and blankets, furniture and carvings, iron and tinwork. Although the shop only lasted for three years, one of the Society's members, also a member of Santa Fe's colony of reform-minded arts patrons, Leonora F. Curtin, opened The Native Market in 1934. Curtin subsidized the shop, running it as a non-profit in hopes that it would eventually become self-sustaining. She employed Hispanic artisans

FIGURE 19.4 Euro-American living room decorated in Santa Fe Style, c. 1940. Photograph by Wyatt Davis. Courtesy Palace of the Governors Photo Archives 68337.

(and salespeople) to work in the shop or in their homes, making quality stock for the shop and filling orders. Artists demonstrating their arts for clientele visiting the shop proved to be a successful marketing strategy (Nunn 2001: 29). Ultimately twelve employees and some three hundred and fifty craftspeople earned their livelihood by supplying The Native Market, which proved to be quite a successful enterprise until 1939 when Leonora Curtin ceased subsidizing the market (Padilla 1996: 42). However, New Mexico's Hispanic arts never proved as popular as the regional Native American arts.

During this period, in spite of the enthusiasm of the wealthy Anglo patrons in northern New Mexico, Hispanic crafts never "caught on" nationally in the way the Indian crafts did. Interest was fairly well limited to the Southwest and southern California, the areas in which the adobe hacienda revival was taking place. The major interest in Hispanic crafts was as furnishings for these comfortable Southwestern-style adobe homes. These crafts were not, as were the Indian, viewed as valuable art objects in themselves purchased with an eye for speculation (Wroth 1977: 6).

A "second cycle of appreciation of Hispanic art took place during the depression of the 1930s, when many villagers lost employment in the outside world and returned home to their small towns ... This took the form of crafts programs organized by the

New Mexico State Department of Vocational Education in 1933" (Cirillo 1998: 24). State vocational schools devoted to providing training in the traditional Hispanic crafts were established in nearly every rural Hispanic community in New Mexico. The artistic products made in the vocational schools were destined for home use in the community or for sale in The Native Market in Santa Fe.

Concurrently the national New Deal art program, composed of several federal programs under the term Works Projects Administration (WPA) from the 1930s into the early 1940s, initiated its own wide sweeping programs. Within the WPA, the Federal Art Project (FAP) was the most ambitious project intended as a relief program for artists and craftspeople, headed by Holger Cahill, an early champion of American folk arts. Selected Hispanic artisans furnished New Mexico public buildings with carved furniture and architectural elements, in addition to tinwork and textiles, all in the spirit of the FAP's mission of art for everyone (Nunn 2001: 8–10).

After Mary Austin's death in 1934, the Spanish Colonial Arts Society fell largely dormant until the 1950s. In 1952, local artist Cady Wells donated his Hispanic arts collection to the Museum of New Mexico, specifying that the museum create a Spanish Colonial Arts department to be headed by E. Boyd, who became the first curator of Spanish Colonial art at the Museum of New Mexico. Upon her appointment Boyd began work to reinvigorate the Society. Boyd moved to the newly opened Museum of International Folk Art, a new museum division of the Museum of New Mexico, in 1953 where, as curator, she continued to build and exhibit a superlative collection of historic New Mexico Hispanic traditional arts for both the museum and the Spanish Colonial Arts Society, whose collection was on loan to the museum. In 2002, the Spanish Colonial Arts Society opened its own museum, the Museum of Spanish Colonial Arts, as a neighbor to the Museum of International Folk Art on Museum Hill, a concentration of museums in Santa Fe.

It was during this era that the third and current cycle in the development of Hispanic arts took place. The Museum of International Folk Art, the Palace of the Governors, and later the Museum of Spanish Colonial Arts, installed numerous exhibitions with accompanying publications that introduced the Hispanic arts to the state's rapidly growing population and tourism industry after the Second World War. In 1989 the Museum of International Folk Art opened its Hispanic Heritage Wing, the first museum gallery in the US dedicated to the presentation of the Hispanic arts.

Teresa Archuleta-Sagel (Rio Grande weaver and scholar) attributes much of the current interest in historic weaving to the 1979 publication of *Spanish Textile Tradition of New Mexico and Colorado* by the Museum of New Mexico Press (reissued in 1994 under the title *Rio Grande Textiles*). In 1976 and 1979, the Museum of International Folk Art in Santa Fe had sponsored workshops in weaving and dyeing, making available for study the museum's extraordinary collection of historic Rio Grande textiles. The 1979 publication was important for Archuleta-Sagel and other weavers because it gave them a "historical context," for the first time, in which to place their own work, inspiring many weavers with a new appreciation and interest in their artistic antecedents (Cirillo 1998: 44).

In 1965, museum curator, E. Boyd, in concert with the renewed Spanish Colonial Arts Society revived the Spanish Market, which until 1971 shared the plaza with the Indian Market, at which point both markets became too big to fit together in the plaza space. The Spanish Colonial Arts Society had originally initiated the Spanish Market in 1926, held during Santa Fe Fiesta weekend, but by the early 1930s, the market lapsed until its revival in 1965. Today the Spanish Market continues to thrive, with 225–250 Hispanic artists selling their arts on the last weekend in July to some eighty thousand visitors on the Santa Fe plaza. For many of these artists, ninety-seven percent of whom are from New Mexico, the Spanish Market is their prime source of annual income. In 2015, the economic impact from the Market yielded $22.8 million for the city, county, and state of Santa Fe, New Mexico. The market is linked with the Museum of Spanish Colonial Art as two of the three programs under the umbrella of the Spanish Colonial Arts Society (M. Magalnick, Personal communication, January 3, 2016).

What does this all mean?

Just at the time when Pueblo Indian pottery was being replaced by metal buckets and Hispanic hand-carved devotional images by mold-made plaster saints, in a small place called Santa Fe, a timely collaboration between the local artisans and the Museum of New Mexico transpired. This was the time when Euro-Americans believed that the demise of Native Americans their cultures and their arts was imminent. American anthropologists raced out to Indian Country to perform "salvage" ethnography in an effort to collect what material culture remained before it all disappeared.

In the Santa Fe region, however, the traditional arts did not disappear. A confluence of initiatives by the Museum of New Mexico staff, incoming and concerned citizens, and purposeful artists created an environment where regional identity in the form of local architecture and traditional crafts, boosted by tourism, gave new respect and created new markets for these arts. "The San Ildefonso Pueblo potters Maria and Julian Martinez were indeed handed a potsherd by anthropologist Edgar Hewett, but the issue is not a white man enlightening Native people about their own archaeological past, it's what the Martinezes did with that potsherd after Hewett gave it to them … They began a period of artistic innovation that continues today" (Bernstein 2011: 130).

The Martinezes were not the only Pueblo pottery family that invested in fine pottery-making as their livelihood, maintaining the tradition of passing on their knowledge and skills to the next generation. In 1974, the Maxwell Museum of Anthropology (at the University of New Mexico) opened an exhibition accompanied by a modest catalog, *Seven Families in Pueblo Pottery*, which identified seven families with multiple generations of potters in several villages, who excelled in their craft. The catalog proved "unexpectedly influential," selling some eighty thousand copies in the next twenty years and serving as a guidebook for non-native pottery collectors, who often would only purchase pottery from a potter who was in the book. When they observed the economic success of those potters included in the catalog, other potters asked for an enlarged edition, while Navajo weavers asked for their own "seven families" book of weavers. Once again a museum had proved influential in the marketplace for traditional arts.

And yet while the marketplace is undoubtedly an essential stimulus to the maintenance and creative development of traditional arts in this region, the value of the arts for the community is more than just an income producer. As Hispanic weaver, Teresa Archuleta-Sagel so aptly puts it:

> We awoke to our own heritage through a desire to create art that reflected our own cultural identity. Our work was an act of self-discovery that stirred intense feelings of pride and self-worth, and the style and tradition in which we worked provided the means to connect with and, in some cases, recreate roots that needed our vigor and vision. We became as midwives attending our community and helping to ensure that it would survive the twentieth century and, indeed, flower in the twenty-first century (Cirillo 1998: 44).

Note

1   In actuality, Santa Fe is the second oldest city in the United States, with St. Augustine, Florida, as the oldest.

References

Batkin, J. (1987), *Pottery of the Pueblos of New Mexico, 1900–1940*, Colorado Springs, CO: The Taylor Museum of the Colorado Springs Fine Arts Center.

Bernstein, B. (2011), "Fired Up: The Poetry, The Politics, The Pressing Place of Pottery at Indian Market," *Santa Fean*, August/September: 127–33.

Bernstein, B. (2012), *Santa Fe Indian Market: A History of Native Arts and the Marketplace*, Santa Fe, NM: Museum of New Mexico Press.

Chapman, K. (1970), *The Pottery of San Ildefonso Pueblo, Albuquerque*, Santa Fe, NM: University of New Mexico.

Cirillo, D. (1998), *Across Frontiers: Hispanic Crafts of New Mexico*, San Francisco, CA: Chronicle Books.

Kidder, A. (1925), "Introduction," in C. Guthe, *Pueblo Pottery Making: A Study at the Village of San Ildefonso*, 1–18, New Haven, CT: Yale University Press.

Marriott, A. (1948), *Maria: The Potter of San Ildefonso*, Norman, OK: University of Oklahoma Press.

Mather, C. and S. Woods (1986), *Santa Fe Style*, New York, NY: Rizzoli International Publications, Inc.

Maxwell Museum of Anthropology (1974), *Seven Families in Pueblo Pottery*, Albuquerque, NM: University of New Mexico Press.

Morley, S. (1915), "Santa Fe Architecture," *Old Santa Fe: A Magazine of History, Archaeology, Genealogy and Biography*, 2 (3): 278–301.

New Mexico Magazine (1938), "New Mexico's Architectural Style Growing in Popularity," April: 48.

Nunn, T. (2001), *Sin Nombre: Hispana and Hispano Artists of the New Deal Era*, Albuquerque, NM: University of New Mexico Press.

Nusbaum, J. (1950), "Vay Morley and the Santa Fe Style," in *Morleyana: A Collection of Writings in Memoriam, Sylvanus Griswold Morley—1883–1948*, 162–73, Santa Fe: The School of American Research and The Museum of New Mexico.

Padilla, C. (1996), "Revival Period Arts and Artists," in D. Pierce and M. Weigle (eds.), *Spanish New Mexico: The Spanish Colonial Arts Society Collection*, vol. 2, 32–47, Santa Fe, NM: Museum of New Mexico Press.

Parezo, N. (1990), "A Multitude of Markets," *Journal of the Southwest*, 32 (4): 563–75.

Spivey, R. (2003), *The Legacy of Maria Poveka Martinez*, Santa Fe, NM: Museum of New Mexico Press.

SWAIA (2014), "The History of Santa Fe Indian Market and the Southwestern Association for Indian Arts,". http://swaia.org/About_SWAIA/History/index.html (accessed November 14, 2017).

Tobias, H. and C. Woodhouse (2001), *Santa Fe: A Modern History, 1880–1990*, Albuquerque, NM: University of New Mexico Press.

Traugott, J. (2007), *The Art of New Mexico: How the West is One*, Santa Fe, NM: Museum of New Mexico Press.

Wilson, C. (1997), *The Myth of Santa Fe: Creating a Modern Regional Tradition*, Albuquerque, NM: University of New Mexico Press.

Wroth, W. (1977), *Hispanic Crafts of the Southwest*, Colorado Springs, CO: Colorado Springs Fine Arts Center.

PART FIVE

Design Futures

Editorial Introduction

Stuart Walker and Martyn Evans

The chapters in this final section focus on the future of culturally significant designs, products, and practices, the role that designers might play in that future, and the potential strategies that might be employed to ensure the healthy and flourishing continuance of these important aspects of our—tangible and intangible—cultural heritage.

We begin with Tom Cassidy's consideration of *Research Approaches for Culturally Significant Design*. The reader is introduced to a variety of research approaches that are applicable for the study of culturally significant designs, products, and practices. Eight approaches are discussed and case studies are provided to illustrate their use. Some have been used many times in the past while others are newer to the field but gaining momentum.

In Amy Twigger Holroyd's chapter, *Digital Transformations, Amateur Making, and the Revitalization of Traditional Textile Crafts,* we are introduced to the ways in which amateur craft communities engage with culturally significant designs, products, and practices, and the importance of digital technologies in supporting this amateur making activity. These issues are explored through a focus on textile crafts such as knitting, sewing, and mending, and one maker's engagement with the tradition of Sanquhar knitting. This chapter draws on interviews with three textile makers, along with the author's previous professional experience. Amy argues that amateur making can play an important role in the revitalization of traditional crafts, especially in post-industrial contexts. Furthermore, she says that digital platforms such as YouTube, Instagram and Ravelry are having a transformational effect on the practices of amateur makers, amplifying their collective ability to share knowledge, develop expertise, and experiment. In this chapter, we see that these emerging cultures of creativity help drive innovation within traditional crafts, enabling them to remain both relevant and vibrant. Also, by recognizing the influential role of digitally enabled amateur making communities, new strategies for revitalization can be developed.

Anna Meroni and Daniela Selloni discuss their work in *Design for Social Innovators*. They suggest that from the first appearance of Creative Communities in the 2000s, many things have changed and the field has matured. Design intervention used to generate social change has resulted in new approaches, new sensibilities, and new tools that designers can use to support local initiatives. Today, "design for social innovation," "community-centered design," "co-design" and "co-production" are more than just buzzwords—they represent new and effective ways for design to make constructive interventions for stimulating local sustainable development. Through a comparative study of three design projects rooted in the local context, this chapter explores the contribution of design in the current transition from creative communities to social innovation ecosystems, and from communities of experience to evolved communities of expertise sharing a service design mindset.

Çağla Doğan offers a reflection on graduate design work in the area of lighting in a chapter entitled, *Integrated Scales of Design and Production for Sustainability*. She presents insights developed from her graduate course in product design for sustainability, which she taught in the Department of Industrial Design at Middle East Technical University (METU) in Ankara, Turkey. Within the scope of this course, students explored the nature of sustainability and its potential implications for product design via a design-centered approach. In this hands-on course, graduate students reflected on the various design considerations in order to use materials effectively, to re-use and re-contextualize components, and incorporate local skills and knowledge. These factors encourage and enable user engagement and participation and can help prolong product lifespans. The chapter presents a comprehensive discussion on the various lighting design explorations that emerged from these reflections on creative design and sustainability and on how the students learned to reflect because of using the *research through design* approach.

Emma Murphy introduces us to the role branding can play in the world of culturally significant artifacts. In *Designing Authentic Brands,* she considers how conventional notions of branding have evolved into what she terms "authentic branding practice." As well as discussing what this means, and what it looks like, she explores design's role in enabling this shift. The chapter provides insights into how these authentic branding practices can be taught, as a way of embedding this thinking into education, so as to affect change in practice. She concludes by considering authentic principles of branding through the use of two examples of empirical fieldwork, and demonstrates how the principles and context of authentic branding can be introduced into design curricula.

Our final chapter is *Strategies for Revitalization of Culturally Significant Designs, Products, and Practices* by Martyn Evans, Amy Twigger Holroyd, Stuart Walker, Tom Cassidy, and Jeyon Jung. It presents a series of successfully employed revitalization strategies, developed through analysis of a wide range of historical examples. Five strategy clusters are presented that underscore how the effective application of design can support revitalization. These clusters provide insight into how design can make constructive contribution by: (1) combining traditional making or use practices with new or reimagined designs; (2) taking traditional design or making practices into new contexts; (3) foregrounding the value of place and provenance in revitalization; (4)

employing appropriate and effective methods of making; and (5) deploying targeted approaches to embed and enhance skills. In addition, broader enabling factors are discussed that underpin how design can reconnect traditions, values, and beliefs with modern ways of living in a sustainable manner. Lastly, the chapter considers the evolving relationship of revitalization and revitalization strategies to the wider research context. A series of emerging themes are identified that will be important for addressing future challenges in the sustainment of culturally significant designs, products, and practices.

20

Research Approaches for Culturally Significant Design

Tom Cassidy

Introduction

Any research approach applied to a study of traditional designs, products, and practices must provide opportunities to explore and understand their cultural significance. This will include ethical, ethnical and spiritual needs, desires and rights of the culture or design ecology concerned. Methods or tools used are often shared within different approaches and this mixing and matching has led to the increasingly popular "bricolage" approach, although this has often been scorned by "old school" researchers (Kincheloe 2001). This chapter describes eight approaches/methodologies that have been used in this sort of research and provides an example for each. Bricolage will be given a relatively light treatment as some would argue it is not yet fully established in this area. Use of archives, museums, and ethnography will also be given light treatments but for the opposite reason—they are well established and fully accepted for this type of research. The eight examples chosen are: Participatory Action Research (PAR); geometric symmetry concepts; Soft Systems Methodology (SSM); grounded theory; bricolage or multi-faceted; use of archives and museums; ethnography.

Participatory Action Research (PAR)

The aims of PAR are achieved through a cyclical process that includes exploration, knowledge construction and implementation at different stages throughout the process. The participants reflect their views through active engagement in critical dialogue and collective reflection, which helps them recognize that they have a stake in the overall project (McTaggart 1997). Accordingly, there are no fixed formulas for designing, practicing, and implementing PAR projects, nor is there an overriding theoretical framework that underpins the PAR process. PAR is a philosophy rather than a methodology and it assists the researcher in developing authentic and effective strategies for collaborating with people in order to improve their lives, effect social change, and reconstruct the meaning and value of their traditional knowledge. Participants engage in collaborative, action-based projects that reflect their knowledge and mobilize their desire (McIntyre 2008). PAR is a recursive process that involves a spiral of adaptable steps that include the following:

- Questioning a particular issue.
- Reflecting on and investigating the issue.
- Developing an action plan.
- Implementing and refining the plan.

Underlying principles specific to PAR are:

- Collective commitment to investigate an issue or problem.
- A desire to engage in self- and collective reflection to gain clarity about the issue under investigation.
- A joint decision to engage in individual and collective action that leads to a useful solution benefitting the people involved. (McIntyre 2008)

In her thesis of 2015, Manju Sugathan explained how she used PAR to produce a framework that could be used for the empowerment of women in rural India.

In the village of Velachery, Kanchipuram District, Tamil Nadu, India, the main source of income is through the weaving of traditional silk saris by the male members of the families. This is a domestic process carried out on handlooms using a warp of approximately twenty-one meters, from which three six-meter sari lengths are produced. This leaves close to three meters of remnant silk yarns on the warp beam. Past efforts to make use of these remnant yarns have been aimed at the production of fashion accessories, such as bracelets and necklaces, which are of low value, only for the local market, and do very little to provide empowerment to the women, which is very much needed.

The aim of the project was to create a framework for a sustainable cooperative model combining the socio-economic and political aspects for setting up a women's cooperative. This would include the technology for production and a marketing strategy.

The objectives were:

- To critically review literature in relation to: empowerment of women and community development, sustainable methods of production, and marketing strategy.
- To investigate the possibility of producing recycled yarn in a workers' cooperative involving the current unpaid labor in the handloom sector (women) in the village.

- To develop an appropriate technology for production and a marketing strategy for the resultant speciality yarn.
- To test consumer response to a sample of yarns and hand-knitted fabrics and garments.
- To formulate a framework that would facilitate the organization of this framework.

The project involved the use of three different textile crafts and was dependent on the active participation of two crafts that were extant and the one that was intended as an appropriate technology to bring about the empowerment of the women. The first craft was handloom weaving practiced by the men in the village, although supported by their unpaid wives. The second extant craft was hand-knitting, which is practiced throughout the world and is very popular in the West. The third was hand-spinning, which would allow the production of a speciality yarn, using the warp remnants as a recycled component mixed with lambswool. The hand-spinning machines could be housed in a single building, which would allow the women to form a cooperative. Also, hand-spinning is a therapeutic activity and this would bring some stress relief for the hard-pressed women.

The participants in this project comprised: the women in the village who had to be involved in the choice of appropriate technology and interested in forming a cooperative; the men of the village, because nothing would be successfully achieved without their full consent, as rural India tends to be a male-dominated society; hand-knitting yarn retailers in the UK who planned the marketing strategy; and hand-knitters in the UK who represented the target market. All these participants were constantly consulted during the research process and they provided very valuable input and ideas throughout.

Sugathan used PAR to:

- question the issue of recycling the silk remnants collected from handlooms to produce a value-added recycled yarn for the hand-knitting market that could help empower women through their involvement in the production process;
- reflect and investigate the issue involving representatives of all participants, at the production and marketing and consumer stages, in order to achieve clarity;
- develop an action plan by choosing and trialing appropriate technology and then combining both quantitative and qualitative data-generating tools;
- review the outcome against the real-life situation to develop a framework that could be adopted in the real world.

Geometric symmetry concepts

As Washburn and Crowe (1988) pointed out, symmetry seems to be a diagnostic feature in the perception of design. A regular repeating pattern may be constructed using a combination of one or more of the four symmetry operations (i.e. translation, rotation, reflection, and glide reflection). The application of symmetry classification to decorated items from archaeological, historic or cultural settings has been developed by a number of anthropologists, archaeologists, and art/design historians. A great quantity of relevant literature indicates that patterns from different cultural settings exhibit their own unique symmetry preferences evidenced by non-random distributions of symmetry classes employed (Hann 1992; Hargittai 1986).

The link between symmetry and culture was explored, in the context of Asian cultures, by van Esterik (1979). He examined symmetry features used in the Ban Chiang pottery of Thailand in order to better understand symbolism and the process of creating symbols by historical communities. Haake (1996) recognized a strong link between particular symmetry characteristics of Javanese batik patterns and the ancient Asian philosophy models of *mancapat* (a model of the cosmos) and dualism (the co-existence of opposites). Summerfield (1996) explored how motifs, structures, and folds in Minangkabau ceremonial garments related to social standards and the rules of *adat*. Yu (1989) revealed the concept of positive and negative on two-fold rotation and bi-lateral reflection in certain Chinese arts and crafts.

A more recent example of this approach is Tantiwong, Hann and Cassidy's paper (2000) that examined symmetry characteristics in traditional Thai textiles. The intention was to test two hypotheses:

(i) While varieties of Thai textiles may fulfil different functions, and are produced using different patterning techniques, symmetry characteristics are nonetheless broadly shared.

(ii) The symmetry characteristics exhibited may be closely associated with and explained in the context of Thai culture and may in some way be manifestations of traditional Thai beliefs and Buddhist philosophy.

They found that symmetry classification offered potential as a tool for analyzing Thai textile patterns and in advancing understandings of the cultural significance of these patterns.

There is little or no evidence to date of design researchers or practitioners using geometric symmetry concepts as a tool for design revitalization. However, the improved understanding of cultural significance that results from this approach may help to throw light on the success of the American designer Jim Thompson's revitalization of the Thai Silk weaving industry. Future research and use of symmetry concepts will lead to new knowledge of cultural significance and may well be useful in understanding how they can be used in the revitalization process.

Soft Systems Methodology (SSM)

Systems thinking was first developed by Checkland (1981) and was primarily aimed at countering the lack of consideration for the user by the computer hardware industry. It has since been applied by business analysts to many forms of activity. Since around 2005, design researchers have made sporadic use of it to address interior and product design issues. The first version introduced by Checkland had seven stages and a number of tools to express issues, ideas, and solutions. However, Checkland also made it clear that researchers could dip in and make use of any of the stages, tools, and methods, and that some might stand alone for specific purposes. SSM can be particularly useful for the revitalization of culturally significant products and practices, which would come under the heading of human activities (particularly the latter) but not for patterns. For clarification: practices, such as craft making, are obviously human activities; products, such as the Quaich shown in Figure 20.1 can be, and often are, used as part of human activities; patterns are observed and enjoyed, or not, but are not human activities in themselves (though eye tracking may alter this, but not to the extent that it would come under the focus of SSM). The stages of SSM can be defined as follows:

1) **Entering the problem situation:** The process starts with the identification and evaluation of a real-world problem or design challenge. The data collected may be qualitative, quantitative or mixed, and the researcher chooses the most appropriate tools or methods to collect this data.

2) **The problem situation expressed:** In this stage, the problem situation is usually expressed using "Rich Pictures" that can reflect and examine the circumstances within the particular system being studied. "Rich Pictures" are particularly useful and attractive to those of us who are visually stimulated, more than or equally as much as textually; they are therefore effective tools for designers to visualize their thinking and record their insight.

3) **Root definition of relevant activity systems:** This is the stating of a hypothesis concerning final improvement of the problem situation by means of an implemented transformation (design solution) and whether it will be feasible or desirable. It is a structured description of a system written by the researcher from the initial research activities and the objective of the system (design solution). Therefore, it has to consider the aim of the transformation, the persons who could affect it or be affected by it, as well as those who would be part of or use the new system. It also identifies other key elements in the transformation that might relate to: the system itself; human activity; and/or the broader environment. To be confident that a given root definition is comprehensive, several criteria need to be specified. The construction of the root definition is an iterative process and each iteration can be tested using the CATWOE test. This test helps ensure that the necessary components of the system are addressed in the root definition. The components are:

- C = **Customers or clients:** Who (or what) benefits from this transformation.

- A = **Actors or agents:** Who is engaged in the system activities and facilitates its operation.

- T = **Transformation:** How is the system, practice or product transformed. This is an essential part of the process of change.

- W = **Weltanschauung:** Worldview.

- O = **Owners:** Who controls the system, practice or product, or could cause it not to exist.

- E = **Environment:** What does this system take as given from the world that surrounds and influences the system, practice or product.

4) **Building a conceptual model** may occur concurrently with the formulation of the root definition. The conceptual model commonly illustrates the relationship between the system activities underpinned by the root definition. Patching (1990) suggests that the development of a conceptual model is illustrated by assembling and structuring the minimum number of verbs necessary to describe each component or activity in the system (commonly expressed in diagrammatic form).

The three final stages of the SSM process are more applicable to business systems but can, in some cases, help with design problems/solutions. They are fairly self-explanatory:

- comparing the new system/practice or product with the existing version;
- deciding on the transformation(s) to be made;
- taking action to improve the existing system.

As an example, the Scottish Quaich was studied using this methodology/approach. The Quaich is a traditional sharing bowl that was used in gatherings to express friendship. They are still used at some ceremonial meetings but mostly they are bought as ornaments because of their decorative qualities; they are normally inscribed with Celtic patterns. However, sales are relatively low and so it was decided that we would take a look at this traditional product and explore what could be done to revitalize sales. The consumer perception of the product and how it would be used were investigated using interviews, focus groups, questionnaires, and observation tools. The participants were drawn from a wide range of backgrounds, including people who understood the meaning and use of a Quaich and those who would not but may be future consumers globally.

To express the nature of the problem in terms of *modern society's acceptance of this product*, the following Rich Picture was developed.

The consumer perception of the product and how it would be used was investigated using interview, focus group, questionnaire and observation tools. This illustrated very well what the problem was and, after developing a root definition and conceptual model, it was decided that the solution could be approached from two angles: the bowl could be divided into two halves and each person would drink from their own side. Also, a re-branding approach could be taken whereby instead of simply calling the product a Scottish Quaich, it could be termed a Scottish Family Quaich or perhaps a Scottish Lovers Quaich. Various other design solutions were also considered.

Grounded theory

Grounded theory is a research method that generates theories inductively on social processes through the analysis of qualitative data. The data are gathered through intensive or in-depth interviews. In this approach, researchers maintain careful field notes and transcriptions of interviews while concurrently working

FIGURE 20.1 Rich Picture. Courtesy Dian Li, School of Design, University of Leeds. © Dian Li.

to integrate the processes of data gathering, data analysis and theory generation; the process used for this type of analysis is known as the *constant comparative method* (Glaser and Strauss 1967). As Glaser and Strauss have emphasized, grounded theory has an underlying premise that the research results must be useful in practice. Design researchers have made good use of this approach for many years. Significantly, it can reveal non-obvious cultural influences in design practice and leadership.

A particularly relevant example of this is the work of C. K. Lee who used a form of grounded theory in his study of design leadership of Taiwanese product design agencies and companies (Lee 2005). The grounded theory approach is normally carried out by researchers who are already experienced in the area being studied. It allows them to probe deeply into the data collected. In Lee's case, he had already had a long career as leader of an industrial design team in Taiwan. He had contemplated that there must be a certain kind of philosophy, which could serve as the source of consistent values that could help govern managerial decisions and actions. The philosophy of Taoism is ubiquitous in Taiwan and Lee's research led him to recognize how it was applied by himself and the fourteen design leaders with whom he had intensive interviews. It is not the aim of this chapter to explain Taoist theory but the following brief examples illustrate how Lee perceived the influence of Taoist philosophy on principles of design leadership:

- **Creative and Holistic Perspectives**: In Taoist philosophy, leaders should be able to look at issues from more creative and holistic perspectives than others. Its relevance to design leadership is that having this perspective could improve the design leaders' ability to recognize highly creative ideas that others may have considered too bold or even regarded as nonsense.

- **Seeing things right into their core nature**: Taoist philosophy encourages individuals to develop enough wisdom to establish the power of insight and perception, which can enable them to look right into the core nature of what they are facing without being distracted or manipulated by their surface or packaging.

- **Receptive like a vast valley**: In encouraging the magnanimity of leaders, Taoist philosophy holds that leaders should be as generous as a vast valley, which can be fully receptive to all inputs, no matter how many. From the Taoist point of view, good leaders should be capable of tolerating a great variety of personalities and even opposing opinions. For good leaders, suggestions should rarely be regarded as nonsense and people should rarely be made unwelcome. As a consequence, all kinds of useful suggestions and opinions will be offered to them; and all sorts of excellent people will be attracted to work for them.

Lee's work offers many more insights but these illustrate some of the main points. John Heider had already written *The Tao of Leadership* (1985) but it was Lee who used grounded theory to show Taoist philosophy's influence within the culture from which it had sprung.

Bricolage or multi-faceted

Bricolage methodology involves the mixing of qualitative data collection techniques to gain a fully informed understanding of the matter at hand. "*Bricoleur*" translates from French as a handyman—someone who "makes use of the tools available to complete a task." The variety of techniques employed in bricolage methodology respects the complexity of the "lived world," and allows researchers to play an active role in collecting data that more accurately represent this world as it really is (Kincheloe and Berry 2004).

The bricolage approach to data collection has been recognized as an effective tool for design researchers (Yee and Bremner 2011). It allows for a multi-faceted study that is capable of embracing the many and varied aspects of culturally significant design. A good example of this approach can be found in the Ph.D. thesis of M. J. Shin (2011) whose study looked at how Korean *bogagi* patterns could be revitalized (reported earlier in this volume).

The aim of this research was to investigate a process to enable the transfer of traditional Korean cultural meanings to design elements and to design fashion *bojagi* prototypes that meet the needs of contemporary target markets. The objectives were as follows:

- To explore the published literature on culture, cultural products, and design management.
- To define the term "cultural reinvention" through a case study of Scottish tartan.
- To explore the current market situation of Korean cultural textile products.
- To propose a process for producing successful cultural products through cultural reinvention.
- To suggest possible design marketing strategies for effective cultural reinvention of traditional Korean *bojagi* textiles.
- To analyse the target consumers' color preferences.
- To develop a Korean *bojagi* website including a new *bojagi* design tool.
- To apply the design tool for producing a range of fashion *bojagi*.
- To evaluate this design tool for consumers and fashion retail experts.

This research required the use of many different approaches and tools. The term "multi-faceted" would also cover this but "bricolage" is becoming increasingly accepted as a term and an approach/methodology for design research. There was no single approach that could fulfil the aims and objectives of this study and therefore the researcher had to dip into and borrow tools and approaches from different methodologies. The important issue is to ensure that the aims and objectives of the study are feasible and set properly and then care has to be taken to ensure that the investigation does not drift away from these due to the adoption of a bricolage approach.

Making use of archives and museums

Archives and museums are of vital importance for the maintenance of culturally significant products and patterns/designs. For example, some researchers believe that differences between levels of "making by hand" in Finland and Estonia are strongly influenced by the plethora of archives in the latter.

Both archives and museums aim to collect and store materials of historical and cultural interest but the main difference is that museums put more emphasis on displaying the materials. Museums also tend to be artifact-based and hold a wide variety of these, whereas archives store all sorts of media and are normally quite specific in their area of specialization. Museums and archives often exist separately but many museums have archives within their structures. It is important to thoroughly plan the visit beforehand before delving into an archive. Compared to the past, the internet has made this much easier for today's researchers. Websites are often well constructed and allow the user to identify specific materials that they wish to inspect. Talking with knowledgeable staff will usually bring excellent rewards, but unfortunately websites do not allow this option.

The Museum of London has a very good historical costume exhibition and an exhaustive costume archive. This is used on a regular basis by fashion and textile students from universities and colleges at all levels as well as by professional costume designers. The biggest problem that the archive has is that the students often want to handle the costumes and would like to be able to deconstruct them to understand how their pattern blocks have been produced. Handling is a major conservation problem and deconstruction is simply impossible.

Zi-Young Kang et al. (2014) worked closely with the staff of the Museum of London costume archive and used the most up-to-date software to produce accurate animated simulations of historical costumes. The aim of this study was to explore a way of recreating costume relics in a digital form and to develop effective and faithful animated simulations for the benefit of museums and their visitors.

The objectives were:

- To establish a theoretical understanding of digital clothing technology and 3D apparel CAD.
- To understand the importance and constraints of historic costume collection.
- To provide an overview of the influence of new media and clarify the status and problems of museums' current practice in applying websites.
- To review methods, strengths, and weaknesses of earlier digital costume projects and establish key concepts for the development of effective digital costume projects.
- To develop prototype digital costumes.
- To evaluate the effectiveness and faithfulness of the costumes both statically and animated.

The results of this work have been received enthusiastically by the staff of the costume archive and the ability for the simulations to be deconstructed (Figure 20.2)

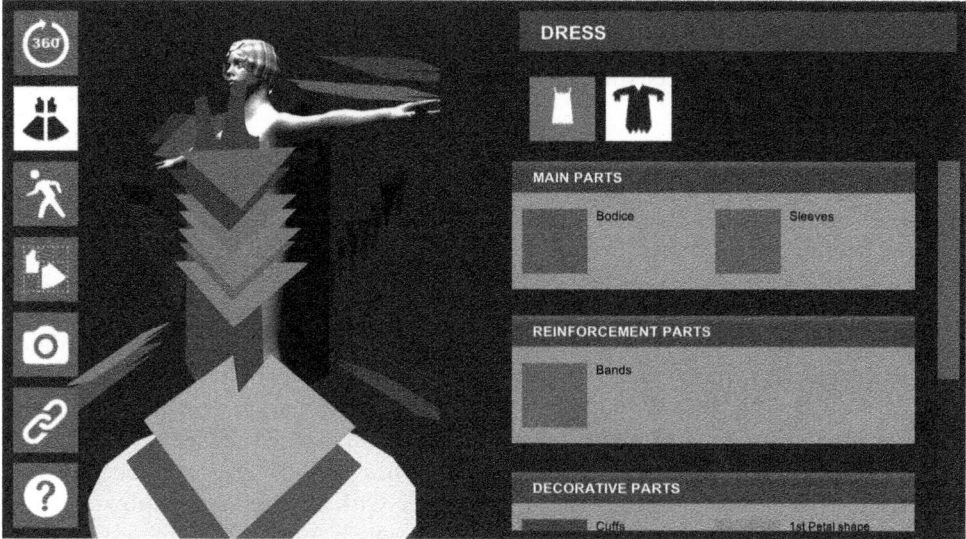

FIGURE 20.2 The simulated garment pattern blocks being removed from the mannequin. Courtesy Zi-Young Kang, University of Leeds. © Zi Young Kang.

will offer excellent educational opportunities for students. It also means that culturally significant costumes will be better conserved and studied by future generations.

Ethnography

This is probably the most obvious approach/methodology to a study of culturally significant design. Indeed, it can be stated that all the previous approaches discussed have elements of ethnography within them. In their excellent book, *Designing and Conducting Ethnographic Research*, Le Compte and Schensul describe ethnography as follows:

> Ethnography is an approach to learning about the social and cultural life of communities, institutions and other settings that: is scientific; is investigative; uses the researcher as the primary tool of data collection; uses rigorous research methods and data collection techniques to avoid bias and ensure accuracy of data; emphasizes and builds on the perspectives of the people in the research setting; is inductive, building local theories for testing and adapting them for use both locally and elsewhere (1999).

For example, if it was decided to explore the possible revitalization of Japanese aesthetics in contemporary design, the researchers would find themselves having to understand the complex politics and networks associated with cultural design in Japan. Much has been written on this subject but the researcher would have to carry out field trips to really understand this and how to avoid the pitfalls that would accompany this phenomenon. Ethnography is more than just another approach, it is an umbrella philosophy and sensitivity that should permeate any study of culturally significant pattern, products, and processes.

Conclusion

The purpose of this chapter has been to introduce various research approaches that are suitable for examining culturally significant designs, products, and practices, and to give examples of their application. The references provided will allow the reader to find out more and to decide which approach/methodology or mix of methodologies they would like to apply in a particular culturally significant research project or indeed, in other types of research. How should the researcher go about choosing the most appropriate approach/methodology for a particular study? There are a plethora of books and articles explaining different approaches and how they may be used and these can be very helpful. However, a researcher with the ability to think outside the box will often see new avenues of study to which an already well-established approach may be applied. For example, the pioneering work of Checkland in the 1970s was a response to what he and his colleagues felt was the overemphasis of the digital age on hard systems, including machines and operating systems. He then went on to produce seminal books and papers showing how systems thinking could be applied to any human activity, although his emphasis was on the business world. In the 1990s. other disciplines were beginning to dip into systems thinking and the design community found that it could be applied in the study of design and design management (e.g., interior design, color forecasting, and product design strategies).

The choice of approach will depend on the experience of the research leader and team, and care should be taken to ensure that the approach/methodology adopted and/or adapted does not preclude the use of methods, tools, and frameworks from other approaches.

The tools used in the application of these approaches include interviews, focus groups, observation, content analysis, rich pictures, and many others. The important issue to consider with these tools is ethics and institutional compliance, and it is interesting to note that questionnaires do not figure in any of the projects discussed. A questionnaire survey is a commonly used tool for both qualitative and quantitative research but it is unlikely to be used for culturally related research due to the non-personal contact aspect, which is important in this sort of research. It is hoped that readers will find the approaches presented in this chapter will give them an appetite for future studies. Finally, the author would like to thank all the individuals whose work has contributed to the chapter, without them it would not have been possible to effectively illustrate the approaches that have been discussed.

References

Checkland, P. (1981), *Systems Thinking, Systems Practice*, Chichester: John Wiley & Sons.
Glaser, B. G. and A. Strauss (1967), *The Discovery of Grounded Theory: Strategies for Qualitative Research*, New York, NY: Aldine.

Haake, A. (1996), "Symmetry of Javanese Batik Patterns," International Symposium on Indonesian Textiles, Jambi, Indonesia.

Hann, M. A. (1992), "Symmetry in Regular Repeating Pattern: Case Studies from Various Cultural Settings," *Journal of the Textile Institute*, 83 (4): 579–90.

Hargittai, I. (1986), "Symmetry: Unifying Human Understanding," *International Journal of Computers and Mathematics with Applications. Part B*, 12B, R13R15.

Heider, J. (1985), *The Tao of Leadership*, Atlanta: Humanics Limited.

Kang, Z.-Y., T. D. Cassidy, T. Cassidy, and D. Li (2014), "Simulation of Historic Costume," International Textiles and Costume Culture Congress, October 24–25, National Chonbuk University, S. Korea.

Kincheloe, J. L. (2001), "Describing the Bricolage: Conceptualizing a New Rigor in Qualitative Research," *Qualitative Inquiry*, December 2001, 7: 679–92.

Kincheloe, J. L. and K. Berry (2004), "Rigour and Complexity in Educational Research. Conducting Educational Research," Maidenhead: Open University Press.

Le Compte, M. D. and J. J. Schensul (1999), *Analysing and Interpreting Ethnographic Data*, London: Altamira Press

Lee, C. K. (2005), "An Investigation of the principles of design leadership," Ph.D. thesis, University of Leeds, Leeds.

McIntyre, A. (2008), *Participatory Action Research: Qualitative Research Methods*, Los Angeles, CA: Sage Publications.

McTaggart, R. (1997), *Participatory Action Research: International Context and Consequences*, Albany, NY: State University of New York Press.

Patching, D. (1990), *Practical Soft Systems Analysis*, London: Pitman.

Shin, M. J. (2011), "Cultural Reinvention: Design Management for Korean Cultural Textile Products," Ph.D. thesis, University of Leeds, Leeds.

Sugathan, M. (2015), "Community Development and Empowerment of Women in Rural India through a Recycling Textile Cooperative," Ph.D. thesis, University of Leeds, Leeds.

Summerfield, A. (1996), "Symbolic meanings in in Minangkabu Ceremonial Cloths," International Symposium on Indonesian Textiles, Jambi, Indonesia.

Tantiwong, P., M. A. Hann, and T. Cassidy (2000), "Symmetry in Thai Textile Patterns," *Ars Textrina*, 33: 29–50.

Washburn, D. K. and D. W. Crowe (1988), *Symmetries of Culture. Theory and Practice of Plane Pattern Analysis*, Seattle, WA/London: University of Washington Press.

Van Esterik, P. (1979), "Symmetry and Symbolism in Bian Chiang Painted Pottery," *Journal of Anthropological Research*, 35 (4): 495–508.

Yee, J. S. R. and C. Bremner (2011), "Methodological Bricolage: What Does It Tell Us About Design?" Doctoral Design Education Conference, May 23–25, Hong Kong Polytechnic, Hong Kong.

Yu, L. X. (1989), "Symmetry in Chinese Arts and Crafts," *Journal of Computers & Mathematics with Applications*, 17 (4–6): 1009–26.

21

Digital Transformations, Amateur Making, and the Revitalization of Traditional Textile Crafts

Amy Twigger Holroyd

Introduction

When considering the revitalization of culturally significant designs, products, and practices, it is easy to assume that the responsibility for such activities must fall squarely on the shoulders of commercial stakeholders. In the course of my research for the Design Routes project, I have gathered an array of examples of revitalization; the vast majority involve products being made for sale, with the success of any such initiative ultimately hinging on its commercial viability. A large body of literature focuses on the potential contribution of traditional crafts to economic and social development (for example Prügl 1996; Richard 2007; Borges 2011), highlighting the fact that in many contexts domestic making practices have been commercialized to provide a source of income as societies adapt to globalization. This overwhelming focus on commercial endeavors can overshadow an important parallel strand of activity: amateur makers producing items for their own use and motivated by non-commercial concerns. A surge of interest in making has recently arisen, encompassing the "maker movement," primarily associated with new technologies such as 3D printing, alongside traditional crafts such as pottery and woodworking. This interest has given rise to an intensification of amateur activity and the emergence of vibrant communities of makers, particularly in post-industrial contexts such as the UK (Dellot 2015). Although Knott (2015) argues that activity by amateurs is essential for the survival and evolution of many craft practices, the role of non-commercial stakeholders in revitalization has received little critical attention. This chapter seeks to address this gap by investigating the ways in which amateur communities engage with traditional craft practices, and with patterns, designs, and products that are linked to particular cultures.

There is a further focus within the chapter: the importance of digital technologies in supporting this amateur making activity. Craft practices—both professional and amateur—have been transformed in recent years through the growth of digital tools and platforms. One aspect of this transformation is the emergence of new technologies to be used in the process of making. Tools such as 3D printers and CNC milling machines provide a novel means of producing objects, while advanced software can be used as part of the design process. There are examples of these technologies being used to engage with culturally significant designs, products, and practices— research by Luscombe and Thomas (2014), for instance, investigated the translation of heraldic engraving patterns into digital design software. In Mexico, Mayan women working with artist Amor Muñoz are blending digital technologies more directly with traditional crafts, combining natural materials with conductive thread to weave solar panels on waist looms (Greer 2016). A different approach can be observed in a recent project from the UK, where the development of a 3D-printed letterpress font has brought innovation to a craft otherwise constrained by antique tools (Steven 2014).

While these technologies have sparked changes in the production of craft artifacts, another type of digital transformation can be observed, which will be the primary focus of this chapter: the enrichment of existing craft cultures through digital platforms. In these cases, the craft practice may not involve any hi-tech equipment; rather, digital technologies are employed to connect practitioners and support effective communication between enthusiasts. Kuznetsov and Paulos explain that such digital communication tools enable "enthusiasts to collaboratively critique, brainstorm and troubleshoot their work, often in real-time" (2010: 1). These tools include social networks such as Twitter, Facebook, and Instagram, specialist sites such as the knitting-related social network Ravelry, and platforms for sharing videos, images, and text such as YouTube and WordPress. As Gauntlett argues, the connective affordances of online spaces have allowed "excited enthusiasts in one corner of the world to inspire and encourage similarly energized individuals elsewhere, with a depth and speed that was not previously possible" (2011: 62).

In this chapter, these digital transformations will be explored through a focus on textile crafts, including knitting, sewing, and mending. Textile culture offers an array of localized traditions, such as—to choose just a few examples from the British Isles—Aran jumpers, English smocks, and Scottish tartan. Although the history of these traditions often involves a surprising degree of conscious invention (Faiers 2008; also see Carden's chapter in this volume), it is fair to say that the patterns and artifacts frequently evoke a strong sense of cultural significance within, and beyond, the communities in question. The making processes themselves are also traditional, in that the knowledge associated with them—even if employed to create non-traditional styles—has been handed down for centuries from one generation to the next. Textiles have an equally long history of amateur activity, with knitting, sewing, and mending having been carried out within the home, whether through necessity or as a hobby (Black 2012; Burman 1999). As with making more broadly, a resurgence in textile practices has taken place in the last ten to fifteen years (Bain 2016; Turney 2009). The cultures surrounding these practices have been significantly transformed during this period; as Bratich and Brush observe, "the knitting circle now meshes with the World Wide Web" (2011: 242). I will look at the role of digital tools in supporting amateur textile craft processes in general before discussing one amateur maker's digitally enabled engagement with a specific local tradition: the two-colored geometric knits associated with the Scottish town of Sanquhar. Having introduced these two areas of focus, I will then discuss a number of issues that emerge, including the relationship between tradition and creativity, the role of digital platforms in supporting craft practices to evolve, and the thorny question of cultural appropriation.

To investigate these themes I will draw on semi-structured interviews with three textile makers: Christine Cyr Clissett, Rosie Martin, and Tom van Deijnen. Each of these makers straddles the blurry line between professional and amateur practice. They make items for themselves to wear, and also support others through books, podcasts, blogs, and workshops. They are, therefore, well placed to discuss the recent resurgence of textile crafts and the use of digital tools and technologies in maker cultures. I will also draw on my own "insider" perspective. As a professional designer-maker, I have several years' experience of supporting amateur knitters through workshops and participatory projects. My previous research has investigated the lived experience of making clothes at home and the reworking of existing knitted garments, considering the contribution of these practices to a sustainable fashion system (Twigger Holroyd 2013).

Supporting textile practices

This section explores the ways in which digital tools and platforms support makers to engage in textile crafts, beginning by considering opportunities for learning. In the past, domestic textile craft skills were transmitted either in person or via printed instructional materials (Black 2012; Emery 2014). "Live" peer-to-peer teaching benefits from personal interaction and feedback, but depends on finding a suitable instructor with the time and patience to share their skills. Printed materials overcome this challenge yet present their own problems, as anyone who has tried to learn a tacit skill such as knitting from a book would probably attest. The web has enabled alternative approaches: videos, for example, offer a "maker's-eye-view" and can, crucially, be paused and repeated as required. YouTube is an incredibly rich resource for textile makers, with countless, freely accessible contributions showing how to carry out a wide range of operations. More structured support is available via sites such as Craftsy, which offers video lessons from expert tutors in various specialist textile techniques. Blogs provide space for makers to share their own methods and solutions, dramatically increasing the diversity of advice available. As interviewee Rosie Martin explained in relation to sewing, these online resources support novice makers to develop their skills:

> The internet, it's full of people giving tips on how they do things, and showing that visually. So that gives people the tools to be able to start. In a way I think it's less intimidating than going to a class, because you're not fearing the judgement of a teacher, or doing something wrong … you're totally in control.

Orton-Johnson suggests the same is true in terms of knitting: "For new knitters online resources are vital sites for learning and 'becoming' a knitter occurs through and with the digital" (2014: 312).

Learning is clearly not just about picking up particular techniques or following step-by-step instructions; when makers connect online to discuss projects and share ideas they also develop their knowledge and skills. Research by Kuznetsov and Paulos into online making communities, including users of the knitting site Ravelry, found "question asking and answering [to be] the core process behind the propagation of methods and ideas" (2010: 7). While the format of these conversations varies according to the platform, it is common for comments to be openly accessible and archived for future reference. Thus, discussions have a secondary audience of "lurkers": visitors who read a conversation thread but do not contribute themselves. As Tom van Deijnen explained, using Ravelry in this way helped him to deepen his engagement with knitting:

> Ravelry's really important for me. In the beginning, I did use it a lot, and I learned a lot of things from it. I learned about techniques, and I learned that there are different approaches. I learned about [author of knitting books] Elizabeth Zimmermann, which I think was really important ... I thought, she sounds like an interesting person.

Many makers use online spaces to share their completed projects with like-minded peers. Social media platforms enable this sharing through the use of hashtags: labels used to help users to find messages relating to a specific topic. Tom van Deijnen described menders posting images of successful repairs on Instagram, using the #visiblemending hashtag to connect with other enthusiasts. Ravelry users, meanwhile, are able to upload images of their completed projects to the site and link them to the site's powerful pattern database. These entries, once aggregated, form an invaluable resource of style adaptations and alternative yarn choices. Makers also share work in progress, benefiting from the feedback and encouragement they receive from their peers. Although many online spaces are characterized by insensitive or even abusive comments, textile craft communities are distinctively supportive. Bain (2016: 63) explains that "One of the striking features of the digital dressmaking community appears to be its inclusivity and positivity." Online knitalongs and sewalongs—projects in which all participants follow the same pattern together, often with guidance from the designer—provide a more intensive form of support. In some cases it is not a specific project but rather an aspect of craft practice that makers choose to share. Rosie Martin described one online project that coordinated contributions from hundreds of makers:

> In November there was something called Sewvember that one sewing blogger [Bimble and Pimble] started. There was a different prompt for every day of the month: technique, sewing space, view, tools. Everyone who participated took their photo and tagged it—and it was so much fun, it was amazing. You're connecting with sewers from all round the world that you'll never meet.

As Christine Cyr Clissett commented, these online connections are particularly valuable if makers do not know fellow enthusiasts in their local area:

I think an interesting component of the current home sewing culture is that blogs are so important. You see what other people are making all over the place. Especially since, maybe, your close friends don't sew. I mean, I think when my grandmother was young, everybody sewed. But now, I'm an anomaly amongst my friends.

The increased visibility of textile practice enabled by the web also contributes to the positive positioning of making in contemporary culture; the successful projects shared via blogs, Instagram, and Ravelry help to build an image of textile crafts as creative and aspirational practices which, in turn, prompts further participation.

Case study: Sanquhar knitting

The digitally enabled support described above encourages makers to engage in textile crafts, and to use these processes to make a diverse range of work. Many initiatives are directly linked to specific local traditions; examples include a blog post with instructions for making traditional Bulgarian martenitsa yarn decorations (Manassiev 2014) and an online video course guiding participants to knit a traditional Shetland hap shawl (Craftsy 2016). In order to consider the interaction between digital transformations and traditional crafts in more detail, I will focus on one specific case: Tom van Deijnen's experiences of engaging with the tradition of Sanquhar knitting.

Sanquhar patterns are intricate geometric two-color designs, primarily used for gloves, which often incorporate the wearer's initials (Future Museum 2012). This tradition emerged in the Scottish town of Sanquhar in the late eighteenth century. It is suggested that the knitters of the town developed the distinctive patterns in order to protect their livelihood from machine-produced alternatives, because "a highly distinctive and well-made garment would still find a buyer" (Future Museum 2012). Although the commercial trade in hand-knitted items was to largely disappear during the nineteenth century, the patterns continued to be handed down from one generation to the next. The patterns were not written down; one Sanquhar knitter, interviewed in 1955, suggested that "there are some bits you can't do unless you've seen them done" (Future Museum 2012). Despite this assertion, in the 1950s Sanquhar knitting was popularized by magazines and commercial knitting patterns, reaching makers far from the town in which it originated. In the 1960s, a series of four leaflets documenting the surviving traditional patterns was produced by the Scottish Women's Rural Institute; more recently, Sanquhar designs have been featured in various books about traditional knitting and thus have reached new generations of knitters across the world (Future Museum 2012).

Tom van Deijnen took up knitting several years ago, initially motivated by the idea of knitting his own version of a scarf he wanted but could not afford. He had learnt to knit as a child and readily reacquainted himself with the craft, assisted by books and local yarn shops along with a range of online resources including, as previously described, Ravelry. His enthusiasm for knitting grew as he developed his knowledge; having learnt to knit socks, he decided to tackle gloves. While browsing patterns on the Ravelry database, he came across one of the Scottish Women's Rural Institute patterns for Sanquhar gloves and was attracted by the design as "they just struck me as beautiful gloves." Tom needed to learn the technique of two-color knitting before attempting the pattern, and did so using instructions in books, tutorials from blogs and YouTube, and information on Ravelry forums. Around the same time he used the web to find a local yarn shop, Prick Your Finger, and discovered an array of enticing yarns produced by specialist British spinners.

Tom soon produced his first pair of Sanquhar gloves (Figure 21.1). He adapted the pattern to suit his desired yarn (Jamieson's of Shetland Spindrift), as it was a little too heavy for the fine gauge of the traditional Sanquhar pattern. He then used several Sanquhar motifs as a border on a pair of socks. On Ravelry, he found the Sanquhar knitting group: a community of fellow enthusiasts, scattered around the world. The discussions within the group supported him to develop his interest further. He gathered information from the Future Museum website, which provides online access to museum collections from south-west Scotland, including the collection of the Tolbooth Museum in Sanquhar. As Tom explained, despite the museum itself being just one small room, its collection of patterns, gloves, and tools is now accessible to anyone with internet access. From the images available on the site, he put together a chart showing a full alphabet of Sanquhar letters (Figure 21.2) and

FIGURE 21.1 Sanquhar gloves knitted by Tom van Deijnen. Courtesy Tom van Deijnen. © Tom van Deijnen.

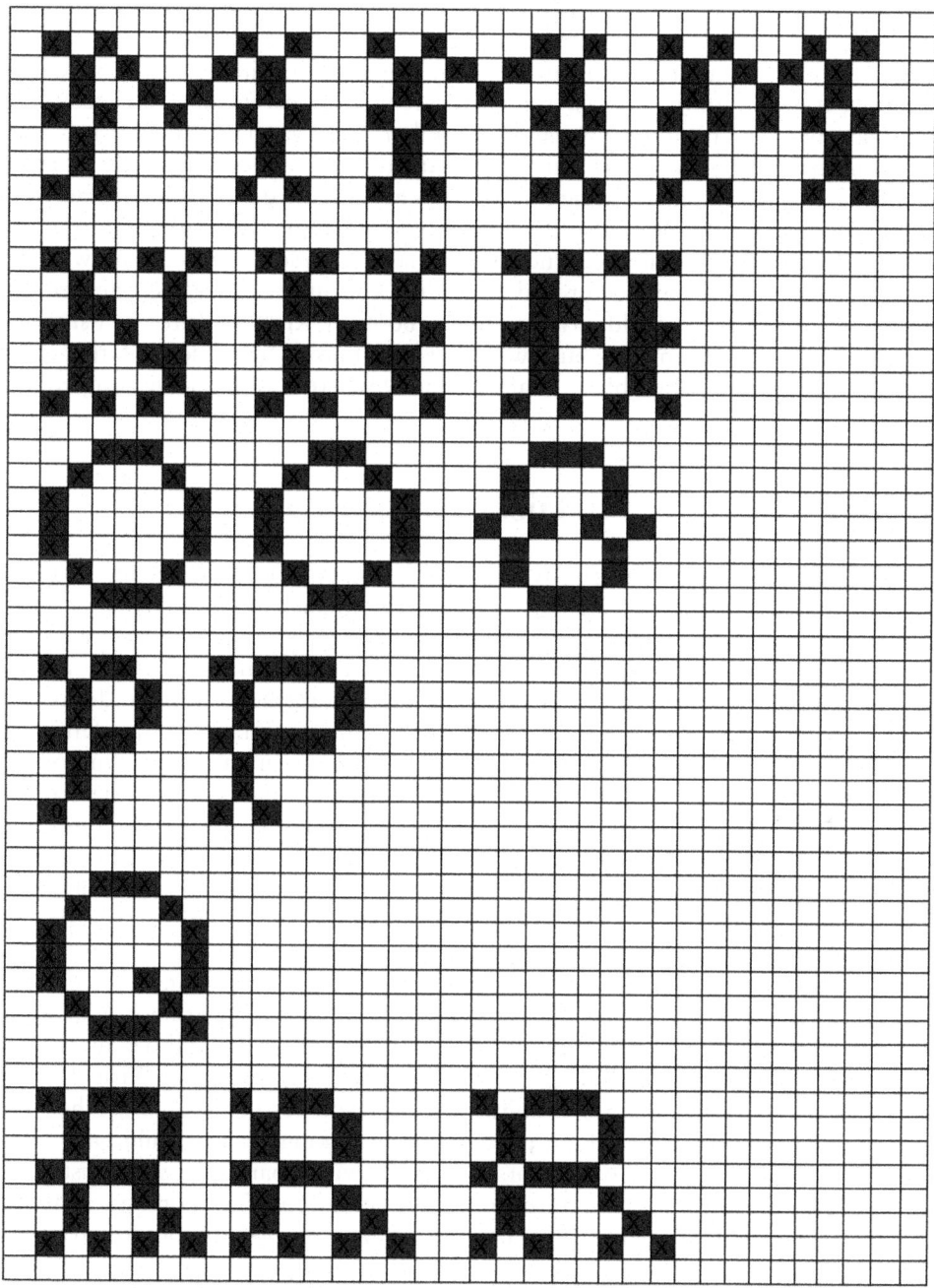

FIGURE 21.2 Excerpt of Sanquhar alphabet chart by Tom van Deijnen. Courtesy Tom van Deijnen. © Tom van Deijnen.

shared it on Ravelry as a free download. He then designed a pattern for a knitted pencil case using the letters and various Sanquhar geometric patterns; this is now for sale online. Remaining, in his own words, "somewhat smitten" by the Sanquhar tradition, Tom has continued his research; a recent blog post included an account of a talk he gave at a knitting study day in Sanquhar itself (van Deijnen 2014).

In this brief case study, we can appreciate the degree to which one maker's engagement with a specific knitting tradition has been enabled by the digital platforms already discussed. Online and offline activity is entangled; digital platforms are used to gather information and, crucially, to share new ideas. I asked Tom whether he thought he would have embraced Sanquhar knitting without the internet. He suggested, "I imagine I would have found the book by Richard Rutt [*A History of Hand Knitting*] and it's in there but I wouldn't have known from the book that there were written patterns available ... that's probably where it would have stopped."

Discussion

Having described the diverse ways in which digital tools are being used by amateur textile makers, we can now consider the impact of this activity in terms of revitalization. As noted, textile crafts have experienced a striking resurgence in recent years, alongside other types of low-tech and hi-tech making. While numerous factors have been discussed in relation to this resurgence—from a desire for nostalgia prompted by an era of austerity to the influence of third-wave feminism (Bain 2016)—it is widely agreed that digital tools have been particularly important (Kuznetsov and Paulos 2010; Orton-Johnson 2014). We have seen that online platforms are supporting amateur enthusiasts to connect and collaborate, and are thus stimulating increased participation and commitment. This is true of craft processes in general terms as well as specific local traditions. Although it may seem that a digitally connected global making culture could stamp out the specificities of local designs and practices, the opposite seems to be happening: the connective power of the internet is driving the appreciation, and even fetishization, of such traditions. Online resources enable craft skills to be passed on regardless of location, and information to be archived for future reference. These capabilities mean that crafts are more resilient and able to survive periodic lapses in popularity. In her interview, Rosie Martin described online sewing resources being used by the "lost generation" of sewers, who did not pick up textile making skills as children.

An important aspect of contemporary craft activity—particularly interesting in terms of traditional crafts—is its culture of experimentation. While domestic activities such as sewing and knitting have long been recognized as opportunities for creativity (Black 2012; Emery 2014), this aspect of textile craft seems to have become more important in recent years. When working with amateur makers I have observed a widespread desire to become "more creative": breaking out from a dependence on pre-designed patterns and producing a broader range of work. A tendency towards experimentation has been identified across a range of digitally enabled amateur making practices; Kuznetsov and Paulos argue that "DIY is a culture that aspires to explore, experiment and understand" (2010: 7). In fact, it is argued that amateur making practices have the potential for greater innovation than professional activity, because they sidestep commercial concerns (Knott 2015). This argument is borne out by the work of Wood, Rust and Horne (2009), who researched the transfer of traditional knife-making skills from professionals to amateurs. Their project involved the development of an online resource offering guidance on making folding knives. As they observe, the amateur makers who engaged with this resource had both the ability and the motivation to approach this craft with a creative mindset:

> One of the ideas behind this research has been the hope that it could help recapture some of the quality of the pre-industrial approach to craft skills, in which artistry and innovation were a normal feature. The industrial craft tradition in many fields of work has tended to emphasise utility and the more creative aspects of the work have devolved to professional designers. This project has shown that we can use new methods to transplant skills outside the industrial setting into the hands of people who have the motivation to innovate (Wood, Rust and Horne 2009: 75).

The issue of creativity is particularly important because traditions—despite being generally thought of as static and unchanging—must evolve in order to remain relevant in the long term. Detailed accounts of specific place-related crafts, such as Bunn's (2011) work on felt-making in Kyrgyzstan and the research by Stankard (2010) into Malaysian hand-woven textiles, describe cultures of innovation. This process of evolution can be endangered by well-meaning attempts at preservation that inadvertently serve to "fossilize" traditions. Craft processes and patterns are frequently documented in professionally published books, for example; although such publications help to capture knowledge that may otherwise be lost, the sense of authority accompanying them can create an implicit sense that the techniques or designs recorded should not be altered. Tom van Deijnen described knitters rejecting any variation on the "authentic" Sanquhar patterns published in the 1960s:

> People get really hung up by these few patterns that were published by the SWRI [Scottish Women's Rural Institute]—like, that's how they should be done. There's no other way. I just don't get it. Even before I went to Sanquhar and saw all the other gloves, I never thought this is the way, and this is the only way.

He went on to point out that the published patterns were merely snapshots of a long and experimental tradition, captured at a particular point in time.

This attitude to the perceived authority of a published document is challenged by the emerging culture of experimentation in craft. It is also challenged by the specific affordances of digital tools. The Ravelry database, for example, which facilitates the display of multiple interpretations of a single pattern, inspires knitters to adopt an inventive approach. More fundamentally, the Ravelry site, like the internet more broadly, offers the ability for makers to "write" as well as "read." Contributions from amateur enthusiasts are able to sit alongside professionally published material, feeding new interpretations into the sea of material available for others to use, remix, and adapt. Thus, the digital tools I have discussed increase the diversity of creative voices being heard and help to restore the organic evolution that is characteristic of any thriving craft.

Despite this positive finding, it must be noted that digital platforms present a new set of challenges in terms of sharing craft knowledge. The intermingling of resources from different cultures increases diversity but can also create confusion. Makers using online crochet resources, for example, frequently encounter a mix of American and British terminology. This is problematic: "double crochet" refers to a different basic stitch in each code. Further problems can arise in terms of the quality of information being shared. For popular craft processes, this is not an issue. The most useful resources will rise up the search rankings, while poorer quality advice will fade into the online abyss. In niche areas where there is little guidance available, however, there is a danger that one person's mistakes or misunderstandings will be passed on to others. Tom van Deijnen described a poor quality online darning tutorial that, given the paucity of information available, is creating problems for novice menders.

The final issue I would like to discuss is that of cultural appropriation. As we have seen, the internet is helping knitting enthusiasts to connect around specific traditions such as Sanquhar knitting. Without the restriction of geographic proximity, these enthusiasts can be spread across the globe; thus, a tradition originally linked to a small Scottish town has started to develop new cultural connections as individuals and groups engage and experiment with its heritage. This cross-cultural migration is nothing new. As knitwear designer Kate Davies argues with reference to Nordic textiles, "knitwear 'traditions' are never completely national or regional in origin, but are always interwoven and interconnected" (2014). In many ways, the new paths being forged for traditional crafts via digital platforms are a cause for celebration: they bring new life to established activities. It is important to be aware, however, that for some the practice of traditional crafts by "outsiders" may be quite contentious. In a recent blog post, knitwear designer Karie Westermann described being criticized by a passer-by for saying she was knitting a Fair Isle cardigan, because she does not originate from Shetland (2014). While responses from other knitters demonstrate this to be an unusually extreme position regarding Fair Isle knitting, the story provides a useful reminder that the appropriation of crafts strongly linked to particular cultures may provoke opposition. This is certainly the case for cultures that have experienced historical oppression and marginalization. Writing about Native American communities, Howes describes appropriation as involving "the alienation, popularization and corruption of native traditions and imagery," and identifies a widespread consensus that this appropriation is "potentially damaging to the survival of native ways of life" (1996: 138). Uwujaren proposes that the line between "appropriate" forms of cultural exchange and damaging cultural appropriation is blurry, but "there needs to be some element of mutual understanding, equality, and respect for it to be a true exchange" (2013). Thus, while the internet offers incredible opportunities for makers to connect with traditions from other cultures, it is vital that these important issues of mutual respect and exchange are borne in mind.

Conclusion

This chapter examines the role of amateur makers in revitalizing traditional crafts, and the ways in which digital tools are supporting this activity. Focusing on textile crafts to explore these issues, I have been concerned both with craft processes in general terms, and with specific designs and products linked to particular cultures—such as the case study of Sanquhar knitting. Digital platforms such as YouTube, Instagram, and Ravelry provide excellent support for amateur textile makers, and have played a vital role in the resurgence of crafts. These platforms support makers to learn, to share, and to collaborate, and as such this prompts further participation and helps crafts to become more resilient. A sense of shared practice is created, which is especially valuable for makers who are geographically isolated from their peers.

The affordances of digital platforms benefit traditions such as Sanquhar knitting: enthusiasts can easily access information about niche areas of practice. Importantly, they are also able to share new ideas and iterations, helping to keep the tradition in motion. Amateurs might, in some contexts, have the motivation and opportunity to be more innovative than professional makers; digital platforms are particularly appropriate for use by this group. While digital spaces present some challenges for traditional crafts, such as the danger of poor quality information being shared, overall the tools discussed help to drive participation, appreciation, and evolution. In many cases, open access to traditional designs and practices drives beneficial cultural exchange; however, makers need to be sensitive to issues around cultural appropriation, particularly when dealing with traditions linked with marginalized communities.

In summary, I propose that amateur making plays an important role in the revitalization of traditional crafts, especially in post-industrial contexts. Digital platforms are having a transformational effect on the practices of amateur makers, amplifying their collective ability to share knowledge, develop expertise, and experiment. Thus, digital tools are contributing to the resurgence of traditional crafts just as much as they are supporting the growth of more obviously "innovative" forms of making.

If we recognize the influential role of amateur making communities in traditional craft cultures, new strategies for revitalization can be developed. Rather than focusing only on approaches that produce commercial goods for sale, designers pursuing the revitalization of traditional crafts can consider initiatives that engage directly with amateur enthusiasts, employing digital tools to reach them. Craft communities that have wholeheartedly embraced the use of digital platforms, such as the textile makers in this study, could provide examples of best practice for other crafts that have yet to fully establish themselves online.

References

Bain, J. (2016), "'Darn right I'm a feminist…Sew what?' The Politics of Contemporary Home Dressmaking: Sewing, Slow Fashion and Feminism," *Women's Studies International Forum*, 54: 57–66.

Black, S. (2012), *Knitting: Fashion, Industry, Craft*, London: V&A Publishing.

Borges, A. (2011), *Design + Craft: the Brazilian Path*, São Paulo: Editora Terceiro Nome.

Bratich, J. Z. and H. M. Brush (2011), "Fabricating Activism: Craft-Work, Popular Culture, Gender," *Utopian Studies*, 22 (2): 233–60.

Bunn, S. (2011), "Felt as a Change-Maker in Contemporary Kyrgyzstan," *Making Futures*, 2. Available online: http://makingfutures.plymouthart.ac.uk/media/75857/bunn_stephanie.pdf (accessed August 10, 2017).

Burman, B. (1999), *The Culture of Sewing: Gender, Consumption and Home Dressmaking*, Oxford: Berg.

Carden, S. (2018), "The Aran Jumper," in S. Walker, et al. (eds.), *Design Roots: Culturally Significant Designs, Products, and Practices*, London: Bloomsbury.

Craftsy (2016), "The Shetland Hap Shawl." Available online: http://www.craftsy.com/class/the-shetland-hap-shawl/4947 (accessed April 8, 2016).

Davies, K. (2014), "Knitwear and Cultural Relativism," *Kate Davies Designs*, October 14. Available online: http://katedaviesdesigns.com/2014/10/14/knitwear-and-cultural-relativism/ (accessed April 8, 2016).

Dellot, B. (2015), *Ours to Master: How Makerspaces Can Help Us Master Technology for a More Human End*, London: RSA Action and Research Centre.

Emery, J. S. (2014), *A History of the Paper Pattern Industry*, London: Bloomsbury.

Faiers, J. (2008), *Tartan*, Oxford: Berg.

Future Museum (2012), "Sanquhar Knitting." Available online: http://www.futuremuseum.co.uk/collections/life-work/key-industries/textiles/sanquhar-knitting.aspx (accessed April 8, 2016).

Gauntlett, D. (2011), *Making Is Connecting*, Cambridge: Polity.

Greer, B. (2016), "Embroidery, Weaving, and the Craftivism of Amor Muñoz," *Creative Live blog*, January. Available online: http://blog.creativelive.com/embroidery-knitting-and-the-craftivism-of-amor-munoz (accessed April 8, 2016).

Howes, D. (1996), "Cultural Appropriation and Resistance in the American Southwest: Decommodifying 'Indianness,'" in D. Howes (ed.), *Cross-Cultural Consumption: Global Markets, Local Realities*, 138–61, London: Routledge.

Knott, S. (2015). "Labour of Love," *Crafts*, July/August: 48–51.

Kuznetsov, S. and E. Paulos (2010), "Rise of the Expert Amateur: DIY Projects, Communities, and Cultures," in *6th Nordic Conference on Human-Computer Interaction*, Reykjavik, October 16–20. Available online: http://www.staceyk.org/hci/KuznetsovDIY.pdf (accessed April 8, 2016).

Luscombe, P. and J. Thomas (2014), "The Petra Sancta Script: Connoisseurship in Digital Engraving," *All Makers Now?* 1: 85–90.

Manassiev, G. (2014), "Martenitsa," *The Saturday Market Project*, February 16. Available online: https://saturdaymarketproject.com/projects/133/martenitsa (accessed April 8, 2016).

Orton-Johnson, K. (2014), "Knit, Purl and Upload: New Technologies, Digital Mediations and the Experience of Leisure," *Leisure Studies*, 33 (3): 305–21.

Prügl, E. (1996), "Home-Based Producers in Development Discourse," in E. Boris and E. Prügl (eds.), *Homeworkers in Global Perspective: Invisible No More*, 39–59, London: Routledge.

Richard, N. (2007), *Handicrafts and Employment Generation for the Poorest Youth and Women*, Paris: UNESCO.

Stankard, S. (2010), "Textile Praxis: The Case for Malaysian Hand-Woven Songket," Ph.D. thesis, Royal College of Art.

Steven, R. (2014), "A2 & New North Press' 3D-printed Letterpress Font," *Creative Review*, September 8. Available online: http://www.creativereview.co.uk/cr-blog/2014/september/a2-new-north-press-3d-printed-letterpress-font (accessed April 8, 2016).

Turney, J. (2009), *The Culture of Knitting*, Oxford: Berg.

Twigger Holroyd, A. (2013), "Folk Fashion: Amateur Re-Knitting as a Strategy for Sustainability," Ph.D. thesis, Birmingham City University, Birmingham.

Uwujaren, J. (2013), "The Difference Between Cultural Exchange and Cultural Appropriation," *Everyday Feminism*, September 30. Available online: http://everydayfeminism.com/2013/09/cultural-exchange-and-cultural-appropriation (accessed April 8, 2016).

van Deijnen, T. (2014), "A Visit to Sanquhar," *Tomofholland*, November 7. Available online: http://tomofholland.com/2014/11/07/sanquhar-visit/ (accessed April 8, 2016).

Westermann, K. (2014), "A Visit from the Knitting Police," *Karie Bookish*, March 12. Available online: http://www.fourth-edition.co.uk/?p=5688 (accessed April 8, 2016).

Wood, N., C. Rust, and G. Horne (2009), "A Tacit Understanding: The Designer's Role in Capturing and Passing on the Skilled Knowledge of Master Craftsmen," *International Journal of Design*, 3 (3): 65–78.

22

Design for Social Innovators

Anna Meroni and Daniela Selloni

From creative communities to social innovators

Design for social innovation, and cultural and technical challenges

Since the beginning of the 2000s, there has been a radical transformation in the way we understand design practice and research, a transformation that mirrors changes occurring in our ways of living and producing value, in our societal systems, and in the way knowledge develops. Changes include: the full acknowledgment of services within the scope of design (Meroni and Sangiorgi 2011); the product-service-system approach; and the growing popularity of design thinking (Buchanan 2015). As a consequence, unprecedented fields of action have emerged in which design is recognized as a contributing discipline. Examples include design for social innovation; activism; policy; democracy; and new venture incubation. We can consider these fields as interconnected and part of the broadening scope of design approaches and purposes.

Clearly, the discourse about design for social innovation has expanded (Manzini 2015) and today design touches on diverse issues, from the definition and development of the solution (assuming that social innovations are forms of service and are subjects for service design), to the creation of capacity building programs for social innovators (i.e. incubation-like programs) (Cautela, Meroni, and Muratovski 2015).

At the beginning of the debate around "creative communities" (Manzini and Jégou 2008; Manzini and Meroni 2014; Meroni 2007) the main concern from a design point of view was how to support "creative minorities" making radical innovations in ways of being and doing (Meroni 2007). As such, the discourse was very much about enabling these groups to more effectively run their initiatives by designing toolkits and interventions aimed at increasing the operability, accessibility and enjoyability of the solution. There was also a strong focus on releasing the "hero" from the effort of carrying things on. Replication was of course an issue, but the main discourse centered on spreading awareness of existing practices in order to stimulate emulation (Manzini and Jégou 2003; Manzini and Jégou 2008).

Today, social innovation is being increasingly acknowledged as a significant driver of change throughout Europe (and beyond). This reflects a paradigm shift in understandings and practices that concern top-down and bottom-up relationships, citizenship and governance, social and commercial entrepreneurship, and profit and non-profit business (European Commission (EC) 2 2013). As part of this shift, design has proven itself in being able to effectively contribute to societal transformation by fostering activism from the bottom-up and advising policy from the top-down.

Put another way, today it is noticeable that social innovation is no longer a minority concern and is not necessarily in opposition to the mainstream. On the contrary, it is actively encouraged and fostered by public administration. It aims to become mainstream and to find a position in society's ecosystem.

New issues have therefore emerged when talking about design for social innovation. These include: expert capacity building; scaling practices up and out; and nurturing an innovation mindset in society at large. More specifically, we see *design* playing a dual role in producing social innovation:

- a cultural role, dealing with desirability (meaning) and acceptability (society);
- a technical role, dealing with feasibility (technology), viability (economy), and ecology (environment).

Simply building upon IDEO's pillars of effective innovation—Desirability, Feasibility, Viability (Brown 2009)—helps to clarify what to consider when fostering, supporting or scaling social innovation through design. The cultural dimension concerns the actual meaning that a certain innovation may convey in a specific society and its acceptability in terms of behaviors, policies, and norms. While the cultural dimension is locally rooted, the technical dimension is more generalizable because it concerns the functioning of the innovation in relation to recurring factors, where the process can be standardized. In fact, a design thinking toolkit can typically serve the purpose of training innovators to design their own service,[1] but it often needs "cultural translation." In other words, the way in which the innovations are co-designed with experts (including designers), users, and stakeholders may require adaptation and explanation in order to fit the cultural specifics of the circumstances in which they are to be used and applied.

In summary, we suggest that there are two main differences between the creative communities of the 2000s and the social innovators of today. The first, which relates to the cultural milieu, is that today's social innovators operate in a more mature socio-behavioral context. The second is more technical and concerns the increased capabilities of the innovators and the features of the innovation. Both result in a new awareness and self-awareness of the whole "social innovation ecosystem" and one's own role in society and economic development.

A new awareness on the part of innovators

Additional factors in the shift from creative communities towards social innovation have been the opportunities offered by ICTs and digital media, which facilitate access to an extensive capital of knowledge and a growing awareness of pressing environmental concerns. Social innovators have a clearer perception of the importance of contemporary environmental challenges for the planet and they feel a responsibility to contribute to the development of a more sustainable way of living, reflecting what is also happening at a general level (World Wide Views on Climate and Energy 2015).

Multi-stakeholder eco-systems

Social innovation ecosystems

We define a social innovation ecosystem as a locally rooted combination of conditions, stakeholders, relations and resources that aim to achieve a communal objective, i.e. a shared purpose. Despite the diversity of motivations and agendas, a social innovation ecosystem includes individual interests but has as its overarching goal the interest of the community. This fosters public value that is, "the total societal value that cannot be monopolised by individuals, but is shared by all actors in society and is the outcome of all resource allocation decisions" (EC 1 2013: 2). It is, therefore, a multi-stakeholder system that can run experiments and projects in specific sectors while testing models and structures of collaboration.

Convergence of action is the key to starting these projects, to increase the effectiveness of the collaboration and to create the conditions that make them possible. Here community-centered design (Manzini and Meroni 2014) supports the co-design of the process and the actions to be taken.

The Milano social innovation ecosystem

In this chapter, we discuss three social innovation projects in the Milan area; therefore, a few notes are needed about the local ecosystem. In the past few years, the local public administration has embarked on improving social innovation in the city through a variety of actions. In conjunction with private organizations, institutions, and foundations, city councils have launched a diverse collection of initiatives for transforming Milan into a smart, sharing city. These take the form of experiments in open government; public incubation, acceleration, and cultural hubs—using public space for temporary initiatives of public value; and asset sharing. This program is called "Milano Smart City" and comprises guidelines, strategic actions, and initiatives aimed at making the city smarter from the point of view of social innovation, i.e. more inclusive and based on the collaboration of multiple stakeholders. The program includes a dynamic set of initiatives, such as cultural events, exhibitions, training programs, and participatory design experiments, demonstrating an unprecedented social and entrepreneurial vitality around these issues.

Three cases of design for social innovation

To exemplify the evolution over time of design for social innovation, we discuss here three case studies in the Milan area, developed by the Polimi DESIS Lab team, within the Department of Design at the Politecnico di Milano. They are action research projects in which three exemplary processes show how social transformation can occur thanks to design contribution.

Coltivando—the convivial garden of Politecnico di Milano

"Coltivando" is the community garden set up within the Bovisa Campus of Politecnico di Milano, developed by a team of researchers, teachers, and postgraduate students in spatial and service design. It originated from two research programs: "Human Cities, reclaiming public spaces" (2010–12), which focused on the regeneration of public spaces and "Feeding Milan—energies for change" (2010–13), which aimed to create short food chain initiatives in the Milanese region. Located on the university campus, it highlights a formerly "hidden" public place (vacant and unused) by adding social and environmental value to the campus and local community (Fassi and Simeone 2013).

The project took over twelve months to develop and is currently an integral part of the university and neighborhood life. It is the result of an extensive co-design process started in a week-long workshop called "Temporary Urban Solutions," in which a group of students created a garden prototype for the community to interact with. This was the first step of a participatory action research activity comprising a set of academic workshops and community consultations that engaged residents and local stakeholders. The aim was to re-design the first garden prototype as a "convivial model," where vegetables are grown in the garden and then distributed throughout the community. To do this, different research actions were implemented:

- outlining the spatial layout to allow both food production and socializing;
- designing the service model to facilitate collaboration;
- adopting a community-centered design approach to engage residents and academic staff;
- shifting from temporary urban solutions to long-term projects. (Fassi and Simeone 2013)

Two years after its launch, Coltivando has thirty permanent members who meet regularly in the garden. It is a place of belonging for the Bovisa community

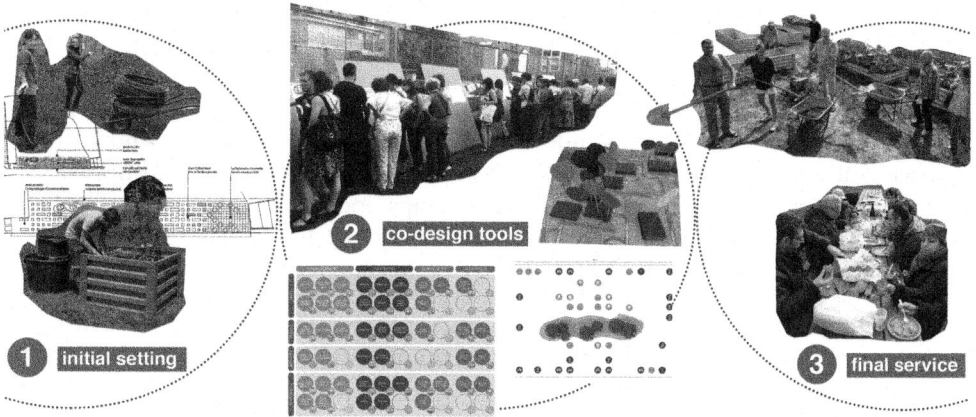

FIGURE 22.1 Coltivando process. Courtesy POLIMI DESIS Lab. © Anna Meroni and Daniela Selloni.

and attracts an ever-increasing number of visitors who sometimes participate in maintenance activities, spend time in the garden, and enjoy being in a public green area (Fassi 2015) (see Figure 22.1). Increasing the responsibility of community members for the tasks to be carried out in the garden has been the way to make it self-sustainable and allow a successful "exit strategy" for the designers who activated the project (Fassi 2015). Coltivando can be seen as a first step in a more extensive regeneration process for the neighborhood. In addition, Coltivando inspired the birth of another research project in 2014, named "CampUS," the aim of which is to spread the experience and competence of Coltivando to other green areas of the town.

Creative Citizens

"Creative Citizens" (Cittadini Creativi) is an action-research project generated within the design doctoral program of the Politecnico di Milano, under the auspices of the Polimi DESIS Lab. It took place within a community of residents in the Zone 4 neighborhood and was located in a local farmhouse, Cascina Cuccagna. This has become a symbol of Milanese activism because it has been saved from dereliction and decay by a group of citizens. The old farmhouse is to become a permanent laboratory for civic participation by offering space, equipment, and opportunities for collaboration (Selloni 2013).

In 2013, Cascina Cuccagna organized residency opportunities for original projects with the same mission. Using the tools of service design research, Creative Citizens responded to the call for the assignment of temporary spaces in the farmhouse by presenting a program that focused on participatory design between designers and local communities.

An experiment that involved a community of thirty citizens meeting each week began in February 2013 and continued until the end of June 2013. The aim of Creative Citizens was to bring the expertise of researchers to the service of ordinary people, creating a laboratory of solutions for daily life, improving existing services and designing new ones, acting as a "semi-public office for service design" and connecting citizens with designers, stakeholders, and institutions. In other words, it created an effective environment for co-designing social innovation (Cantù and Selloni 2013).

The project consisted of a series of co-design sessions dealing with four different service areas: sharing networks, administrative advice, food systems and cultural activities, all of which were connected to simple daily tasks and to existing services and places, such as time banks, purchasing groups, local shops, museums, markets, and fairs. The four service areas were organized in four cycles, each of them consisting of three creative sessions, which can be seen as steps on a progressive path:

- A *warm up session*, to familiarize participants with the topic by presenting practices from all over the world. It aimed to inspire people and offer visions of an alternative way of life.

- A *generative session*, a sort of collective brainstorming bringing together citizens' desires and insights of good practice.

- A *prototyping session* whose objective was to move from an ideal service to a real one, identifying the local resources that could be involved in the development of the service.

The final result of Creative Citizens is a collection of six everyday services co-designed with the local people:

1. *Augmented Time Bank:* a system for exchanging skills and small tasks, within condominium blocks and the neighborhood as a whole, starting with Cuccagna Time Bank.

2. *Object Library*: a physical and digital space for bartering, borrowing, gifting, and renting goods in the neighborhood.

3. *Citizens' Desk*: a service for orientation and procedural first aid, in various domains: legal, fiscal and architectural/building advice.

4. *Facecook*: a neighborhood food network, connecting restaurants, markets, shops, and local residents.

5. *Local Distribution System*: an alternative distribution network to connect Zone 4 with the peri-urban area, based on the principles of disintermediation and participated logistics.

6. *Zona 4 Cicerons*: places in Zone 4 selected and explained by citizen-guides, who organize unconventional tours to discover hidden or forgotten places.

These services may be regarded as public-interest services (Selloni 2014). They were co-designed with local people and, responding to individual interests session by session, they were expanded to become public interests. Each service had a citizen "hero," someone who became a stalwart advocate for it, who emerged spontaneously during the work sessions. The need and the value for a "service hero" was specifically recognized at the end of the process, when a set of "ready-to-use" solutions were made available to the community (see Figure 22.2); without the personal commitment of the "hero," these services might never have been developed.

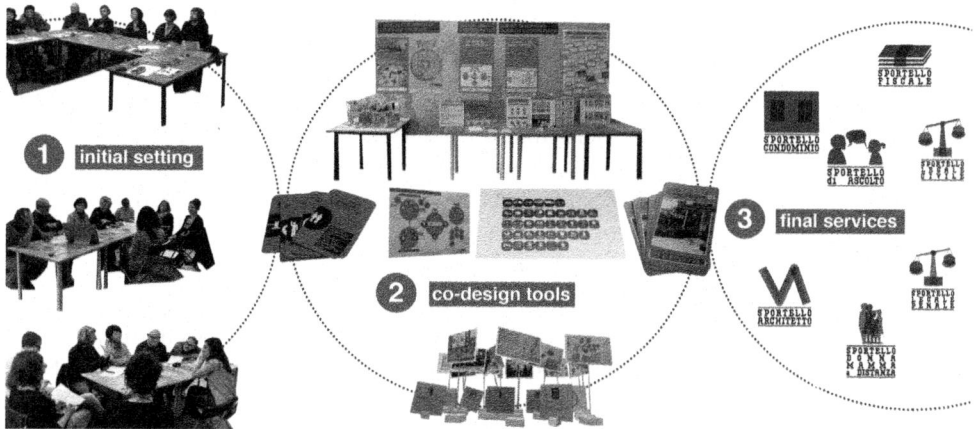

FIGURE 22.2 Creative Citizens process. Courtesy POLIMI DESIS Lab. © Anna Meroni and Daniela Selloni.

Each service is now at a different stage of development and it is possible to identify three possible progressions:

- to envisage an intersection with the public sector (Citizens' Desk);
- to foster the birth of original service start-ups (Object Library);
- to join existing services provided within the Cascina Cuccagna (Augmented Time Bank).

These paths are currently evolving and generating other kinds of ventures, which will become subjects for observations and analysis in further research.

Feeding Milan—Energies for Change

"Feeding Milan—Energies for Change" ("Nutrire Milano—Energie per il cambiamento") is an action research project funded by local institutions (Fondazione Cariplo, a bank foundation with the Comune di Milano and Provincia di Milano) and developed through a partnership between Slow Food Italia, the Department of Design of Politecnico di Milano, and the Università di Scienze Gastronomiche. The project ran from 2010 to 2013.

The service design team from Polimi DESIS Lab brought together a multidisciplinary group of agriculturalists and gastronomists to create a network of interconnected services based on the principles of a short food chain, multifunctionality, and collaboration among stakeholders (Irving et al. 2007). This also connected consumers in the town directly with farmers in the peri-urban area of Agricultural Park South, on the southern edge of the town. It led to a network of services that work in synergy, following the principles of economies of scope (Panzar and Willig 1981). These services operate on a collaborative basis and are inspired by the idea of offering a rich and convivial experience (Illich 1973). More specifically, as Manzini and Meroni (2013) state, conviviality is the underlying principle of the whole project, not only as a way of eating together, but actually as a way of creating pleasurable and collaborative relationships in every activity. The project experimented with diverse initiatives, such as:

- **The Earth Market**: A farmers' market for local producers, organized according to the principles of Slow Food, where products are "good, clean and fair." Currently, it takes place twice a month and includes instructive workshops, taste laboratories, street kitchens, and convivial tables where visitors can come together and eat.

- **Ideas Sharing Stall**: A stand within the Earth Market where designers discuss emerging ideas for new services with visitors and participants, asking for comments and inviting creative contributions. By using a set of boundary objects (Star 1989), visitors have the opportunity to co-design and personalize the ideas already available and to provide their insight.

- **The Farmer's Food Box**: A weekly delivery service of local fruit and vegetables. The box is delivered to convenient collection points, such as a neighborhood shop, bar, cultural center, school, office, or some other regular meeting point. Prototyped in 2011 and 2012, this service unfortunately experienced several logistical difficulties in evolving into a self-sufficient activity and is no longer working.

- **The Collaborative Supermarket—SuperCo-op**: A supermarket based on a co-operative principle to distribute high-quality, fresh, local produce at affordable prices, due to the work being carried out by customers/members. Developed as a feasibility study, it is now waiting to find the right context for its implementation.

- **The Local Distribution System**: A platform that aims to answer the urgent and unmet demand for B2B logistics, connecting local producers with restaurants and food shops. After several scenarios and micro-experimentations, there is now a start-up company working on it, integrating the assets of different stakeholders and creating synergies with the market.

- **The Local Bread Chain**: Production of bread entirely at the local level, from the growing of grain to final produce. Commercialized at a fixed price, the project has set high standards for everyday consumption and bread is produced and distributed by different bakers across the Milanese area.

- **Zero-mile tourism**: A set of services in which farms offer hospitality and accommodation to urban tourists. An initial series of activities, prototyped by students in the School of Design at Politecnico di Milano, has inspired independent initiatives run by the farmers themselves.

Five years have passed since the inception of Feeding Milan and we are now able to analyze the results. While some services have been successful, several have not evolved into long-lasting activities: to fully exploit the legacy of the project, a start-up, MiCibo, has recently been created by two members (the "heroes") of Slow Food who took part in the Feeding Milan project (Altuna et al. 2015). This is one outcome of the social innovation movement activated by this project (see Figure 22.3). It is possible to argue that Feeding Milan worked as a platform for diverse activity models and *modus operandi* that now form the basis of a new territorial ecology.

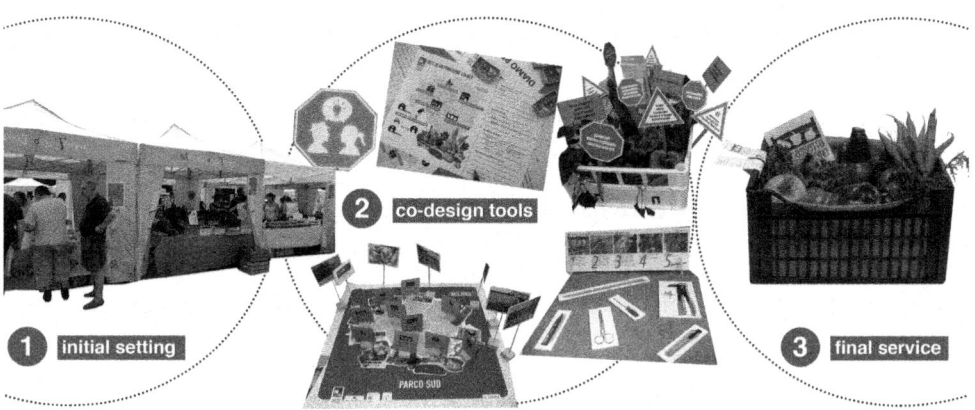

FIGURE 22.3 Feeding Milan process. Courtesy POLIMI DESIS Lab. © Author

Three cases of design for social innovation, three evolutions

These three cases show different paths for implementing social innovations and transforming them into mature, long-lasting experiences. They can be regarded as progressive examples of the development of a social innovation ecosystem through the use of service design, where both cultural and technical dimensions were empowered:

- **Coltivando** started with the idea of utilizing an unused public space on the Politecnico campus. From the first initiative of a small group of activists, it evolved into a cohesive and robust community that was able to spread its knowledge and share its practices, as the CampUs project shows. Coltivando generated a self-governing community in which the "exit strategy" of the design research group was properly prepared, leaving the stage to a new community of experts of active citizens and local associations.

- **Creative Citizens** focused initially on research objectives specifically related to the experimentation of a set of co-design tools, but then the process unexpectedly produced a shift from engaging to empowering people (Cantù and Selloni 2013) and originated six different collaborative services. They are currently evolving into various forms, located in a hybrid space between public and private, market and society, amateur and professional, profit and non-profit.

- **Feeding Milan,** because of its scale and complexity, exemplifies many possible evolutions, but for the purposes of this chapter, we want to highlight the path followed by the start-up MiCibo. This shows the evolution of a social innovation practice into an enterprise, which is benefitting from the network created by the research project. This start-up represents an important outcome because it reflects an idea of "local economy" based on food, agriculture, tradition and culture where multifunctional farming, de-mediated food chains, and urban activism merge (Manzini and Meroni 2013).

Discussion: The service design mindset

Design supporting social innovators

A recent European Commission-funded project provided us with the opportunity to conceptualize part of what we have been doing during this time—based on design for social innovation and projects such as the three discussed above. TRANSITION[2] (Transnational Network for Social Innovation Incubation, 2013–16) aims to research and determine a common methodology to support the social innovators in a group of innovation-based incubators structured into a European Social Innovation Incubation Network (ESIIN).

The main outcome of this project is, in fact, the definition of the Social Innovation Journey SIJ (Davalli, De Coninck, and Marengo 2015), a shared incubation path that takes an innovation from infancy to maturity, and eventually to its replication/diffusion. In short, this path mixes and matches methods and tools from strategic design, service design and co-design with social and collaborative formats in order to have them embedded in the solution. By taking the innovators through a journey to understand the "who, what, how and why" of their initiative, it acts as a Socratic process (learning by asking questions and developing answers) aiming at individual empowerment and an increasing awareness of the practicability of their own initiative, its impact, and its social and economic potential. In other words, the SIJ aims at maximizing the technical competence of the innovator by providing customized assistance (in the form of group training, one-to-one mentoring, or peer-to-peer interaction, according to the circumstances) in an expert capacity-building process, which includes tools from service and strategic design integrated with other disciplines.

The SIJ is not, of course, the only methodology for accelerating social innovations, but it has definitely capitalized on the experience of several cutting-edge programs by some of the most renowned social innovation and incubation centers.[3] The same is true for the local context of Milan, where the number of acceleration programs launched in the last few years by local alliances of public and private entities (local administrations, big companies, foundations, and the third sector) in conjunction with incubators has produced a generation of social innovation experts. They are very much aware of global conditions (sustainability and social issues, and economic transformation), of their potential, and have developed an "expertise" that spread naturally through person-to-person (P2P) networking. This expertise is creating a culture of innovation in society, the other fundamental factor we have pinpointed for creating an effective social innovation ecosystem.

Institutions such as universities and public administrations play a crucial role in creating this culture via different actions. As a research group based in a design university, we see ourselves (the Polimi DESIS Lab) as an integral component of the local social innovation ecosystem. As such, we can reflect on our role in contributing to both its technical and cultural growth. Design can contribute in the following ways:

- **Incubating innovations:** The SIJ systematizes lessons learnt from all the previous projects (including Coltivando, Creative Citizens, Feeding Milan) with a special emphasis on creating an expert capacity-building process for people with an already developed social and environmental awareness.

- **Finding unexpected opportunities for (social) innovation**: Coltivando, for example, was born from an experimental envisioning and fast-prototyping process conducted by design students with the neighborhood, in which diverse hypothetical solutions were proposed and tested with the local people, until the current one was determined.

- **Giving voice to stakeholders**: By orchestrating and setting up ad hoc co-design situations that can effectively involve not only the most pro-active members of the society but also the "unusual suspects," stakeholders who are less familiar with participation in innovation. Creative Citizens brought citizens from a neighborhood together around common interests; Coltivando sat citizens around the same table as local administrators and university staff; and Feeding Milan "intercepted" a wide range of people at a market stall in order for them to think about the future of food for the city.

- **Creating shared visions for the future**: Feeding Milan is an example of a long-term field experiment where fast prototyped services indicated future directions for possible service systems. Design helped to visualize and create an overarching scenario, which evolved over time, and a shared meaning of public value, where stakeholder engagement was crucial.

A service design mindset

In conclusion, we can summarize these three cases of social innovation as projects in which design operated as an empowerment agent for a value-creating process with both cultural and technical dimensions. These cases have also illustrated the nature and function of a local social innovation ecosystem where a design university acts alongside and among very diverse stakeholders.

It is now worth discussing in greater depth how this form of empowerment-by-design can take place. According to the research project TEPSIE (Davies and Simon 2013), and building on the study of McLean and Andersson (2009), it is possible to distinguish subjective empowerment (*feeling able* to influence decisions) and objective or *de facto* empowerment (*actually being able* to influence an outcome or a decision). Within the three cases presented, we can observe a common path that progressively provides citizens with subjective empowerment and lays the foundations for delivering objective empowerment.

In spite of their diversity in terms of topic, length, and member participation, the co-design sessions held within Coltivando, Creative Citizens, and Feeding Milan engendered the feeling of being able to influence/control/orient a situation. This first phase has been fundamental in inspiring people, enhancing imagination and hope, and offering visions of better ways of living together. However, it was the adoption of a service design approach, with its specific and actionable methods and tools integrating different disciplines that actually raised participants to the level of objective empowerment. By doing so, they developed an authentic expertise, i.e. a conscious and transferable knowledge, which enabled them to transform ideas into working services and make things happen, influencing the outcome and further decisions, and making them aware that they are part of a bigger ecosystem.

What characterizes the shift from creative communities with a unique experience to social innovation ecosystems with shared, transferable expertise is, ultimately, this awareness, which enhances the confidence of social innovators in understanding the context and making things happen through planned strategies. More specifically, we like to talk about a "service design mindset" as a way of seeing behaviors and unused assets as potential services, and of being able to conduct and replicate a design process. We think this service design mindset represents a fundamental achievement for current social innovators and may be seen as their distinguishing feature with regard to past experiences of creative communities.

In addition, we may also argue that the service design mindset builds upon the concept of service-dominant logic (Vargo and Lusch 2008) transferring it to social innovation. As Margolin (2012) states, design is a propositional activity and this is fully reflected by the projects discussed here: the basis of the proposition was a service (or a system of services), together with the cultural and technical process required to co-design, prototype and implement it within complex systems.

The unquestionable positivity and relative ease of diffusion of this mindset must not, however, generate overconfidence or simplistic interpretations of the phenomena. The very high rate of failure for service-based start-ups (Clarysse, Wright, and van Hoven 2015; Marmer et al. 2012) demonstrates several possible shortcomings in the production of self-sustainable ventures, which are even more risky in the social ambit, where revenues are regulated by social criteria. Instead, we can welcome the dissemination of this service design mindset in social innovation ecosystems as a cultural achievement; a subjective and objective empowerment of the community, in which design can play an important role.

Notes

1   Examples include: DYI-Development Impact and You http://diytoolkit.org; TRANSITION-The Social Innovation Journey http://transitionproject.eu/learning-outcomes/; The Social Design Method Menu https://fieldstudio.wordpress.com/methods-menu/.

2   European Research Project TRANSITION—Transnational Network for Social Innovation Incubation (2013–16), a thirty-month action supported by the European Commission's Seventh Framework Programme for research, technical development and demonstration, under the grant agreement n. 604849.

3   TRANSITION partners: European BIC Network (EBN), Belgium; The Young Foundation, UK; NESTA, UK; Social Innovation Park, Spain; Politecnico di Milano—Department of Design, Italy; PRICE, France; SEA, Portugal; WestBIC, Ireland; Social Innovation eXchange (SIX), UK.

References

Altuna, N., C. Dell'Era, L. Landoni, and R. Verganti (2015), "Developing Innovative Visions through Collaboration with Radical Circles," in L. Collina, L. Galluzzo, and A. Meroni (eds.), *Proceedings of CUMULUS Spring Conference 2015—The Virtuous Circle*

Design Culture and Experimentation, Politecnico di Milano 3–7 June, Milan: McGraw Hill. Digital Publication from: http://cumulusmilan2015.org/proceedings/

Brown, T. (2009), *Change by Design*, New York, NY: HarperCollins.

Buchanan, R. (2015), "Worlds in the Making: Design, Management, and the Reform of Organizational Culture," *Shè-Ji. The Journal of Design, Economics and Innovation*, Autumn, 1: 1–80.

Cantù, D. and D. Selloni (2013), "From Engaging to Empowering People: A Set of Co-design Experiments with a Service Design Perspective," *Social frontiers: the next edge of social innovation research*. Research papers for a major new international social research conference, London: NESTA.

Cautela, C., A. Meroni, and G. Muratovski (2015), "Design for Incubating and Scaling Innovation," in L. Collina, L. Galluzzo, and A. Meroni (eds.), *Proceedings of CUMULUS Spring Conference 2015—The Virtuous Circle Design Culture and Experimentation, Politecnico di Milano 3–7 June*, Milano: Mc Graw Hill. Available online: http://cumulusmilan2015.org/proceedings/ (accessed August 1, 2016).

Clarysse, B., M. Wright, and J. Van Hoven (2015), *A Look Inside Accelerators. Building Businesses*, London: NESTA.

Davalli, C., V. De Coninck, and C. Marengo (2015), "Scaling Social Innovation. DENISI—TRANSITION: experiences and first success stories of the two European networks of incubators of social innovation," Transition Project. Available online: http://transitionproject.eu/scaling-social-innovation-experiences-and-first-success-stories-of-the-two-european-networks-of-incubators-for-social-innovation/ (accessed August 1, 2016).

Davies, A. and J. Simon (2013), "The Value and Role of Citizen Engagement in Social Innovation," a deliverable of the project: *"TEPSIE" European Commission—7th FP*, Brussels: European Commission.

European Commission 1 (EC1)—DG Communications Networks, Content and Technology (2013), "A vision for public services." Available online: http://ec.europa.eu/newsroom/dae/document.cfm?doc_id=3179 (accessed August 1, 2016).

European Commission 2 (EC2)—DG Regional and Urban Policy and DG Employment, Social affairs and Inclusion (Ed) (2013), "Guide to Social Innovation," working paper. Available online: http://ec.europa.eu/regional_policy/sources/docgener/presenta/social_innovation/social_innovation_2013.pdf (accessed August 1, 2016).

Fassi, D. (2015), "Coltivando—the Convivial Garden of Politecnico di Milano," *A Case Study from the State of the Art Work Package of the EU research Human Cities—Challenging the City Scale (2014–2017)*.

Fassi, D. and G. Simeone (2013), "Spatial and Service Design meet up at Coltivando Convivial Garden at the Politecnico di Milano," *DRS // CUMULUS 2013—The 2nd International Conference for Design Education Researchers*, Oslo: Oslo and Akershus University College of Applied Sciences.

Illich, I. (1973), *Tools for Conviviality*, New York: Harper and Row.

Irving, J., S. Milano, B. Minerdo, and G. Novellini (2007), *Terra Madre: 1,600 Food Communities*, Bra, Italy: Slow Food Editore.

Manzini, E. (2015), *Design, When Everybody Designs*, Cambridge, MA: MIT Press.

Manzini, E. and F. Jégou (2003), *Sustainable Everyday: Scenarios of Urban Life*, Milano: Edizioni Ambiente.

Manzini, E. and F. Jégou (2008), *Collaborative Services. Social Innovation and Design for Sustainability*, Milan: Polidesign.

Manzini, E. and A. Meroni (2013), "Design for Territorial Ecology and a New Relationship between City and Countryside: The Experience of the Feeding Milano Project," in S. Walker and J. Giard (eds.), *The Handbook of Design for Sustainability, 237–54*, London: Bloomsbury.

Manzini, E. and A. Meroni (2014), "Catalysing Social Resources for Sustainable Changes. Social Innovation and Community Centred Design," in C. Vezzoli, C. Kohtala, and A. Srinivasan (eds.), *Product-Service System Design for Sustainability*, 362–79, Sheffield: Greenleaf Publishing.

Margolin, V. (2012), "Design and Democracy in a Troubled World," lecture at the School of Design, Carnegie Mellon University, Pittsburgh, PA, April 11.

Marmer, M., H. Bjoern Lasse, E. Dogrultan, and R. Berman (2012), "Startup Genome Report Extra on Premature Scaling. A Deep Dive into Why Most High Growth Startups Fail' v 1.2," startupgenome.cc. Available online: http://startupgenome.cc/pages/startup-genome-report-extra-on-premature-scal (accessed August 1, 2016).

McLean, S. and E. Andersson (2009), *Activating Empowerment: Empowering Britain from the Bottom-up*, London: Involve & Ipsos MORI.

Meroni, A. (ed.) (2007), *Creative Communities. People Inventing Sustainable Ways of Living*, Milano: Polidesign

Meroni, A. and D. Sangiorgi (2011), *Design for services*, Farnham: Gowerpublishing.

Panzar, C. J. and D. R. Willig (1981), "The Economies of Scope," *The American Economic Review*, 71 (2), 268–72.

Selloni, D. (2013), "The Experience of Creative Citizens," *Touchpoint—The Journal of Service Design*, 5 (2): 86–9.

Selloni, D. (2014), "Designing for public-interest services. Citizen participation and collaborative infrastructures in times of societal transformation," Ph.D. thesis, XXVII Cycle, Politecnico di Milano, Italy.

Star, S. L. (1989), "The Structure of Ill-Structured Solutions: Boundary Objects and Heterogeneous Distributed Problem Solving," in L. Gasser and M. Huhns (eds.), *Distributed Artificial Intelligence—Vol. 2*, 37–54, San Francisco, CA: Morgan Kaufman.

Vargo, S. L. and R. F. Lusch (2008), "Service-dominant Logic: Continuing the Evolution," *Journal of the Academy of Marketing Science*, 36 (1): 1–10.

World Wide Views on Climate and Energy (2015), "From the World's Citizens to the Climate and Energy Policymakers and Stakeholders," *Results Report*. Available online: http://climateandenergy.wwviews.org (accessed August 1, 2016).

23

Integrated Scales of Design and Production for Sustainability with a Focus on Graduate Design Work in Lighting

Çağla Doğan

Introduction

Since 2011, Product Design for Sustainability has been offered annually as a practice-oriented and design-led graduate course in the Department of Industrial Design at Middle East Technical University (METU). In addition to a literature search of selected articles and class presentations and discussions, an important component of the course is the *research through design* phase in which design students focus on various sustainability approaches and reflect on the design considerations discussed throughout the course sessions (Doğan 2012: 313). The students redefine and re-contextualize objects through sketches, mock-ups, and working models. The chosen product category is household lighting (ceiling, wall, or mood). Within the context of the course, students prepare their design solutions for class presentation, including a working model, a presentation board, and an oral summary of the main phases of their design proposals, including their reflections on, and insights into, the design process. The presentation also involves an assessment of the design solution and its adherence to sustainability considerations, and key conclusions and findings from the research through design activity. The design solutions and explorations focus mainly on "integrated scales of design and production for sustainability" approach (Doğan 2007: 20, 2014: 196; Doğan and Walker 2008: 277, 285–8; Walker 2006: 136), with the intention of incorporating greater localization into the design process, and so to develop solutions that are:

- aesthetically adaptable for local needs, tastes, and preferences (Walker 2011: 158–61) by facilitating user comprehension and engagement in the design and use phases, and enabling product personalization through a "halfway" design approach (Fuad-Luke 2009: 95), so as to generate variety and diversity;

- tailored to local/regional materials and manufacturing capabilities to encourage post-use services at local batch-production scale, such as repair, re-use/upgrading, and recovery.

Taking into account these sustainability considerations, the course takes a holistic approach to encouraging product-user interaction and participation by enabling and empowering users (Manzini 2007: 240–1) in the design, use, and post-use phases, which in turn aims to prolong the product lifespan (Cooper 2010: 13–14; Papanek 1999: 48). A hands-on approach to the exploration of sustainability considerations is adopted while developing design solutions. In a comprehensive review and assessment of the design outcomes of the course between 2011 and 2015, three interrelated factors emerged that were taken into consideration by the students in their design solutions, as listed below. The first factor aims to enable the end users as active participants, while the last two lean towards empowering local producers within the design process:

- Do-it-Yourself (DIY) approach focusing on personalization through user involvement and engagement in adapting, updating, and using products, and including product templates for design details;

- design solutions empowering and enabling local and/or craft skills and tacit knowledge;

- design solutions empowering and enabling local skills and tacit knowledge through the incorporation of flexible technologies.

The DIY approach has the potential to address sustainability considerations (e.g. the effective use of resources and materials, product maintenance, repair and upgrading, product personalization for local needs and tastes etc.), and to actively involve end users in the design process. The level of this involvement, including the required mental and physical effort, also determines the nature of user engagement. Product personalization, in this sense, enables the end user to modify, renew, and upgrade the design solutions (Mugge, Schoormans, and Schifferstein 2009: 468–9) considering local needs, preferences, and tastes. Consequently, the design solution evolves over time, which strengthens the bond between the user and the product, resulting in "emotional durability" (Chapman 2009: 32–3), which prolongs the "psychological lifespan" of a product (Verbeek and Kockelkoren 1998: 29–30). The second and third factors focus primarily on empowering local small-scale producers, taking advantage of their skills and knowledge, and provide design solutions that support post-use services. These factors also determine the design considerations, bringing about a rethinking of the roles of the designer, user, and producer. For instance, in the first factor in which product personalization is the main focus, the designer's intention is to provide the end user with a "halfway" design solution (Fuad-Luke 2009: 95, 100–1) rather than a finished product, meaning that the end user engages actively in the design process and adapts the product according to her/his preferences and aesthetic considerations. This sustainability approach emerges in reply to criticisms of the design of mass-produced products as being compact and inaccessible, and preventing people from repairing and/or upgrading their products, or maintaining them properly. In this regard, the notion of product personalization proposes a design direction that helps the design students explore and rethink the nature of products and their design details, encouraging them to come up with design solutions that are both aesthetically and technologically adaptable. This open-source approach to design also redefines the role of people as active participants in the design, use, and post-use phases.

In the second and third factors, the role of the designer has particular emphasis on re-vitalizing and re-valuing local and/or craft skills through the creation of design solutions that are tailored to local materials and manufacturing capabilities. This integrates various scales of design and production, and explores the relationships that exist among batch production, mass production, craft, and open design (i.e. democratization of the design process by enabling non-designers to adapt designs tailored to their needs and preferences). There are several design examples in which product designers make use of craft skills in their design solutions, and in these cases, the designers work closely with craftspeople to produce their design work at the small-scale production level (Er and Kaya 2008: 173; İngin 2006: 34–7). In such collaborations, the designers co-create and develop their design solutions while being involved in the production process, leading to the creation of unique design pieces. This approach is most commonly found in such fields as jewelry, home accessories, and furniture, which provide inspiring examples of how new generation designers are keen to engage in close collaboration with craftspeople in the development and materialization of their designs. However, the design explorations within the course context take a different stance, proposing a new path for the incorporation of these skills into the design process. Rather than adopting these skills entirely, the course aims to rethink and re-contextualize them, and in doing so, reconsiders and re-envisages the designer's role in bringing together various scales of production through design.

Revaluing crafts and small-scale production through design solutions is particularly significant for the revitalization and sustaining of local skills and knowledge. As this is related directly to the well-being of society, which empowers the culture of local production and design, it increases the potential for creating high-skilled employment at the local and regional levels. Within the course context, the design solutions following this path explore the potential of incorporating local materials and product skills into the design, such as embroidery, knitting, lacework etc. Lastly, the third factor is aimed primarily at the rethinking and integration of new flexible technologies, such as three-dimensional (3D) printing, into the design process, and explores the use of more environmentally benign materials, such as locally sourced clay.

The importance of the notion of localization for sustainability has led to the recent emergence of a number of inspirational approaches that encourage integrated scales of design and production. One example of these is Open Structures, which is an open-source platform based on a shared modular grid that allows people from various disciplines and interests to contribute to the development of design parts, components, and structures (openstructures.net n.d.). The platform enables people to re-use or re-contextualize the relevant product parts with the help of 3D printing and rapid prototyping. For instance, a 3D-printed part that has been designed and produced based on the shared grid can be adapted to different products, and this has the potential to serve as a connection detail, bringing together mass-produced and locally produced parts. This approach is shared and discussed broadly within the context of the course, and its implications for product design and integrated scales of design and production for sustainability approaches.

Rethinking sustainability considerations through design and designing leads to a creative way of externalizing and interpreting existing theories and approaches, as well as the consequent assessment of design decisions and their reflection on design (Gaver 2012: 938; Schön 1983: 69). Exploring local materials, re-using or re-contextualizing existing products or parts, integrating and assessing new flexible technologies, and discussing their implications for local needs, preferences, and tastes through design are the features of the main methodology in the research through design approach phase adopted within the context of the course. Each phase of the design process, from exploration, research and ideation to design detailing, requires a hands-on approach, meaning that the design students face real challenges, experience personally the direct effects of their decisions, and interpret the implications of these for sustainable product design. For instance, if they propose a specific local and/or craft skill to be integrated into their design solutions, they should explore the main limitations and opportunities for the application of that skill in the local context, and investigate the related materials and production capabilities. In this regard, they are encouraged to choose a design scenario that focuses on enabling people and/or producers.

The design explorations phase, entitled the Conceptual Notions of Sustainable Products, is a five-week process scheduled at the end of the course. During this phase, the students gain feedback and insights through class discussions and design critiques, and make further iterations and improvements to their design solutions. These critique sessions are particularly valuable, in that the students are given the opportunity to familiarize themselves with the range and diversity of design interpretations that are visualized by mock-ups, sketches, and working models. Each student may interpret and reflect on sustainable design considerations differently, and so by being actively involved in the class discussions, they are given the opportunity to explore further their design solutions and potential directions, and to assess them based on the sustainability considerations set out at the beginning of the research through design phase. These main factors are discussed and presented in the following sections, with design solutions developed and presented within the course context provided as exemplary cases considering their implications for sustainability.

Do-It-Yourself (DIY) approach focusing on personalization through user involvement and engagement

Social Tree is a conceptual design solution in which the main focus was on product personalization through user intervention, with the user being encouraged to make, adapt, and update the design aesthetically (Figure 23.1a). Initially, the user assembles the product parts provided to form the main structure, and then threads a piece of string through the cutouts within the design detail. The user then alters the design for the purpose of personalization by adding materials to the main structure, such as photos, notes etc. The solution encourages active user participation in the design process by offering a design solution that can evolve and change over time with the incorporation of personal belongings. The student initially proposed this design exploration as a DIY project, however it also involves flexible technologies such as laser cutting in the preparation and production of the main components, and in this sense, adopts a more hybrid approach that could be tailored to small-scale production.

Sparkholes is a Do-It-Yourself (DIY) design concept in which the main emphasis is on product personalization (Figure 23.1b). The product can be made out of paper-based materials, such as corrugated cardboard of various thicknesses and material properties. The users are provided with a template that can be downloaded from a designated website that presents folding and cutting details for the development

FIGURE 23.1 (a) Social Tree lighting design by Alper Karadoğaner, 2014. © Alper Karadoğaner; and (b) Sparkholes lighting design by Güzin Şen, 2013. © Güzin Şen. Courtesy Department of Industrial Design, Middle East Technical University.

of a frame that fits onto a box. The frame can be adapted using a web-based application that aims to transform photos into preferred sizes of dots, allowing the user to transform photos or images that are personal and meaningful to them. The transformed pattern can be printed onto a sheet of A5 paper, after which the user simply pins the printed pattern to make openings in the paper, creating light and shade. The simple transformation of a box into a lighting design that enables personalization has merits in terms of its ease of applicability.

Re-lace is a ceiling lamp concept comprising electrical components and a large piece of molded lace (Figure 23.2a). The design concept provides a wide-range of potential product adaptations by employing a simple but engaging making process in which a starch-based powder with added water is applied to mold and fix the lace onto flexible forms of various sizes, such as balloons. Similarly, *Lace Lighting* is a wall lamp that re-contextualizes lace through the use of a metal sieve mold and a laser-cut wooden base into which LED electrical components and small magnets are set (Figure 23.2b). After the molding process, a metal hoop is placed onto the inner edges of the molded lace with the help of detachable rings. The hoop holding the molded lace, as the lampshade, can be attached to the laser-cut base with the help of magnets. This design detail enables the end user to re-use the lace or replace it with a new one of a different pattern. The first example proposes a DIY scenario in which the end user produces and personalizes the entire product following simple instructions; while in the second example, the use of molded lace is developed further involving a design kit (i.e. a metal sieve and rings, electrical components and magnets embedded on a laser-cut panel, and design instruction manual) that is provided to enable product personalization.

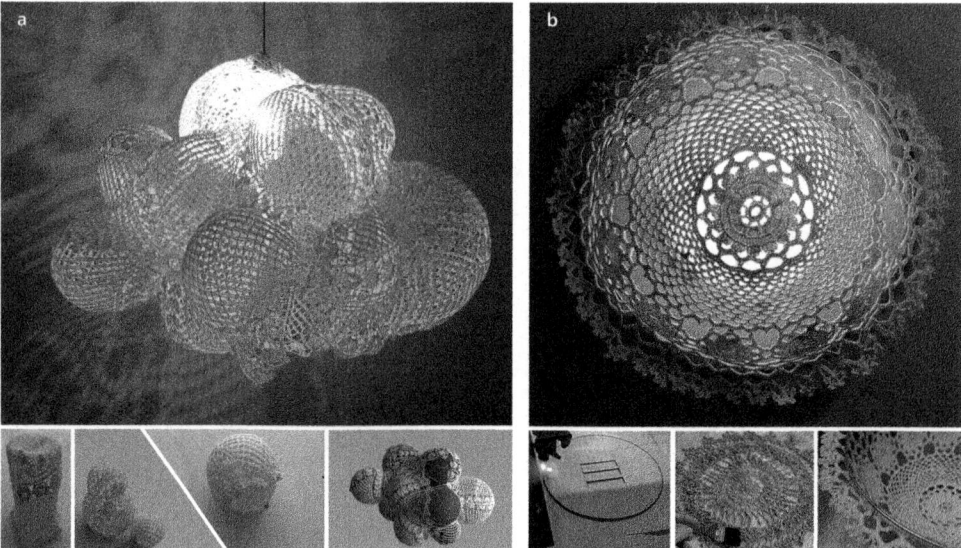

FIGURE 23.2 (a) Re-lace lighting design by Nazlı Terzioğlu, 2013. © Nazlı Terzioğlu; and (b) Lace lighting design by Gizem Hediye Eren, 2015. © Gizem Hediye Erem. Courtesy Department of Industrial Design, Middle East Technical University.

An important consideration in these design solutions is the prevention of any irreversible changes or damage to the lace. Through a simple making process, the lace is transformed into a culturally relevant object without losing the initial inherent meaning and value of the item that may have been passed down through generations. Furthermore, through the design, the re-used lace is transformed into a more visible and relevant piece of everyday life, and that transformation re-conceptualizes and personalizes the traditional craft of needle lace as a locally significant and valuable craft. This process also has the potential of revaluing an item that may otherwise be kept out of sight and forgotten in a drawer, box, or hope chest (dowry chest). As a result of its practical and engaging transformation, the proposed design solutions can evolve over time, and can be renewed into new forms and patterns in line with evolving local needs and tastes.

Design solutions empowering and enabling local and/or craft skills and tacit knowledge

The *Orbit* lighting design concept aims to take advantage of culturally relevant local skills and knowledge (Figure 23.3a), bringing together locally produced parts with off-the-shelf electrical components. A wooden sieve forms the main structure of the lighting concept, which also includes a base made out of corrugated cardboard that contains cut-outs that allow the wooden sieve to be attached to the base; felt for the shade; thread (used to form the main shape of the shade); and electrical components. The product parts are intended to be kept in their original state, in

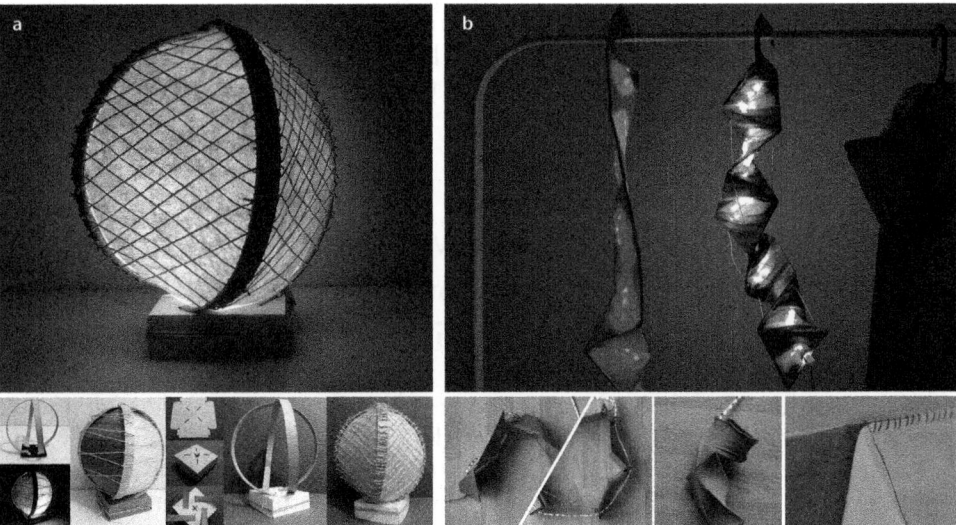

FIGURE 23.3 (a) Orbit lighting design by Dilruba Oğur, 2014. © Dilruba Oğur; and (b) Suspended lighting design by Yekta Bakırlıoğlu, 2013. © Yekta Bakırlıoğlu. Courtesy Department of Industrial Design, Middle East Technical University.

line with environmental considerations with no applications of surface finishing or coloring. Following this approach, the details are also kept simple, involving no adhesives or permanent connections. This concept embodies design details that permit re-use and repair at the local-batch production scale, and at the idea generation phase, various knotting techniques and materials for the frame and base were explored. The felt shading can also be replaced with alternative materials and fabrics, or can be eliminated completely according to user needs and preferences. The knotting process requires specific craft skills, and while that process can contribute to the diverse application of various patterns, it can also limit its adaptation at the individual level, or to certain users with specific hand skills. This proposal supports small-scale workshops that can empower women's collectives as a feasible medium in which to explore and materialize the potential variations and alternatives offered.

The main intention in the *Suspended* design concept is to re-use LED strips and to include locally available fabrics in the design (Figure 23.3b). Through the development process, the design concept evolved into a product that can be tailored in accordance with diverse user needs and preferences. Like *Orbit*, *Suspended* requires some specific skills and tacit knowledge in the cutting and stitching of fabric based on a pattern developed and provided by the designer. With the application of specific design details, the components of the product are attached together permanently; however, the basic making process would provide a small-scale producer with the possibility of adapting this to create alternative lighting solutions, as exemplified above. The components include a re-used LED strip made out of a flexible circuit and a silicon cover. The LED strip is produced for one-use, or is disposable, and can be cut into pieces and used in accordance with the main purpose or needs of the product, fitting into a desired context and/or product. Each lighting component on the strip can be functional, and thus can be re-used. Although LEDs can be long-lasting, the adhesives on the back of the strip can lose their adherence over time, meaning that a complex product part, eventually, is turned inevitably into waste. The *Suspended* design concept presents an alternative approach to re-use through the application of locally available fabrics for the shade and cardboard for structure, all of which are attached together using local skills.

Design solutions empowering and enabling local skills and tacit knowledge through the incorporation of flexible technologies

With the emergence of the maker movement (i.e. empowering people in designing and making processes via adopting open design and DIY approaches), flexible technologies such as 3D printing and laser cutting become more influential, providing designers with great possibilities in the rethinking of the entire design and production process. Although the nature of these technologies is more in line with local-batch production, their current applications are on the whole geared more towards mass-production and customization. This, in turn, supports mass-consumption through the rapid production of customizable features for products that are available online for purchase that allow the user to choose from various and diverse features. The use of non-reusable or non-recyclable plastic-based materials for filaments, and the global outsourcing of production through the internet closely resemble current design, mass-production and consumption patterns, and so this current and mainstream utilization undervalues its initial promise as an open-source, accessible, and personalized design and production process. Based on these discussions, one of the students adopted a more contemporary and critical approach to incorporating 3D printing into the design process, following a path that was more in line with the sustainability considerations discussed throughout the course (Figure 23.4). This design solution embraced a more sustainable approach by exploring clay, a natural and locally available material for the 3D printing of the lampshade. The initial aim of the project was to revalue the material and to explore means of its re-use several times over through melting and reprinting. The lampshade is put together with off-the-shelf

FIGURE 23.4 3D Printed Lampshade by Efe Alpay, 2013. © Efe Alpay. Courtesy METU.

electrical components. The production phase, which involved experimenting with a natural material, offered the greatest challenge in terms of deciding on the right mixture of water and clay, fabrication parameters such as material thickness, build speed, layer thickness etc. Although the exploratory design solution presented here is a work-in-progress, it opens up new possibilities for materialization and reflection on the notion of sustainable product design.

Conclusions, insights, and future directions

Throughout the Product Design for Sustainability course, various means of incorporating sustainability considerations (e.g. personalization, localization, engaging use etc.) into the design process are presented in the examples developed and presented. These range from DIY design solutions that make effective use/re-use of materials and/or product parts and enable product personalization, to those that take advantage of local craft skills and knowledge, and utilize flexible technologies such as 3D printing at the local batch-production scale. The students are encouraged to select and focus on specific design and production scenarios, and to discuss and interpret the roles of users, designers, and producers. Each solution, in this regard, is developed in line with the scenarios considered by the students. These explorations aim primarily at empowering the participation of end users and/or producers at the local batch-production scale.

The design solution involves people in the design process more actively through product personalization and user engagement, and in this regard, the proposed solutions presented here hold many possibilities for product adaption and variation (e.g. *Sparkholes, Re-Lace, Lace Lighting, Orbit, Suspended, 3D Printed Lampshade* and *Social Tree*). Design explorations that engage people in the design, use, and post-use phases also aim to strengthen the emotional bond between the product and the user, thus prolonging the product lifespan. As a consequence, the users are able to adapt these design solutions according to their changing needs and tastes, thus locally relevant solutions are able to evolve over time.

One of the most significant outcomes from the course is the incorporation of flexible production technologies into the designs, such as 3D printing and laser cutting, which support product personalization and adaptation at the local scale. These also encourage the students to examine and materialize design solutions through a more exploratory approach using different materials (e.g. clay via 3D printing) and design details (e.g. production of actual DIY drawing templates, laser-cut parts). Such technologies also enable the students to combine mass-produced product parts with locally produced items to incorporate greater localization into the design and production process.

The design solutions presented in this chapter exemplify the various paths internalized by the students during the research through design phase within the context of the course, which aim to bring together both theory and practice. One of the main challenges in the research through design approach related to sustainability is that the students tend to have difficulties in developing a critical approach to their work and going beyond the conventional notions of product design, production, and consumption. Rethinking these notions by way of a more exploratory approach to sustainability would appear to be both novel and challenging for them. The students' conventional and sometimes judgemental approach towards their initial design solutions in the idea generation phase may at first limit the desired exploratory nature of sustainable solutions. To overcome this, active class participation is encouraged, allowing them to reflect further on their design solutions and considerations of sustainability, which results in design critiques that give more emphasis to the design process rather than the outcome itself.

Full documentation of the entire design process is an important feature of the research through design process, helping the students incorporate their insights and experiences into their designs through daily logs, sketches etc. When the students realize their solutions evolve incrementally and confidently with the help of class discussions and design critiques, their engagement and motivation in this phase becomes more visible, which positively affects the facilitation of the research through design sessions. Throughout the design-led sessions, the students are encouraged to adopt a more hands-on development approach, meaning that they explore with actual materials and product parts. This experimentation also helps them realize the opportunities and barriers affecting the sustainability considerations.

The outcomes may also be developed further through feedback and insights garnered from local people, craftspeople, and/or small-scale producers. To strengthen this connection between the students and the local context, in spring 2015, the course was supported by a one-week intensive workshop entitled Essence of Place facilitated by Professor Stuart Walker and Çağla Doğan, which focused on the old city of Ankara, particularly Ankara Castle and its environs. The workshop gave the students the opportunity to observe, examine, and explore various local craftspeople at work (hammock maker, gourd lamp maker etc.), which was valuable for the students, giving them a deeper understanding of local craft skills and knowledge that can then be applied to the development of their design directions. Although this workshop was not linked directly to the research through design phase of the course, some of the students were greatly influenced by that experience. In future, it is possible that the course will be supported by similar workshops and/or field observations, with the aim of developing, assessing, materializing, and presenting design solutions that have a wider impact on re-vitalizing local craft skills, and making them more relevant and valuable in our everyday life. Similarly, design solutions that focus on product personalization can be encouraged in such a way that the involvement of potential end users in the design process can be more effective. As such, sustainable and open design solutions can be experienced, adapted, and assessed by potential end users, and further iterations based on the findings of the approach can be made. Active involvement of and instant feedback from potential users, and reflection on design and designing, would result in more profound discussions related to the sustainability considerations, with significant implications for our current notions of design, production, and consumption. Such alternative design solutions and reflections can also highlight potential and inspiring directions that may be adopted for future research and design in line with the personal, social, environmental, and personal strands of sustainability.

References

Chapman, J. (2009), "Design for (Emotional) Durability," *Design Issues*, 25 (4): 29–35.

Cooper, T. (2010), *Longer Lasting Products: Alternatives to the Throwaway Society*, Farnham: Gower Publishing Limited; Burlington: Ashgate Publishing Group.

Doğan, Ç. (2007), "Product Design for Sustainability: Integrated Scales of Design and Production," Ph.D. diss., Faculty of Environmental Design, University of Calgary, Alberta, Canada.

Doğan, Ç. (2012), "Product Design for Sustainability: Development of a New Graduate Course in Industrial Design," *Journal of the Faculty of Architecture*, 29 (2): 312–29.

Doğan, Ç. (2014), "Design Education for Sustainability: A Design Studio Project on the Re-contextualization of the Wind-up Radio," *International Journal of Sustainable Design*, 2 (3): 195–209.

Doğan, Ç. and Walker, S. (2008), "Localization—the Design and Production of Sustainable Products," *International Journal of Product Development*, 6 (3/4): 276–89.

Er, Ö. and Ç. Kaya (2008), "Problems or Opportunities? Overcoming the Mental Barrier for Socially Responsible Design in Turkey," *The Design Journal* 11 (2): 170–6.

Fuad-Luke, A. (2009), *Design Activism: Beautiful Strangeness for a Sustainable World*, Sterling: Earthscan.

Gaver, W. (2012), "What Should We Expect from Research Through Design?" *CHI 2012 Conference Proceedings*, 937–46, May 5–10, Austin, Austin, TX.

İngin, A. K. (2006), *Made in Şişhane: Istanbul, Küçük Üretim ve Tasarım Üzerine/on Istanbul, Small-scale Production and Design*, İstanbul: Pandora Yayınları.

Manzini, E. (2007), "Design Research for Sustainable Social Innovation," in R. Michel (ed.), *Design Research Now: Essay and Selected Projects*, 233–45, Berlin: Birkhäuser Verlag AG.

Mugge, R., J. P. Schoormans, and H. N. Schifferstein (2009), "Emotional Bonding with Personalised Products," *Journal of Engineering Design*, 20 (5): 467–76.

Openstructures.net (n.d.), "Can We Design Hardware Like How We Design Software?" Available online: http://openstructures.net/pages/2 (accessed July 14, 2015).

Papanek, V. (1999), *The Green Imperative—Ecology and Ethics in Design and Architecture*, New York, NY: Thames and Hudson.

Schön, D. A. (1983), *The Reflective Practitioner: How Professionals Think in Action*, New York, NY: Basic Books.

Verbeek, P. P. and P. Kockelkoren (1998), "The Things That Matter," *Design Issues*, 14 (3): 28–42.

Walker, S. (2006), *Sustainable by Design: Explorations in Theory and Practice*, London: Earthscan.

Walker, S. (2011), *The Spirit of Design: Objects, Environment and Meaning*, London: Earthscan.

24

Designing Authentic Brands

How Designerly Approaches Can Craft Authentic Brand Identity

Emma Murphy

Introduction[1]

Ask most people what they think is meant by branding and they usually describe it as the name of a product, advertising, selling, or simply a logo (see, for example, Davis and Baldwin 2006; Gordon and Langmaid 1988). At a more sophisticated level, a brand might be seen as a message conveyed not just in slogans but in behavior too (see, for example, Aaker 1996; Smythe, Dorward, and Reback 1992). Recently there has been a rise in so-called "genuine" brands, which try to convey a message of tradition, authenticity, and heritage (see, for example, Beverland 2004); however, the slightest probe beneath the surface suggests their publicized values stop at the boardroom, the labor practices that bring you your jeans, or the tax deals behind your morning coffee. So-called authenticity is only skin deep—yet clever design can mask this so we believe it to be authentic (here, design is being used in a surface-level, tactical manner).

Despite the rise of "the brand" and the deluge of identities, logos, and corporate straplines in today's globalized consumer landscape, our towns and cities are becoming more homogenous and indistinguishable from others, not just in our own countries, but also around the world (Vidal 2003). Stirling has many of the same shops as Seattle and Shanghai, Lisbon the same cafes as London. In effect, we are living in a monoculture (Michaels 2011).

The branding practices that create these surface-level brands are not, as this chapter will argue, "authentic" and such a process does not create authentic brands. This is because their provenance and authenticity is only skin deep and the principles they convey do not permeate into their organization, culture, mission, visions, and values. While there may have been a designed brand identity at a surface level, this chapter argues that this is not authentic branding practice. There are however organizations, from sole traders to start-ups and established businesses, that base their activities on deep-rooted values they will not compromise. These values permeate their brand at every level and are manifested through the design of the brand. These are regarded in this research as *authentic* brands.

But what exactly is authentic branding practice, and how does it differ from conventional notions of branding? What is design's role in conventional branding, and in authentic branding? How can we educate our design and marketing students to understand authentic branding, so that this practice can become embedded within contemporary branding practice? In order to answer these questions, this chapter is split into four sections. Section (i) outlines conventional notions of branding and its relationship to design; section (ii) outlines traditional notions of design and how design is changing; and section (iii) outlines, by drawing upon empirical fieldwork, what the author proposes to be authentic branding (a) by design and (b) by silent design. The former is illustrated through workshops with small- and medium-sized enterprises (SMEs) and micro businesses, and the latter via a series of interviews conducted with entrepreneurs in Orkney. The chapter concludes with a section on design education (iv), which details how we can embed the principles of authentic branding in the curriculum. It is anticipated that this chapter can prompt discussion about how we can start to embed authentic and meaningful branding practices into the curriculum through design to help (a) better communicate the strategic relationship between design and branding, and (b) embed authentic branding practices in education, so that this can permeate branding practice in industry.

(i) Branding and design: The old model

Before detailing the idea of *authentic* branding as something contemporary, it is worth considering whether branding has ever been regarded as an authentic practice. Early notions of branding are often related to the practice of marking cattle with a tag to identify who owned them. A mark was applied to the surface to differentiate between similar products (Neumeier 2005), and in the case of the cattle it was literally branded onto their skin. With this in mind, branding symbolizes the act of application to something already in existence, rather than the creation of something authentically conceived. The origination of the term branding (e.g. surface-level application) could therefore be viewed as being partly responsible for many of the negative assumptions around branding practice. This is particularly true for contexts such as corporate social responsibility and sustainability (see, for example, Hillestad, Xie, and Haugland 2010; Harris and de Chernatony 2001). This chapter aims to convey that branding practices have moved on from this. In a similar way, these notions of application and surface-level treatment are something design is also trying to dispel.

But what relationship does design have to this conventional model of branding? In the past, design (much like branding) was seen as something aesthetic, which was applied to the product or service, rather than something that could play a strategic role in the creation of brands, products, and services from the beginning (Murphy 2010).

(ii) How design has evolved branding into an authentic practice

Design has moved from being viewed merely as application or an aesthetic intervention at the surface level, after a product, service or idea has been developed, to an activity that is strategic, e.g. employed from the outset, purposeful, and permeating all levels. Design, when it was employed tactically could be said to make inauthentic branding possible, e.g. it could be used in a surface-level manner. In its contemporary strategic role, however, design practice is employed from the outset of the development of a new product or service, meaning that branding practice itself starts from the outset. Brand identity is conceived and manifested from the outset, rather than being tacked on or dreamt up as an add-on. So how has design moved branding towards a more authentic practice?

One way in which it has done this is through a demonstration of the roles that design can play—and indeed the things that can be designed. For example, consider design is no longer viewed as an activity geared towards only creating tangible artifacts (e.g. products, objects, graphics, interfaces), but is now regarded as a way of developing the intangible: services, experiences, interfaces, strategies—even futures. Previous work by the author (Murphy 2010) has referred to this development as the tacit-explicit-tacit dimension of design, e.g. it's not just products and interiors and graphics that are designed; it is services, experiences, interactions, and even organizations. This shares Brown's proposal that design now has a more strategic role as opposed to a tactical role:

> Historically, design has been treated as a downstream step in the development process—the point where designers, having played no earlier role in the substantive work of innovation, come along and put a beautiful wrapper around the idea … Now however, rather than asking designers to make an already developed idea more attractive to consumers, companies are asking them to create ideas that better meet consumers' needs and desires. The former role is tactical and results in limited value creation; the latter is strategic, and leads to dramatic new forms of value (2008: 86).

When organizations that are new to the concept of brand identity embark upon their first branding activity (employing design in a tactical manner), it is doubtful as to whether their branding practice could be considered authentic. The market is full of examples of design used in a tactical way, at the surface level, where seductive or slick graphics are applied to an already existing brand, which requires selling and hype. The assumption here may be that a good design can sell a bad product, yet in truly authentic branding this is not the case. Here, branding is more than a logo and a strapline; it's a culture and a practice that holistically consider the brand from beginning to end, tangible and intangible, internal and external. So what does a truly authentic approach to branding look like, and how is design used?

(iii) Brand-new notion of branding: An authentic approach by design

(a) Strategic design

In the previous scenario, it has been proposed that design, when historically or poorly used at a tactical level, can mask a bad brand or even "fake" authenticity. In contrast, when design is employed strategically, e.g. from the outset, this can help an organization adopt a more holistic approach to its branding practice, which this chapter argues is a more authentic way of branding. Brand manifestation through the use of strategic design can help an organization better understand itself through various touchpoints: it can help re-frame organizational values; identify which aspects of their brand don't match up (e.g. the consistency gap); plan an effective design strategy to then communicate this brand internally and externally; and employ brand values to underpin decision making and drive future development. The approach taken by the team the author worked with in industry was just this—a fundamentally *authentic* practice.

By way of a definition, an authentic approach to branding, or the practice of designing authentic brands is a way of understanding an organization before forming the design brief, which helps organizations better understand themselves. This in turn, helps them to use design strategically, e.g. from the outset, rather than as decoration or sticking plaster solution. Among my colleagues, there was a deeply-rooted belief that the practice of branding informed good design, and that if an organization didn't know its brand, it would be ill-equipped to communicate with its stakeholders. Before any design work could take place, and essentially as a pre-design stage, time has to be taken for conceiving, consolidating, and communicating an organization's brand. It is this idea of brand manifestation through design that this chapter wishes to offer up for discussion as authentic branding. To clarify this further, designing an authentic brand means:

- design is embedded from the outset, e.g. not as a wrap around;
- each element of the brand is considered internally and externally;
- brand values are communicated effectively through design.

Rampersad (2008) has previously identified the notion of personal authentic branding, and offered an approach for aligning personal values to ensure consistency. This authentic notion of branding, however, is not linked to design—which is why, essentially, any design work that follows could be seen as not authentic—because it designs over what has already been conceived. Ind alludes to this, referring to the design system within corporate identity as being "names, graphics, slogans and language" (1990). Davis and Baldwin (2006) highlight the importance of a designer knowing the context of the brand that they are designing for—but again, this implies a designer is involved much later in the process.

It is this notion of translating brand from the tacit, e.g. core values, beliefs, into the explicit, e.g. language, service, interior. It is this translation and holistic approach—in a designerly way—that enables this authentic approach to branding. This designerly approach to branding is not something that marketers apply to a product or service, but is something that is built from the fundamental origins of the organization. It is a way of fundamentally understanding an organization's brand and how it is manifested through its various touchpoints, and then considering how all these touchpoints can better reflect this brand. Authentic branding is not a way to sell, but a way to understand and, as an ongoing practice, can ensure that all aspects of an organization are being communicated consistently.

With this in mind, it can be argued that a brand has nowhere to hide—and that an authentic approach leaves no room for gimmicks or add-ons—it all has to hang together. Irregularities and impostor material will stand out. There are several authors whose work complements this approach (see, for example, Abbing 2010; Neumeier 2005; Ries and Ries 2004).

Workshop with SMEs and microbusinesses

In order to consider the relevance and value of the practice of authentic branding to organizations, this concept was introduced to organizations to inform its development. In May 2014, an in-depth participatory workshop was organized for representatives from five SMEs and microbusinesses, with business support organizations in attendance. Ten participants gathered for a one-day design workshop to help them scope out the opportunity for design to be utilized for strategic advantage in their organizations. The first step was to explore their brand values using collage, prototyping, and mapping techniques. All the participants said that when they learned that what they had just been through was effectively an exercise about branding, they were surprised as they understood branding to be something different. They had imagined the notion of branding to be about spin involving advertising and selling a story. What they took away from the experience was that branding was about considering the organization as a whole, its reason for existence (manifesto, mission, vision, values, core business) and to start to identify all the ways in which their brand is manifested—e.g. through space, employee behavior, uniforms, language, services, experience etc. This workshop experience gave the organizations an audit tool to identify where design could be used to help them to authentically understand and communicate their brands in a more holistic and strategic way.

Here, design is being proposed as the link that has moved conventional branding into the practice of authentic branding and, as such, the above can be regarded as authentic branding enabled by the application of strategic design.

Yet, as initial primary research has uncovered, there are principles of authenticity in brands that haven't explicitly been driven by a design approach from the outset, or with any explicit design intervention. The author, however, presents these as being enabled through the practice of "silent design" (Gorb and Dumas 1987).

(b) Examples of authentic branding through silent design

Silent Design was a term first coined by Gorb and Dumas:

> A great deal of design activity goes on in organizations which is not called design. It is carried out by individuals who are not called designers, and who would not consider themselves to be designers. We have called this Silent Design (1987: 152).

In late 2015, a week-long field trip was undertaken in a remote part of Scotland involving ten interviews and accompanying site visits with local organizations, enterprise support, and academics. The purpose of this field trip was to gain insights into ways of doing business in rural Scotland and to understand how this may differ from mainland business culture. The field trip aimed to develop initial portraits of indigenous business people in a remote location and to uncover, using qualitative ethnographic approaches, how these organizations essentially "did business." What were their values around business interactions? How did they operate? What is business culture in these areas?

The following is an excerpt from the field notes:

> One powerful observation from our trip is that the brands and industry may attract people to this particular place, but it's the place and the people that keeps them there. Arts & Craft Cultures are often curated and communicated within a framework of wider value that not only sells the product/service but tells a wider story that includes the history, landscape and people behind it … we have started to develop an understanding that that there is a particular business culture indigenous to the land, its people, and its social dynamics, and that there is something unique and special about the place.

What is interesting to note here is that we hadn't gone out to draw any particular conclusions with regard to branding, but were struck by the nature of these organizations, their unique qualities, and connection to the land. Their authenticity and their brand values reflected a lot of the principles of authentic branding, but this had been done by people who weren't professionally trained designers, and who weren't in a formal or recognized design role. We acknowledge that further research is required, but due to the opportunistic nature of the fieldwork and the unexpected connection it had to authentic branding, we felt it useful to include this as an example of organizations that indicated authentic branding practice through design—but this time, through silent design.

Considering the observations around authentic branding first conceived through work in industry, and then explored through research with organizations who (a) had benefited from design intervention, and (b) had not been involved with any design intervention, what can we take forward? How can we embed the principles of authentic branding practice into the curriculum so that it becomes normal practice? The next section will now give insight into current and ongoing work about how these principles of authentic branding are being taught to postgraduate management students studying design.

(iv) Implications for education: How to teach authentic business practice through design?

A traditional management or business approach may be to teach conventional notions of branding, still using a tactical view of design. The example given here is novel because it concerns management students learning about design and its role in business—in this case, the role of design in authentic branding practice. If we are to help businesses move towards understanding authentic branding practice using design, it's important that this mindset is embedded within the curriculum. In this example, by learning about design and its role in organizations through live projects, these management students are learning alternative ways of framing organizational problems, and how to craft appropriate approaches to research as a way of framing these problems. Instead of learning something as temptingly linear as "the five key approaches of design thinking," students are developing skills to be able to take any problem or context they find themselves in, or may in the future find themselves managing, and to use a designerly approach to (a) understand the context, and (b) craft an appropriate response. This is a contrast to a limited toolbox approach and the notion of problem solving. Using a designerly approach, complex problems are understood, analyzed, and made explicit rather than reduced to simple elements and a solution. We propose that this is beneficial to the students as it provides them with a competitive edge of being more dynamic and creative management graduates, who think in a non-linear and dynamic way. This is the context in which the author has started to teach the principles of authentic branding. Although the material for this curriculum is still under development, four core activities are being developed to encourage students to consider these alternative business ways of thinking:

1. Workshops on crafting authentic brands: e.g. the notion of collage, mapping, modeling, and making, to develop a way for organizations to conceive their brand and to develop their brand proposition based on futuristic and emerging insights. This allows for propositional brand models to be built using service design principles. Participants have reported that the action of making and modeling has allowed them to identify opportunities for business models quickly, which allows for more traditional approaches to development (e.g. then developing the business case around these physical propositional models).

2. Lectures forming a series entitled *brand manifestation through design*: In this series of lectures, participants are introduced to the practice of conducting brand audits using design approaches. They identify touchpoints for how brand values are communicated and offer insights into (a) inconsistencies and (b) where design could be used to help a brand be more consistent. After having written this chapter, this series will now move on to look at designing authentic brands, e.g. considering how design approaches can be used from the outset—rather than to enrich what's already been done.

3. Research methods series: In this series of lectures, participants are introduced to how to integrate design research approaches with marketing research approaches—traditional social sciences methods (such as interviews and observation) vs creative approaches (laddering, artifact analysis, cultural probes etc).

4. Developing a series of workshops that seek to introduce discussions on what constitutes a designerly approach to management. These workshops are currently taking place, and are proving to be rich discussion spaces. So far, the principles of a designerly approach to management are (a) user-centeredness, (b) engendering empathy,(c) crafting bespoke responses to the context and (d) creative research methods that value insights over data.

These four activities show how the principles of authentic branding through design can be taught within the curriculum and demonstrate how designerly approaches can draft authentic brand identity.

Conclusion

Although this research is in its developmental stages, the insights to date have provided rich material with which to inform live research activity and to dynamically enhance the curriculum.

Until now, conventional views of branding have maintained a strong connection to selling and marketing. Similarly, conventional notions of brand identity consider this as something applied to a product or service, rather than real attributes and assets that grow with the product or service from the outset. While design was also viewed as tactical and as an add-on, it could be argued that design aided this inauthentic, surface level approach to branding. However, as design evolved into a more strategic role, a process embedded from the outset, which permeates all parts of the brand identity (organizational values, mission, color palette, packaging, work ethic, organizational culture, language, material, look and feel etc.), it has enabled branding practice to be more authentic—growing from the outset rather than as an add-on. Strategic design and silent design have both been identified as types of design that have created this notion of authentic branding practice.

Finally, this chapter outlined how the principles behind authentic branding are being taught to management students. This chapter concludes by calling for these principles to be developed as part of the wider mission of design to enrich management practice.

Note

1   Some of the research underpinning this chapter has been conducted in collaboration with the Institute of Design Innovation at the Glasgow School of Art, UK.

References

Aaker, D. (1996), *Building Strong Brands*, New York, NY: The Free Press.
Abbing, E. R. (2010), *Brand Driven Innovation: Strategies for Development and Design*, Lausanne: AVA Publishing.

Beverland, M. (2004), "Uncovering 'theories-in-use': Building Luxury Wine Brands," *European Journal of Marketing*, 38 (3/4): 446–66.

Brown, T. (2008), "Design Thinking," *Harvard Business Review*, 86 (6): 84–92.

Davis, M. and J. Baldwin (2006), *More than a Name: An Introduction to Branding*, Lausanne: AVA publishing.

Gorb, P. and A. Dumas (1987), "Silent Design," *Design studies*, 8 (3): 150–6.

Gordon, W. and R. Langmaid (1988), "'A Great Ad Pity They Can't Remember the Brand'– True or False?" *31st MRS Conference Proceedings*, 15–46. London: PRS.

Harris, F. and L. de Chernatony (2001), "Corporate Branding and Corporate Brand Performance," *European Journal of Marketing*, 35 (3/4): 441–56.

Hillestad, T., C. Xie, and S. A. Haugland (2010), "Innovative Corporate Social Responsibility: The Founder's Role in Creating a Trustworthy Corporate Brand Through 'Green Innovation,'" *Journal of Product & Brand Management*, 19 (6): 440–51.

Ind, N. (1990), *The Corporate Image: Strategies for Effective Identity Programmes*, London: Kogan Page.

Michaels, F. S. (2011), *Monoculture: How One Story is Changing Everything*, Kelowna, BC: Red Clover Press.

Murphy, E. (2010), "Learning to Practice: A Case Study in Dynamic Learning at the Interface of Design and Business," Ph.D. thesis, University of Dundee, Dundee.

Neumeier, M. (2005), *The Brand Gap*, Vancouver: Peachpit Press.

Rampersad, H. K. (2008), "A New Blueprint for Powerful and Authentic Personal Branding," *Performance Improvement*, 47 (6): 34–7.

Ries, A. and L. Ries (2004), *The Origin of Brands: Discover the Natural Laws of Product Innovation and Business Survival*, New York, NY: Harper Collins.

Smythe, J., C. Dorward, and J. Reback (1992), *Corporate Reputation*, London: Century.

Vidal, J. (2003), "How Lie of the Land is Belied by the Bland," *The Guardian*, June 21.

25

Strategies for Revitalization of Culturally Significant Designs, Products, and Practices

Martyn Evans, Amy Twigger Holroyd, Stuart Walker, Tom Cassidy, and Jeyon Jung

Introduction

Culturally significant designs, products and practices (CSDPP) are found in every society, country, and culture, and are tangible, durable, and portable artifacts that are linked to particular places, employ traditional making processes or are embedded in local ways of life. Their cultural significance is derived from social, historical, and aesthetic characteristics valued by a particular community over time and transmitted from generation to generation. Cultural significance "is not static and continually transforms and innovates" (Cominelli and Greffe 2012: 245) while its importance derives from the wealth of knowledge and skills that are transmitted through it from one generation to the next (UNESCO 2016).

Drawing upon the work undertaken as part of a major Arts and Humanities Research Council (AHRC)-funded research project entitled 'Design Routes', as well as subsequent AHRC projects 'Living Design' and 'Design Ecologies', we have explored how design can make a meaningful contribution in developing and revitalizing CSDPP to make them relevant to the needs of people today. Many such CSDPP can be seen to be out of step with contemporary society and, as a result, have become marginalized.

Increasingly, the importance of such traditions is being reassessed (for example, see Lazzeretti 2012; Zukin 2012) as their rich historical links with community and culture mean they have much to offer in terms of identity, well-being, and the promotion of cultural diversity (Cominelli and Greffe 2012). Invigorating the current international discussion in CSDPP, Lazzeretti notes an emerging contemporary trend where communities "look at their past history to create the capacity to resist threats and to transform critical situations into opportunities for change and growth" (2012: 230). While this notion of change and growth is also an important driver of the revitalization of CSDPP, there is a need to balance social and economic progress such that the very traditions, heritage, and meanings that are valued are not forgotten in the name of progress (Brown 2005). By not doing so there is a danger of stripping the enduring value from the contexts that give meaning in the first place.

When considering how to revitalize CSDPP and make them relevant to contemporary lifestyles, there is a need to identify approaches, or more purposefully, strategies that respect tradition and provide viable and effective means to create sustainable futures. Given the vast number of examples of CSDPP that we have identified, a structured approach to the organization and communication of these strategies is essential. The development of a taxonomy of revitalization strategies provides a structured mechanism to formalize these strategies such that they can be readily understood and thus actionable. This chapter presents five clusters of cognate strategies that underscore how the effective application of contemporary design can support successful revitalization. In addition to the aforementioned clusters, the chapter discusses broader enabling factors that underpin how design can reconnect traditions, values and beliefs with modern ways of living in a sustainable manner.

Making sense of revitalization—a taxonomy

As a means of making sense of the plethora of approaches that have been used to revitalize CSDPP, the authors analyzed and categorized over four hundred historical designs, products, and making practices, which demonstrated successful revitalization in one form or another. Secondary sources were identified where examples conformed to the working criteria generated as part of the project, namely CSDPP are: tangible, durable, and portable artifacts that are linked to particular places; employ traditional making processes; or are embedded in local ways of life. Examples also needed to demonstrate a level of successful revitalization where the tradition on which the revitalization was based was maintained in a recognizable form. Given that Brown (2005) notes successful revitalization needs to value the traditions, heritage, and meanings on which the cultural significance is based, the notion of success was introduced to both acknowledge the sustainment of cultural significance as well as maintaining the positive connection between the "original" and the "revitalized."

Acknowledging the complexity and messiness of the data that this process generated, both in terms of the diverse nature of the contexts, approaches, and motivations involved, as well as the scale, scope, and timescales of revitalization identified, data analysis was framed around a taxonomy of revitalization strategies.

Developed by iterative analysis and close attention to the relationship of these examples to the traditions upon which they build, the taxonomy contains four classification levels.

1. The primary level of the hierarchical taxonomy comprises three categories: designs, products, and practices. The categorization refers to the element of tradition on which the revitalization is primarily based.

   - *Designs* refers to traditional patterns or forms.
   - *Products* refers to traditional artifacts.
   - *Practices* refers to traditional processes of making (and use).

2. The second level comprises *clusters (of revitalization strategies):* groups of cognate strategies brought together to provide a high-level understanding of the key approaches available to support revitalization.

3. The third level comprises revitalization *strategies:* distinct approaches used to pursue revitalization of designs, products, or practices.

4. The fourth level contains specific examples of successfully revitalized culturally significant designs, products, and practices from diverse contexts, cultures, and timeframes.

The taxonomy aimed to provide a structured entry point to enable users to be aware of the breadth of approaches that can be applied to undertake revitalization, support a focused consideration of which revitalization strategies could be of maximum benefit, and provide examples of successful revitalization to help visualize the contribution that design can make. The introduction of the clusters level specifically aimed to draw together individual strategies into cognate groupings and as a result make them more accessible and actionable. Extensive analysis of the successful historical examples of revitalized designs, products, and making practices enabled iterative development of strategies and associated clusters. This process involved visual mapping (Collins 2010; Gray and Malins 2004) combined with thematic analysis (Gibbs 2007; Silverman 2006) to refine and synthesize the clusters into an understandable and accessible form. This iterative development balanced the need for a manageable number of clusters while recognizing that they needed to be representative of the breadth of the identified revitalization strategies. Finally, multiple examples of a given revitalization strategy needed to evident before the strategy was considered for inclusion in the taxonomy, i.e. all strategies need to have multiple successful examples. The revitalization clusters identified are:

- *Sustain Through Design*—combine traditional making or use practice with new or reimagined design.
- *Transpose Tradition*—take traditional design or making practice into a new context.
- *Value of Place*—foreground the value of place and provenance.
- *Production Processes*—employ appropriate and effective methods of making.
- *Skills*—employ targeted approaches to embed and enhance skills.

In addition to these clusters, a series of connected enabling factors was identified, which support and underpin how design can reconnect traditions, values, and beliefs with modern ways of living in a sustainable manner. These enabling factors are structured around three themes: (1) *Promotion*—spread awareness and appreciation via effective promotion, (2) *Enterprise*—employ effective business, organization, and finance models, (3) *Research and Education*—learn about traditions, meanings, and contemporary relevance. This chapter now explores the above revitalization clusters and associated strategies, and then considers how the broader enabling factors support revitalization through design.

Sustain through design

This cluster combines traditional making or use practices with new or reimagined designs. Strategies include:

Remix design elements linked to traditional making practice: This strategy involves the creative exploration of design elements, including two-dimensional patterns and motifs, or three-dimensional forms, which are linked to a traditional making practice. The exploration may create new prototypes, to then be put into production. Alternatively, experimentation may take place during the production process to create one-off variations on a central theme. The remixing process may be driven by aesthetic considerations, or perhaps by the need to develop a simplified design that can be produced more quickly. When remixing these design elements, contemporary needs and preferences should be considered. Researching designs that have been used in the past, in order to enrich the vocabulary of design elements to be used, enhances the effectiveness of this strategy.

Reintroduce design associated with traditional making practice: In many contexts, the pressures of modernization and globalization have led to the loss of traditional designs. This strategy involves the reintroduction of designs used in the near or distant past, enriching the visual vocabulary used by makers. These designs are often two-dimensional patterns and motifs that frequently carry cultural meaning. When reintroducing these design elements, there may be value in remixing them and combining them in new ways. Before they can be reintroduced, these designs and their meanings first need to be researched and understood by the designer. In order to flourish in the contemporary context, the revitalized products need to carry appeal today, thus, it may be important to consider how the story behind the reintroduced designs is communicated.

Rework design to meet contemporary needs: In this strategy, products are reworked with the needs and preferences of the contemporary target market in mind. This target market may be local to the place in which the products are made, or geographically distant. In this case, it is especially important that research is carried out. Traditional products can often be adapted to suit the consumers in the target market; this adaptation may be in terms of aesthetics involving styling garments in a way that corresponds with contemporary fashions in the target market, for example.

Adaptations may be required in terms of size: contemporary lifestyles may demand that items for use in the home are reduced in size to suit families with limited space. A reworked design could respond to people's desire to make things themselves, rather than buying ready-made products. The history of an adapted product is likely to be an important element of the narrative surrounding it.

Mashup with "external" traditional design elements: For this strategy, the designer revitalizes a traditional making practice by blending—or "mashing up"—traditional two- or three-dimensional design elements from elsewhere. These design elements may be from a similar product, from another type of traditional product, or from some other source of local visual material. When reimagining these design elements, contemporary needs and preferences should be kept in mind. If not employed with care, this strategy can have negative impacts. For example, Borges (2012) describes stylistic motifs associated with traditions from European countries having become widespread on embroideries and surface decoration on artisanal objects across Brazil, partly due to design leaflets given free with paint and paintbrushes. As she explains, this results in "a remarkable dissociation between the everyday life of the artisans and their work" (Borges 2012: 97).

Introduce fresh aesthetic to traditional making practice: Here the designer creates a new aesthetic for traditional making practices, while keeping within an established product type. The novel design may be a three-dimensional form or two-dimensional pattern, and could incorporate contemporary iconography. Elements of traditional design may be included, but given a fresh "look." This type of work can help a traditional craft to evolve in aesthetic terms and may potentially broaden its appeal. Common sources of inspiration for new designs are local flora, fauna, and architectural features. The use of such inspiration can help to ground new products in a specific location. If overused, there is a danger that this strategy could lead to the loss of traditional designs.

Create new product based on traditional archetype: This strategy starts from the perspective of the user, who has a yearning for traditional material culture, yet requires the convenience and ease of use of contemporary products. Taking this forward, the designer can develop a new interpretation of a traditional archetype, drawing on modern materials and technologies to create a solution that references user practices from the past. In order for customers to appreciate the hybrid nature of the new products created, it will be important to communicate the narrative surrounding the new design effectively.

Transpose tradition

This cluster takes traditional designs or making practices into new contexts. Strategies include:

Reinterpret traditional pattern using new making practice: This strategy involves traditional two-dimensional patterns and motifs being transposed to a new context using a new, often non-traditional, making process. This new making process may be an alternative artisanal craft but often an industrial process with capacity for mass production is employed, although it may be possible to combine industrial processes with craft techniques. Digital technologies may be involved, enabling traditional patterns to be explored using the latest methods of making. Such approaches can be used to experiment with patterns in terms of scale, color, and application. It is common for patterns with roots in a craft process to be used as the basis for new textile designs that are mass-produced using industrial methods. Although there are examples of this strategy being used effectively to revitalize a culturally significant pattern, if used carelessly it can have negative effects. Cheap mass-produced imitations can erode the market for traditional products made using craft techniques, and therefore harm the livelihoods of artisans. Appropriating traditional patterns without due care for their cultural meaning—especially spiritual meaning—can result in a disconnection with tradition.

Reinterpret traditional form using new making practice: This strategy involves the forms of traditional products being transposed to a new context using a non-traditional making process. As with the preceding strategy, the new making process may be an alternative artisanal craft but an industrial process with capacity for mass production is frequently employed. Increasingly digital technologies are playing a key role enabling traditional forms to be explored using the latest methods of making. When reinterpreting a traditional form, contemporary needs and preferences should be kept in mind. The practice of reinterpreting traditional three-dimensional forms is less common than that of reinterpreting traditional patterns yet the same factors should be considered, e.g. cheap mass-produced imitations can erode the market for traditional products made using craft techniques, appropriating traditional forms without due care for their cultural or spiritual meaning could cause offense. It is important, therefore, to understand the history and meaning of any traditional form considered for revitalization.

Apply traditional making practice to new product type: This strategy involves the use of a traditional making practice to produce an entirely new type of product. This allows traditional craft knowledge to be applied to products for non-traditional contexts, such as consumer electronics and healthcare applications. This strategy is driven by a vision to see the potential of a making process in terms of a new application. To be effective, these new products need to consider the inherent characteristics of the specific making process. Contemporary needs and preferences should also be kept in mind. How the story behind the new design is communicated may be an important consideration. If successfully employed, this strategy can help traditional craft practices to find new purposes and applications, beyond the creation of low volume, upmarket luxury items.

Transfer traditional making practice to new material: This strategy involves the combination of a traditional making practice with an unconventional material. It may be prompted by the local availability of alternative materials, the attraction of new materials in terms of aesthetic or performance, or simply the maker's curiosity. This approach can help a traditional making practice to adapt to changing conditions and in doing so the look and characteristics of the new products may attract new customers. Therefore, contemporary needs and preferences should be kept in mind, and how the story behind the new product is conveyed is another consideration. Depending on the characteristics of the new material, it may be useful to also explore the strategies that consider production processes. If overused, there is a danger that this strategy could lead to the loss of tacit knowledge relating to traditional and local (especially natural) materials.

Value of place

This cluster foregrounds the value of place and provenance as an intrinsic aspect of the revitalization process. Strategies include:

Introduce traditional making practice in new place: This strategy embraces the fact that culturally significant products frequently have complex histories, with traditions spreading across the globe through trade and migration. While many making practices are firmly embedded in particular cultural contexts, they can also spring up in new places, thus, some traditions that we consider to be long standing have actually been introduced by outsiders through relatively recent interventions. As the making practice becomes embedded in the community, it may gain cultural significance. The use of this strategy may be prompted by individuals or communities wishing to engage in a particular making practice. It may be prompted by someone seeing the opportunity for a particular making practice to thrive in a new location— perhaps due to an abundance of relevant materials or the transferable skills of the local people. When making practices are being introduced in new locations, it is important that they are allowed to adapt to local conditions and the desires and preferences of the local makers. Attention should also be paid, of course, to the needs and preferences of those who will use the products and the communication of the story behind this new approach.

Reintroduce lost making practice in relevant historical location: This strategy involves the revitalization of a making practice in the location with which it was historically associated. While modernization has led to many localized crafts dying out, accessing this rich heritage can be an effective means of regenerating a locally distinctive material culture. Reintroduction initiatives may be small or large in scale, craft-based or much more industrial, yet the connection with history and tradition usually presents a compelling narrative. In order to avoid simply creating a pastiche of the past, it is important to allow the making practice to evolve and adapt to the contemporary context. While it may be productive to reintroduce traditional designs associated with the lost making practice, it could also be interesting to explore new product types, new materials, and novel designs. Whatever the approach to design, attention should be paid to the needs and preferences of those who will use the products.

Utilize local materials: This strategy involves the use of local materials—shaped using traditional craft processes or industrial methods—to create a strong connection between product and place. Local materials carry an inherent sense of provenance, which can be heightened through sensitive design and effective promotion. Materials will often be locally abundant, may be naturally occurring, and may require specialist care during the process of growing and harvesting. Alternatively, it may be a type of commercial or domestic waste that can be repurposed to create something new. In some cases, the material may come from a specific source—a particular tree or building, for example—that carries its own historical significance. Contemporary needs and preferences of potential users should be kept in mind when working with local materials. Depending on the characteristics of the material, it may be useful to also explore strategies related to production processes.

Production process

This cluster employs appropriate and effective methods of making. Strategies include:

Develop production capability to increase output: This strategy aims to increase the volume of output of a particular maker. This might be in terms of increasing the volume of work produced, by making an established making process quicker and more efficient or by increasing the workforce. A common approach in terms of textiles is to make items with thicker yarns or threads to increase the yield for a given amount of production effort. Another interpretation could be to produce work that is larger in scale. Alternatively, the aim may be an increase in the variety of work that can be produced, through the improvement of tools and equipment. In many cases, this enhancement will require the use of new technologies—although any technological solution must be appropriate to the context in which it is to be used. Improvements will often be strongly linked to the development of makers' skills. When considering enhancing production capability, it is important to also think about demand for the finished products. If not handled sensitively, there is a danger a drive to increase volume and variety could lead to the loss of tacit knowledge, craft skill, and understanding of the meanings associated with complex designs.

Improve quality and consistency of production process: This strategy aims to improve an established production process to create better quality and more consistent products. Initiatives of this type may also aim to improve makers' working conditions and reduce the impact of production on the environment. In many cases, this enhancement will require the use of new technologies. Improvements will often be strongly linked to the development of makers' skills. Another approach involves the redesign of products to eliminate areas of weakness during transit. When thinking about improving quality and consistency, it is important to also think about the expectations of the market. Craft skill and associated tacit knowledge may be lost if not handled sensitively. Furthermore, the introduction of inappropriate technology could have detrimental consequences for makers.

Enhance production process using new technology: This strategy involves the fusion of new technologies with established craft processes to generate reinvented methods of making. Emergent approaches are likely to produce items with a novel aesthetic. This process might involve learning new skills or collaborating with other makers from an area outside normal working practices. If a design is entirely transposed to a new making practice this will align with either the *reinterpret traditional pattern using new making practice* strategy, or the *reinterpret traditional form using new making practice* strategy in the Transpose Tradition cluster.

Skills

This cluster employs targeted approaches to embed and enhance skills. Strategies include:

Transmit making skill from person to person: This strategy focuses on initiatives that support the transfer of skills between people who work together. Some of these initiatives will cater for complete beginners while others support makers with well-developed skills. Some will have a professional and commercial focus, while others will cater for amateur makers. Initiatives will vary in terms of time, from short drop-in workshops to much more extended learning experiences. Workshops and other "live" group-based making experiences support the transfer of tacit and contextual knowledge relating to particular craft traditions. Two-way interaction also more readily encourages an experimental approach to making, in comparison with documented one-way instruction. Place is frequently important in "live" interactive experiences. For example, a course may take place in a location with which a craft tradition is strongly linked, and participants may be attracted to take part in order to gain an "authentic" experience of that place, especially while on holiday. On the other hand, "live" experiences depend on access to skilled instructors, and this may limit choice.

Create and access enduring record of skilled making practice: This strategy focuses on transferring skills via instructional materials such as books, patterns, and online resources. These instructional materials employ a "one-way" broadcast approach rather than a dialogue, as the makers using them do not have easy or direct access to the experts who created them. Some instructional materials will cater for absolute beginners while others support makers with well-developed skills, and this variation will be reflected in the design of the images, text, and materials offered. While such instructions are most frequently created by experienced professionals, the internet offers a readily accessible platform for amateurs to provide support to fellow enthusiasts. The advantage of one-way instruction is that it enables large numbers of non-professional makers to access high-quality information developed by experienced makers, and to engage in making practices that may be connected to distant cultures. The trade-off for this access is that some of the contextual knowledge transmitted through situated two-way dialogue will be missing. Furthermore, there is a danger that the act of documenting instructions for a particular craft tradition will standardize the tradition, preventing it from evolving. Many instructional materials guide makers through a fixed step-by-step process to produce a set outcome. Although this has some value in many contexts, skilled instructors are able to encourage others to experiment around a craft tradition.

Design material, tool or kit to support development of making skill: This strategy involves the creation and application of material, such as a tool or kit, to support the development of making skills. The aim here is to create a supportive environment with actionable tools or kits that scaffold and assist the development of making skills. These kits may be simple or complex but tend to provide support for novice or intermediate makers so are often quite basic. A popular form of such tools or kits introduces makers to a particular skill or process from first principles and supports the notion of "distributed competence," where support actions for novices provide a guide to follow that ultimately helps groups to learn. There is a danger here where such kits may reduce making skills to a series of steps, which can result in a lack of deeper understanding of a given making skill and the breadth of knowledge required to employ it successfully.

Develop skill to complement making practice: This strategy develops complementary skills to support making practices. Typically, this can be in the form of organized courses or workshops, sometimes delivered to multiple cohorts of makers, that increase knowledge and understanding of business or enterprise practices. Examples include enhancing customer service, establishing and running cooperatives, marketing, developing products for specific markets etc. In such instances, approaches tend to complement well-developed making skills but also extend the knowledge and understanding required to develop sustainable enterprises, identify new market opportunities, increase business awareness etc. When successful, such approaches become embedded in particular contexts and build traditions that can continue over a number of years. Peer learning is also used to transfer understanding of business skills between cohorts of makers and expert facilitators. A key focus is to develop business skills within artisans such that they become self-sufficient rather than need ongoing support.

Beyond clusters towards enabling factors

As we move the focus away from individual designs, products, and practices towards the context that enables revitalization, we have identified broader enabling factors whose presence supports revitalization through design. These interrelated factors support the development of conditions that, when combined appropriately with individual strategies, create a fertile context in which revitalization can be fostered and, as a result, helps to sustain the cultural values attached to designs, products, and practices. The effectiveness of the revitalization strategies (which focus directly on individual designs, products, and practices) is enhanced when combined with enabling factors. We have conceptualized these enabling factors around three themes: (1) Promotion, (2) Enterprise, and (3) Research and Education.

Promotion

Targeted, purposeful, and effective promotion is important when attempting to spread awareness and appreciation of CSDPP. While the motivation for undertaking promotion activities can be context dependent, a central theme is the need to ensure that the value of a given design, product or practice is conveyed to its target audience and thus support their sustainment. In some instances, showcasing making practices and products may aim to increase awareness, capture and document for future generations, and create interest rather than result in commercial gain. Such awareness-raising approaches can act as a precursor for more commercially focused activities, which often explicitly try to create time-bound focal points that maximize revenue through strategic selling opportunities. Clearly there is overlap and complementarity between raising awareness and creating focal points to maximize revenue, and often these approaches are connected into a broader promotion strategy. Examples of focal points that maximize revenue include craft trails where artisans provide opportunity to visits individual studios; international festivals that bring together artisans to sell their work to visitors; and curated stores that represent a portfolio of master-craftspeople that create work that connects to contemporary lifestyles. Other promotion approaches include the use of "champions" who act as ambassadors for a particular making practice or product type, often highlighting heritage and meaning generated from the connection to a particular locale or context. Many of the promotion approaches seek to convey compelling narratives that engage audiences, raise interest, and create meaningful connections between artisans, their work, and relevant audiences. Frequently these narratives place the artisan at the center of the story as a means of humanizing the particular craft, tradition or locale aiming to connect on an emotional level. The use of compelling narratives can be extended to create strong brand identities, which have the potential to connect effectively to many of the revitalization strategies discussed earlier. Often the key priority for the aforementioned promotion approaches is to help artisans to raise awareness to first, sustain their particular CSDPP and, second, help them to make a reasonable living out of it. As such, promotion approaches can be seen to underpin revitalization strategies but are critical to sustaining both the design, product or practice and the livelihood of the artisan.

Enterprise

While many believe that artisans are driven solely by the passion for their creative practice, effective business, organization, and finance models are important in fostering sustainable enterprise models that support CSDPP. Some approaches aim to directly benefit makers through the creation of enterprises that connect activities (such as integrated supply chains, marketing and promotion etc.) through "co-ops," collaborations or collectives that maximize economies of scale by bringing together artisans in cognate groups. Community- or policy-led initiatives can also be effective in establishing interconnected schemes or lead to new organizations that again help to create contexts in which individual makers can link up and promote place-based enterprises. The "One Village One Product" (OVOP) initiative started in Japan in the late 1970s aimed to revitalize the rural economy. The original focus of OVOP was to encourage villages in the Oita region to identify a product unique to that region and develop it to national and global standards, thereby establishing a locally embedded, authentic offer that could be readily communicated to customers. In recent years, this approach has been transferred to other Asian, African, and Latin American countries as it is portable, adaptable, and can be embedded in a given locale. The OVOP approach has evolved into direct-intervention, state-level policy to alleviate poverty in rural communities. Other enterprise approaches include development of new "route-to-market" models that enable makers to sell directly to consumers. While some models utilize digital technologies (such as Etsy, a peer-to-peer (P2P) e-commerce website focused on handmade or vintage items and supplies, as well as unique factory-manufactured items) some approaches are more traditional (such as Nest, which aims to make craft valuable by integrating modern innovation and training into heritage techniques, bringing advocacy and data-driven business development to global artisans and homeworkers with the goal of empowering women, alleviating poverty, and preserving cultural traditions). Finally, there is an increasing interest in taking advantage of all possible sources of finance often beyond traditional models. Crowdfunding (the practice of funding a project by raising many small amounts of money from a large number of people, typically via the internet) was used by shoe company Markhor, via a successful Kickstarter campaign, to reimagine 1800-year old Pakistani shoe-making techniques combining indigenous craftsmanship with immaculate attention to detail to create a contemporary range of shoes. Within the broad Enterprise category, we see a range of emerging business models, networks, collaborations and initiatives that may well exploit digital technologies to complement more traditional approaches, demonstrating the need for CSDPP to evolve in response to environmental conditions to ensure sustainment.

Research and Education

Increasingly, research and educational activities to support revitalization of CSDPP have gathered momentum as contemporary appreciation and relevance of traditions and their meaning have increased. While research and education activities are often conducted independently, there is also increasing interest in their interrelationship. One key area of research activity involves gathering and documenting traditional design, products, and practices as a precursor to revitalization activities. Here, the archiving of traditional artifacts and associated practices can form a valuable resource that helps contemporary understanding and as a result, underpins reinterpretation for modern lifestyles. Such resource building can help to increase awareness of the value of traditions and thus enable the learning about histories, meanings and value of CSDPP. Combined resource building and learning opportunities are effective in providing a reference point for revitalization by providing a historical context that helps to develop in-depth yet nuanced understanding of the development of a given CSDPP. For example, the Daopo Huang Weaving Museum in Shanghai brings together an extensive collection of cotton and spinning and weaving technologies from the thirteenth century pioneered by Daopo Huang combined with a workshop that provides opportunities to try out centuries-old spinning and weaving techniques. This resource acts as a living museum that maintains an understanding of Daopo Huang's ground-breaking weaving techniques and makes them available for today. Given the historical and cultural importance of many CSDPP, the understanding of such traditions is appropriated into art and design education in numerous ways.

The Estonian Native Crafts Department in the University of Tartu aims to represent the local and native traditions and values that strengthen the sense of identity of Estonia by integrating traditional craft techniques into contemporary functional milieus. Students are able to study at undergraduate and postgraduate levels in Estonian native textiles, construction or metalwork with a combined historical and practice-based curriculum that produces the next generation of artisans well-versed in traditional Estonian crafts. The final area of activity in research and education is that of academic research where researchers from a wide variety of fields, including the creative arts and design, but also ethnography, anthropology, business, and history for example, study CSDPP to both understand their importance historically and culturally but also as a resource that can inform contemporary understanding of material culture. The driver for this book was the Design Routes project that aims to understand how design can make a meaningful contribution to the revitalization of CSDPP and in doing so increase their perceived value today. Design Routes has revealed a significant amount of academic research in this area reinforcing the increasing recognition of the value of traditions and practices that employ manual skill, and an understanding of materials, designs, and techniques that are culturally relevant.

Interconnections, interdependencies, and messiness

The interconnection between the Promotion, Enterprise, and Research and Education enabling factors provides a rich context to support the sustainment of CSDPP. By considering these enabling factors as a series of interconnected rather than independent approaches, there is scope to proactively develop a fertile context in which revitalization can be fostered by focusing on actioning new initiatives in combination with strategies outlined above under the individual research clusters. There is clear evidence that the revitalization of CSDPP does not occur in isolation, and often the combination of a number of revitalization strategies and enabling factors are required to effectively achieve sustainment of a given design, product, or associated practice. For example, effective promotion is often needed to communicate to specific audiences a newly developed design, product or practice that may then result in a new enterprise model. Alternatively, a new design (created by applying a traditional making practice to a new product type) may require research in a particular archive and engagement with academic researchers who are active in an area of relevance.

The interconnectedness and interdependencies of such approaches can be challenging for craft makers to understand, in that it isn't always easy to ascertain in what order revitalization activities need to take place, what the priorities should be, and how best to develop the new while retaining and respecting tradition. This chapter sets out a palette of options available to support revitalization rather than providing a prescriptive process to follow. Given the wide range of cultures and traditions our research has considered, and the diversity in approaches under the banner of CSDPP, a one-size-fits-all approach would be doomed to fail. Often there is a need to move between a micro and macro perspective—moving from exploring the individual design, product or process being revitalized to considering the broader cultural context in which the revitalization is situated. To achieve sustainable, meaningful, and valuable revitalization, craft makers need to (i) recognize the interconnectedness and interdependencies of individual revitalization strategies that result in a messiness that reflects reality rather than a simplified model of cultural manifestation, and (ii) be willing to explore more than one particular revitalization strategy (and/or enabling factor) as innovation can result from interaction between particular strategies, rather than concentrating on one in particular. While the notion of messiness may be challenging, this is an important consideration in revitalization as the historical and cultural context of a particular CSDPP often represents a series of interconnected yet serendipitous events that, with hindsight, may not conform to a particular logic or clear rationale. In essence, messiness is an underlying characteristic of revitalization as this reflects the history upon which revitalization is based.

Reflecting design roots

This final section considers the evolving relationship of revitalization and revitalization strategies and enabling factors with the broader research context in which we have been engaged. While it does not aim to act as a synthesis of all potential aspects of research related to CSDPP, it does aim to highlight a selected number of key issues that are of particular relevance to future research challenges. It is structured around four themes: (1) looking back to look forward, (2) the influence of (evolving) technologies, (3) the creative ecology, and (4) limits, extents, and focal points.

Looking back to look forward

In the revitalization of CSDPP, understanding of historical contexts is critical to being able to respect and value heritage, and use this understanding as a trigger for reimagining for the future. This process of looking backwards to look forward involved three key elements:

a) *Understanding the role of locale:* All artifacts are a result of numerous ideas, events, and activities but, importantly for our research, the historical context in which artifacts are placed may have had a significant influence on their development. Availability of a particular material in a geographic region can shape the development of a particular artifact and as such often becomes synonymous with a particular region and its inhabitants. The availability of raw material over time may mean that these resources become a critical factor in what can be produced by the regions' inhabitants. For example, Pueblo Pottery is associated with Native American people of the Southwest United States exemplified by inhabitants of New Mexico where suitable clay is available on the settlements, or Pueblos, where they live. Each Pueblo has slightly different clay, which has shaped the color and style of pottery each Pueblo produces. Understanding the history of the region means that it is possible to understand the development and individuality of the pottery produced by each Pueblo.

b) *Recognize that tradition is relative:* No culture is static and, over time, what is deemed to be traditional changes. It is relative to the timeframe that is being considered. While some believe that a tradition can only evolve over a specific time period (for example, when passed between three generations), others see tradition as more dynamic and constantly evolving. The key issue here for the revitalization of CSDPP is not what becomes considered authentic after a minimum timeframe, rather that traditions become valued over time and become embedded in situated ways of life. This means that, to an extent, the notion of tradition is constructed in relation to how it is valued by a particularly community rather than how long it has been around. The connection to a given community and locale can override the length of time is has been recognized.

c) *Tomorrow is different from yesterday:* Awareness of a historical context is an important factor in revitalization but this alone is not sufficient to plot a successful path into the future for the sustainment of a particular CSDPP. We have seen that the historical success of a particular artifact does not guarantee an ongoing demand and sustainable livelihood for craft makers as tastes change. What was once popular and valued by a particular community (or target consumer) evolves over time as lifestyles change. This may be due to the zeitgeist of the time, the cyclical nature of trends and material culture, or just a reaction to what the older generation valued. The assumption that what was once valued and able to sustain a maker culture will still continue to be valued is dangerous and likely to result in the potential demise of a particular CSDPP. What can be recognized from numerous historical examples is that while a particular type of artifact is, and continues to be, valued, it does not necessarily mean that future generations will continue to purchase this artifact. There is a need to reimagine the past for future generations while respecting the very traditional values and heritage that connected in the first place, as without this, there is a disconnect between what people used to value and the contemporary lens through which they view the past.

The influence of (evolving) technologies

As we have explored the need to understand a given history to be able to move forward effectively, there is a corresponding need to continually reassess the role of technology in the sustainment of CSDPP. Like culture, technology does not stand still and while huge value is placed on the maintenance of the use of authentic technologies and associated processes required to produce a culturally significant artifact, what actually is authentic is a moving picture. Authenticity is interpreted differently in different contexts. Clearly, cultural significance is dependent on notions of authenticity and how value is placed on such traditions but without evolution of technology (or, in some instances, revolution) many CSDPP would have disappeared. The influence of technology and mechanization in the textile industry, for example, revolutionized the production of cotton and, many claim, was critical to the Industrial Revolution. Without the adoption of mechanized spinning and weaving technologies in the seventeenth and eighteenth centuries, the world that we know today may be unrecognizable. Yet this raises an interesting question for our research, namely "when does a new technology become considered authentic?" In many respects the mechanism of cotton production in the Industrial Revolution has become absorbed into the cultural milieu and is now seen as part of its tradition. The notion of traditional cotton production is wedded to a range of technologies invented in the seventeenth and eighteenth centuries but if these technologies had not been adopted at the time, what we take for granted as being authentic and traditional production techniques would be vastly different. If that were the case, who is to know what we would now consider to be authentic? The influence of technology and, importantly, new technologies on the sustainment of CSDPP cannot be overstated. Technology has shaped how we product, consume, and conceptualize material culture, and it has had a profound effect on revitalization and sustainment of culturally significant products.

Within the revitalization clusters and associated strategies discussed previously, it is clear that technology has enabled new and previously unimaginable artifacts to be created often by impacting on the making processes. For example, within the Transpose Tradition cluster, the "Reinterpret Traditional Pattern Using New Making Practice" or "Reinterpret Traditional Form Using New Making Practice" strategies are reliant upon new production technologies (increasingly using digital technologies) that have opened up new possibilities and, as a result, enable new Enterprise opportunities. While it is clear that technology can be a powerful enabler of revitalization, care needs to be taken to ensure that the value placed on tradition and cultural meaning are not lost in the name of progress. There needs to be acknowledgement of the tension between tradition and progress when introducing technologies to support new forms of revitalization. Yet, it is important to recognize that many technologies that were once seen as new have been absorbed into tradition over time.

The creative ecology

Designs and products that emerge from place-based practices may be culturally significant if they contribute to a sense of local identity. However, locally produced designs and products need not be distinctive in terms of their materials, processes, aesthetics, or skills. Often, very similar examples are to be found in other places around the world. However, if through materials, patterns or design, or indeed through their use, there arises a sense of cultural particularity associated with custom and tradition, this can contribute to a sense of identity and strengthen the cultural contribution of such artifacts. Moreover, if they serve to continue a tradition that is rooted in the history and culture of people and place, this will further add to their significance. Design Routes has explored examples of such designs and products, their origins and history, and their characteristics and mutually reinforcing relationships in order to understand the context, or creative ecology, in which they exist.

The broader context in which revitalization occurs, and the corresponding positive conditions required to support a sustainable environment conducive to successful revitalization, involves many interconnected factors. While individually they may not be able to support revitalization, their collective contributions can foster a suitable environment in which this can take place. While this chapter has largely focused on individual revitalization strategies (and three enabling factors), our research has revealed a broad set of factors that form a such a creative ecology. We define a creative ecology thus:

A creative ecology consists of an interrelated set of situated factors that enable culturally significant creative practices to flourish. *Intrinsic factors*, comprising priorities, perceptions, motivations, values, responsibilities, and outlooks of those involved, are supported by *extrinsic factors* involving connections to, and interactions among, associated organizations, resources, and activities.

The notion of a creative ecology helps to structure how we may understand the conditions that enable culturally significant practices (like those described in this chapter and more broadly in this book) to flourish. Consideration of individual factors can be useful in decoding the underlying structure of a given context. The constituent factors of a creative ecology include: *History* (religion, significant conflicts, indigenous cultures, transportation, migration etc.); *Geography* (climate, geology, flora, fauna, landscape etc.); *Economy* (primary and secondary income sources, trade routes, bartering traditions etc.); *Education and Training* (educational institutions, peer-to-peer training, intergenerational learning, museums, archives etc.); *Competencies* (knowledge (of history, place, materials, economy), skills (know-how, experience), ideas and vision embedded in region etc.); *Resources* (materials and tools (local/gathered, imported/bought) etc.); *Policy* (local/regional policy, planning regulations, promotion of tradition and place-making, funding for promotion and support programs etc.); *Hospitality* (suitable accommodation, hotels, campsites, restaurants, tours etc.); *Cultural Events* (music, theater, dance, festivals, sport etc.); and *Communications* (geographic isolation/proximity, transport infrastructure etc.).

The creative ecology places the individual artisan (craft maker etc.) at its core, and can be considered to encompass the range of contextual factors needed for creative practices to flourish. The creative ecology for a given locale can be adapted to suit the particular requirements of that context and some factors may not be relevant. Conversely there may be a need to introduce new factors required to accommodate the nuances of the context being considered. The interdependency of the identified factors reflects the particular characteristics of a given creative ecology. Finally, serendipity can play an important role in how a particular ecology has developed (and will continue to develop) but this is normally alongside a range of purposeful activities that have been undertaken with the aim of shaping the ecology into a preferred state. This interplay is something that may not be easy to understand or predict.

As we have demonstrated, cultural significance is established through notions of place, retained or archived meanings, people, practices (both traditional and modern) and an effective way to investigate, and to further revitalize, cultural significance is through an understanding of the myriad ecologies evident in particular cultural contexts. Creative ecologies is an effective lens to explore cultural significance providing a complex, overlapping infrastructure in which taxonomies, traditions, notions of place, production, skills, strategies etc. populate, and can be deployed further to understand the revitalization and the sustainment of cultural significance.

Limits, extents, and focal points

The final theme encompasses the limits, extents, and focal points of revitalization, and is concerned with how best to constrain the many factors that play a role in the sustainment of CSDPP.

It would be naïve to assume that revitalization can be readily understood or undertaken without first taking into account the range of factors that play a role in sustainment, be it successful or otherwise. Limits need to be placed on what is, or is not, considered to be critical when bringing together the information that underpins revitalization activities as, without some form of boundaries, there is a danger of moving too far away from the traditions, heritage, and meanings on which the cultural significance is based. At the outset of revitalization, there are two key considerations that can help to establish limits for these activities, namely, what is driving the need for revitalization and what information is critical to support revitalization? By exploring these two considerations, working boundaries can be established by drawing out and clearly understanding the inputs to revitalization. Without such an understanding, it is hard to know what should and should not be taken into account moving forward. This leads on to the second aspect of this theme, extents.

Once the inputs have been established through consideration of limits, the next step is to establish some extents for activities by considering what should be excluded from revitalization? This directly addresses the notion of "mission-creep" in that porous boundaries to revitalization activities can result in the watering down of the cultural significance of a particular design, product or practice by not having established where revitalization activities should end. By establishing the scope of the activities, a more efficient and, as a consequence, more effective revitalization can be conducted. In establishing the extent of revitalization activities, it is important to determine those aspects that need to be preserved as they are and, through a process of elimination, those aspects that need to be updated and improved.

The final aspect of this theme is that of focal points, which responds to consideration of what are the consequences of not undertaking revitalization? If we have already established the inputs to the process, and the extent of the revitalization activities, consideration needs to be given to the consequence(s) of not attempting to sustain a particular CSDPP. While this may seem a slightly radical approach, all options should be considered to ensure that revitalization does not become the default. For example, if revitalization is not attempted, will the particular design, product or practice fade or, will other consequences emerge? This may involve its evolution into a new form that has a better chance of achieving longevity or being better aligned to contemporary lifestyles. An underlying point here is that not all CSDPP can be sustained and new forms do emerge through necessity and innovation. The focal points of revitalization can be useful in identifying what actions that should not be pursued as much as those that should.

Postscript

This chapter has explored a range of strategies that have been employed successfully to revitalize culturally significant designs, products, and practices, and contextualizes these activities in a broader cultural ecology. The scope of the chapter is vast. It has encompassed many approaches that have emerged through the three years of the Design Routes project and has been informed by subsequent work on the Living Design and Design Ecologies projects. As our understanding has developed through the process of conducting research into CSDPP, the opportunities for design to contribute to successful revitalization have seemingly decreased and increased in equal amounts. While this may seem oxymoronic or counterintuitive, the reality is that revitalization requires an in-depth understanding of the culture in which the design, product or practice is based before any design-led intervention can successfully take place. Design can make a meaningful contribution to revitalization but it needs to work in consort with other disciplines and recognize the interplay between the past and the future. To maximize revitalization possibilities, attention needs to be given to what Lazzeretti (2012) notes is the need to create capacity to transform critical situations into opportunities for change. This ambition is one that has the potential to underpin the central thrust of this chapter and sustain culturally significant designs, products, and practices, and make them vital once again. Design can, and will, make a meaningful contribution to this endeavor.

References

Borges, A. (2012), *Design and Craft: The Brazilian Path*, São Paulo: Terceiro Nome.

Brown, M. (2005), "Heritage Trouble: Recent Work on the Protection of Intangible Cultural Property," *International Journal of Cultural Property*, 12: 40–61.

Collins, H. (2010), *Creative Research: The Theory and Practice of Research for the Creative Industries*, Lausanne: AVA Publishing.

Cominelli, F. and X. Greffe (2012), "Intangible Cultural Heritage: Safeguarding for Creativity," *City, Culture and Society*, 3 (4): 245–50.

Gibbs, G. (2007), *Analyzing Qualitative Data*, London: Sage Publications Ltd.

Gray, C. and J. Malins (2004), *Visualizing Research: A Guide to the Research Process in Art and Design*, Abingdon: Routledge.

Lazzeretti, L. (2012), "The Resurge of the 'Societal Function of Cultural Heritage'. An Introduction," *City, Culture and Society*, 3 (4): 229–33.

Silverman, D. (2006), *Interpreting Qualitative Data: Methods for Analyzing Talk, Text and Interaction*, London: Sage Publications Ltd.

UNESCO (2016), "Text of the Convention for the Safeguarding of the Intangible Cultural Heritage." Available online: http://www.unesco.org/culture/ich/en/convention (accessed August 21, 2016).

Zukin, S. (2012), "The Social Production of Urban Cultural Heritage: Identity and Ecosystem on an Amsterdam Shopping Street," *City, Culture and Society*, 3 (4): 281–91.

INDEX

Please note that page references to Figures will be in *italics*, while references to Tables will be in **bold'**.